"Well-written. It describes the test exactly."

> *Carol Lewis*
> *Detroit, Michigan*

"We recommend that anyone taking the FAA Entrance Examination should utilize the Air Traffic Controller book by Arco."

> *Charles Richie*
> *Federal Aviation Administration*
> *Washington, DC*

"I highly recommend Arco's *Air Traffic Controller*. It has made my job of teaching air traffic control a lot easier."

> *Peter De Marco*
> *Teacher of Air Traffic Control*
> *Former Air Traffic Controller*

"I recommend the book to all my students who plan on an air traffic career."

> *Professor Donald Fagin*
> *University of Pennsylvania*

"I found the Air Traffic Controller book to be a great help in taking the exam."

> *Robert Tower*
> *Denver, Colorado*

"I took the exam once without using Arco's Air Traffic Controller book and did not pass. The second time around I used the book and passed with a qualifying score."

> *S. Goldfarb*
> *Westminster, Colorado*

"I've seen so many people fail the air traffic exam without knowing about this book. I recommend it to anyone taking the test who wants to get a good score."

> *Thomas G. Doerr*
> *Former Air Traffic Controller*

"Mr. Turner's book has made taking the test a whole lot easier."

> *Robert Covelli*
> *Long Island, New York*

AIR
TRAFFIC
CONTROLLER

Dr. James E. Turner
Air Traffic Controller
President/CEO, Aviation Education Systems, Inc.

New York   London   Toronto   Sydney   Tokyo   Singapore

We would like to thank the Federal Aviation Administration for some of the materials and photographs used in this book.

Third Edition

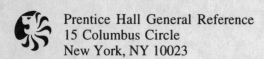Prentice Hall General Reference
15 Columbus Circle
New York, NY 10023

An Arco Book

ARCO and PRENTICE HALL are registered trademarks
of Prentice-Hall, Inc.
Colophon is a trademark of Prentice-Hall, Inc.

Library of Congress Cataloging-in-Publication Data

Turner, James E., 1942-
      Air traffic controller / James E. Turner. -- 3rd ed.
          p.   cm.
      Rev. ed. of: Air traffic controller qualifying test. c1991.
      At head of title: Arco.
      "An Arco book" — T.p. verso.
      ISBN 0-671-86398-3
        1. Air traffic controllers--United States. 2. Air traffic
    control--United States--Examinations, questions, etc.   I. Turner,
    James E., 1942-   Air traffic controller qualifying test.
    II. Title
    TL725.3.T7T88 1994
    629. 136'6'076--dc20   93-46244
                                                                                CIP

Manufactured in the United States of America

1 2 3 4 5 6 7 8 9 10

First, To the Air Traffic Control Professional who has for as long as I remember made it work;

To a few of the beginners who look and wonder and not understand why;

And, of course, to the majority of the others, the ones who commit to this profession and realize that they have joined a group of the most dedicated individuals in the world.

CONTENTS

Introduction To
Air Traffic Control Systems

This book can help you become an air traffic control specialist. It can facilitate your learning an important professional skill that will always be in great demand. No book—not this one nor any other—can give you the desire to work hard enough to master the field of air traffic control. But if you want to succeed, and have the necessary determination, this book can help you a great deal.

Why would you want to be an air traffic controller? Only you know the answer, but I can think of several reasons that make sense to me. Controllers do interesting and important work. They usually work in pleasant surroundings with other smart people. They go home feeling they have done a good day's work and their work amounts to something. They work in the field of aviation—one of the most dynamic and glamorous fields of employment available.

When I was FAA Administrator, 250 million people a year used the air transportation system. Today, only a little more than ten years later, the number of passengers has grown to 450 million. That tells you something about what is happening. More people are enjoying flying. Flying used to be what a few selected business people did. Now the typical passenger is as likely to be a grandmother going to visit the kids or taking off for a vacation in Europe.

Flying has also grown safer over the years. When jets first began flying, people said they flew so fast they would be uncontrollable, and they would be crashing into each other all the time. But the air traffic system has gotten safer every year. Why? Because the airplanes are better built, whether they are jets, turboprops, or piston-powered, and their engines are more reliable. Just as important, we have learned by experience how to avoid most accidents. Not that accidents can't happen any more; people still make mistakes and reliable systems still break down occasionally. And people still fall in their bathtubs, too. But thanks to a lot of very well trained professional people—such as pilots, mechanics, and air traffic controllers—accidents are much less likely now than ever before.

Air traffic control is an equal opportunity field. Many women are doing very well as controllers. Recently I asked a senior controller at a TRACON (see glossary of terms) whether men or women were better controllers. He said there is no difference in ability or quality. People of many different backgrounds are becoming controllers. If you think you can be a good controller, you probably can. But not everyone has the stamina, the ability, and the attitude to become a successful air traffic controller. If you succeed, I am sure you will be very proud that you did.

When you do become a controller, you will be well paid. Your pay will depend on your level of proficiency, your skill in handling traffic at the busiest terminals, and your ability to work under pressure. Let's face it: The controller's job is sometimes a stressful one. Don't try to be a controller if you can't handle a reasonable amount of stress. Many people thrive on it, and take pride in their ability to "keep 'em flying" in bad weather as well as good.

Your pay and working conditions may depend on where you work. Many people like to work near their home towns. This may be possible, but you must decide whether you are willing to move farther away if it means more responsibility and more money. It only stands to reason that the toughest jobs pay the most, so you may need to decide whether it is more important to be near the old stomping grounds or to follow opportunity wherever it may lead.

Many controllers enter training from high school. But there are advantages to having some college work, and there are co-op programs in some parts of the country that allow you to combine work and college. Check this out; it may be just what you want.

As I said earlier, aviation is a prestige field. Being a part of aviation brings satisfaction to many people because it is so important to our way of life. Aviation is a homegrown American product. We started it, and we are still the leader. Among other things, this means that many countries send people here for training and to learn how we manage our aviation industry, how we operate the air traffic control system, and much more. This means also that you may have the opportunity to be an ambassador for the United States as you bring your knowledge to other people. You will have one great advantage. Because of the strong role that the United States has played ever since the beginning of flight at Kitty Hawk, English is the worldwide language of air traffic control. This doesn't mean we shouldn't learn other languages, but it does mean that in a crunch as well as for routine work, your language is the one that the system uses.

Most of the talk you hear about aviation is directed to the airline industry and the large airplanes built to serve the major airlines' customers. But aviation spans the whole gamut from the small single seater to the jumbo jet with hundreds of passengers. There are individuals out there flying their own planes for business or for pleasure. There are small commuter planes carrying a handful of passengers, mid-size planes serving mid-size cities and towns, and hundreds of large planes working from the hubs and other mega-airports of the nation. As an air traffic controller, you will lean how all these different carriers blend to form the mosaic of the world's largest aviation system.

Also, don't forget that there are many airplanes out there that don't enter the air traffic control system, except by mistake. As long as they follow the rules and stay out of controlled airspace, they are welcome. One of your jobs is to see that they operate safely and don't get into places where they don't belong. Of course, if they get into trouble, you, like any other public-spirited citizen, must use your skills to help them avoid accidents and loss of life.

So dig in and learn as much as you can from this book. It is designed to help you prepare for your training later on. When you are accepted, you know you probably have what it takes to be a success in this field of aviation services. If you apply yourself and are willing to work, you too can proudly take your place in a profession that is always essential, frequently a lot of fun, and also well paid.

I wish you success in your venture.

During the past twenty years, dramatic changes have taken place within the Federal Aviation Administration: New approaches to human behavior and an ever-increasing complexity in aviation technology have reshaped the air traffic system.

When I started, the world of air traffic control and the people in it were different than I had expected. I can remember being sent to Oklahoma, where the FAA's training school is located. On hot days, people would listen to reports on the radio, preparing themselves for what was to me an unknown phenomenon called a tornado. They listened intently, but went about their business with an equanimity that reminded me of life in New York. On many a night I would return from school to my rented apartment, telling my wife that this job was not for me, that I thought we should give it up. Her reaction was always the same: "O.K., I'll start to pack." Well, I stayed, and became part of one of the most unique occupations anyone could ever undertake—Air Traffic Control.

My first assignment was the New York Center. This was to be the true beginning of my learning process, the place where I learned the meaning of the word "trainee."

The center had a profound effect on me: it formed my commitment to making changes that were so necessary to the agency. Back then, there was nothing that resembled today's outstanding programs in human relations. You were a trainee, and it was your responsibility to do what was necessary to get "checked out." This process involved some rather frustrating duties.

For example, one of the aids we didn't have back then were alphanumerics (aircraft informational display information on the radar). Trainees had the task of placing little plastic strips called "shrimpboats" onto the radar screen to tell the aircraft's identity, its direction, and anything else that could be written in a two-inch square. Another of our jobs was to post, throughout the facility, all the flight progress strips into all the different sectors the aircraft was going to pass through.

I can still remember the days that I tried to get to work as early as possible in order to sign up for training. If you were late or just on time your name would be on the bottom of the list for that day and you would probably not get very much training. I learned to clean radar scopes and to carry six cups of coffee for the members of my crew. I had a "godfather" back then. . .everyone did. He was the person who was responsible for you, and for your training. You followed him around and did what he told you to do. He was the person who determined if you had what it took to be a controller—or if you didn't fit in.

Such "training" persisted, and the trainees that made it became instructors themselves and perpetuated the same philosophy. The failure rate, always extremely high (due in part to this type of training), started to increase in the late seventies and early eighties. The agency became aware of the seriousness of the problem and confronted it. Some of the controllers who had experienced all those frustrations and had made commitments to bring about change were now given the opportunity to show that there were indeed those in Air Traffic Control who did care about people. Steps were taken to change the philosophy of the controller in the field. Training programs now had to be written with consideration for the individual as well as for his knowledge of the job. Instructors or "godfathers" could no longer be placed in the training role just because they were journeymen controllers.

It became apparent that there were many people within the agency who had the same feelings as I did about change. Still, there were roadblocks, people fighting change, critics who thought we were heading in the wrong direction and that the quality of the controller would not be what it had been in the "old days." But we proved them wrong by showing that someone cared, and that we were willing to correct the errors in the system, giving new life to the agency while getting back better controllers.

Today I feel that in a small way I have helped to bring about some of the changes in the air traffic training field. What I see in the faces of the people that I've trained, and in their character, makes me confident that the air traffic control field will never go back to the "old days." These new people will continue to make changes for the better, proving to everyone that this is not just *another* job—it's the greatest job in the world. It was a crazy world back then.

GOOD LUCK IN AIR TRAFFIC!

—JAMES TURNER

ACKNOWLEDGMENTS

Many people helped in the construction of this book. A few of them will be mentioned here, but I am no less grateful to all the rest.

To John Foundos, my first crew chief, a man who cared about people, a real believer from the beginning. And to the guys on my first crew at the Common I; they showed me that there were plenty of good people in the agency.

And to Joe Del Balzo, the executive director for systems development for the FAA. I believe I owe him the most thanks, for everything from his notes of encouragement to his continued belief in my ideas and projects. He made the changes that were necessary. He will always be there for someone. Thanks, Joe.

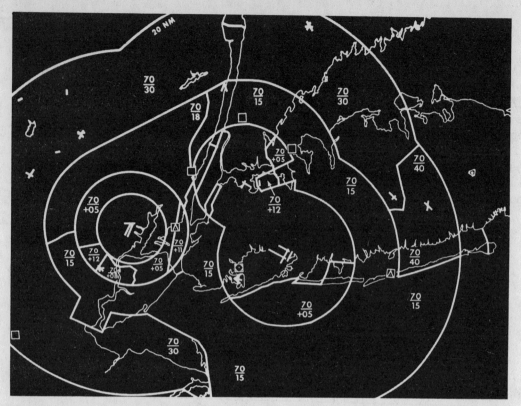

Static map mounted above radar screen displays Class B airspace covered by air traffic controllers at the New York TRACON.

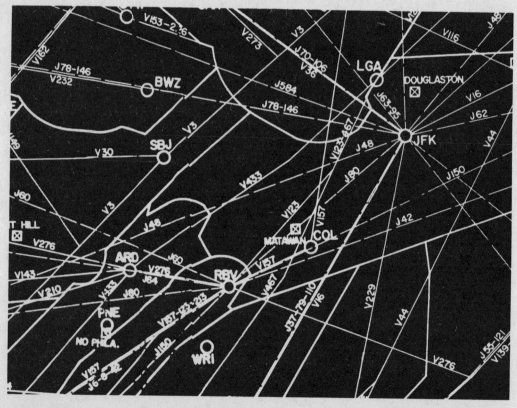

Static flight approach chart mounted above radar screen displays aircraft flight paths in the New York TRACON vicinity.

PART ONE

How to Become an Air Traffic Controller

"The Spirit of St. Louis" making its very first takeoff at San Diego, April 28, 1927, with Charles Lindbergh at the controls. After completing the flight tests, Lindbergh departed for St. Louis on May 10, arriving in a record-setting 14 hours, 25 minutes. He flew to Long Island on May 12. His total flying time from coast to coast set a new air record: 21 hours, 45 minutes.

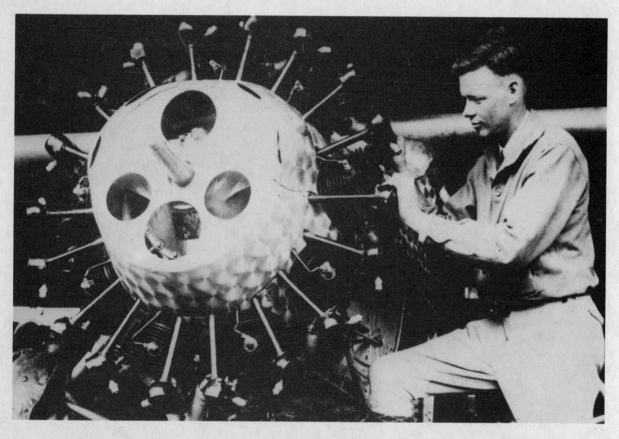

Charles A. Lindbergh looks over his "super-inspected" 223 horsepower Wright Whirlwind engine in an airfield hangar on Long Island a few days before his trans-Atlantic flight. (Photo courtesy Smithsonian Institution National Air and Space Museum)

"The first flight lasted only twelve seconds, a flight very modest when compared with that of birds, but it was, nevertheless, the first in the history of the world in which a machine carrying a man had raised itself by its own power into the air in free flight, had sailed forward on a level course without reduction in speed, and had finally landed without being wrecked."

—Wright brothers' description of the birth of powered flight at Kitty Hawk, N.C., December 17, 1903

FAA HISTORY

The FAA, now an operating arm of the Department of Transportation, traces its ancestry back to the Air Commerce Act of 1926, which led to the establishment of the Aeronautics Branch (later reorganized as the Bureau of Air Commerce) in the Department of Commerce with authority to certify pilots and aircraft, develop air navigation facilities, promote flying safety and issue flight information. The government acted just in time. In May of 1927, Charles Lindbergh bridged the North Atlantic in 33½ hours, generating new interest and enthusiasm for aviation in both Europe and the United States.

Aviation continued to grow and expand at a very rapid rate in the decade following Lindbergh's flight, creating a need for new machinery to regulate civil flying. The result was the Civil Aeronautics Act of 1938, which established the independent Civil Aeronautics Authority with responsibilities in both the safety and economic areas of civil aviation. In 1940, the machinery was readjusted and the powers previously vested in the Civil Aeronautics Authority were shared by a new Civil Aeronautics Authority (CAA), which was placed under an Assistant Secretary in the Department of Commerce, and the semi-independent Civil Aeronautics Board (CAB), which had administrative ties to the Department of Commerce but reported directly to Congress.

The CAA performed yeoman service during World War II, but proved unequal to the task of managing the airways in the years after the war due to the tremendous surge of civil air traffic and the introduction of new high-performance aircraft. In 1958, Congress passed the Federal Aviation Act, which created the independent Federal Aviation Agency with broad new authority to regulate civil aviation and provide for the safe and efficient utilization of the nation's airspace.

In April 1967, the Federal Aviation Agency became the Federal Aviation Administration (FAA) and was incorporated into the new Department of Transportation, which had been established to give unity and direction to a coordinated national transportation system. The FAA's basic responsibilities are still the same. And even while working with other administrations within the Department of Transportation in long-range transportation planning, the FAA continues to concern itself primarily with the promotion and regulation of civil aviation to insure safe and orderly growth.

One of the FAA's principal responsibilities is the operation and maintenance of the world's largest and most advanced air traffic control and air navigation system. Today half of the agency's work force of approximately 50,000 people are engaged in some phase of air traffic control. They staff some 464 airport control towers, 21 air route traffic control centers, and 175 flight service stations.

John F. Kennedy Airport: This is an example of a busy airport terminal area.

An aerial view of LaGuardia Airport. If you look closely you can see a departure off the end of Runway 31.

Civil aviation careers in the federal government are found within the Department of Transportation, the Federal Aviation Administration (FAA), and a growing number of other federal departments and agencies. All of the jobs come under the auspices of the federal civil service. Wage scales are determined by Congress, which, from time to time, adjusts the pay levels to bring them in line with comparable jobs in private business and industry. Salaries for federal civil service employees are divided into two categories:

General Schedule—for those employees who perform administrative, managerial, technical, clerical, and professional jobs and who are paid on an annual basis
Federal Wage System—for those employees who perform jobs associated with the trades and crafts and who are paid wages on an hourly basis

Most federal civil service employees in the aviation field are covered by the General Schedule, and their salaries vary according to their grade level (GS-1 through GS-18). Within each of the grades provided in the General Schedule, provision is made for periodic pay increases based on an acceptable level of performance coupled with an acceptable level of competence. Forty hours constitutes a normal work week. Additional payment is called premium pay and is made for shift work involving duty between 6 p.m. and 6 a.m. and for work during Sundays and holidays.

TABLE 1. GENERAL SCHEDULE OF ANNUAL SALARY RATES

GENERAL SCHEDULE — Department of Transportation — EFFECTIVE JANUARY 1991

GRADE	52 Weeks Waiting Period				104 Weeks Waiting Period			156 Weeks Waiting Period		
	Step 1	2	3	4	5	6	7	8	9	10
GS-1	$10,581	$10,935	$11,286	$11,637	$11,990	$12,197	$12,544	$12,893	$12,910	$13,232
2	11,897	12,180	12,574	12,910	13,053	13,437	13,821	14,205	14,589	14,973
3	12,982	13,415	13,848	14,281	14,714	15,147	15,580	16,013	16,446	16,879
4	14,573	15,059	15,545	16,031	16,517	17,003	17,489	17,975	18,461	18,947
5	16,305	16,849	17,393	17,937	18,481	19,025	19,569	20,113	20,657	21,201
6	18,174	18,780	19,384	19,992	20,598	21,204	21,810	22,416	23,022	23,628
7	20,195	20,862	21,541	22,214	22,887	23,560	24,233	24,906	25,579	26,252
8	22,367	23,113	23,859	24,605	25,351	26,097	26,843	27,589	28,335	29,081
9	24,705	25,529	26,353	27,177	28,001	28,825	29,649	30,473	31,297	32,121
10	27,206	28,113	29,020	29,927	30,834	31,741	32,648	33,555	34,462	35,369
11	29,891	30,887	31,883	32,879	33,875	34,871	35,867	36,863	37,859	38,855
12	35,825	37,019	38,213	39,407	40,601	41,795	42,989	44,183	45,377	46,571
13	42,601	44,021	45,441	46,861	48,281	49,701	51,121	52,541	53,961	55,381
14	50,342	52,020	53,698	55,376	57,054	58,732	60,410	62,088	63,766	65,444
15	59,216	61,190	63,164	65,138	67,112	69,086	71,060	73,034	75,008	76,982
16	69,451	71,766	74,081	76,396	78,190	79,438*	81,708*	83,978*	85,470*	
17	79,762*	82,420*	85,078*	85,470*	85,500*					
18	86,682*									

*The rate of basic pay payable to employees at these levels is limited to $78,200, the rate payable for Level V of the Executive Schedule.

NOTE: The entry grade for Air Traffic Control Specialists is GS-7

AIR TRAFFIC CONTROL CAREERS

The Federal Aviation Commission projects a 30% rise in the volume of air traffic over the next ten years. During this same period, more than half of the current Air Traffic Control work force will become eligible to retire. This means that the demand for qualified candidates to fill Air Traffic Control positions will continue to increase.

Nature of the Work

The definition most often used to describe an Air Traffic Control Specialist is "a professional who provides for the safe, orderly and expeditious flow of air traffic both in the air and on the ground." This definition may sound simple but the job of the Air Traffic Control Specialist is a highly complicated and exacting one. It demands practical men and women with special characteristics. A controller's work is divided into three specializations: (1) Center, (2) Terminal, and (3) Station.

CENTER. Center controllers direct aircraft operating under Instrument Flight Rules en route along the airways for the purpose of assuring proper separation between the aircraft and minimizing delays arising from traffic congestion. They issue instructions, clearances, advice, and information to aircraft, maintain a progressive check of aircraft movement, initiate search and rescue action's to locate overdue aircraft and direct the dispersal of aircraft in a military emergency. Center controllers are assisted in their work by computer-fed radar as they maintain voice communications with the flight crews aloft. An individual permanently assigned to a Center could progress to the GS-13 or 14 level.

TERMINAL. Terminal controllers are concerned with controlling aircraft in the vicinity of airports for the purpose of assuring proper separation between aircraft and minimizing delays resulting from traffic congestion. They give traffic control instructions to aircraft operating under Visual and Instrument Flight Rules and provide flight assistance to assure safe and expeditious movement of traffic. An individual permanently assigned to a tower could progress to a GS-11, 12, 13, or 14 level.

STATION. Station specialists provide information about weather, air navigation and airport conditions to pilots before and during flight. They relay traffic control conditions to pilots before and during flight. They also relay traffic control instructions and other information between pilots and air traffic control facilities, provide information to pilots in distress, orient lost pilots, and initiate search and rescue actions to locate overdue aircraft. An individual permanently assigned to a Flight Service Station could progress to the GS-9, 10, or 11 level. (For further information about the work of Flight Service Station personnel, see Part Four of this book.)

Working Conditions

Controllers normally work a forty-hour week in FAA control towers and centers using radios, radar, electronic computers, telephones, and other devices for communications. Shift work is necessary. Each controller is responsible, at separate

times, for giving instructions to aircraft. These individual duties are rotated among the staff about every two hours at busy locations. At peak times, controllers must work rapidly. Mental demands increase as traffic mounts, especially when poor flying conditions occur and traffic stacks up. Radar controllers usually work in semi-darkness.

While the salary scale for controllers is determined by the U.S. Congress, certain other conditions of work are covered by agreements between the controllers and the FAA. The contract negotiated by the National Air Traffic Controllers Association, which went into effect in May of 1989, provides for more frequent rest breaks, more flexible vacation and leave policies, and more flexible work schedules, including greater opportunity for part-time employment.

Where The Jobs Are

The FAA employs over 17,000 controllers at air traffic centers and towers and Flight Service Stations located throughout the nation. Some jobs are available outside the contiguous United States in Alaska, Hawaii, Puerto Rico, the Virgin Islands, and American Samoa. IMPORTANT: Employees must be able to relocate to meet staffing requirements.

Qualification Requirements

To qualify, you must meet the criteria listed below:

- Pass the written test PLUS 3 years of general experience, or 4 years of college, or any combination of education and experience equaling 3 years of general experience; or

- Pass the written test PLUS 4 years of college PLUS 1 year of graduate study or Superior Academic Achievement; or

- Pass the written test PLUS one of the following:
  (1) civilian or military facility rating in ATC involving the active control of air traffic in a center or terminal, or (2) past or present FAA air carrier dispatcher certificate, or (3) past or present instrument flight rating, or (4) past or present FAA certificate as a navigator or armed forces navigator/bombardier, or (5) past or present pilot rating with 350 hours of flight time, or (6) past or present rating as an Aerospace Defense Command Intercept Director, or (7) specialized experience as described in the following information.

Experience

General experience is any progressively responsible work which demonstrates your potential for learning and performing air traffic control work. The work can be administrative, technical, or other types of employment.

Specialized experience is military or civilian air traffic control work which demonstrates possession of the knowledge, skills, and abilities needed to perform air traffic control work.

Education

Qualifying education is successfully completed study in a college or university leading to a bachelor's or higher degree.

In combining education and experience, 1 year (30 semester or 45 quarter hours) of undergraduate study is equivalent to 9 months of general experience. Thus, if you had 60 semester hours (90 quarter hours) of college study, you could substitute it for 18 months of general experience, and you would need another 18 months of qualifying work experience to meet the 3-year requirement.

Students who will complete the amount of education needed to qualify within 9 months of the test date may apply and be selected, but they must complete the study before they can begin work.

Superior Academic Achievement. Applicants who have a bachelor's degree and score 70 through 75 on the written test may still qualify for GS-7 positions if they have attained a high academic standing. The agency will require proof of academic standing before appointing you. This does not apply to applicants with scores above 75.

Age Limitation

In May 1972, the 92nd Congress of the United States of America passed Public Law 92-297, giving recognition to the unusually high standards required of FAA air traffic controllers. Consequently, you must be no older than age 30 when entering on duty as an air traffic control specialist in the tower or center option. This age limitation does not apply in the flight service station option. On the basis of extensive studies and experience, it has been determined that the unique skills and abilities necessary for the control of air traffic begin to decline at a relatively early age.

Citizenship

You must be a U.S. citizen at the time you apply for an ATCS position.

Written Aptitude Test

All applicants must take a written aptitude test to measure their ability to learn and perform air traffic work. This test primarily measures your ability to think abstractly and spatially. Your knowledge of aviation and air traffic will also be measured; however, you can make the maximum score on the test (100) with no knowledge of aviation at all. The test requires approximately 4 hours to take, plus additional time for forms completion. **Your written test score establishes your eligibility for employment referral for a period of 18 months. You may not retest during this period.**

Applying for the Test

Your first step is to complete an application form like the one shown on page 10 (Figure 1). You may request the application from one of the Federal Job Information/Testing Centers listed in Appendix I of this book. (See "Office of Personnel Management Addresses and Telephone Numbers.") Mail the application form to the OPM office which is located closest to the city where you wish to be tested.

The OPM office will notify you when and where the test will be given. Tests are given at least once every 3 months. Additional forms will be mailed to you to complete and take to the test location.

In many metropolitan areas, the test is regularly administered without pre-scheduling. Call the OPM office in your area for a recorded message which will include information on walk-in testing, if available.

You may also contact the FAA Employment Offices listed in Appendix II for more information on the hiring process.

Test Scoring

You will be tested, your score sheets will be computer scanned and graded, and a computer record will be established. Your records will then be referred to the Special Examining Unit (SEU) located at the Federal Aviation Administration's Mike Monroney Aeronautical Center in Oklahoma City, Oklahoma. As soon as your computer record is established, you will receive a Notice of Results indicating your score.

Scores range from 70 to 100 with up to 10 points added for individuals entitled to veterans preference.

Figure 1. APPLICATION FOR WRITTEN TEST

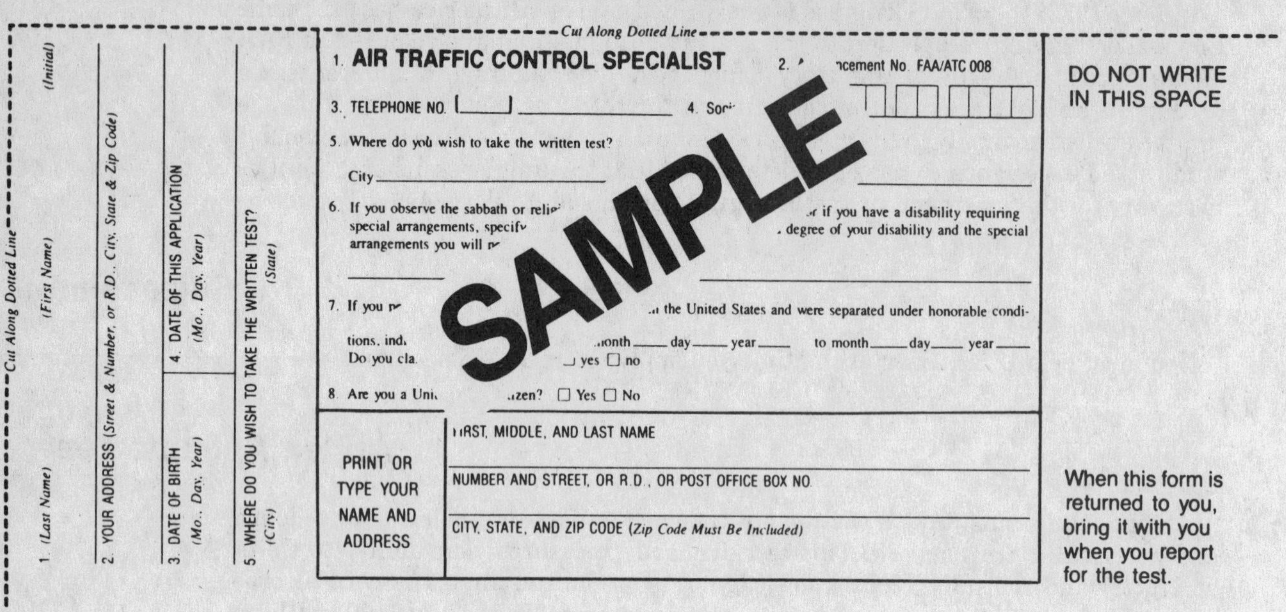

Cut Along Dotted Line

1. (Last Name) (First Name) (Initial)

2. YOUR ADDRESS (Street & Number, or R.D., City, State & Zip Code)

3. DATE OF BIRTH (Mo., Day, Year)

4. DATE OF THIS APPLICATION (Mo., Day, Year)

5. WHERE DO YOU WISH TO TAKE THE WRITTEN TEST? (City) (State)

Cut Along Dotted Line

1. AIR TRAFFIC CONTROL SPECIALIST 2. A…ncement No. FAA/ATC 008

3. TELEPHONE NO. ( ) 4. Soc…

5. Where do you wish to take the written test?

City

6. If you observe the sabbath or reli… …or if you have a disability requiring special arrangements, specify… …degree of your disability and the special arrangements you will n…

7. If you … …in the United States and were separated under honorable conditions, ind… …month ___ day ___ year ___ to month ___ day ___ year ___
Do you cla… ☐ yes ☐ no

8. Are you a Uni… …izen? ☐ Yes ☐ No

PRINT OR TYPE YOUR NAME AND ADDRESS

FIRST, MIDDLE, AND LAST NAME

NUMBER AND STREET, OR R.D., OR POST OFFICE BOX NO.

CITY, STATE, AND ZIP CODE (Zip Code Must Be Included)

DO NOT WRITE IN THIS SPACE

When this form is returned to you, bring it with you when you report for the test.

SAMPLE

New Controller Screening Tests

Applicants who have scored 90 or more points on the written aptitude test will be eligible to be chosen for the new computerized aptitude screening tests.

Under this new procedure, applicants must undergo a one-week computerized testing process at the FAA Academy. Only applicants who score high on these tests will be eligible for training. Travel expenses to the Academy in Oklahoma City will be paid by the FAA for all participants.

Measuring Controller Aptitude

Designed by the FAA specifically for the air traffic controller profession, the screen tests different aptitudes including memory, the ability to visualize the relationship of objects to one another, the ability to do several complex tasks at the same time, the ability to sort and prioritize important tasks, and the ability to analyze situations quickly and to plan ahead. The tests look somewhat like video games and can involve simulated airspace scenarios.

Applicants are given three to four days of practice time before testing begins to ensure a level-playing field for all participants. A candidate's prior familiarity with computer or video games should not affect test results.

Training

Trainees receive substantive instruction at the FAA Academy in Oklahoma before going on to further training at field facilities. However, those who fail to complete training are separated or reassigned from controller positions. The FAA conducts upgrading training programs for controllers continuously. Training in air traffic control goes on long after the controller reaches the full performance level.

The ARTS IIIA system processes incoming signals and produces a continuous alphanumeric display which tags each blip on the display with aircraft identity, speed and altitude.

A modern air traffic facility.

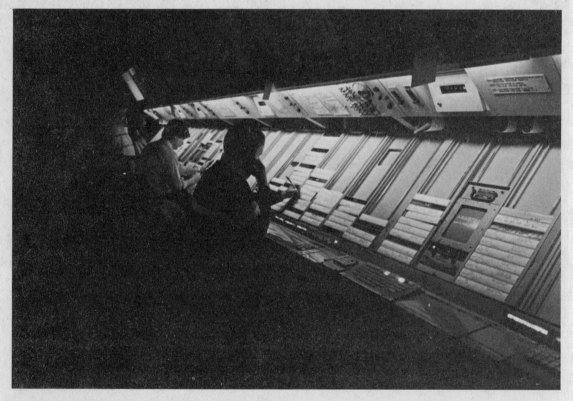

Controllers working on flight progress strips.

Controller working air traffic at a TRACON.

Two weather radar displays used for weather observations and tracking.

Opportunities for Advancement

Promotion from a trainee to a higher-grade professional controller depends upon the employee's performance and satisfactory progression in the training program. Trainees who do not successfully complete their training courses are separated or reassigned from their controller positions. Advances in grade (with accompanying increases in salary) for successful trainees are fairly rapid, but grades above GS-14 are limited to managerial positions of team supervisor, assistant chief, staff officer, and chief. During the first year, trainees are on probation, and then they may advance from back-up positions to primary positions of responsibility. It takes a controller from three to six years to reach the full performance level. Some professional controllers are selected for research activities with the FAA's national aviation facilities experimental center in Atlantic City, New Jersey. Some are selected to serve as instructors at the FAA Academy in Oklahoma City, Oklahoma.

APPLYING FOR A GOVERNMENT JOB

The Office of Personnel Management (OPM) operates area offices and federal job information and testing centers throughout the country. (See Appendix I for a list of these area offices.) These offices provide individuals with a centralized location for information on filing procedures and on federal government employment opportunities.

Area offices release test date information and conduct exams. They are responsible for recruiting functions and for the referral of qualified individuals to employing agencies in their own geographic area. They serve as a liaison between the federal government and the public.

APPLYING FOR THE ATC WRITTEN EXAM AND FOR WORK AS AN AIR TRAFFIC CONTROLLER

The application form for the written test for the position of Air Traffic Control Specialist was shown on p. 10. You may also have to fill out the following forms to apply for the written examination and to apply for federal employment. You can obtain these forms from any Office of Personnel Management (OPM) Federal Job Information Center (FJIC). These centers are listed in the white pages of major metropolitan area telephone directories under "Federal Government." (See Appendix I for a current OPM address listing.)

Let's examine each form.

1. OPM FORM 5000-B—ADMISSION NOTICE (See Figure 3, page 17.)
This form is completed and forwarded by the applicant to the U.S. Office of Personnel Management. It serves the following purposes:
a. It is used by OPM to notify an applicant where and when to report for the written examination and to send the applicant all the necessary forms for completion prior to the test.
b. It is used to admit the applicant to the test site indicated on the form.

2. SF-171—APPLICATION FOR FEDERAL EMPLOYMENT (Figure 4, pages 18–22.)
This form asks for general information about the applicant: availability for employment, military service and veteran preference information, work experience, education, and any special skills and/or accomplishments the applicant may have or have attained. The applicant's qualifications for a position are determined based on a review of this form; filling it out should be taken very seriously and done with great care. This form is given to applicants after the written exam is scored.

3. OPM FORM 1203–M—OCCUPATIONAL SUPPLEMENT FOR AIR TRAFFIC CONTROL POSITIONS (See Figure 5, pages 23–26.)
This form is furnished at the test site. It is coded and reviewed by a scanner, and the information compiled is used in determining eligibility, availability, and other facts about the applicant. For example, it asks you to select the regions where you would prefer to work. (See Figure 2 on page 16.) Information obtained from this form is used, along with the applicant's written test results, to determine referral for ATC vacancies.

4. OPM FORM 1170-17—SUPPLEMENTAL QUALIFICATIONS STATEMENT— LIST OF COLLEGE COURSES AND CERTIFICATE OF SCHOLASTIC ACHIEVEMENT (See Figure 6, pages 27–30.)
This form documents the college courses an applicant has taken and is used to support Form SF–171 in satisfying the qualifications requirements of the position(s) being applied for. Courses are listed by appropriate academic field, and information must be filled in on completion dates, grades attained and credits received. This form also contains a portion on scholastic achievement, which may be applicable in qualifying for a higher grade level (in this case a GS-7) based on academic standing. Proof in support of this form (transcripts, employment records, etc.) is required before any appointment is made.

All the forms that you will be completing are very important. Take your time filling them out; work slowly and with great care. These forms will be part of your record for the rest of your career in the FAA.

FIGURE 2. FAA REGIONAL BOUNDARIES

As the map shows, there are 11 FAA regions. Be sure to apply where you are willing to work because transfers between regions rarely occur before the controller reaches full performance level.

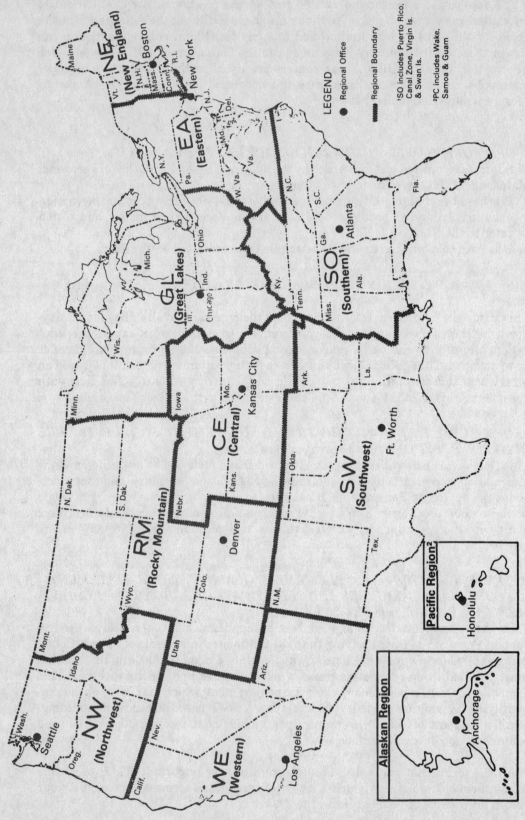

FIGURE 3. OPM FORM 5000-B ADMISSION NOTICE

Type or Print in Ink

1. Title of Examination

2. Social Security Number

3. Announcement No. (If appropriate)

4. Where do you wish to take written test?
   City   State   Examining Point No.

5. Birth Date
   (month)   (day)   (year)

6. Telephone No. (Include Area Code)

7. Where are you willing to work?
   State:

8. If you have performed active duty in the armed forces of the United States, separated under honorable conditions, indicate periods of service:
   From: (month, day, year)   To: (month, day, year)

9. City: State:
   Check here if you observe the Sabbath or religious holiday on a day other than Sunday (specify day) or have a disability that will require special or individual testing arrangement. Specify the nature and degree of your disability and the special arrangements you will need.

10. Do you claim veteran preference? ☐ No ☐ Yes If yes, based on:
    ☐ (1) Active duty in the armed forces of the U.S. during the period December 7, 1941, through July [...] than 180 consecutive days of active duty (other than for training) in the armed forces of the U.S. any p[...] after January 31, 1955 and before October 15, 1976, or (3) after service in a campaign for which a c[...] been authorized
    ☐ Your status as: (1) a disabled veteran or a veteran who was awarded the Purple Heart for wounds or injur[...] action, (2) a spouse of a deceased veteran who has not remarried, (3) the spouse of a veteran who h[...] connected disability which disqualifies the veteran for civil service appointment, or (4) the widowed, [...] separated mother of an ex-service son or daughter who died in action or who is totally and permanently a[...]

11. Are you a United States citizen? ☐ YES ☐ NO

DO NOT WRITE IN THIS SPACE

Give Address Where You Wish To Be Notified of Time and Place For Examination.

Name (First, middle and last)

Address (Number and street, or R.D., or post office box no.)

City, state and Zip Code (ZIP Code must be included)

CHECK COPY TO BE SURE IT IS LEGIBLE

This card will be returned to you. Bring it with you when you report for the written test.

ADMISSION NOTICE

IMPORTANT — READ INSTRUCTIONS ON THE OTHER SIDE

IDENTIFICATION MAY BE REQUIRED FOR WRITTEN EXAMINATIONS
The Federal Government Is An Equal Opportunity Employer

OPM Form 5000-B
(Rev. 10-80)

SAMPLE

FIGURE 4. SF-171—APPLICATION FOR FEDERAL EMPLOYMENT

Standard Form 171
Application for Federal Employment

Read The Following Instructions Carefully Before You Complete This Application

- **DO NOT SUBMIT A RESUME INSTEAD OF THIS APPLICATION.**

- **TYPE OR PRINT CLEARLY IN DARK INK.**

- IF YOU NEED MORE SPACE for an answer, use a sheet of paper the same size as this page. On **each** sheet write your name, Social Security Number, the announcement number or job title, and the item number. Attach all additional forms and sheets to this application at the top of page 3.

- If you do not answer **all** questions fully and correctly, you may delay the review of your application and lose job opportunities.

- Unless you are asked for additional material in the announcement or qualification information, **do not attach** any materials, such as: official position descriptions, performance evaluations, letters of recommendation, certificates of training, publications, etc. Any materials you attach which were not asked for may be removed from your application and will **not** be returned to you.

- We suggest that you **keep a copy** of this application for your use. If you plan to make copies of your application, we suggest you leave items **1, 48** and **49** blank. Complete these blank items each time you apply. **YOU MUST SIGN AND DATE, IN INK, EACH COPY YOU SUBMIT.**

- **To apply for a specific Federal civil service examination** (whether or not a written test is required) **or a specific vacancy in a Federal agency:**

  -- Read the announcement and other materials provided.

  -- Make sure that your work experience and/or education meet the qualification requirements described.

  -- Make sure the announcement is open for the job and location you are interested in. Announcements may be closed to receipt of applications for some types of jobs, grades, or geographic locations.

  -- Make sure that you are allowed to apply. Some jobs are limited to veterans, or to people who work for the Federal Government or worked for the Federal Government in the past.

  -- Follow any directions on "How to Apply". quired, bring any material you are instruc sion. For example, you may be instructed 171 to the test." If a written test is not requi and all other forms required by the announc the address specified in the announcement.

Work Experience *(Item 24)*

- Carefully complete each experience block you need to describe your work experience. Unless you qualify based on education alone, **your rating will depend on your description of previous jobs. Do not leave out any jobs you held during the last ten years.**

- Under **Description of Work**, write a **clear** and **brief**, but **complete** description of your **major** duties and responsibilities for each job. Include any supervisory duties, special assignments, and your accomplishments in the job. We may verify your description with your former employers.

- If you had a major change of duties or responsibilities while you worked for the same employer, describe each major change as a separate job.

Veteran Preference in Hiring *(Item 22)*

- **DO NOT LEAVE Item 22 BLANK.** If you do **not** claim veteran preference place an "X" in the box next to "**NO PREFERENCE**".

- You **cannot** receive veteran preference if you are retired or plan to retire at or above the rank of major or lieutenant commander, **unless** you are disabled or retired from the active military Reserve.

- To receive veteran preference your separation from active duty must have been under honorable conditions. This includes honorable and general discharges. A clemency discharge does not meet the requirements of the Veteran Preference Act.

- Active duty for training in the military Reserve and National Guard programs is not considered active duty for purposes of veteran preference.

- To qualify for preference you must meet **ONE** of the following conditions:

  1. Served on active duty anytime between December 7, 1941, and July 1, 1955; (If you were a Reservist called to active duty between February 1, 1955 and July 1, 1955, you must meet condition 2, below.)

     or

  2. Served on active duty any part of which was between July 2, 1955 and October 14, 1976 or a Reservist called to active duty between February 1, 1955 and October 14, 1976 **and** who served for more than 180 days;

     or

  3. Entered on active duty between October 15, 1976 and September 7, 1980 or a Reservist who entered on active duty between October 15, 1976 and O   r 13, 1982 **and** received a Campaign Badge or Expediti   al **or** are a disabled veteran;

     or

  4.   d Forces after September 7, 1980 or entered   enlistment on or after October 14, 1982 **and:**

     a.   nths of continuous active duty or the full period   dered to active duty, or were discharged under 10   1171 or for hardship under 10 U.S.C. 1173 **and** received   were entitled to receive a Campaign Badge or Expeditionary Medal; **or**

     b.   are a disabled veteran.

- If you meet one of the four conditions above, you qualify for 5-point preference. If you want to claim 5-point preference **and** do not meet the requirements for 10-point preference, discussed below, place an "X" in the box next to "**5-POINT PREFERENCE**".

- If you think you qualify for 10-Point Preference, review the requirements described in the Standard Form (SF) 15, Application for 10-Point Veteran Preference. The SF 15 is available from any Federal Job Information Center. The 10-point preference groups are:

  -- Non-Compensably Disabled or Purple Heart Recipient.

  -- Compensably Disabled (less than 30%).

  -- Compensably Disabled (30% or more).

  -- Spouse, Widow(er) or Mother of a deceased or disabled veteran.

  If you claim 10-point preference, place an "X" in the box next to the group that applies to you. **To receive 10-point preference you must attach a completed SF 15 to this application together with the proof requested in the SF 15.**

Privacy Act Statement

The Office of Personnel Management is authorized to rate applicants for Federal jobs under sections 1302, 3301, and 3304 of title 5 of the U.S. Code. Section 1104 of title 5 allows the Office of Personnel Management to authorize other Federal agencies to rate applicants for Federal jobs. We need the information you put on this form and associated application forms to see how well your education and work skills qualify you for a Federal job. We also need information on matters such as citizenship and military service to see whether you are affected by laws we must follow in deciding who may be employed by the Federal Government.

We must have your Social Security Number (SSN) to keep your records straight because other people may have the same name and birth date. The SSN has been used to keep records since 1943, when Executive Order 9397 asked agencies to do so. The Office of Personnel Management may also use your SSN to make requests for information about you from employers, schools, banks, and others who know you, but only as allowed by law or Presidential directive. The information we collect by using your SSN will be used for employment purposes and also may be used for studies, statistics, and computer matching to benefit and payment files.

Information we have about you may also be given to Federal, State and local agencies for checking on law violations or for other lawful purposes. We may send your name and address to State and local Government agencies, Congressional and other public offices, and public international organizations, if they request names of people to consider for employment. We may also notify your school placement office if you are selected for a Federal job.

Giving us your SSN or any of the other information is voluntary. However, we cannot process your application, which is the first step toward getting a job, if you do not give us the information we request. Incomplete addresses and ZIP Codes will also slow processing.

DETACH THIS PAGE — NOTE SF 171-A ON BACK

SAMPLE

Application for Federal Employment—SF 171

Read the instructions before you complete this application. *Type or print clearly in dark ink.*

Form Approved
OMB No. 3206-0012

GENERAL INFORMATION

1 What kind of job are you applying for? *Give title and announcement no. (if any)*

2 Social Security Number

3 Sex ☐ Male ☐ Female

4 Birth date *(Month, Day, Year)*

5 Birthplace *(City and State or Country)*

6 Name *(Last, First, Middle)*

Mailing address *(include apartment number, if any)*

City   State   ZIP Code

7 Other names ever used *(e.g., maiden name, nickname, etc.)*

8 Home Phone — Area Code Number

9 Work Phone — Area Code Number Extension

10 Were you ever employed as a civilian by the Federal Government? If **"NO"**, go to **Item 11.** If **"YES"**, mark each type of job you held with an **"X".**

☐ Temporary ☐ Career-Conditional ☐ Career ☐ Excepted

What is your **highest** grade, classification series and job title?

Dates at **highest** grade: FROM   TO

AVAILABILITY

11 When can you start work? *(Month and Year)*

12 What is the lowest pay you will not be cc than you indic... Pay $ _____

13 In what geographic area(s) are you willing to w...

14 Are you willing to work: **YES NO**

A. 40 hours per week *(full-time)*? . . . .
B. 25-32 hours per week *(part-time)*? . . . .
C. 17-24 hours per week *(part-time)*? . . . .
D. 16 or fewer hours per week *(part-time)*? . . . . . .
E. An intermittent job *(on-call/seasonal)*? . . . .
F. Weekends, shifts, or rotating shifts?. . . . .

15 Are you willing to take a temporary job lasting:

A. 5 to 12 months *(sometimes longer)*? . . . .
B. 1 to 4 months? . . . .
C. Less than 1 month?. . . . .

16 Are you willing to travel away from home for:

A. 1 to 5 nights each month?. . . . .
B. 6 to 10 nights each month?. . . . .
C. 11 or more nights each month?. . . . .

MILITARY SERVICE AND VETERAN PREFERENCE

17 Have you served in the United States Military Service? *If your only active duty was training in the Reserves or National Guard, answer "NO".* If **"NO"**, go to item 22. . . . .   **YES NO**

18 Did you or will you retire at or above the rank of major or lieutenant commander?. . . . .

THE FEDERAL GOVERNMENT IS AN EQUAL OPPORTUNITY EMPLOYER
PREVIOUS EDITION USABLE UNTIL 12-31-90

Page 1

FOR USE OF EXAMINING OFFICE ONLY

Date entered register

Form reviewed:
Form approved:

Option	Grade	Earned Rating	Veteran Preference	Augmented Rating

☐ No Preference Claimed
☐ 5 Points *(Tentative)*
☐ 10 Pts. *(30% Or More Comp. Dis.)*
☐ 10 Pts *(Less Than 30% Comp. Dis.)*
☐ Other 10 Points

Initials and Date

☐ Disallowed ☐ Being Investigated

FOR USE OF APPOINTING OFFICE ONLY

Preference has been verified through proof that the separation was under honorable conditions, and other proof as required.

☐ 5-Point ☐ 10-Point--30% or More Compensable Disability ☐ 10-Point--Less Than 30% Compensable Disability ☐ 10-Point--Other

Signature and Title

Date

SAMPLE

...Y SERVICE AND VETERAN PREFERENCE *(Cont.)*

Were you discharged from the military service under honorable conditions? *(If your discharge was changed to "honorable" or "general" by a Discharge Review Board, answer "YES". If you received a clemency discharge, answer "NO".)* If **"NO"**, provide below the date and type of discharge you received.   **YES NO**

Discharge Date *(Month, Day, Year)*   Type of Discharge

20 List the dates *(Month, Day, Year)*, and branch for all **active duty** military service.

From	To	Branch of Service

21 If all your active military duty was after October 14, 1976, list the full names and dates of all campaign badges or expeditionary medals you received or were entitled to receive.

22 Read the instructions that came with this form before completing this item. When you have determined your eligibility for veteran preference from the instructions, place an **"X"** in the box next to your veteran preference claim.

☐ NO PREFERENCE

☐ 5-POINT PREFERENCE -- You must show proof when you are hired.

10-POINT PREFERENCE -- If you claim 10-point preference, place an **"X"** in the box below next to the basis for your claim. **To receive 10-point preference you must also complete a Standard Form 15, Application for 10-Point Veteran Preference, which is available from any Federal Job Information Center. ATTACH THE COMPLETED SF 15 AND REQUESTED PROOF TO THIS APPLICATION.**

☐ Non-compensably disabled or Purple Heart recipient.
☐ Compensably disabled, less than 30 percent.
☐ Spouse, widow(er), or mother of a deceased or disabled veteran.
☐ Compensably disabled, 30 percent or more.

NSN 7540-00-935-7150   171-109

Standard Form 171 (Rev. 6-88)
U.S. Office of Personnel Management
FPM Chapter 295

WORK EXPERIENCE *If you have no work experience, write "NONE" in A below and go to 25 on page 3.*

23 May we ask your present employer about your character, qualifications, and work record? *A "NO" will not affect our review of your qualifications. If you answer "NO" and we need to contact your present employer before we can offer you a job, we will contact you first. . . . .*

YES	NO

24 READ **WORK EXPERIENCE** IN THE INSTRUCTIONS BEFORE YOU BEGIN.

- Describe your current or most recent job in Block **A** and work backwards, describing each job you held **during the past 10 years.** If you were **unemployed** for longer than **3 months** within the past 10 years, list the dates and your address(es) in an experience block.

- You may sum up in one block work that you did **more than 10 years ago.** But if that work **is related** to the type of job you are applying for, describe each related job in a separate block.

- INCLUDE VOLUNTEER WORK *(non-paid work)*.--If the work *(or a part of the work)* is like the job you are applying for, complete **all** parts of the experience block just as you would for a paying job. You may receive credit for work experience with religious, community, welfare, service, and other organizations.

- INCLUDE MILITARY SERVICE--You should complete **all** parts of the experience block just as you would for a non-military job, including all supervisory experience. Describe each major change of duties or responsibilities in a separate experience block.

- IF YOU NEED MORE SPACE TO DESCRIBE A JOB--Use sheets of paper the same size as this page (be sure to include **all** information we ask for in **A** and **B** below). On **each** sheet show your name, Social Security Number, and the announcement number or job title.

- IF YOU NEED MORE EXPERIENCE BLOCKS, use the SF 171-A or a sheet of paper.

- IF YOU NEED TO UPDATE (ADD MORE RECENT JOBS), use the SF 172 or a sheet of paper as described above.

A Name and address of employer's organization *(include ZIP Code, if known)*

Dates employed *(give month, day and year)*

From: To:

Salary or earnings

Starting $ per

Ending $ per

Average number if hours per week

Number of employees you supervise

Your reason for wanting to leave

Your immediate supervisor
Name   Area Code   Telephone No.

Exact title of your job

If Federal employment *(civilian or military)* list series, grade or rank, and, if promoted in this job, the date of your last promotion

Description of work: Describe your specific duties, responsibilities and accomplishments in this job, **including** the job title(s) of any employees you supervise. *If you describe more than one type of work (for example, carpentry and painting, or personnel and budget), write the approximate percentage of time you spent doing each.*

SAMPLE

For Agency Use (skill codes, etc.)

B Name and address of employer's organization *(include ZIP Code, if known)*

Dates employed *(give month, day and year)*

From: To:

Salary or earnings

Starting $ per

Ending $ per

Average number of hours per week

Number of employees you supervised

Your reason for leaving

Your immediate supervisor
Name   Area Code   Telephone No.

Exact title of your job

If Federal employment *(civilian or military)* list series, grade or rank, and, if promoted in this job, the date of your last promotion

Description of work: Describe your specific duties, responsibilities and accomplishments in this job, **including** the job title(s) of any employees you supervised. *If you describe more than one type of work (for example, carpentry and painting, or personnel and budget), write the approximate percentage of time you spent doing each.*

For Agency Use (skill codes, etc.)

Page 2   IF YOU NEED MORE EXPERIENCE BLOCKS, USE SF 171-A *(SEE BACK OF INSTRUCTION PAGE).*

← ———— **ATTACH ANY ADDITIONAL FORMS AND SHEETS HERE**

EDUCATION

25 Did you graduate from high school? *If you have a GED high school equivalency or will graduate within the next nine months, answer "YES".*

26 Write the name and location *(city and state)* of the last high school you attended or where you obtained your GED high school equivalency.

YES   If "YES", give month and year graduated or received GED equivalency: . . . .
NO   If **NO**, give the highest grade you completed: .

27 Have you ever attended college or graduate school?   **YES**   **NO**   If "YES", continue with **28**. If **NO**, go to **31**.

28 NAME AND LOCATION *(city, state and ZIP Code)* OF COLLEGE OR UNIVERSITY. *If you expect to grad-uate within nine months, give the **month** and **year** you expect to receive your degree:*

Name	City	State	ZIP Code	MONTH AND YEAR ATTENDED From	To	NUMBER OF CREDIT HOURS COMPLETED Semester	Quarter	TYPE OF DEGREE *(e.g. B.A., M.A.)*	MONTH AND YEAR OF DEGREE
1)									
2)									
3)									

29

CHIEF UNDERGRADUATE SUBJECTS *Show major on the first line*	NUMBER OF CREDIT HOURS COMPLETED Semester	Quarter
1)		
2)		
3)		

30

CHIEF GRADUATE SUBJECTS *Show major on the first line*	NUMBER OF CREDIT HOURS COMPLETED Semester	Quarter
1)		
2)		
3)		

31 If you have completed any **other courses or training** related to the kind of jobs you are applying for *(trade, vocational, Armed Forces, business)* give information below.

NAME AND LOCATION *(city, state and ZIP Code)* OF SCHOOL	MONTH AND YEAR ATTENDED From	To	CLASS-ROOM HOURS	SUBJECT(S)	TRAINING COMPLETED YES	NO
School Name 1)						
City	State	ZIP Code				
School Name 2)						
City	State					

SPECIAL SKILLS, ACCOMPLISHME~~NTS~~

32 Give the title and year of any honors, awards or ~~...~~ examples are: skills with computers or other m~~...~~ professional or scientific societies; patents or inven~~...~~ . List your special qualifications, skills or accomplishments that may help you get a job. *Some ~~...~~ant publications (do not submit copies); public speaking and writing experience; membership in*

33 How many words per minute can you:

TYPE?   TAKE DICTATION?

Agencies may test your skills before hiring you.

34 List **job-related** licenses or certificates that you have, such as: *registered nurse; lawyer; radio operator; driver's; pilot's; etc.*

LICENSE OR CERTIFICATE	DATE OF LATEST LICENSE OR CERTIFICATE	STATE OR OTHER LICENSING AGENCY
1)		
2)		

35 Do you speak or read a language other than English *(include sign language)?* **Applicants for jobs that require a language other than English may be given an interview conducted solely in that language.**   **YES**   **NO**   If "YES", list each language and place an "X" in each column that applies to you. If "NO", go to **36**.

LANGUAGE(S)	CAN PREPARE AND GIVE LECTURES Fluently	With Difficulty	CAN SPEAK AND UNDERSTAND Fluently	Passably	CAN TRANSLATE ARTICLES Into English	From English	CAN READ ARTICLES FOR OWN USE Easily	With Difficulty
1)								
2)								

REFERENCES

36 List three people who are not related to you and are not supervisors you listed under **24** who know your qualifications and fitness for the kind of job for which you are applying. At least **one** should know you well on a personal basis.

FULL NAME OF REFERENCE	TELEPHONE NUMBER(S) *(Include Area Code)*	PRESENT BUSINESS OR HOME ADDRESS *(Number, street and city)*	STATE	ZIP CODE
1)				
2)				
3)				

Page 3

SAMPLE

BACKGROUND INFORMATION -- *You must answer each question in this section before we can process your application.*

37 Are you a citizen of the United States? *(In most cases you must be a U.S. citizen to be hired. You will be required to submit proof of identity and citizenship at the time you are hired.)* If **"NO"**, give the country or countries you are a citizen of: _____ | YES | NO |

> **NOTE: It is important that you give complete and truthful answers to questions 38 through 44.** If you answer **"YES"** to any of them, provide your explanation(s) in **Item 45. Include** convictions resulting from a plea of nolo contendere *(no contest)*. **Omit:** 1) traffic fines of $100.00 or less; 2) any violation of law committed before your 16th birthday; 3) any violation of law committed before your 18th birthday, if finally decided in juvenile court or under a Youth Offender law; 4) any conviction set aside under the Federal Youth Corrections Act or similar State law; 5) any conviction whose record was expunged under Federal or State law. We will consider the date, facts, and circumstances of each event you list. In most cases you can still be considered for Federal jobs. However, **if you fail to tell the truth or fail to list all relevant** events or circumstances, this may be grounds for not hiring you, for firing you after you begin work, or for criminal prosecution (18 USC 1001).

	YES	NO
38 During the last **10 years**, were you **fired from any job** for any reason, did you **quit after being told that you would be fired**, or did you leave by mutual agreement because of specific problems?.		
39 Have you **ever** been convicted of, or forfeited collateral for **any felony violation?** *(Generally, a felony is defined as any violation of law punishable by imprisonment of longer than one year, except for violations called misdemeanors under State law which are punishable by imprisonment of two years or less.)*		
40 Have you **ever** been convicted of, or forfeited collateral for **any firearms or explosives violation?**		
41 Are you **now** under charges for **any** violation of law?		
42 During the **last 10 years** have you forfeited collateral, been convicted, been imprisoned, been on probation, or been on parole? Do **not** include violations reported in 39, 40, or 41, above.		
43 Have you **ever** been convicted by a military **court-martial?** If no military service, answer **"NO"**.		
44 Are you **delinquent** on any Federal debt? *(Include delinquencies arising from Federal taxes, loans, overpayment of benefits, and other debts to the U.S. Government **plus** defaults on Federally guaranteed or insured loans such as student and home mortgage loans.)*		

45 If **"YES" in:** **38** - Explain for each job the problem(s) and your reason(s) for leaving. Give the employer's name and address.
   39 through 43 - Explain each violation. Give place of occurrence and name/address of police or court involved.
   44 - Explain the type, length and amount of the delinquency or default, and steps you are taking to correct errors or repay the debt. Give any identification number associated with the debt and the address of the Federal agency involved.
   NOTE: If you need more space, use a sheet of paper, and include the item number.

Item No.	Date (Mo./Yr.)	Explanation	Mailing Address
			~~Em~~ployer, Police, Court, or Federal Agency
			City State ZIP Code
			Name of Employer, Police, Court, or Federal Agency
			City State ZIP Code

SAMPLE

		YES	NO
46 Do you receive, or have you ever applied for retirement pay, pension, or other pay based on military, Federal civilian, or District of Columbia Government service?			
47 Do any of your relatives work for the United States Government or the United States Armed Forces? Include: *father; mother; husband; wife; son; daughter; brother; sister; uncle; aunt; first cousin; nephew; niece; father-in-law; mother-in-law; son-in-law; daughter-in-law; brother-in-law; sister-in-law; stepfather; stepmother; stepson; stepdaughter; stepbrother; stepsister; half brother; and half sister.*			

If **"YES"**, provide details below. If you need more space, use a sheet of paper.

Name	Relationship	Department, Agency or Branch of Armed Forces

SIGNATURE, CERTIFICATION, AND RELEASE OF INFORMATION

YOU MUST SIGN THIS APPLICATION.   Read the following carefully before you sign.

- A false statement on any part of your application may be grounds for not hiring you, or for firing you after you begin work. Also, you may be punished by fine or imprisonment (U.S. Code, title 18, section 1001).
- If you are a male born after December 31, 1959 you must be registered with the Selective Service System or have a valid exemption in order to be eligible for Federal employment. You will be required to certify as to your status at the time of appointment.
- I **understand** that any information I give may be investigated as allowed by law or Presidential order.
- I **consent** to the release of information about my ability and fitness for Federal employment by *employers, schools, law enforcement agencies and other individuals and organizations, to investigators, personnel staffing specialists, and other authorized employees of the Federal Government.*
- I **certify** that, to the best of my knowledge and belief, **all** of my statements are true, correct, complete, and made in good faith.

48 SIGNATURE *(Sign each application in dark ink)*	**49** DATE SIGNED *(Month, day, year)*

Page 4

FIGURE 5. FORM 1203-M

FORM APPROVED
OMB NO. 3206-0040

FORM **B**

**OCCUPATIONAL SUPPLEMENT FOR
AIR TRAFFIC CONTROL POSITIONS – 2152**

US Office of Personnel
Management

PAGE **1**

DO NOT FOLD, STAPLE, TEAR OR PAPER CLIP THIS FORM.
DO NOT SUBMIT PHOTOCOPIES OF THIS FORM.
This form can be processed only if you:
1) Use a number 2 (or softer) lead pencil.
2) Completely blacken the circle corresponding to your response choice.
3) Completely erase any mistakes or stray marks.
Read the instructions for each item carefully before completing that item.

Recording information that does not accurately reflect your availability, employment preferences, and qualifications may cause you to lose consideration for some positi'

1 NAME

BATCH NUMBER (BNO)
FOR OFFICE USE ONLY

USE ONLY A NUMBER 2 (or softer) LEAD PENCIL.

NAME: _____
(Please Print)

3 DATE OF BIRTH (DOB)

MONTH DAY YEAR

4 DATE (DAV) AVAILABLE TO START WORK

JAN   This year
FEB
MAR   Next
APR   year
MAY
JUN
JUL
AUG
SEP
OCT
NOV
DEC

WRITE YOUR RESPONSE IN THE BOXES AND
BLACKEN THE APPROPRIATE CIRCLES.

EXAMPLES

4
JAN   This year
FEB
MAR   Next
APR   year
MAY
JUN
JUL
AUG

18
Alaskan Region
Central Region
Eastern Region
Southwest Region
Western-Pacific
Hawaiian Islands

2 0 1 – 3 7

SAMPLE

1 SOCIAL SECURITY NUMBER (SSN)

6 ...ALITY FOR (WSA) ... POSITIONS

Occasionally the Department of Defense (DOD) hires air traffic controller trainees to work in military air traffic control facilities. If your name is referred to a DOD agency, you will continue to receive consideration for FAA jobs. Indicate your availability for DOD jobs by blackening the appropriate circle below.

ARE YOU AVAILABLE
FOR DOD JOBS?

○ YES   ○ NO

7 DATE OF WRITTEN TEST

Write in the date you are scheduled to take the ATC written test and blacken the corresponding circles below.
Note: You may take the test only once during an open period.

MONTH DAY YEAR

5 OCCUPATIONAL SPECIALTIES (OSP)

Refer to the current announcement for Air Traffic Control Positions for descriptions of the three specialties, for information on the maximum entry age restriction for the TOWER and EN ROUTE CENTER specialties, and for any other restrictions on which specialties you may apply for.

If you select either the TOWER or EN ROUTE CENTER specialties, you may be considered concurrently for both specialties and selected for either specialty, depending on the hiring needs of the FAA.

Blacken the circle beside each specialty for which you wish to be considered:

○ TOWER (001)   ○ FLIGHT SERVICE STATION (003)

○ EN ROUTE CENTER (002)

OCCUPATIONAL SUPPLEMENT NO. 2152 OPM FORM 1203-M Rev. Nov 83

2152

279988

Figure 5—continued

Figure 5—continued

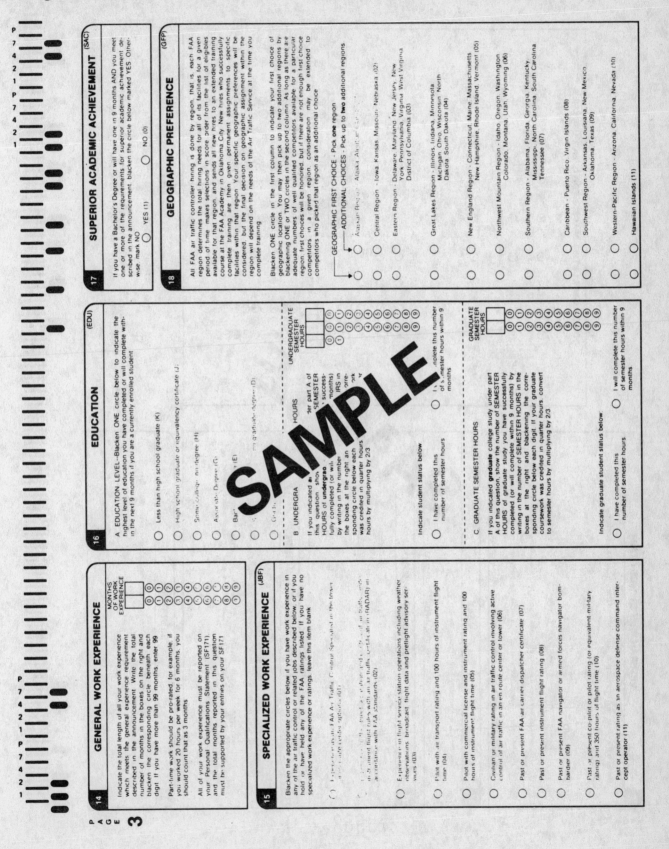

Figure 5—continued

DO NOT MARK IN THIS SPACE – FOR OFFICE USE ONLY

AVP= ① NV ② TP ③ XP ④ CP ⑤ XP ⑥ CP-S

ASB= ① None ② OK ③ Hold ④ Clear

EIC= ○ IA ○ ID ○ IG ○ IH ○ IJ ○ IO ○ IS

EIA= EL ES IK
001 ○ ○ ○
002 ○ ○ ○
003 ○ ○ ○

RAT

TSC

510A   510B   157   512

IMPORTANT NOTES

DO **NOT** SUBMIT PHOTOCOPIES OF THIS FORM.

YOUR NOTICE OF RESULTS WILL CONTAIN INSTRUCTIONS ON HOW TO CHANGE INFORMATION SUBMITTED ON THIS FORM.

---

19 VETERAN PREFERENCE CLAIM (VET)

Blacken the circle next to the claim you made on the attached application.

① - No preference claimed

② - 5 points preference claimed

③ - 10 points preference claimed (award of a Purple Heart or noncompensable service-connected disability)

④ - 10 points compensable disability preference claimed (disability rating of less than 30%)

⑤ - 10 points other (wife husband, widow, widower, mother preference claimed)

⑥ - 10 points compensable disability preference claimed (disability rating of 30% or more)

20 SEX (SEX)

Blacken the circle corresponding to your sex.

Ⓜ MALE Ⓕ FEMALE

FOR STATISTICAL INFORMATION ONLY

21 FEDERAL EMPLOYMENT

Blacken the circle below that describes your Federal employment status.

○ Currently employed by Federal government as a civilian

○ Formerly employed by Federal government as a civilian

○ Never employed by Federal government as a civilian

22 BACKGROUND INFORMATION (SB1)

Mark YES below if you:
- are **not** a citizen of the United States, OR
- have been fired or quit after being notified that you would be fired, in the last 5 years, OR
- have been imprisoned, convicted, forfeited collateral (in the last 7 years), or are now under charges for any offense you must identify on your SF171 (Personal Qualifications Statement)

Otherwise, mark NO below

Ⓨ YES Ⓝ NO

23 SIGNATURE

I certify that all of the information on this form is true, complete, and correct to the best of my knowledge and belief.

_____   _____
Signature   Date Signed

PAGE 4

279988

SAMPLE

FIGURE 6. FORM 1170/17

SUPPLEMENTAL QUALIFICATIONS STATEMENT

LIST OF COLLEGE COURSES AND CERTIFICATE OF SCHOLASTIC ACHIEVEMENT

Complete and submit this Form with your Personal Qualifications Statement

Form Approved
OMB No. 3206-0038

1. Name (Last, First, M.I.)

2. Birth date (Month, year)

3. Social Security Number

4. Position for which you are applying (Include options, if any)

5. List the undergraduate and/or graduate college degrees you ha... (Give name of degree, name of college or university granting degree, and date received or to be received)

6. State your major undergraduate course(s) of study

6a. State your major graduate course(s) of study

PART I — COLLEGE COURSES

List below by appropriate academic field (e.g., biology, mechanical engineering, economics, sociology, etc.) all courses you have taken (including those failed) which appear to satisfy the qualification requirements of positions for which you are applying. List graduate and undergraduate courses separately. Credits for each category should be totaled to determine if you meet the minimum course requirements.

Indicate academic field:

DESCRIPTIVE TITLE	COMPLETION DATE	GRADE	CREDIT HOURS			DESCRIPTIVE TITLE	COMPLETION DATE	GRADE	CREDIT HOURS		
			SEM	QTR	CLASS ROOM				SEM	QTR	CLASS ROOM
TOTAL						TOTAL					

Indicate academic field:

U.S. Office of Personnel Management

OPM Form 1170/17 (Rev. 5/84)

Figure 6—continued

(2)

Indicate academic field:

DESCRIPTIVE TITLE	COMPLE- TION DATE	GRADE	CREDIT HOURS		
			SEM	QTR	CLASS ROOM
TOTAL					

Indicate academic field:

DESCRIPTIVE TITLE	COMPLE- TION DATE	GRADE	CREDIT HOURS		
			SEM	QTR	CLASS ROOM
TOTAL					

Indicate academic field:

DESCRIPTIVE TITLE	COMPLE- TION DATE	GRADE	CREDIT HOURS		
			SEM	QTR	CLASS ROOM
TOTAL					

Indicate academic field:

DESCRIPTIVE TITLE	COMPLE- TION DATE	GRADE	CREDIT HOURS		
			SEM	QTR	CLASS ROOM
TOTAL					

Figure 6—continued

(3)

MISCELLANEOUS COURSES

DESCRIPTIVE TITLE	COMPLETION DATE	GRADE	CREDIT HOURS			DESCRIPTIVE TITLE	COMPLETION DATE	GRADE	CREDIT HOURS		
			SEM	QTR	CLASS ROOM				SEM	QTR	CLASS ROOM
TOTAL						TOTAL					

SAMPLE

PART — STATEMENT AND CERTIFICATION

The Office of Personnel Management is autho_____ _____ of Chapter 13 (Special Authority) and sections 3301 and 3304 of Chapter 33 (Examination, Certification, and Appointment) of Title 5 of the _____ _____ollect the information on this form.

Executive Order 9397 (Numbering System for Fe___ al Accounts Relating to Individual Persons) authorizes the collection of your Social Security Number (SSN). Your SSN is used to identify this form with your basic application. It may be used for the same purposes as stated on the application.

The information you provide will be used primarily to determine your qualifications for Federal employment. Other possible uses or disclosures of the information are:

1. To make requests for information about you from any source; (e.g., former employers or schools), that would assist an agency in determining whether to hire you;

2. To refer your application to prospective Federal employers and, with your consent, to others (e.g., State and local governments) for possible employment;

3. To a Federal, State, or local agency for checking on violations of law or other lawful purposes in connection with hiring or retaining you on the job, or issuing you a security clearance;

4. To the courts when the Government is party to a suit; and

5. When lawfully required by Congress, the Office of Management and Budget, or the General Services Administration.

Providing the information requested on this form, including your SSN, is voluntary. However, failure to do so may result in your not receiving an accurate rating, which may hinder your chances for obtaining Federal employment.

ATTENTION – THIS STATEMENT MUST BE SIGNED
Read the following paragraph carefully before signing this Statement

A false answer to any question in this Statement may be grounds for not employing you, or for dismissing you after you begin work, and may be punishable by fine or imprisonment (U.S. Code, Title 18, Sec. 1001). All statements are subject to investigation, including a check of your fingerprints, police records, and former employers. All the information you give will be considered in reviewing your Statement and is subject to investigation.

CERTIFICATION	Signature *(Sign in ink)*	Date Signed
I CERTIFY that all of the statements made in this Statement are true, complete, and correct to the best of my knowledge and belief, and are made in good faith.		

COMPLETE PART III ON THE NEXT PAGE IF YOU
CLAIM SUPERIOR ACADEMIC ACHIEVEMENT

Figure 6—continued

(4)

PART III — SCHOLASTIC ACHIEVEMENT

NOTE: This part is for the use of college students and graduates who may qualify for some GS-7 and GS-9 positions on the basis of undergraduate scholastic achievement, as provided in an open announcement. *See the appropriate announcement for complete requirements.* If you do not wish to qualify on this basis or if you do not meet the requirements below, do not complete this part. In any case, YOU MUST SIGN YOUR NAME AFTER THE CERTIFICATION STATEMENT AT THE BOTTOM OF PAGE 3.

A. COLLEGE OR CLASS STANDING. Must be in upper third of the college or university, or major subdivision such as School of Engineering, School of Business Administration, etc.

NUMBER IN CLASS _____   YOUR STANDING _____

B. COLLEGE GRADE AVERAGE. Must equal a "B" average (2.90 on a 4.0 scale) or better for *all* undergraduate courses, or equal "B +" (3.5) or better in courses comprising the major field of study, completed during the period specified in the announcement under which you file. If the announcement permits a choice of computing periods, you may use the one which gives you the best average. In any case you should indicate the method used by check mark in the appropriate box in item 1 *and* in item 2 below, *and* compute your average in the space provided at the bottom of this page.

1. (Check one) ☐ "B" average for all undergraduate courses
   ☐ "B +" average in major field of study
2. (Check one) ☐ All 4 years   ☐ First 3 years   ☐ Last 2 years*
   ☐ At time of filing *(In some announcements this is the only computing period permitted.)*

*NOTE: For those announcements which permit you to qualify on the basis of a grade average during the last 2 years of the undergraduate curriculum, you may be rated provisionally eligible if you are a senior student, provided yo͟u ͟͟͟͟͟ the required average in the junior year. You will be required to submit evidence at the time of appointment that you maintaiṉ͟͟͟ ͟͟ed average during your senior year.

Most colleges have "A," "B," "C," and "D" as passing grades and compute o͟͟͟͟͟͟͟͟ 4, 3, 2, 1 scale. In computing your grade point average, round to the first decimal place (e.g., 2.95 = 3.0, 2 ͟͟͟͟͟͟͟͟͟͟͟ r, the 2.90 average may not be achieved by rounding up a lower average. If your college uses a different system ͟͟͟͟͟͟͟ ͟ow how it compares with the "A," "B," "C," "D" system.

NO. OF SEMESTER OR QUARTER HOU͟͟ ͟͟͟͟͟͟͟͟ "A" _____ X 4 = _____

NO. OF SEMESTER OR QUARTER H͟͟ ͟͟͟͟͟GRADE OF "B" _____ X 3 = _____

NO. OF SEMESTER OR QUARTER HOU͟ ͟ITH A GRADE OF "C" _____ X 2 = _____

NO. OF SEMESTER OR QUARTER HOURS WITH A GRADE OF "D" _____ X 1 = _____

NO. OF SEMESTER OR QUARTER HOURS FAILED _____ X 0 = _____

TOTAL (1) _____   TOTAL (2) _____

GRADE POINT AVERAGE _____
Total (2) divided by Total (1)

C. HONOR SOCIETY MEMBERSHIP. Must be one of the national honorary scholastic societies meeting the minimum requirements of the Association of College Honor Societies (other than freshman scholarship honor societies).

Name of honor society and date you were elected to membership _____

NOTE—Many colleges and universities offer courses of study which have disposed, in whole or in part, of traditional grading systems in favor of pass/fail or similar systems. If your grades are more than 10 percent pass/fail, you may claim credit under the scholastic achievement provision only on the basis of class standing or membership in a national honorary society. Proof of class standing should be in the form of a statement in writing from the institution's registrar, the dean of the applicant's course of study, or the appropriate department head or chairman. This statement of class standing must be based on a suitable measure of the student's academic performance, such as the results of a comprehensive examination or an overall faculty assessment, and must indicate the basis of the judgment. Class standing must be based on the candidate's standing in his college or university or a major subdivision of the university (e.g., the College of Business Administration, the College of Arts and Sciences, etc.). Subdivisions of colleges, such as the History Department, are not recognized as subdivisions for this purpose. This proof should not be submitted with your application, but will be required by your hiring agency before you may report for work.

BE SURE TO SIGN THIS FORM AT THE BOTTOM OF PAGE 3.

✿ U.S. GOVERNMENT PRINTING OFFICE: 1984-779-846

Government Employment Benefits and Special Job Requirements

Age Limitations

In May 1972, the 92nd Congress of the United States passed public law 92-297 giving recognition to the unusually high standards required of FAA Air Traffic Controllers. In accordance with the law, you must be under age 31 prior to entering duty as an Air Traffic Control Specialist in the tower or center option (this age limitation does not apply for the flight service station option). The age limitation rule was established on the basis of extensive studies and experience, in which it was determined that the unique skills and abilities necessary for the control of air traffic begin to decline at a relatively early age.

Appointment

Career-conditional: Most new appointments in the federal service are of this type. Such an appointment leads to a career appointment at the end of three years. Career-conditional employees serve a probationary period of one year.

Career: This is a permanent type of appointment. At the end of three years of satisfactory service, career-conditional employees automatically receive career (permanent) appointments.

Probationary Period

The first year of employment in federal service, or the first year after receiving a new appointment from a civil service commission register, is considered the probationary period. During the first year of employment, your ability, attitude, and work habits are carefully observed. This is done to determine your suitability for retention in federal service. At any time during your probationary or trial period you may be separated if it appears that your employment would not be in the best interest of the FAA.

Nepotism

It is the policy of the FAA that close relatives may not be assigned to any position in which one relative may directly or indirectly supervise, control, or influence the work or the employment status of the other relative or the affairs of the organizational unit in which the other relative is employed.

Annual ATCS Medical Examination

Once employed as an Air Traffic Control Specialist, you will be required to pass an annual medical examination. Annual examinations will be performed at FAA medical facilities or those of other agencies, or when this is not possible, by an approved aviation medical examiner or specialist. The cost of the examination is paid by the agency.

If you fail to meet the established medical requirements you will be disqualified from controlling air traffic. If this occurs, several alternatives are available. You may be retired under the provisions of the disability retirement program if you qualify; you may be placed in another position (other than air traffic) if vacancies exist and you meet the qualifications; or you may be terminated if you cannot be accommodated by any of the above.

FAA Administrative Reassignment and Relocation Policy

If selected for appointment, you must be available for temporary assignment for as long as 60 to 90 days (over and above training at the academy), and you must be willing to accept permanent assignments anywhere in the U.S. as the needs of the service require. It is the policy of the FAA to use its employees in localities where they desire to work. To the maximum extent the conditions of the work will permit, the FAA will honor employee wishes. In addition, in the interests of economy, it is the policy of the agency to avoid unnecessary assignments and reassignments. However, past experience tells us that changes in workload, changes in technology, and other unforseen circumstances do make necessary occasional reassignments and relocations.

It is the FAA's policy, therefore, insofar as the needs of the service require the employee's assignment or reassignment to a new locality or temporary detail away from home, that the employee agrees to and expresses willingness to accept such orders as a condition of initial and continued employment with the FAA. *This means that if the FAA wants you somewhere else, you must go. The chances are slim but not unknown. Also in such reassignments or transfers, transportation and moving expenses are usually paid by the agency.*

Payment of Travel Costs

If selected from a civil service register or given a veteran's readjustment appointment, you must pay travel expenses associated with relocation to your first duty station. In addition you must bear the cost of travel to your interview and medical examination.

Pay

Normally the FAA has 26 pay periods a year; pay checks are received every two weeks. (You should receive your first check within three weeks after reporting to duty station.)

In addition to your base salary, you may receive additional compensation as follows:

HOLIDAY AND SUNDAY PAY. You will receive extra pay for required work performed on holidays and Sundays.

NIGHT PAY. If your regular duty tour includes work between the hours of 6:00 p.m. and 6:00 a.m., you will receive extra pay, called night differential.

OVERTIME PAY. If you work in excess of 8 hours in a day or 45 hours in the administrative work week, you are entitled to overtime pay.

COST OF LIVING ALLOWANCE. A cost of living allowance is provided for general schedule employees assigned to certain duty posts, such as Alaska, Hawaii, or Puerto Rico.

REVITALIZATION PAY (HOUSE JOINT RESOLUTION 599). You may be eligible for certain types of additional premium pay in connection with the performance of ATCS duties.

Within Grade Step Increases

You may get an increase in salary without a change in position or grade. There are steps in the salary range for each grade to which you progress after periods of satisfactory service. These increases are called "within grade step increases." Increases are granted either yearly, every two years, or every three years depending upon your length of time in the present grade.

Promotion

The FAA follows the policy of promotion from within the agency when filling higher grade Air Traffic Control Specialist (ATCS) positions. As a result, opportunities for promotion are excellent; in fact, many key FAA officials began their careers as ATCSs. Promotions, however, are by no means automatic.

Early in your FAA career as an ATCS you will typically receive one or more noncompetitive promotions. To earn one of these promotions you must satisfy all civil service requirements and meet exacting standards of training and proficiency established by the FAA. Later in your career you will have opportunities to win further advancement by competing for vacant positions with other qualified employees under the agency's merit promotion program.

Unions

There are labor organizations within the FAA. As an FAA employee you have a right to join or refrain from joining any of the existing organizations.

Payroll Deductions

The FAA will automatically deduct federal taxes (and state taxes if you work in a state that has an agreement with the U.S Treasury Department for such withholdings). In addition, as a general schedule employee, you are subject to the Retirement Act and a percentage of your base pay is deducted and deposited to your account to provide you with income upon retirement.

If you choose to join a union, your dues can be deducted if you so authorize from your salary. If you elect to be covered by a health plan and/or life insurance, these too will be deducted from your salary. You may also have allotments deducted for deposit in financial institutions, such as credit unions or banks. United States saving bonds may be purchased voluntarily through the payroll savings plan. This can be an automatic deduction if authorized by you.

Military Reserve Status

As an Air Traffic Control Specialist (GS-9 and above) you will not be considered available for active military service in time of war or national emergency. If you are already a reservist and are promoted to the GS-9 level, the FAA must report to your reserve office that you are not available for active military service. An exception may be recommended if your absence for reserve training or mobilization will not disrupt the activity of the FAA facility to which you are assigned.

Vacation and Sick Leave

You will earn annual leave, for vacation and other purposes which require time away from your job, according to the number of years (civilian plus creditable military service) you have been in federal service: 13 days for the first 3 years, 20 days a year for the next 12 years. After 15 years, you can earn 26 days of annual leave each year. You may carry a maximum of 240 hours of unused annual leave over into a new leave year. Any annual leave in excess of 240 hours that is not used prior to the end of the leave year will be forfeited.

Sick leave is earned at the rate of 13 days a year. You can use this leave when incapacitated because of illness, injury, or pregnancy and confinement, and for appointments with a doctor, dentist, or optician. Sick leave that is not used will be saved for future use; it is one of the best forms of insurance you can have in case of extended periods of illness.

Holidays

In addition to your annual leave, you will receive holiday benefits for each federal holiday. There are currently 10 paid holidays each year.

Health Insurance

When you are appointed to a position in the FAA, you have the opportunity to enroll in a group health benefits plan, with better rates and protection than you normally can get as an individual. Ordinarily, you must enroll within 31 days following appointment if you desire coverage. You get guaranteed protection for yourself and your family that cannot be canceled by the plan. There are no medical examinations, generally no waiting period, and no restrictions because of age or physical condition.

There is a choice of plans, so that you can get the kind and amount of protection you actually need and want. The government contributes toward the cost of your plan, while you pay your share of the cost through payroll deductions. Protection continues after retirement (if you meet the length of service and other requirements) at the same cost as for active employees. The cost of this insurance is deducted from your annuity. Participation in the program will ensure that you have a good program of protection against the cost of illness.

Life Insurance

Unless you elect to decline the benefit, you will be covered by term life insurance without taking a physical examination. Two kinds of insurance are provided—life insurance and accidental death and dismemberment insurance—in amounts which usually are at least $2,000 more than your annual base pay. The minimum amount of each kind of protection is $10,000. The Government pays one-third of the premium cost, and you pay the remainder.

If you enroll for the basic life insurance, you may purchase optional insurance for which you pay the full premiums, also through payroll deductions. You may elect coverage under one or more of the following options:

- Option A—an additional $10,000; or
- Option B—an amount equal to one, two, three, four, or five times your annual basic pay (rounded to the next $1,000); or
- Option C—coverage for eligible family members ($5,00 for your spouse and $2,500 for each dependent child).

Retirement

GENERAL OVERVIEW. New employees are covered by the Federal Employees' Retirement System (FERS). This system provides that, in addition to Social Security coverage, you will be covered by a guaranteed Basic Annuity and be eligible to participate in a Thrift Savings Plan. The Thrift Savings Plan is a tax-deferred savings plan similar to an Individual Retirement Account.

TABLE 2. RETIREMENT ELIGIBILITY

Type of Retirement	Minimum Age	Years of Service Required	Special Requirements
Optional	62	5	None
Optional	60	20	None
Optional	55	30	None
Optional for ATCS occupation subject to PL 92-297 and PL99-335	50 Any age	20 25	Must have been actively engaged in, or the immediate supervisor of one who is engaged in, the separation and control of air traffic or the providing of pre-flight, inflight, or airport advisory service to aircraft operators for entire service period, all of which must have been civilian service.
Disability	Any age	CSRS-5 FERS-1½	Must be totally disabled to do your work or other work to which you may be assigned. A disability retirement application must be approved by the Office of Personnel Management on the basis of a medical examination.

Individuals who were civil service employees prior to January 1, 1984, may be covered under a different retirement plan (i.e., Civil Service Retirement System or CSRS). Check with the employment office considering you for employment to see which rules apply in your case.

SPECIAL PROGRAMS LEADING TO FAA EMPLOYMENT

Cooperative Education Programs

Cooperative education has been defined as "a process of education which formally integrates a student's academic study with productive work experiences in cooperating employer organizations." Through the interaction of study and work experiences, the student enhances academic knowledge, personal development and professional preparation.

ACADEMIC COURSEWORK. The following major courses of study are acceptable for the Air Traffic Control program: aeronautics, avionics, communications, air traffic control, and aviation sciences.

ADVANTAGES TO CO-OP PROGRAMS. Cooperative education programs have several strong advantages:

1. They provide financial support while teaching work-related skills.
2. They provide invaluable work experience that can be added to your resume after graduation.
3. They provide a direct channel into federal employment with the FAA.

After graduation and successful completion of the program, the FAA can offer participants permanent employment at the GS–7 level. These developmental positions in the career competitive service lead to higher grade levels of GS–9 through G–14.

ENTRY REQUIREMENTS. To be eligible for the Air Traffic Control co-op program, a student must:

- be a U.S. citizen
- have completed at least 60 semester hours of academic work
- currently have a 2.0 or better grade point average
- pass the FAA Air Traffic Controller written examination

The Airway Science Program

The Airway Science Program was designed by the Office of Personnel Management and the FAA. A specific college-level curriculum (see Figure 7 on pages 38–39) was developed by the University Aviation Association and the FAA to respond to the needs generated by the revision of the national airspace system. The curriculum was designed to meet normal university academic and accreditation requirements, to be easily adapted to existing aviation-related programs, to have the flexibility to allow educational institutions the option of offering any of five areas of concentration according to their individual resources, and to be attractive to students seeking careers in both government and the aviation industry. Applicants who successfully complete this curriculum are eligible to fill positions at the GS–7 level in one or more specializations. In addition, other education, training or experience may be substituted, as will be later discussed.

CURRICULUM REQUIREMENTS FOR SPECIFIC JOBS. Table 3 lists the different areas of concentration available under the Airway Science curriculum, each area leading to an aviation job specialty.

TABLE 3.

Curriculum	Job Specialization
Airway Science Management	Air Traffic Control Specialist
Airway Electronics Systems	Electronics Technician
Airway Computer Science	Computer Specialist or Air Traffic Control Specialist
Aircraft Systems Management	Aviation Safety Inspector (general aviation operations) or Air Traffic Control Specialist
Aviation Maintenance Management	Aviation Safety Inspector (general aviation airworthiness)

Although the primary method of qualifying for Airway Science positions is through successful completion of an approved curriculum, other training, education or experience may be substituted provided you can demonstrate the equivalency of your training, education or experience to the knowledge, skills, abilities and other characteristics provided by the Airway Science curriculum.

Students who will complete the amount of education needed to qualify within 9 months may apply and be selected, but they must complete their study before they can begin work.

SPECIAL CONDITIONS OF EMPLOYMENT. There are some special conditions of employment in this program:

Applicants must be physically and mentally able to efficiently perform the essential functions of the position without hazard to themselves or others. Depending on the essential duties of a specific position, usable vision, color vision, hearing, or speech may be required. However, in most cases a specific physical condition or impairment will not automatically disqualify an applicant for appointment. The loss or impairment of a specific function may be compensated for by the satisfactory use of a prosthesis or mechanical aid. Reasonable accommodation may also be considered in determining an applicant's ability to perform the duties of a position. Reasonable accommodation may include, but is not limited to: the use of assistive devices, job modification or restructuring, provision of readers and interpreters, or adjusted work schedules. In addition, applicants for aviation safety positions which require participation in the operation of an aircraft must (1) possess a current, valid medical certificate in accordance with the regulations of the FAA, and (2) pass recurrent medical examinations as prescribed by the FAA.

Air Traffic Control Specialist applicants must pass a rigorous physical examination by a medical examiner designated and paid for by the government. A detailed list of medical examiners may be obtained from the FAA regional office in your area.

FIGURE 7. AIRWAY SCIENCE CURRICULUM

CORE SAMPLE CURRICULUM

General Studies	Sem. Hrs.	Management	Sem. Hrs.
English Composition	3	Principles of Management	3
Technical Writing	3	Organizational Behavior	3
Economics	6	Techniques of Supervision	3
Government	3		9
Psychology	3		
Humanities	3		
History	3	Aviation	
Speech	3	Introduction to Aeronautics	3
	27	Aviation Legislation	3
Math/Science/Technology		Flight Safety	3
Algebra/Trigonometry	3	Air Traffic Control	3
Calculus	3	The National Airspace System	3
Physics	8		15
Geography	4		
Statistics	3	Area of Concentration	
Chemistry	4	(see following)	40
	25		
Computer Science		Total	125
Introduction to the Computer	3		
Computer Programming I	3		
Computer Science Elective	3		
	9		

AREAS OF CONCENTRATION SAMPLE CURRICULA

Airway Science Management		Airway Electronics Systems	
Introduction to Sociology	3	Theory of Electronics	3
Theories of Personality	3	Calculus II	3
Psychology of Communication	3	Math Analysis	3
Introduction to Interpersonal Communication	3	Microprocessor Theory and Application	3
Communication Theory and Models	3	Advanced Computer Programming	3
Introduction to Adminis-trative Problems	3	Solid State Devices	3
Air Transportation	3	Integrated Circuits	3
Airport Management	3	Engineering Drawing	2
Theories of Personnel Management	3	Electrical Circuits	3
Concepts of Air Transport Utilization	3	Digital Logic Application	3
Labor/Management Relations	3	Advanced Logic Analysis	3
Operations Management	2	Reliability and Maintain-ability Theory and Systems Engineering	3
Management Decisionmaking	2	Electrical and Power Principles	2
Approved Electives	3	Approved Electives	3
	40		40

Figure 7—continued

Airway Computer Science	Sem. Hrs.	Aircraft Systems Management	Sem. Hrs.
Computer Programming II	3	Commercial Pilot Certification	5
Advanced Computer Programming	3	Instrument Rating	5
Computer Operating Systems	3	Multi-engine Rating	1
Assembler Language Programming	3	CFI-Airplance	5
Data Structures	3	CFI-Instruments	3
Computer Methods and Applications I	3	Advanced Aerodynamics and Aircraft Performance	3
Computer Methods and Applications II	3	Advanced Aircraft Systems	3
Introduction to Microcomputers	3	Meteorology	3
Introduction to Office Automation	3	Weather Reporting and Analysis	3
Theory of Programming Languages and Complex Construction	3	Aviation Management	3
Mathematical Modeling and Computer Simulation	4	Air Transportation	3
Computer Architecture	3	CFI-Multi-engine	3
Approved Electives	3		40
	40		

Aviation Maintenance Management

	Sem. Hrs.
Engineering Drawing	2
Aircraft Materials	2
Propulsion	6
Propulsion Laboratory	6
Structures	6
Structures Laboratory	6
Aircraft Systems	3
Avionics Systems	3
Reliability and Maintainability Theory and Systems Engineering	3
Approved Electives	3
	40

TRAINING. All eligibles appointed to these positions will adhere to the same FAA training requirements as those established for any new entrant. Airway Science selectees entering into the Air Traffic Program must undergo formal training at the FAA Academy at Oklahoma City.

MOVING EXPENSES. Appointees must pay their own transportation and moving expenses to their first duty station.

INTERVIEW. Interviews may be required of applicants. The purpose of the interview is to evaluate certain personal characteristics to determine if an applicant possesses the essential qualities to successfully perform the duties of the position. Applicants may be questioned during the interview about information in their applications. The interview will be held in the applicant's geographic area. Expenses connected with travel to the interview will be the applicant's responsibility.

SPECIAL JOB CONSIDERATIONS. Most aviation safety inspector positions require considerable overnight travel.

SALARY. All positions begin at the GS–7 level. Current salary information may be obtained from a Federal Job Information Center.

JOB LOCATIONS. Positions are available in the continental U.S., Alaska, Hawaii, and the Caribbean. You may designate as many as three geographic areas on OPM Form 1203–X, Employment Availability Statement (KEES), using the instructions listed in the insert. Assignments may be made to any location within an area depending on the needs of the FAA.

AGE RESTRICTIONS. Regarding Air Traffic positions, a maximum age limit of 30 at the time of initial appointment to towers and centers has been established. No age limit applies to other positions that have been listed.

APPLICATION PROCEDURES. Applicants need the following forms: SF–171, Personal Qualifications Statement; a copy of the applicant's current college transcript to date; OPM form 1203–X, Employment Availability Statement (KEES); AC form 3330–77, Airway Science Supplemental Qualification Statement; and if you want to claim a 10-point veteran preference, standard form 15 with documentary proof as required. Forms may be obtained from any Office of Personnel Management (OPM) Federal Job Information Center (FJIC). Offices are listed under "Federal Government" in the white pages of telephone directories. Send your completed forms to:

> Department of Transportation
> FAA Mike Monroney Aeronautical Center
> Special Examination Unit Staff for
>   the Office of Personnel Management
> P.O. Box 25082—Attn: AAC-80
> Oklahoma City, OK 73125

FAA Collegiate Training Initiative

This recent test program funded by the FAA allows graduates of selected postsecondary programs to bypass the Academy in Oklahoma City and be placed directly into the field. Each program's curriculum must meet or exceed FAA Academy curriculum standards. There are five schools currently participating in the program. Students in this program do not have to take the FAA written examination.

Minnesota Technical College System Air Traffic Control Training Center. Also called the Minnesota Air Traffic Control Training Center (MnATCTC), the school offers a six-month (two-quarter) program focusing on enroute control. Applicants must have completed a two- or four-year college-aviation program or a two- or four-year program in any field and an aviation-related course. For more information, contact:

> Admissions Office
> Minnesota Technical College System
> Air Traffic Control Training Center
> 10100 Flying Cloud Drive
> Eden Prairie, MN 55347-4016
> 612-832-6968
> 1-800-475-2828 (outside Minneapolis-St. Paul metro area)

University of Alaska (Anchorage). The University of Alaska offers an A.A.S. degree in Air Traffic Control. Full-time students can complete the program in 21 months. For more information, contact:

> Air Traffic Control Department
> University of Alaska, Anchorage
> ORCA Building
> 1515 East 13th Avenue
> Anchorage, AK 99501
> 907-272-3500

Community College of Beaver County (Pennsylvania). The school offers a two-year Associate Degree major in Air Traffic Control. The program provides training in the application of non-radar enroute air traffic control procedures as well as control tower operator training and experience. Graduates receive an FAA Control Tower Operator (CTO) certificate and a private pilot certificate. For more information, contact:

> Community College of Beaver County
> Aviation Sciences Center
> 125 Cessna Drive
> Beaver Falls, PA 15010-1060
> 412-847-7000

University of North Dakota (Grand Forks). The school offers a four-year B.S. Air Traffic Control program. The intensive curriculum includes business and management courses in addition to its rigorous studies in air traffic control operations. The school's ATC-2000 complete training system combines advanced computing technology with a fully integrated voice communications network. For more information, contact:

University of North Dakota
Center for Aerospace Science
University and Tulane
Grand Forks, ND 58202-8216
701-777-2791

Hampton University (Virginia). The school currently offers a two-year degree program in Air Traffic Control that will soon be transitioned to a four-year program. Hampton's Terminal and Enroute Airspace Management/Air Traffic Control curriculum (TEAM/ATC) utilizes computer-assisted instruction, interactive video-disc technology, radar simulation, and lectures to train students. An important facet of the curriculum is the integration of human factors skills into the coursework. For more information, contact:

Hampton University
Airway Science Department
TEAM/ATC
Hampton, VA 23668
804-727-5418

Sample Curriculum from Hampton College

The innovative TEAM/ATC program at Hampton College is one of the five programs in the FAA's Collegiate Training Initiative. All of these schools are providing an exciting new approach to controller training.

TEAM/ATC PROGRAM
TWO-YEAR COURSE CURRICULUM

First Semester

ATC 301 – Tower Operations I
ATC/CRM 315 – Tower Lab I
ATC 321 – Aviation Theory I

Second Semester

ATC 302 – Tower Operations II
ATC/CRM 316 – Tower Lab II
ATC 322 – Aviation Theory II

Third Semester

ATC 401 – Terminal Operations I
ATC/CRM 415 – Terminal Lab I
ATC 421 – Aviation Safety

Fourth Semester

ATC 402 – Terminal Operations II
ATC/CRM 416 – Terminal Lab II
ATC 422 – Aviation Management

Fifth Semester

ATC 423 – Contemporary Aviation
  Projects
ATC 431 – Enroute Operations
ATC/CRM 445 – Enroute Lab

Sixth Semester

ATC 432 – ATC Facility Applications
ATC 446 – ATC Facility Lab
ATC/CRM 499 – Combined ATC
  Operations

TEAM/ATC PROGRAM
COURSE DESCRIPTIONS

ATC 301 – Tower Operations I: 4.0

Fundamental control tower operations with emphasis on aircraft operating under visual flight rules. The course includes procedures, phraseology, aircraft separation, airport traffic patterns, night operations, control tower positions, responsibilities, and equipment. Corequisites: ATC 315 and CRM 315. Prerequisite or corequisite: ATC 321.

ATC 302 – Tower Operations II: 4.0

Advanced control tower operations. Includes, but is not limited to, simultaneous parallel runway operations, instrument clearances, IFR departure and arrival procedures and separation criteria, helicopter operations, and emergency procedures. Corequisite: ATC 316 and CRM 316. Prerequisite or corequisite: ATC 322. Prerequisite: ATC 301.

ATC 315 – Tower Lab I: 4.0

Laboratory simulations utilizing an airport layout and control tower cab mock-up to support fundamental tower operations comprising taxi, takeoff, and landing of aircraft. Includes phraseology, procedures, and separation of aircraft flying under visual conditions. Corequisites: ATC 301 and CRM 315.

ATC 316 – Tower Lab II: 4.0

Laboratory simulations utilizing an airport layout and control tower cab mock-up to support Tower Operations II. Students will utilize procedures, phraseology, and separation criteria to apply their knowledge and understanding of the more complex control tower operations. Corequisites: ATC 302 and CRM 316.

ATC 321 – Aviation Theory I: 3.0

Provides foundational aviation knowledge required for application in ATC 301 and ATC 315. Subjects include aircraft recognition, nomenclature and performance; temperature and altitude factors; the National Airspace System; Federal Aviation Regulations and publications; navigational aids; basic navigation concepts; enroute and approach chart symbology and usage; and pilot/controller terminology and phraseology.

ATC 322 – Aviation Theory II: 3.0

Advanced navigation, including RNAV, LORAN, GPS, MLS, and "glass cockpits." Aviation weather, including basic concepts and nomenclature, cloud classifications, air masses, fronts, and the jet stream; weather hazards, including thunderstorms, turbulence, windshear, microbursts, fog, precipitation, and icing; weather reports and forecasts. The hemispheric cruising altitude rules. Aerodynamics, including the forces affecting an aircraft in flight, axes of motion and control surfaces, flight loads, and stability. Single-engine and multi-engine aircraft emergencies. Prerequisite: ATC 321.

ATC 401 – Terminal Operations I: 4.0

Fundamental terminal operations utilizing radar and non-radar procedures and equipment. Course will include control and separation of aircraft in the terminal area with emphasis on the safe, expeditious flow of arriving and departing traffic transitioning between enroute centers and the control tower environment. Corequisites: ATC 415 and CRM 415. Prerequisite: ATC 301.

ATC 402 – Terminal Operations II: 4.0

Advanced terminal operations utilizing radar and non-radar procedures and separation. Course will include emergency radar procedures, operations within Airport Radar Service Areas and Terminal Control Areas, simultaneous parallel runway operations, and the utilization of the more complex airspace around larger airports. Corequisites: ATC 416 and CRM 416. Prerequisite: ATC 401.

ATC 415 – Terminal Lab I: 4.0

Fundamental laboratory simulations in support of Terminal Operations I. This course will utilize radar air traffic control simulators by which students will apply their knowledge, skill, and understanding of terminal procedures. Corequisites: ATC 401 and CRM 415.

ATC 416 – Terminal Lab II: 4.0

Advanced laboratory simulations in support of ATC 402. Students will utilize radar simulators to apply their knowledge and understanding of complex radar procedures and their ability to safely control traffic in a terminal environment. Corequisites: ATC 402 and CRM 416.

ATC 421 – Aviation Safety: 3.0

A broad overview of the factors associated with the safe operation of air traffic with emphasis placed upon the role of air traffic controllers, pilots, airline management, and maintenance personnel in fostering aviation safety. Certain aspects of aviation will be explored in depth, to include human factors, weather phenomena, communications, and aircraft design. Additionally, aircraft accident investigation procedures as a means of preventing future accidents will be explored. Prerequisite: ATC 322.

ATC 422 – Aviation Management: 3.0

Management techniques and administrative functions as applied to the aviation industry. Includes current issues and future trends in aviation from the viewpoint of airlines management, airport management, and the Federal Aviation Administration. Emphasis will be placed upon the manager's role in problem identification and solutions. Additionally, legislation of the aviation system will be addressed. Prerequisite: ATC 322.

ATC 423 – Contemporary Aviation Projects: 3.0

An examination of the factors affecting the future of the aviation industry. Includes topics associated with the expected implementation of the National Airspace System Plan, advancements in aircraft design and equipment, airport planning to support the anticipated growth in air traffic, and problems facing the aviation professional of tomorrow. Prerequisite: ATC 402.

ATC 431 – Enroute Operations: 4.0

Specific procedures, criteria, and regulations regarding the control of enroute traffic. Course will consist of movement of aircraft in both the radar and non-radar environment, aircraft limitations at higher altitudes, and traffic management including coordination with terminal facilities and flow control. Also, aircraft performance characteristics peculiar to high-altitude operations. Corequisites: ATC 445 and CRM 445. Prerequisite: ATC 402.

ATC 432 – ATC Facility Applications: 3.0

Procedures, regulations, and airspace applicable to specific existing air traffic control facilities. Includes actual airport environments, arrival and departure routes, and preparation for controlling real-life traffic scenarios. Corequisites: ATC 446, ATC 499, and CRM 499. Prerequisite: ATC 431.

ATC 445 – Enroute Laboratory: 4.0

Radar and non-radar enroute laboratory in support of ATC 431. Students will utilize laboratory equipment to apply their knowledge and understanding of enroute procedures. Corequisites: ATC 431 and CRM 445.

ATC 446 – ATC Facility Lab: 4.0

Simulated radar laboratory exercises in support of ATC 432. Students are expected to employ procedures in existence at a selected air traffic control facility to control aircraft movement. Simulations will be based upon actual traffic scenarios at that facility. Corequisite: ATC 432.

ATC 499 – Combined ATC Operations: 4.0

Utilizing the radar air traffic control laboratory, students will apply their knowledge and ability to control traffic at both enroute and terminal facilities. This course will simulate actual traffic situations in which aircraft are coordinated and transferred from controller to controller both within a given facility and between adjacent facilities. Corequisites: ATC 432 and CRM 499.

CRM 315 – Crew Resource Management I: 1.0

Correlation between aviation safety and effective and efficient intra- and inter-facility crew coordination among controllers and between controllers and pilots. Includes identification of available crew resources and effective resource management strategies. Corequisite: ATC 315.

CRM 316 – Crew Resource Management II: 1.0

Advanced correlation of aviation safety and effective and efficient intra- and inter-facility crew coordination among controllers and between controllers and pilots. Includes identification of personal impact on available resources. Corequisite: ATC 316.

CRM 415 – Teambuilding I: 1.0

Correlation between teambuilding skills and aviation safety and the practical application of these skills in ATC courses. Emphasis on transferability of skills to the workplace. Corequisite: ATC 415.

CRM 416 – Teambuilding II: 1.0

Advanced correlation between teambuilding skills and aviation safety and the practical application of these skills in ATC courses. Emphasis on transferability of skills to the workplace. Corequisite: ATC 416.

CRM 445 – Communications Skills and Stress Management: 1.0

Correlation between interpersonal communication skills and stress management with aviation safety. Practical application of these skills in ATC courses with emphasis on transferability of skills to the workplace. Corequisite: ATC 445.

CRM 499 – Consolidated CRM: 1.0

Integration of Crew Resource Management concepts and skills with effective intra- and inter-facility controller communications—coping with specific controller/controller, supervisor/controller, controller/pilot scenarios. Emphasis on transferability to the workplace. Corequisite: ATC 499.

PART TWO

About the Air Traffic Controller Examination

The 4-hour Air Traffic Controller written test consists of three separate subtests. The first test is designed to assess your aptitude as an air traffic controller; the second test is intended to assess your ability to perceive spatial relationships; and the third test is intended to assess your knowledge of air traffic control work. The test is scored by machine, and you will receive a separate answer sheet (see Figure 8 on page 48) on which you are to indicate your answers.

Test 1. Air Traffic Controller Aptitude Questions

This test consists of drawings that simulate a radar scope depicting characteristic patterns of air traffic. Each problem contains a drawing of a particular flight path and aircraft flying on it. A table containing information about the altitude, speed and route of flight of each aircraft accompanies each drawing. Your job will be to answer questions which make use of this flight information. The questions ask for identification of potential midair collisions, differences in the route of flight of the aircraft, distances between aircraft, compass headings of different aircraft and changes in the route of flight. Some preliminary instructions necessary to correctly read the information provided in the problems will be given to you at the test site before you start the exam.

A typical example of the kind of information provided in the test problems is given on page 49. The drawing shows the flight paths that aircraft must follow. Changes in the route of flight can only occur at the intersection between the two routes. Each double slash displayed on the route of flight represents the aircraft traveling in the particular direction indicated by the trailing dots. Below or to the side of the problem you will be given a table containing critical flight information about each aircraft. The number by each slash on the drawing allows the matching of flight information to the correct aircraft. The flight information lists the altitude, speed in miles per hour, and the route of the aircraft.

QUESTION ANALYSIS. For Test 1 questions, keep in mind the following:

1. The drawings will indicate where to locate the aircraft. There will be a double slash on the screen that will represent what an aircraft looks like when you see it on the real radar screen. The slashes will all be numbered so that you can solve the requested problem.

2. The aircraft will all be moving. You will be able to determine this by looking at the target and seeing how the dots behind the slashes are moving. Remember the aircraft is moving away from the dots which are supposed to represent the target trail, a function that occurs on the real presentation.

3. The route of flight of the aircraft, or path that it will be traveling, is shown by the black lines that are crossing the screen. They will be drawn between the capital letters.

4. The figures around the scope depict the compass rose. This shows the direction of travel: N (North), SW (Southwest), SE (Southeast) and so on. You will be asked to determine the direction of some of the aircraft, and by looking at the compass rose you can give an accurate answer.

FIGURE 8. SAMPLE ANSWER SHEET

	A B C D E		A B C D E		A B C D E		A B C D E
1	⋮ ⋮ ⋮ ⋮ ⋮	21	⋮ ⋮ ⋮ ⋮ ⋮	41	⋮ ⋮ ⋮ ⋮ ⋮	61	⋮ ⋮ ⋮ ⋮ ⋮
2	⋮ ⋮ ⋮ ⋮ ⋮	22	⋮ ⋮ ⋮ ⋮ ⋮	42	⋮ ⋮ ⋮ ⋮ ⋮	62	⋮ ⋮ ⋮ ⋮ ⋮
3	⋮ ⋮ ⋮ ⋮ ⋮	23	⋮ ⋮ ⋮ ⋮ ⋮	43	⋮ ⋮ ⋮ ⋮ ⋮	63	⋮ ⋮ ⋮ ⋮ ⋮
4	⋮ ⋮ ⋮ ⋮ ⋮	24	⋮ ⋮ ⋮ ⋮ ⋮	44	⋮ ⋮ ⋮ ⋮ ⋮	64	⋮ ⋮ ⋮ ⋮ ⋮
5	⋮ ⋮ ⋮ ⋮ ⋮	25	⋮ ⋮ ⋮ ⋮ ⋮	45	⋮ ⋮ ⋮ ⋮ ⋮	65	⋮ ⋮ ⋮ ⋮ ⋮
6	⋮ ⋮ ⋮ ⋮ ⋮	26	⋮ ⋮ ⋮ ⋮ ⋮	46	⋮ ⋮ ⋮ ⋮ ⋮	66	⋮ ⋮ ⋮ ⋮ ⋮
7	⋮ ⋮ ⋮ ⋮ ⋮	27	⋮ ⋮ ⋮ ⋮ ⋮	47	⋮ ⋮ ⋮ ⋮ ⋮	67	⋮ ⋮ ⋮ ⋮ ⋮
8	⋮ ⋮ ⋮ ⋮ ⋮	28	⋮ ⋮ ⋮ ⋮ ⋮	48	⋮ ⋮ ⋮ ⋮ ⋮	68	⋮ ⋮ ⋮ ⋮ ⋮
9	⋮ ⋮ ⋮ ⋮ ⋮	29	⋮ ⋮ ⋮ ⋮ ⋮	49	⋮ ⋮ ⋮ ⋮ ⋮	69	⋮ ⋮ ⋮ ⋮ ⋮
10	⋮ ⋮ ⋮ ⋮ ⋮	30	⋮ ⋮ ⋮ ⋮ ⋮	50	⋮ ⋮ ⋮ ⋮ ⋮	70	⋮ ⋮ ⋮ ⋮ ⋮
11	⋮ ⋮ ⋮ ⋮ ⋮	31	⋮ ⋮ ⋮ ⋮ ⋮	51	⋮ ⋮ ⋮ ⋮ ⋮	71	⋮ ⋮ ⋮ ⋮ ⋮
12	⋮ ⋮ ⋮ ⋮ ⋮	32	⋮ ⋮ ⋮ ⋮ ⋮	52	⋮ ⋮ ⋮ ⋮ ⋮	72	⋮ ⋮ ⋮ ⋮ ⋮
13	⋮ ⋮ ⋮ ⋮ ⋮	33	⋮ ⋮ ⋮ ⋮ ⋮	53	⋮ ⋮ ⋮ ⋮ ⋮	73	⋮ ⋮ ⋮ ⋮ ⋮
14	⋮ ⋮ ⋮ ⋮ ⋮	34	⋮ ⋮ ⋮ ⋮ ⋮	54	⋮ ⋮ ⋮ ⋮ ⋮	74	⋮ ⋮ ⋮ ⋮ ⋮
15	⋮ ⋮ ⋮ ⋮ ⋮	35	⋮ ⋮ ⋮ ⋮ ⋮	55	⋮ ⋮ ⋮ ⋮ ⋮	75	⋮ ⋮ ⋮ ⋮ ⋮
16	⋮ ⋮ ⋮ ⋮ ⋮	36	⋮ ⋮ ⋮ ⋮ ⋮	56	⋮ ⋮ ⋮ ⋮ ⋮	76	⋮ ⋮ ⋮ ⋮ ⋮
17	⋮ ⋮ ⋮ ⋮ ⋮	37	⋮ ⋮ ⋮ ⋮ ⋮	57	⋮ ⋮ ⋮ ⋮ ⋮	77	⋮ ⋮ ⋮ ⋮ ⋮
18	⋮ ⋮ ⋮ ⋮ ⋮	38	⋮ ⋮ ⋮ ⋮ ⋮	58	⋮ ⋮ ⋮ ⋮ ⋮	78	⋮ ⋮ ⋮ ⋮ ⋮
19	⋮ ⋮ ⋮ ⋮ ⋮	39	⋮ ⋮ ⋮ ⋮ ⋮	59	⋮ ⋮ ⋮ ⋮ ⋮	79	⋮ ⋮ ⋮ ⋮ ⋮
20	⋮ ⋮ ⋮ ⋮ ⋮	40	⋮ ⋮ ⋮ ⋮ ⋮	60	⋮ ⋮ ⋮ ⋮ ⋮	80	⋮ ⋮ ⋮ ⋮ ⋮

Example

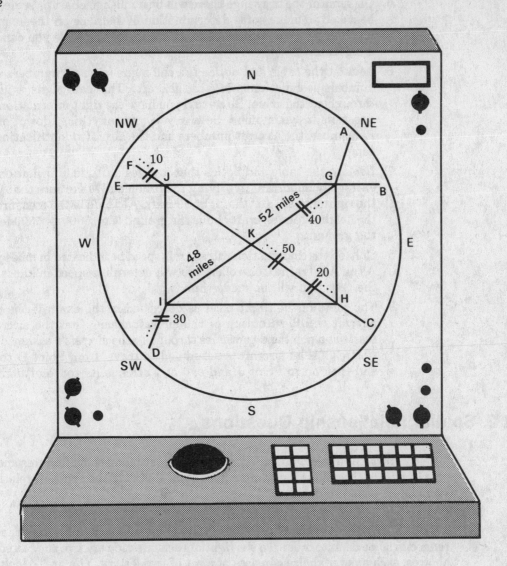

AIR TRAFFIC CONTROL FLIGHT INFORMATION			
Aircraft	**Altitude**	**Speed**	**Route**
10	5000	300	FJKH
20	5500	300	HKJF
30	5000	450	DIKG
40	6000	450	GKID
50	6000	300	FJKH

Note: Figure *not* drawn to scale.

5. On some of the drawings there will be a mileage chart or scale. You will be asked to make some determination of distance on the exam. If you lay your pencil or a piece of paper alongside the scale you can measure a distance.

6. Look at the table and notice the call signs (aircraft numbers or letter-number designations) of the aircraft. The call signs will change throughout the exam. Be certain you have the right information for each question in your mind before you put anything down on paper. Remember, the aircraft numbers and the aircraft identification are the same.

7. Look at the table and notice that it gives altitude information. This is extremely important in solving the problems. Make sure that you have the right altitude for the right aircraft. Altitude is the measurement of the height of the aircraft above the ground (e.g., 5500 = 5500 feet above the ground).

8. Only on the examination will aircraft speed be indicated in miles per hour. As an Air Traffic Controller, you will determine speed in knots. But for the test, you will be using mph.

9. The route of the flight path as described in the exam is the path the aircraft will fly. Routing of the aircraft means that the aircraft path starts at a point and continues through to the aircraft's assigned destination (e.g., if an aircraft is scheduled to travel from Point D to Point I and then on to Point J and end at F, this is its route of flight).

Test 2. Spatial Relationship Questions

In this test, the questions deal with relationships among sets of figures and among sets of letters. The following sample questions illustrate the types of relationships you will be asked to discover.

LETTER SERIES. In these questions, you are given a series of letters that are arranged in some definite order. To the right of each question are five suggested answer choices; each answer choice consists of a set of two letters. You are to look at each letter series and determine what its order is and then from the suggested answers at the right select the set that gives the next two letters in the series in their correct order. Let's look at two sample problems.

Example 1

X C X D X E X   (A) F X   (B) F G   (C) X F   (D) E F   (E) X G

In this question, the series consists of X's alternating with letters in alphabetical order. The next two letters would be F and X. The correct answer is A.

Example 2

A B D C E F H   (A) G H   (B) I G   (C) G I   (D) K L   (E) I H

For the above question, the letters in the letter series are arranged in pairs, the first pair in their usual order and the next pair in reverse order. The last letter given in the series is H, which is the second letter of the reversed ordered pair G–H. The first missing letter must therefore be G. Since the next pair of letters must be I–J, the second of the missing letters must be I. Since the answer is G I, answer C is correct.

QUESTION-ANSWERING STRATEGY. For answering Letter Series questions, you will find it a great help to write out the entire alphabet (see below) and keep this in front of you during the test. The key to each question can be picked out much more easily by using this visual reference.

A B C D E F G H I J K L M N O P Q R S T U V W X Y Z
1 2 3 4 5 6 7 8 9 10 11 12 13 14 15 16 17 18 19 20 21 22 23 24 25 26

SYMBOL CLASSIFICATION. Each of these questions consists of two sets of symbols. You are asked to find the one rule that (A) explains the similarity of the symbols within each set, and (B) also explains the difference between the sets.

Let's look at an example. Which of the five suggested answers can best be substituted for the question mark in Set 2?

Example 1

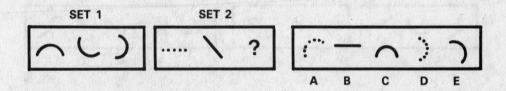

The general rule for the above question is that all of the symbols are lines. The symbols in Set 1 are similar because they are all curved lines; the symbols in Set 2 are similar to each other and different from the symbols in Set 1 because they are all straight lines. Therefore B is the correct answer. Please note that the type of line (dotted or solid) is a detail that has nothing to do with the rule for solving the problem.

Example 2

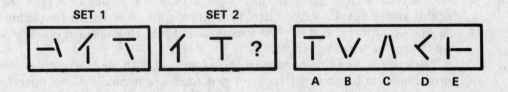

For the above question, the general rule for both sets is that all the symbols consist of two lines. In Set 1 all the symbols are made up of lines that do not touch each other. In Set 2 all the symbols are made up of lines that are touching. Therefore D is the correct answer. Please note that the length of the lines is a detail that is irrelevant to the rule for solving the problem.

Example 3

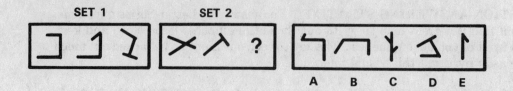

In example 3, the general rule is that all the symbols in both sets are made up of
lines that touch each other. In Set 1 all of the symbols consist of three lines that
touch; in Set 2 all of the symbols consist of two lines that touch. Therefore E is the
correct answer. Note the fact that some of the lines' touching and some of the lines'
crossing is a detail that has nothing to do with answering the question.

Example 4

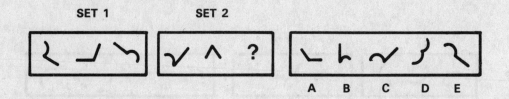

In the above example, the general rule for both sets is that all the symbols are made
up of lines that form an angle. In Set 1, all of the symbols consist of lines that form
an obtuse angle (greater than 90°). In Set 2, all of the symbols consist of lines that
form an acute angle (less than 90°). Therefore B is correct. Note that the shape of
the lines in the symbols is a detail that has nothing to do with the rule for solving
the problem.

Test 3. Air Traffic Control Knowledge Questions

In this test you will be asked to answer questions that draw upon knowledge
related to air traffic control work. The test serves as an indicator of your possession
of this knowledge. However, there is no knowledge requirement for taking the Air
Traffic Controller Exam nor is it a requirement for being selected into the Air Traffic Controller training program.

The questions in this portion of the exam deal with air traffic rules, air traffic
procedures, in-flight traffic control procedures, communications operating procedures, flight assistance service procedures, air navigation and aids to navigation,
and aviation weather.

Scoring

For Tests 1 and 3, incorrect answers will not affect your total score. On Test 3 you can receive additional points on your total score by answering questions correctly.

FORMULA FOR TEST 3

Number of Questions Answered Correctly	Points Added to Total Score
52–55 questions	3 points
56–59 questions	5 points
60–63 questions	10 points
more than 63 questions	15 points

General Techniques

1. "Check & Go"—Don't spend too much time on a difficult question (keep a watch with you during the exam); otherwise you could miss several questions by running out of time. Be sure to check off the number on the answer sheets so you don't subsequently come back and put the answer in the wrong box.

2. Be Conscious of the Time Factor—In most sections of the test you have about 30 seconds per question. Budget your time accordingly and "put time in your pocket" on the easy questions.

3. Be Aware of the Penalty for Incorrect Answers—More points are deducted for incorrect answers than for skipped questions, so it does not pay to guess on the major portions of the test. On the air traffic knowledge portion, which is extra credit only, guessing is advised.

4. When the examiner indicates that the time limit for a section is almost up, go back to the questions you skipped in that section and try to solve them.

5. Once you have chosen an answer, don't go back and change it unless you are positive that the first answer is incorrect. Studies have shown that the first answer is most often the best choice.

6. Familiarize yourself with the test directions and sample answer sheets given in this book. You will save yourself time on the real test by understanding the directions beforehand and by knowing how to fill out the answer sheets.

7. Be certain that you fill in the correct answer box on your answer sheet. In other words, if you are answering question 10, be certain that you mark your answer next to number 10. If you want to change an answer, make sure that you erase the old answer completely. Since the exami-

nation is graded by machine, you must be certain to follow this last bit of advice. A machine cannot tell the difference between a light erasure and a smudge. If the machine sees what it thinks are two or more marks for an answer, it won't give you credit or it will mark the answer as wrong.

8. Remember to get a good night's sleep before the exam and eat a light breakfast. If you are tired or sluggish, you won't be as sharp as you normally are.

9. Under no circumstances is cheating condoned. It is a serious offense and will disqualify you immediately.

Air Traffic Control Aptitude Test Techniques

1. When given questions other than "conflict" problems, there is only one correct answer; stop when you find it (unless "all of the above" is given as a choice). For example, in question 2 on page 67, since the correct answer is A, there is no need to examine choices B, C, or D.

2. Read questions carefully. For example, note the word "opposite" in question 6 on page 67.

3. Be alert for questions referring back to starting points, such as question 1, page 87.

4. For problems involving distance be sure to use the edge of a paper and mark off miles; don't use finger joints or eyeball mileages. See question 1, page 89.

5. For aircraft time or distance problems such as question 5, page 93, always use the following calculations:

   - Divide the aircraft speed by 60 to get miles flown per minute—e.g., a 400 mph aircraft divided by 60 equals 6.67 miles per minute.

   - Then divide the distance to be flown by miles per minute to determine how long it takes a given aircraft to fly a specified distance.

6. Solve "conflict" problems using the following sequence of steps:

   - Check the table first for pairs of altitudes.
   - If more than one pair of altitude conflicts occur, check the routes to see if there are any common letters—common letters in routes indicate conflictions.
   - If there are still two or more possible pairs of aircraft conflicts, look at the radar chart to determine the answer. For example, in question 6, page 69, aircraft 50 has passed the point of conflict with aircraft 40, leaving 10 and 20 as the only possible pair.

7. Skip a question if you find it too difficult and return to it if you can.

Letter Series Techniques

1. Use logical reasoning; question 7 on page 98 was answered by reading the letters to yourself and completing the logical flow. If you can't see it, go to technique #2.

2. Use the numbering technique to find pattetns that do not appear logically (see page 106). Write the number of each letter under the appropriate letter. If you still don't see the answer, go to technique #3.

3. Skip the question and return to it later, using technique #4.

4. Extend your analysis to look for a pattern—for example, see the explanation for question 13 on page 107.

Symbol Classification Techniques

1. There are common patterns in the questions:
   Straight Lines vs. Curved Lines
   Obtuse vs. Acute Angles
   Solid vs. Dotted Lines
   Open Figures vs. Closed Figures
   Circles vs. Squares or Triangles
   Touching Lines vs. Non-Touching Lines
   Parallel Lines
   Numbers of Straight or Curved Lines

2. Pacing procedures:
   Look at Box 1 for the pattern.
   Look at Box 2 for the pattern variation.
   Look at Box 3 for the oddball and fit it into the question mark.

Air Traffic Knowledge Test Techniques

To study for the air traffic knowledge portion, do the test beginning on page 129 by looking up the correct answers and ignoring the incorrect responses. Read the "Introduction to Air Control Systems" section in this book. These techniques should help you recall correct responses on the multiple choice test without cluttering up your mind with useless information.

PART THREE

Full-Length Sample Examination

This sample test differs from the actual 4-hour exam in length and time allocation per test section. It gives you ample practice in each test area in the aptitude and knowledge sections.

> The questions contained in this examination illustrate the types of questions you may encounter on the Air Traffic Controller exam. They are **NOT** intended to represent an actual ATC examination.

ANSWER SHEETS
AIR TRAFFIC CONTROLLER EXAMINATION

Test 1   Part I

FIGURE A

	A B C D E		A B C D E		A B C D E		A B C D E
1	⋮ ⋮ ⋮ ⋮ ⋮	3	⋮ ⋮ ⋮ ⋮ ⋮	5	⋮ ⋮ ⋮ ⋮ ⋮	7	⋮ ⋮ ⋮ ⋮ ⋮
2	⋮ ⋮ ⋮ ⋮ ⋮	4	⋮ ⋮ ⋮ ⋮ ⋮	6	⋮ ⋮ ⋮ ⋮ ⋮	8	⋮ ⋮ ⋮ ⋮ ⋮

FIGURE B

	A B C D E		A B C D E		A B C D E		A B C D E
1	⋮ ⋮ ⋮ ⋮ ⋮	3	⋮ ⋮ ⋮ ⋮ ⋮	5	⋮ ⋮ ⋮ ⋮ ⋮	7	⋮ ⋮ ⋮ ⋮ ⋮
2	⋮ ⋮ ⋮ ⋮ ⋮	4	⋮ ⋮ ⋮ ⋮ ⋮	6	⋮ ⋮ ⋮ ⋮ ⋮	8	⋮ ⋮ ⋮ ⋮ ⋮

FIGURE C

	A B C D E		A B C D E		A B C D E		A B C D E
1	⋮ ⋮ ⋮ ⋮ ⋮	2	⋮ ⋮ ⋮ ⋮ ⋮	3	⋮ ⋮ ⋮ ⋮ ⋮	4	⋮ ⋮ ⋮ ⋮ ⋮

FIGURE D

	A B C D E		A B C D E		A B C D E		A B C D E
1	⋮ ⋮ ⋮ ⋮ ⋮	3	⋮ ⋮ ⋮ ⋮ ⋮	5	⋮ ⋮ ⋮ ⋮ ⋮	7	⋮ ⋮ ⋮ ⋮ ⋮
2	⋮ ⋮ ⋮ ⋮ ⋮	4	⋮ ⋮ ⋮ ⋮ ⋮	6	⋮ ⋮ ⋮ ⋮ ⋮		

FIGURE E

	A B C D E		A B C D E		A B C D E		A B C D E
1	⋮ ⋮ ⋮ ⋮ ⋮	3	⋮ ⋮ ⋮ ⋮ ⋮	5	⋮ ⋮ ⋮ ⋮ ⋮	6	⋮ ⋮ ⋮ ⋮ ⋮
2	⋮ ⋮ ⋮ ⋮ ⋮	4	⋮ ⋮ ⋮ ⋮ ⋮				

FIGURE F

	A B C D E		A B C D E		A B C D E		A B C D E
1	⋮ ⋮ ⋮ ⋮ ⋮	3	⋮ ⋮ ⋮ ⋮ ⋮	5	⋮ ⋮ ⋮ ⋮ ⋮	6	⋮ ⋮ ⋮ ⋮ ⋮
2	⋮ ⋮ ⋮ ⋮ ⋮	4	⋮ ⋮ ⋮ ⋮ ⋮				

FIGURE G

	A B C D E		A B C D E		A B C D E		A B C D E
1	⋮ ⋮ ⋮ ⋮ ⋮	3	⋮ ⋮ ⋮ ⋮ ⋮	5	⋮ ⋮ ⋮ ⋮ ⋮	6	⋮ ⋮ ⋮ ⋮ ⋮
2	⋮ ⋮ ⋮ ⋮ ⋮	4	⋮ ⋮ ⋮ ⋮ ⋮				

FIGURE H

	A B C D E		A B C D E		A B C D E		A B C D E
1	⋮ ⋮ ⋮ ⋮ ⋮	3	⋮ ⋮ ⋮ ⋮ ⋮	5	⋮ ⋮ ⋮ ⋮ ⋮	6	⋮ ⋮ ⋮ ⋮ ⋮
2	⋮ ⋮ ⋮ ⋮ ⋮	4	⋮ ⋮ ⋮ ⋮ ⋮				

Tear Out Along This Line

FIGURE I

	A B C D E			A B C D E			A B C D E			A B C D E
1	:: :: :: :: ::		4	:: :: :: :: ::		6	:: :: :: :: ::		8	:: :: :: :: ::
2	:: :: :: :: ::		5	:: :: :: :: ::		7	:: :: :: :: ::		9	:: :: :: :: ::
3	:: :: :: :: ::									

Test 1   Part II

FIGURE A

	A B C D E			A B C D E			A B C D E			A B C D E
1	:: :: :: :: ::		4	:: :: :: :: ::		7	:: :: :: :: ::		9	:: :: :: :: ::
2	:: :: :: :: ::		5	:: :: :: :: ::		8	:: :: :: :: ::		10	:: :: :: :: ::
3	:: :: :: :: ::		6	:: :: :: :: ::						

FIGURE B

	A B C D E			A B C D E			A B C D E			A B C D E
1	:: :: :: :: ::		4	:: :: :: :: ::		7	:: :: :: :: ::		9	:: :: :: :: ::
2	:: :: :: :: ::		5	:: :: :: :: ::		8	:: :: :: :: ::		10	:: :: :: :: ::
3	:: :: :: :: ::		6	:: :: :: :: ::						

FIGURE C

	A B C D E			A B C D E			A B C D E			A B C D E
1	:: :: :: :: ::		3	:: :: :: :: ::		5	:: :: :: :: ::		7	:: :: :: :: ::
2	:: :: :: :: ::		4	:: :: :: :: ::		6	:: :: :: :: ::		8	:: :: :: :: ::

FIGURE D

	A B C D E			A B C D E			A B C D E			A B C D E
1	:: :: :: :: ::		8	:: :: :: :: ::		15	:: :: :: :: ::		22	:: :: :: :: ::
2	:: :: :: :: ::		9	:: :: :: :: ::		16	:: :: :: :: ::		23	:: :: :: :: ::
3	:: :: :: :: ::		10	:: :: :: :: ::		17	:: :: :: :: ::		24	:: :: :: :: ::
4	:: :: :: :: ::		11	:: :: :: :: ::		18	:: :: :: :: ::		25	:: :: :: :: ::
5	:: :: :: :: ::		12	:: :: :: :: ::		19	:: :: :: :: ::		26	:: :: :: :: ::
6	:: :: :: :: ::		13	:: :: :: :: ::		20	:: :: :: :: ::		27	:: :: :: :: ::
7	:: :: :: :: ::		14	:: :: :: :: ::		21	:: :: :: :: ::			

Test 2   Part I (Letter Series)

SECTION 1

	A B C D E		A B C D E		A B C D E		A B C D E
1	:: :: :: :: ::	8	:: :: :: :: ::	14	:: :: :: :: ::	20	:: :: :: :: ::
2	:: :: :: :: ::	9	:: :: :: :: ::	15	:: :: :: :: ::	21	:: :: :: :: ::
3	:: :: :: :: ::	10	:: :: :: :: ::	16	:: :: :: :: ::	22	:: :: :: :: ::
4	:: :: :: :: ::	11	:: :: :: :: ::	17	:: :: :: :: ::	23	:: :: :: :: ::
5	:: :: :: :: ::	12	:: :: :: :: ::	18	:: :: :: :: ::	24	:: :: :: :: ::
6	:: :: :: :: ::	13	:: :: :: :: ::	19	:: :: :: :: ::	25	:: :: :: :: ::
7	:: :: :: :: ::						

SECTION 2

	A B C D E		A B C D E		A B C D E		A B C D E
1	:: :: :: :: ::	8	:: :: :: :: ::	14	:: :: :: :: ::	20	:: :: :: :: ::
2	:: :: :: :: ::	9	:: :: :: :: ::	15	:: :: :: :: ::	21	:: :: :: :: ::
3	:: :: :: :: ::	10	:: :: :: :: ::	16	:: :: :: :: ::	22	:: :: :: :: ::
4	:: :: :: :: ::	11	:: :: :: :: ::	17	:: :: :: :: ::	23	:: :: :: :: ::
5	:: :: :: :: ::	12	:: :: :: :: ::	18	:: :: :: :: ::	24	:: :: :: :: ::
6	:: :: :: :: ::	13	:: :: :: :: ::	19	:: :: :: :: ::	25	:: :: :: :: ::
7	:: :: :: :: ::						

SECTION 3

	A B C D E		A B C D E		A B C D E		A B C D E
1	:: :: :: :: ::	8	:: :: :: :: ::	14	:: :: :: :: ::	20	:: :: :: :: ::
2	:: :: :: :: ::	9	:: :: :: :: ::	15	:: :: :: :: ::	21	:: :: :: :: ::
3	:: :: :: :: ::	10	:: :: :: :: ::	16	:: :: :: :: ::	22	:: :: :: :: ::
4	:: :: :: :: ::	11	:: :: :: :: ::	17	:: :: :: :: ::	23	:: :: :: :: ::
5	:: :: :: :: ::	12	:: :: :: :: ::	18	:: :: :: :: ::	24	:: :: :: :: ::
6	:: :: :: :: ::	13	:: :: :: :: ::	19	:: :: :: :: ::	25	:: :: :: :: ::
7	:: :: :: :: ::						

Test 2   Part II (Symbol Classification)

SECTION 1

	A B C D E		A B C D E		A B C D E		A B C D E
1	:: :: :: :: ::	7	:: :: :: :: ::	13	:: :: :: :: ::	19	:: :: :: :: ::
2	:: :: :: :: ::	8	:: :: :: :: ::	14	:: :: :: :: ::	20	:: :: :: :: ::
3	:: :: :: :: ::	9	:: :: :: :: ::	15	:: :: :: :: ::	21	:: :: :: :: ::
4	:: :: :: :: ::	10	:: :: :: :: ::	16	:: :: :: :: ::	22	:: :: :: :: ::
5	:: :: :: :: ::	11	:: :: :: :: ::	17	:: :: :: :: ::	23	:: :: :: :: ::
6	:: :: :: :: ::	12	:: :: :: :: ::	18	:: :: :: :: ::		

SECTION 2

	A B C D E		A B C D E		A B C D E		A B C D E
1	:: :: :: :: ::	5	:: :: :: :: ::	9	:: :: :: :: ::	13	:: :: :: :: ::
2	:: :: :: :: ::	6	:: :: :: :: ::	10	:: :: :: :: ::	14	:: :: :: :: ::
3	:: :: :: :: ::	7	:: :: :: :: ::	11	:: :: :: :: ::	15	:: :: :: :: ::
4	:: :: :: :: ::	8	:: :: :: :: ::	12	:: :: :: :: ::		

SECTION 3

	A B C D E		A B C D E		A B C D E		A B C D E
1	:: :: :: :: ::	5	:: :: :: :: ::	9	:: :: :: :: ::	13	:: :: :: :: ::
2	:: :: :: :: ::	6	:: :: :: :: ::	10	:: :: :: :: ::	14	:: :: :: :: ::
3	:: :: :: :: ::	7	:: :: :: :: ::	11	:: :: :: :: ::	15	:: :: :: :: ::
4	:: :: :: :: ::	8	:: :: :: :: ::	12	:: :: :: :: ::		

Test 3

	A B C D E		A B C D E		A B C D E		A B C D E
1	:: :: :: :: ::	21	:: :: :: :: ::	41	:: :: :: :: ::	61	:: :: :: :: ::
2	:: :: :: :: ::	22	:: :: :: :: ::	42	:: :: :: :: ::	62	:: :: :: :: ::
3	:: :: :: :: ::	23	:: :: :: :: ::	43	:: :: :: :: ::	63	:: :: :: :: ::
4	:: :: :: :: ::	24	:: :: :: :: ::	44	:: :: :: :: ::	64	:: :: :: :: ::
5	:: :: :: :: ::	25	:: :: :: :: ::	45	:: :: :: :: ::	65	:: :: :: :: ::
6	:: :: :: :: ::	26	:: :: :: :: ::	46	:: :: :: :: ::	66	:: :: :: :: ::
7	:: :: :: :: ::	27	:: :: :: :: ::	47	:: :: :: :: ::	67	:: :: :: :: ::
8	:: :: :: :: ::	28	:: :: :: :: ::	48	:: :: :: :: ::	68	:: :: :: :: ::
9	:: :: :: :: ::	29	:: :: :: :: ::	49	:: :: :: :: ::	69	:: :: :: :: ::
10	:: :: :: :: ::	30	:: :: :: :: ::	50	:: :: :: :: ::	70	:: :: :: :: ::
11	:: :: :: :: ::	31	:: :: :: :: ::	51	:: :: :: :: ::	71	:: :: :: :: ::
12	:: :: :: :: ::	32	:: :: :: :: ::	52	:: :: :: :: ::	72	:: :: :: :: ::
13	:: :: :: :: ::	33	:: :: :: :: ::	53	:: :: :: :: ::	73	:: :: :: :: ::
14	:: :: :: :: ::	34	:: :: :: :: ::	54	:: :: :: :: ::	74	:: :: :: :: ::
15	:: :: :: :: ::	35	:: :: :: :: ::	55	:: :: :: :: ::	75	:: :: :: :: ::
16	:: :: :: :: ::	36	:: :: :: :: ::	56	:: :: :: :: ::	76	:: :: :: :: ::
17	:: :: :: :: ::	37	:: :: :: :: ::	57	:: :: :: :: ::	77	:: :: :: :: ::
18	:: :: :: :: ::	38	:: :: :: :: ::	58	:: :: :: :: ::	78	:: :: :: :: ::
19	:: :: :: :: ::	39	:: :: :: :: ::	59	:: :: :: :: ::	79	:: :: :: :: ::
20	:: :: :: :: ::	40	:: :: :: :: ::	60	:: :: :: :: ::	80	:: :: :: :: ::

AIR TRAFFIC CONTROLLER EXAMINATION
Test 1   Part I

Time: 30 minutes

DIRECTIONS: *This test consists of drawings that simulate a radar scope depicting characteristic patterns of air traffic. Each problem contains a drawing of particular flight paths and aircraft flying on those routes. A table containing information about the altitude, speed, and route of each aircraft accompanies each drawing. Your task will be to answer questions that make use of this flight information.*

IMPORTANT: In order to properly answer a number of the questions in both parts of Test 1, you must be aware of the criteria by which two aircraft are determined to be "in conflict." For this test, planes are to be considered in conflict if they are separated by less than 1000 feet of vertical space (altitude) while approaching the same geographical point along their flight paths.

Assume all distances given are correct when it is indicated that the figure is *not* drawn to scale.

For more information concerning this term—and for definitions of other terms appearing in these tests—refer to the Glossary.

FIGURE A

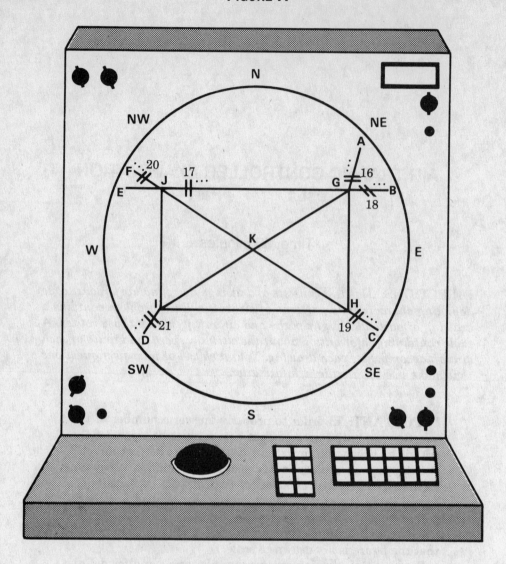

AIR TRAFFIC CONTROL FLIGHT INFORMATION			
Aircraft	Altitude	Speed	Route
16	5000	480	AGB
17	5000	480	GJE
18	6000	240	BGHID
19	5000	240	CHKJF
20	6000	240	FJKHC
21	5000	240	DIKGA

Figure A Questions

1. Are Aircraft 16 and 17 flying at the same altitude and speed?
   (A) Yes   (B) No

2. Which aircraft are flying at the same altitude but at different speeds?
   (A) 16 and 19   (B) 17 and 18   (C) 18 and 20   (D) 19 and 21

3. Will Aircraft 19 and 20 conflict?
   (A) Yes   (B) No

4. What is the approximate direction from Point J to Point D?
   (A) East   (B) North   (C) South   (D) Northeast

5. At the speed of 240 mph, four miles per minute, how many minutes will Aircraft
   19 need to go 48 miles?
   (A) 2   (B) 7   (C) 17   (D) 12

6. What is the opposite of the approximate direction from Point J to Point K?
   (A) Southeast   (B) Southwest   (C) Northwest   (D) East

7. Which airways form a figure that most resembles the letter X?
   (A) JKH/IKG   (B) FJKHC/DIKGA   (C) GKID/CHKJ   (D) IKGA/HKJF

8. Which aircraft will conflict?
   (A) 21 and 20   (B) 19 and 21   (C) 20 and 19   (D) 18 and 16

END OF FIGURE A.
GO TO FIGURE B.

FIGURE B

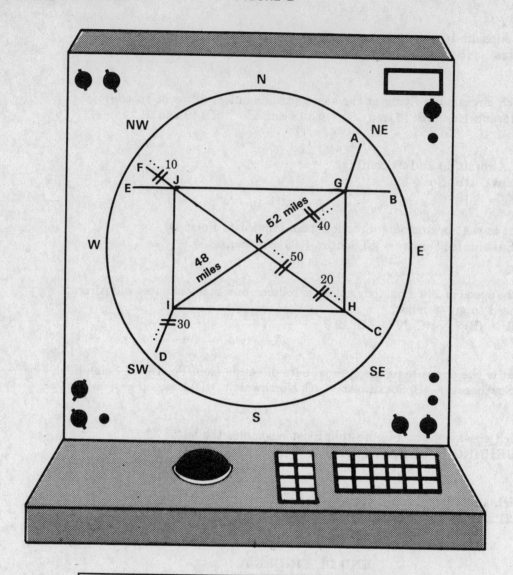

AIR TRAFFIC CONTROL FLIGHT INFORMATION			
Aircraft	Altitude	Speed	Route
10	5000	300	FJKH
20	5500	300	HKJF
30	5000	450	DIKG
40	6000	450	GKID
50	6000	300	FJKH

Note: Figure *not* drawn to scale.

Figure B Questions

1. Which aircraft are flying in the *same direction* on the same routes?
   (A) 20 and 50   (B) 10 and 50   (C) 40 and 10   (D) 30 and 20

2. Which aircraft are flying at the *same speed toward each other* on routes that follow the same path?
   (A) 30 and 10   (B) 40 and 20   (C) 50 and 40   (D) 20 and 50

3. What is the approximate number of miles from Point G to Point H?
   (A) 35   (B) 62   (C) 48   (D) 52

4. Approximately how many minutes does Aircraft 30 need to fly from Point I to Point K?
   (A) 6   (B) 9   (C) 11   (D) 10

5. What is the approximate number of miles from Point J to Point G?
   (A) 85   (B) 100   (C) 120   (D) 125

6. Which aircraft will conflict?
   (A) 10 and 20   (B) 40 and 50   (C) 30 and 40   (D) 10 and 50

7. Which aircraft flies a route to the northwest?
   (A) 30   (B) 10   (C) 50   (D) 20

8. Which aircraft ends its route in a direction that is the opposite of southwest?
   (A) 50   (B) 10   (C) 20   (D) 30

END OF FIGURE B.
GO TO FIGURE C.

FIGURE C

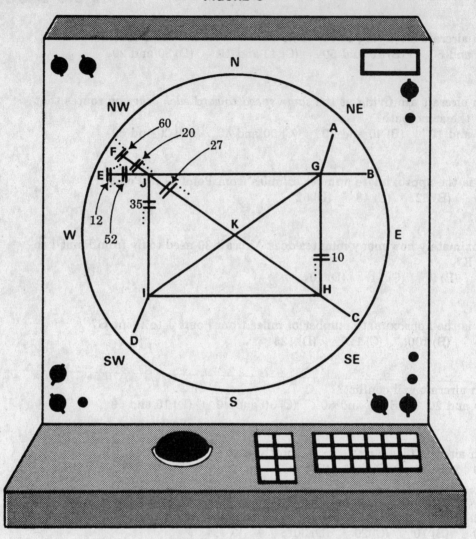

AIR TRAFFIC CONTROL FLIGHT INFORMATION			
Aircraft	Altitude	Speed	Route
10	7000	360	HGJE
20	6000	450	HKJF
12	4000	240	DIJE
27	4000	240	HKJE
35	5000	480	DIJF
52	5000	300	EJGB
60	9000	390	FJKH

Figure C Questions

1. Which aircraft will conflict?
   (A) 35 and 52   (B) 10 and 20   (C) 27 and 60   (D) None

2. Which aircraft flies a route that forms a figure resembling the number 7?
   (A) 12   (B) 60   (C) 10   (D) 52

3. Which aircraft are flying toward each other on routes that follow the same path?
   (A) 12 and 52   (B) 10 and 20   (C) 35 and 52   (D) 20 and 60

4. In what direction is Aircraft 10 moving?
   (A) NE   (B) NW   (C) South   (D) North

END OF FIGURE C.
GO TO FIGURE D.

FIGURE D

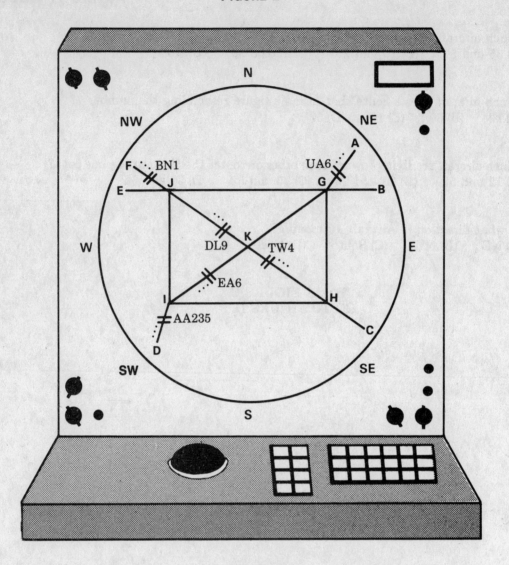

AIR TRAFFIC CONTROL FLIGHT INFORMATION			
Aircraft	**Altitude**	**Speed**	**Route**
BN1	14,000	450	FJGB
AA235	23,000	450	DIKGA
TW4	18,000	430	HKJ
UA6	23,000	480	AGKID
EA6	18,000	430	IKG
DL9	19,000	465	JKH

Figure D Questions

1. Which aircraft will conflict?
   (A) BN1 and UA6   (B) AA235 and EA6   (C) DL9 and TW4
   (D) AA235 and UA6

2. Which aircraft fly routes that form an X?
   (A) EA6 and TW4   (B) BN1 and TW4   (C) DL9 and TW4
   (D) UA6 and EA6

3. Will DL9 and TW4 conflict?
   (A) Yes   (B) No

4. In what direction is EA6 traveling?
   (A) NE   (B) NW   (C) SW   (D) SE

5. If DL9 continues on its present path, which fixes (lettered points on the drawing) will it pass over?
   (A) KHC   (B) KGA   (C) KID   (D) KJF

6. Will EA6 and UA6 conflict?
   (A) Yes   (B) No

7. Will EA6 and DL9 conflict?
   (A) Yes   (B) No

END OF FIGURE D.
GO TO FIGURE E.

FIGURE E

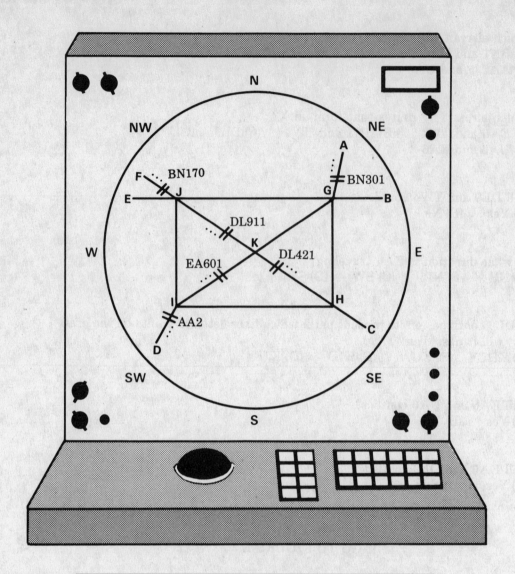

AIR TRAFFIC CONTROL FLIGHT INFORMATION			
Aircraft	Altitude	Speed	Route
BN170	16,000	450	FJGB
AA2	23,000	450	DIKGA
DL421	18,000	430	HKJ
BN301	23,000	480	AGKID
EA601	18,000	430	IKG
DL911	19,000	465	JKH

Figure E Questions

1. In what direction is EA601 flying?
   (A) Southwest   (B) North   (C) Northeast   (D) South

2. Which two aircraft are flying at the same altitude but at different speeds?
   (A) AA2 and BN170   (B) BN301 and AA2
   (C) DL911 and BN170   (D) EA601 and DL911

3. In what direction is DL421 traveling?
   (A) NW   (B) SE   (C) SW   (D) SE

4. What is the altitude difference between DL421 and BN170?
   (A) 1,000 feet   (B) 2,000 feet   (C) 3,000 feet   (D) 4,000 feet

5. EA601 must turn in what direction at Fix K to get to Fix F?
   (A) SW   (B) SE   (C) NE   (D) NW

6. BN170 must climb how many thousand feet to arrive at 24,000?
   (A) 2,000   (B) 4,000   (C) 6,000   (D) 8,000

END OF FIGURE E.
GO TO FIGURE F.

FIGURE F

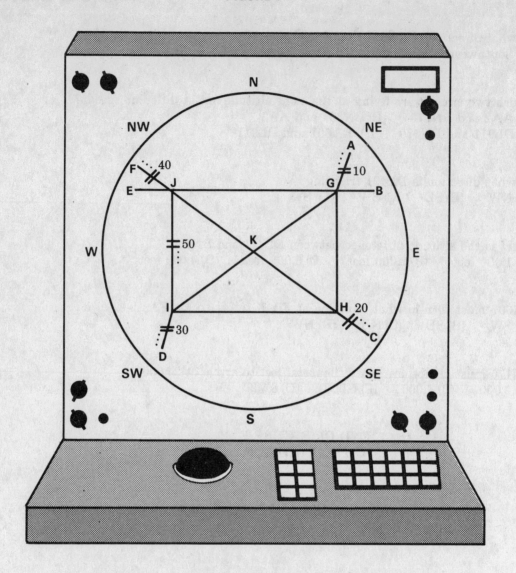

AIR TRAFFIC CONTROL FLIGHT INFORMATION			
Aircraft	Altitude	Speed	Route
10	6000	240	AGKID
20	6000	240	CHKJF
30	5000	280	DIJGB
40	5000	280	FJKHC
50	7000	190	DIJGB

Figure F Questions

1. Which aircraft will conflict?
   (A) 20 and 40   (B) 50 and 10   (C) 10 and 20   (D) 40 and 50

2. What is the opposite of the approximate direction in which Aircraft 50 is flying?
   (A) South   (B) Southeast   (C) Northwest   (D) North

3. Aircraft 20 is flying in what direction?
   (A) Northwest   (B) Northeast   (C) North   (D) West

4. Will Aircraft 20 conflict with Aircraft 30?
   (A) Yes   (B) No

5. Can Aircraft 30 climb to any of the following altitudes and not conflict with another aircraft?
   (A) 6000   (B) 7000   (C) 8000

6. Aircraft 40 is flying in what direction?
   (A) NE   (B) NW   (C) SW   (D) SE

END OF FIGURE F.
GO TO FIGURE G.

FIGURE G

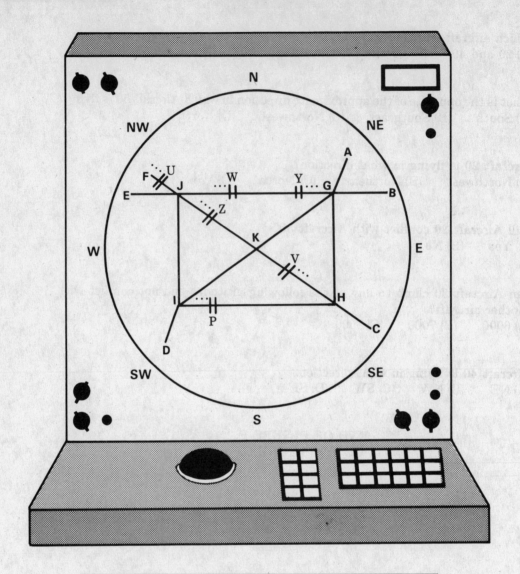

AIR TRAFFIC CONTROL FLIGHT INFORMATION			
Aircraft	**Altitude**	**Speed**	**Route**
U	7000	310	FJGA
V	8000	440	HKJE
W	8000	420	JGHC
P	7000	280	DIHC
Y	7000	320	AGJE
Z	9000	320	JKHC

Figure G Questions

1. Which aircraft will conflict?
   (A) U and Y   (B) U and Z   (C) P and Y   (D) V and W

2. Will Aircraft P and U conflict?
   (A) No   (B) Yes

3. What is the opposite of the approximate direction from Point I to Point H?
   (A) North   (B) South   (C) East   (D) West

4. What is the direction in which Aircraft W is traveling?
   (A) NE   (B) E   (C) SE   (D) W

5. What is the difference in the airspeed between Aircraft U and Aircraft P?
   (A) 10   (B) 20   (C) 30   (D) 40

6. Will Aircraft P and Z conflict?
   (A) Yes   (B) No

END OF FIGURE G.
GO TO FIGURE H.

FIGURE H

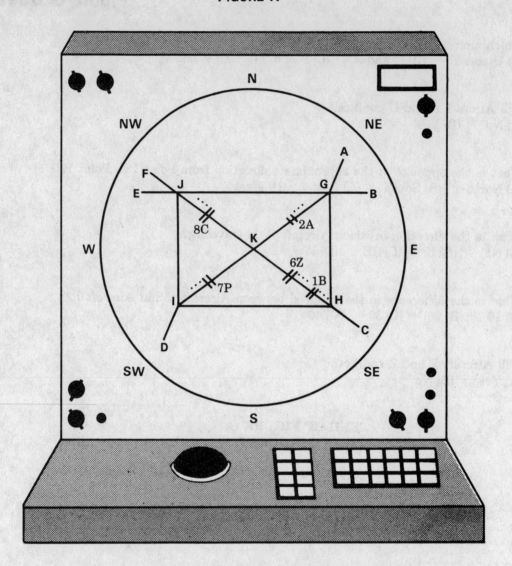

AIR TRAFFIC CONTROL FLIGHT INFORMATION			
Aircraft	**Altitude**	**Speed**	**Route**
1B	5000	300	CHKJ
2A	3000	210	GKID
6Z	3000	210	CHKJ
8C	4000	250	JKHC
7P	2000	180	IKJF

Figure H Questions

1. Which aircraft flies a route to the southwest?
   (A) 1B   (B) 6Z   (C) 7P   (D) 2A

2. How far apart is Aircraft 2A from Aircraft 1B in altitude?
   (A) 1000 feet   (B) 2000 feet   (C) 3000 feet   (D) 4000 feet

3. Which aircraft fly the same route?
   (A) 2A, 8C, 1B   (B) 1B, 6Z, 8C   (C) 6Z and 7P   (D) 6Z and 2A

4. About how many feet apart are Aircraft 1B and 8C?
   (A) 500   (B) 1500   (C) 2500   (D) 1000

5. Aircraft 7P will fly in what direction?
   (A) Northeast   (B) Northwest and Southeast
   (C) Northeast and Northwest   (D) Southwest

6. Will Aircraft 7P and 8C cross Point K?
   (A) Yes   (B) No

END OF FIGURE H.
GO TO FIGURE I.

FIGURE I

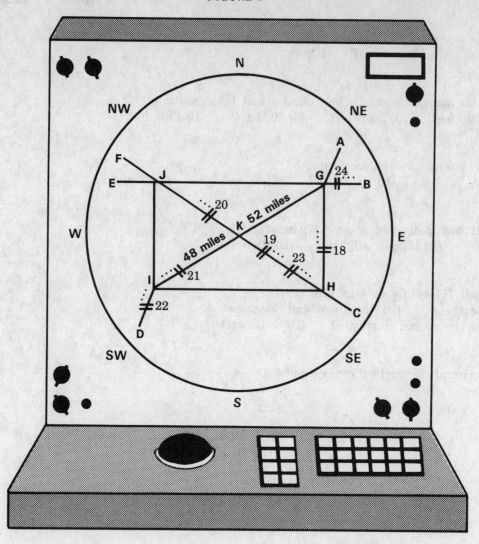

AIR TRAFFIC CONTROL FLIGHT INFORMATION			
Aircraft	Altitude	Speed	Route
20	6000	290	JKHC
21	3000	110	IKG
22	4000	155	JID
19	4000	175	HKGB
23	6000	290	CHKJ
18	10,000	400	AGHID
24	9000	300	BGKID

Note: Figure *not* drawn to scale.

Figure I Questions

1. Which aircraft are flying routes that together form a figure that most resembles the letter X?
   (A) 23 and 24   (B) 21 and 22   (C) 24 and 20   (D) 20 and 21

2. Which aircraft will conflict?
   (A) 20 and 23   (B) 19 and 20   (C) 21 and 22   (D) 18 and 21

3. How long will it take Aircraft 21 from its present position to get to Point K?
   (A) 23 min.   (B) 20 min.   (C) 27 min.   (D) 17 min.

4. Which aircraft flies the longest route?
   (A) 24   (B) 18   (C) 21   (D) 22

5. Are Aircraft 22 and 21 flying in the same direction?
   (A) Yes   (B) No

6. Which aircraft are flying at the same altitude and the same speed?
   (A) 18 and 24   (B) 22 and 19   (C) 20 and 23   (D) 19 and 23

7. Which aircraft are flying at the same altitude but at different speeds?
   (A) 22 and 19   (B) 23 and 20   (C) 18 and 24   (D) 21 and 22

8. At a speed of 400 mph, how many minutes will it take Aircraft 18 to go 120 miles?
   (A) 22 min.   (B) 18 min.   (C) 14 min.   (D) 13 min.

9. What is the opposite of the approximate direction from Point K to Point D?
   (A) North   (B) Northeast   (C) Southwest   (D) South

END OF TEST 1 PART I.

Answer Key—Test 1   Part I

FIGURE A

1. A	3. B	5. D	7. A	8. B
2. A	4. C	6. C		

FIGURE B

1. B	3. D	5. A	7. D	8. D
2. D	4. A	6. A		

FIGURE C

1. A	2. C	3. D	4. D

FIGURE D

1. D	3. B	5. A	6. B	7. B
2. A	4. A			

FIGURE E

1. C	3. A	4. B	5. D	6. D
2. B				

FIGURE F

1. C	3. A	4. B	5. C	6. D
2. A				

FIGURE G

1. A	3. D	4. B	5. C	6. B
2. A				

FIGURE H

1. D	3. B	4. D	5. C	6. A
2. B				

FIGURE I

1. D	3. D	5. B	7. A	9. B
2. A	4. B	6. C	8. B	

AIR TRAFFIC CONTROLLER EXAMINATION
Test 1   Part II

Time: 30 minutes

DIRECTIONS: *This test consists of drawings that simulate a radar scope depicting characteristic patterns of air traffic. Each problem contains a drawing of particular flight paths and aircraft flying on those routes. A table containing information about the altitude, speed, and route of each aircraft accompanies each drawing. Your task will be to answer questions which make use of this flight information.*

NOTE: In answering questions in this part, assume:

(A) Aircraft must be 1,000 feet apart in altitude for safety while flying over the same geographical point, and

(B) All aircraft leave the starting point at the same time.

For some questions in Part 2, you will have to utilize a measuring scale that appears next to the figure diagram to determine your answers. Keep in mind that distance is measured *along indicated flight paths.*

FIGURE A

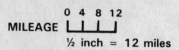

MILEAGE

0 4 8 12

½ inch = 12 miles

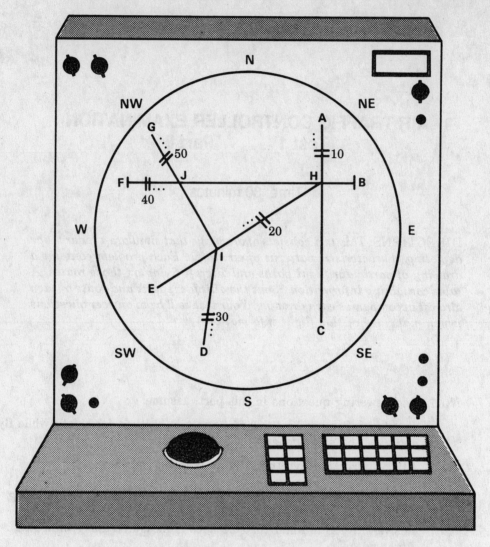

AIR TRAFFIC CONTROL FLIGHT INFORMATION			
Aircraft	Altitude	Speed	Route
10	5000	300	AHC
20	5500	300	EIHB
30	5000	450	DIJF
40	6000	450	BHJF
50	6000	450	GJHB

Figure A Questions

1. At their starting points, which two aircraft are the farthest distance away from the first intersection?
   (A) 20 and 30   (B) 10 and 40   (C) 50 and 10   (D) 40 and 50
   (E) 20 and 10

2. Which aircraft flies a route to the south?
   (A) 40   (B) 10   (C) 30   (D) 20   (E) 50

3. Which aircraft will conflict?
   (A) 10 and 40   (B) 30 and 40   (C) 20 and 50   (D) 30 and 50   (E) 20 and 40

4. By the end of its route, which aircraft has traveled the shortest distance?
   (A) 50   (B) 30   (C) 10   (D) 40   (E) 20

5. Which aircraft flies directly west?
   (A) 50   (B) 30   (C) 40   (D) 20   (E) 10

6. Which aircraft will conflict?
   (A) 10 and 40   (B) 10 and 30   (C) 40 and 50   (D) 30 and 20   (E) None

7. Which pair of aircraft does not travel over the same intersection at any point?
   (A) 20 and 50   (B) 30 and 40   (C) 30 and 50   (D) 10 and 30
   (E) 10 and 20

8. Aircraft 30 will end its flight in what direction?
   (A) East   (B) West   (C) Southeast   (D) Northwest   (E) South

9. Which aircraft will conflict?
   (A) 30 and 40   (B) 20 and 40   (C) 10 and 30   (D) 40 and 50
   (E) 30 and 50

10. Which aircraft flies northeast over the longest distance?
    (A) 20   (B) 50   (C) 10   (D) 40   (E) 30

END OF FIGURE A.
GO TO FIGURE B.

FIGURE B

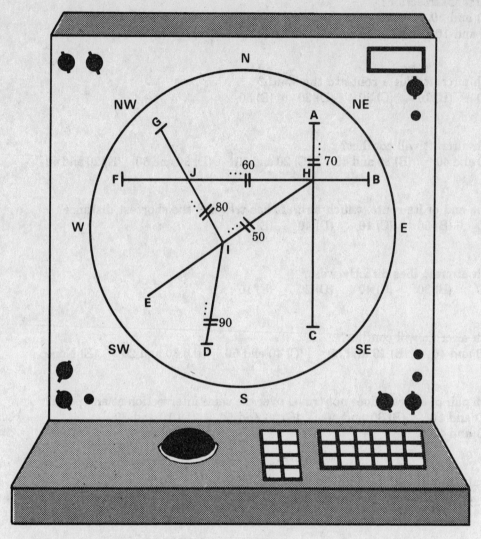

AIR TRAFFIC CONTROL FLIGHT INFORMATION			
Aircraft	Altitude	Speed	Route
50	28,000	500	DIHB
60	27,000	350	GJHB
70	29,000	500	AHB
80	27,000	500	FJI
90	28,000	500	BHID

Figure B Questions

1. Approximately how many miles is Aircraft 50 from Point I?
   (A) 19   (B) 16   (C) 12   (D) 10   (E) 11

2. In approximately what direction is Aircraft 90 traveling?
   (A) East   (B) Southeast   (C) South   (D) North   (E) Northeast

3. What is the approximate number of miles from Point I to Point H?
   (A) 53   (B) 30   (C) 49   (D) 35   (E) 50

4. Which aircraft travels south, then directly east?
   (A) 90   (B) 70   (C) 50   (D) 80   (E) 60

5. Which aircraft will conflict?
   (A) 50 and 70   (B) 70 and 90   (C) 80 and 50   (D) 60 and 80   (E) None

6. Approximately how long will it take Aircraft 50 to go from Point I to Point H?
   (A) 4 mins.   (B) 2 mins.   (C) 12 mins.   (D) 10 mins.   (E) 15 mins.

7. Aircraft 70 flies a route south then east; how many degrees will Aircraft 70 turn to go east?
   (A) 115   (B) 60   (C) 120   (D) 90   (E) 125

8. Which two aircraft travel over the same intersection at some point in their routes?
   (A) 50 and 70   (B) 70 and 60   (C) 60 and 80   (D) 70 and 90
   (E) All of the preceding

9. Which aircraft begins its route traveling east and then turns southeast?
   (A) 90   (B) 50   (C) 60   (D) 80   (E) 70

10. Which aircraft will conflict?
    (A) 50 and 60   (B) 50 and 90   (C) 70 and 80   (D) 80 and 90   (E) None

END OF FIGURE B.
GO TO FIGURE C.

FIGURE C

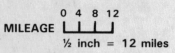

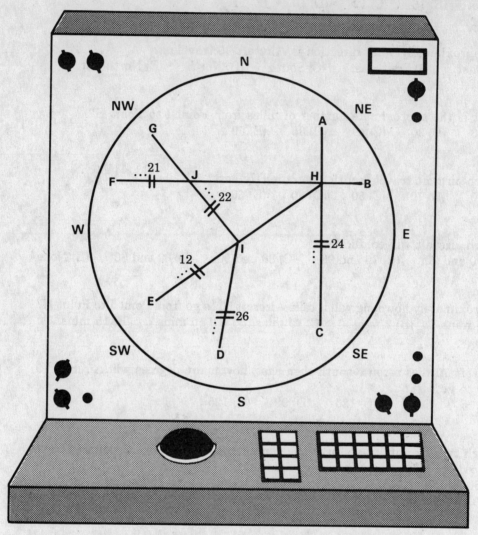

AIR TRAFFIC CONTROL FLIGHT INFORMATION			
Aircraft	Altitude	Speed	Route
12	6000	200	EIHA
21	7000	400	FJHB
22	6000	400	GJIH
24	7000	400	CHJF
26	8000	440	DIJF

Figure C Questions

1. Which aircraft travels a route that does not change direction?
   (A) 26   (B) 12   (C) 24   (D) 22   (E) 21

2. Will Aircraft 22 and 26 conflict?
   (A) Yes   (B) No

3. How many miles does Aircraft 21 travel on its route?
   (A) 90   (B) 78   (C) 63   (D) 82   (E) 85

4. Aircraft 12 travels:
   (A) East then south   (B) Southeast then west   (C) Northeast then north
   (D) Northeast then northwest   (E) East only

5. Will Aircraft 24 and 26 conflict?
   (A) Yes   (B) No

6. Which aircraft fly routes that most resemble the letter Y?
   (A) 24 and 12   (B) 26 and 24   (C) 21 and 22   (D) 12 and 21   (E) None

7. There is possibility of a collision between Aircraft:
   (A) 22 and 26   (B) 22 and 12   (C) 24 and 26   (D) 21and 12   (E) None

8. Which aircraft travels from west to east?
   (A) 12   (B) 26   (C) 21   (D) 24   (E) None

END OF FIGURE C.
GO TO FIGURE D.

FIGURE D

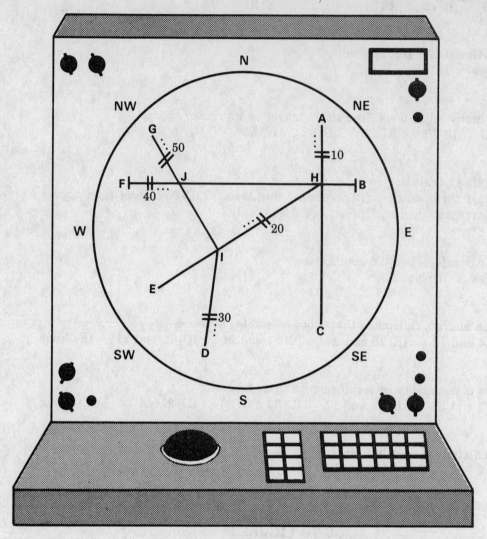

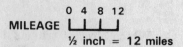

MILEAGE

0 4 8 12

½ inch = 12 miles

AIR TRAFFIC CONTROL FLIGHT INFORMATION			
Aircraft	Altitude	Speed	Route
10	5000	300	AHC
20	5500	300	EIHB
30	5000	450	DIJF
40	6000	450	BHJF
50	6000	300	GJHB

Figure D Questions

1. What is the approximate distance between Aircraft 30 and 20?
   (A) 50 miles   (B) 40 miles   (C) 30 miles

2. Aircraft 40's distance from Point J is:
   (A) 20 miles   (B) 15 miles   (C) 8 miles

3. Assuming present time is 1001Z, Aircraft 40 will reach Point F at what time?
   (A) 1003Z   (B) 1004Z   (C) 1002Z

4. Aircraft 10 is traveling in what direction?
   (A) South   (B) Southeast   (C) Southwest

5. From its present position how long will it take Aircraft 30 to reach Point J?
   (A) 5 minutes   (B) 10 minutes   (C) 3 minutes

6. When Aircraft 10 and 20 cross, by how many feet will they be separated?
   (A) 550   (B) 500   (C) 1,000

7. How many miles does Aircraft 50 have to travel to reach Point J?
   (A) 5   (B) 10   (C) 15

8. What is the distance between Aircraft 50 and Aircraft 30?
   (A) 40 miles   (B) 59 miles   (C) 63 miles

9. Aircraft 50 is traveling in what direction?
   (A) South   (B) Southeast   (C) Southwest

10. Aircraft 30 is traveling in what direction?
    (A) East   (B) Northwest   (C) Southeast

11. How long will it take Aircraft 30 to reach Point I?
    (A) 2 minutes   (B) 9 minutes   (C) 4 minutes

12. How far does Aircraft 30 have to travel to reach Point I?
    (A) 18 miles   (B) 12 miles   (C) 22 miles

13. How long will it take Aircraft 50 to reach Point J?
    (A) 1 minute   (B) 4 minutes   (C) 6 minutes

14. Is Aircraft 10 separated from Aircraft 30?
    (A) Yes   (B) No

15. Which aircraft flies a route that ends to the south?
    (A) 30   (B) 40   (C) 10

16. How long will it take Aircraft 10 to reach Point C?
    (A) 13 minutes   (B) 10 minutes   (C) 5 minutes

17. Will Aircraft 10 and 20 conflict?
    (A) Yes   (B) No

18. Name two aircraft that form a letter V when they cross.
    (A) 30 and 40   (B) 40 and 50   (C) 10 and 50

19. Which two aircraft fly a route that most resembles the letter T?
    (A) 10 and 40   (B) 40 and 30   (C) 20 and 30

20. When Aircraft 20 reaches Point H, Aircraft 10 will be how many miles south of Point H?
    (A) 1 mile   (B) 9 miles   (C) 4 miles

21. When Aircraft 10 reaches Point H, what will the distance be between Aircraft 10 and 20?
    (A) 16 miles   (B) 18 miles   (C) 12 miles

22. How long will it take Aircraft 40 to reach Point F?
    (A) 1 minute   (B) 4 minutes   (C) 5 minutes

23. Will Aircraft 30 and 50 conflict?
    (A) Yes   (B) No

24. Name three aircraft that form a triangle when they cross.
    (A) 30, 40 and 20   (B) 30, 20 and 10   (C) 10, 50 and 40

25. Which two aircraft fly a route that most resembles the letter Y?
    (A) 10 and 20   (B) 10 and 40   (C) 40 and 50

26. If Aircraft 10 was routed AHIE, would it be separated from Aircraft 20?
    (A) Yes   (B) No

27. When Aircraft 50 reaches Point J, what will the distance be between Aircraft 50 and 40?
    (A) 10 miles   (B) 14 miles   (C) 7 miles

END OF TEST 1 PART II.

Answer Key—Test 1   Part II

Figure A

1. A	3. C	5. C	7. D	9. D
2. B	4. C	6. C	8. B	10. A

Figure B

1. D	3. B	5. E	7. D	9. D
2. C	4. B	6. A	8. E	10. B

Figure C

1. E	3. C	5. B	7. B
2. B	4. C	6. D	8. C

Figure D

1. C	7. A	13. A	19. A	25. C
2. C	8. A	14. A	20. B	26. B
3. C	9. B	15. C	21. C	27. B
4. A	10. B	16. B	22. A	
5. A	11. A	17. A	23. B	
6. B	12. A	18. B	24. A	

AIR TRAFFIC CONTROLLER EXAMINATION
Test 2   Part I
LETTER SERIES

DIRECTIONS: *In these questions, you are given a series of letters that are arranged in some definite order. To the right of each question are five suggested answer choices; each answer choice consists of two sets of letters. You are to look at each letter series and determine what its order is and then from the suggested answers at the right select the set that gives the next two letters in the series in their correct order.*

Letter Series—Section 1

Time: 15 minutes

1. E E G I I K M ___ ___   (A) MN (B) OO (C) OQ (D) MO (E) NM

2. S H R I Q J P ___ ___   (A) KO (B) KL (C) OK (D) PK (E) ON

3. G N V H O W I ___ ___   (A) PJ (B) XJ (C) IP (D) PX (E) XG

4. P P G R R I T ___ ___   (A) TT (B) UV (C) UU (D) TU (E) TK

5. E E A E E B E ___ ___   (A) EE (B) EF (C) CE (D) FE (E) EC

6. A R C S E T G ___ ___   (A) HI (B) HU (C) UJ (D) UI (E) IV

7. A V A W A X A ___ ___   (A) ZA (B) YZ (C) YW (D) AZ (E) YA

8. X C X D X C X ___ ___   (A) XB (B) XA (C) XF (D) XG (E) DX

9. T G H U E F V ___ ___   (A) DC (B) DW (C) DE (D) CD (E) CW

10. D J H N L R ___ ___   (A) XT (B) OU (C) TX (D) PX (E) PV

11. J M K N L O M ___ ___   (A) PQ (B) PN (C) NM (D) NP (E) MM

12. C F I L O R ___ ___   (A) XW (B) UX (C) UU (D) UT (E) TU

13. B D F H J L ___ ___   (A) NP (B) OP (C) PN (D) PO (E) OP

14. A B Z C D Y E ___ ___   (A) XG (B) XW (C) FW (D) FX (E) FG

15. R L S M T N U ___ ___   (A) OV (B) UV (C) VW (D) OW (E) VO

16. L C D L E F L ___ ___   (A) LG (B) GH (C) LE (D) FG (E) GG

17. F G G F H H F ____ ____   (A) FF   (B) FI   (C) II   (D) IF   (E) JJ

18. M N O M N O M ____ ____   (A) MN   (B) NO   (C) NM   (D) ON   (E) OM

19. A B D E G H J ____ ____   (A) KL   (B) LN   (C) JM   (D) LM   (E) KM

20. R R S S T T U ____ ____   (A) UU   (B) UV   (C) US   (D) VW   (E) UW

21. A B C B D F C F I D H L E ____ ____ (A) OJ   (B) PO   (C) OT   (D) QD   (E) JO

22. C D C E C F C G C ____ ____   (A) HC   (B) IC   (C) ID   (D) DH   (E) CH

23. J O L Q N S ____ ____   (A) PU   (B) PT   (C) UT   (D) VT   (E) TT

24. C M D O E Q F S G ____ ____   (A) PU   (B) HS   (C) HU   (D) UH   (E) SM

25. A V A W A X A ____ ____   (A) ZA   (B) YZ   (C) YA   (D) AZ   (E) AY

END OF SECTION 1.
GO TO SECTION 2.

Letter Series—Section 2

Time: 15 minutes

1. C E H L Q O L ____ ____   (A) QO   (B) EC   (C) NQ   (D) GD   (E) HC

2. F G D I B K L ____ ____   (A) IN   (B) JH   (C) AM   (D) NJ   (E) CF

3. Z X U Q O L H ____ ____   (A) FC   (B) FB   (C) DA   (D) EB   (E) GD

4. D F H H E G I I F H J ____ ____   (A) JG   (B) GG   (C) GI   (D) JI   (E) LL

5. C D F G J K O ____ ____   (A) PT   (B) PU   (C) TX   (D) TZ   (E) SX

6. A G L M L Q R ____ ____   (A) QR   (B) QW   (C) RW   (D) QV   (E) RQ

7. A C F H K M P ____ ____   (A) SV   (B) RT   (C) RU   (D) SU   (E) QR

8. M P N Q O R P ____ ____   (A) SQ   (B) GR   (C) TQ   (D) QS   (E) SR

9. F R H T J V L ____ ____   (A) MN   (B) WY   (C) XN   (D) NW   (E) XM

10. T G T H T I T ____ ____   (A) LT   (B) JT   (C) IM   (D) TL   (E) TJ

11. H G F K J I N ____ ____   (A) ML   (B) PO   (C) LM   (D) OP   (E) MO

12. S H R I Q J P ____ ____   (A) KO   (B) KL   (C) OK   (D) PK   (E) ON

13. J H N L R P V ____ ____   (A) TX   (B) SZ   (C) TZ   (D) SY   (E) ZT

14. M K H E K I F ____ ____   (A) MG   (B) HI   (C) JD   (D) CM   (E) CI

15. C E I O C F K ____ ____   (A) QC   (B) RC   (C) CP   (D) RZ   (E) CQ

16. Y X V T S Q O N L J I ____ ____   (A) HF   (B) HG   (C) GE   (D) FE   (E) GF

17. R N P T P R V ____ ____   (A) SU   (B) RT   (C) XZ   (D) ZX   (E) TR

18. C D H F J H L ____ ____   (A) JM   (B) IN   (C) JN   (D) KM   (E) IM

19. A D F G J L M ____ ____   (A) PR   (B) PQ   (C) OP   (D) NP   (E) OR

20. G I K H J L I ____ ____   (A) KL   (B) JK   (C) JL   (D) JM   (E) KM

21. B D C E G F H ____ ____   (A) GI   (B) IK   (C) JI   (D) JL   (E) JH

22. A B D E G H J ____ ____   (A) KL   (B) LN   (C) JM   (D) LM   (E) KM

23. R P N L J H F ____ ____   (A) EC   (B) DC   (C) EB   (D) DB   (E) ED

24. T G H U E F V ____ ____   (A) DC   (B) DW   (C) DE   (D) CD   (E) CW

25. Q J R K S L T ____ ____   (A) UL   (B) MU   (C) LU   (D) MN   (E) LM

END OF SECTION 2.
GO TO SECTION 3.

Letter Series—Section 3

Time: 15 minutes

1. Y X V T S Q O N L J I ____ ____   (A) HF   (B) HT   (C) GE   (D) FC   (E) GI

2. E G T H J T K ____ ____   (A) LT   (B) MT   (C) LM   (D) TL   (E) MN

3. H G F K J I N ____ ____   (A) ML   (B) PO   (C) LM   (D) OP   (E) MO

4. Q G R I S K T ____ ____   (A) UL   (B) MU   (C) LU   (D) MN   (E) LM

5. A B Z C D Y E ____ ____   (A) XG   (B) XW   (C) FW   (D) FX   (E) IG

6. R L S M T N U ____ ____   (A) OV   (B) UV   (C) VW   (D) OW   (E) VO

7. L C D L C F L ____ ____   (A) LG   (B) GH   (C) LC   (D) CH   (E) GG

8. M N O M N O M ____ ____   (A) MN   (B) NO   (C) NM   (D) ON   (E) OM

9. A K B J C I D ____ ____   (A) EG   (B) HE   (C) EA   (D) EH   (E) GE

10. Y V W T U R S ____ ____   (A) PQ   (B) PO   (C) QO   (D) QR   (E) WU

11. M L N K O J P ____ ____   (A) IH   (B) IQ   (C) QH   (D) QM   (E) OP

12. F G I J L M O P ____ ____   (A) QR   (B) PQ   (C) PR   (D) QS   (E) RS

13. G I K J L N ____ ____   (A) HM   (B) IK   (C) LN   (D) NM   (E) MO

14. B C D E F G H ____ ____   (A) GI   (B) IK   (C) IJ   (D) JL   (E) HL

15. R P N L J H F ____ ____   (A) CC   (B) DC   (C) CB   (D) DB   (E) EP

16. T G H U E F V ____ ____   (A) DC   (B) DW   (C) DO   (D) CD   (E) CW

17. J H N L R P V ____ ____   (A) TX   (B) SZ   (C) TZ   (D) SY   (E) ZT

18. S H R I Q J P ____ ____   (A) KO   (B) KL   (C) NK   (D) OK   (E) ON

19. H N V I O W J ____ ____   (A) PJ   (B) XJ   (C) IP   (D) PX   (E) XQ

20. F G G F H H F ____ ____   (A) FF   (B) FI   (C) II   (D) IF   (E) JJ

21. A C D B E G H ____ ____   (A) FI   (B) EC   (C) IK   (D) JH   (E) JL

22. H G S T F E U ____ ____   (A) VC   (B) VD   (C) VW   (D) WE   (E) VE

23. Y Z X W U V T ____ ____   (A) QR   (B) QS   (C) SR   (D) RQ   (E) SQ

24. B Y X C D W V ____ ____   (A) FE   (B) WV   (C) FU   (D) EF   (E) EV

25. R Y Z X Y W X ____ ____   (A) WW   (B) WV   (C) ZY   (D) VX   (E) VW

END OF TEST 2 PART I.

Answer Key—Letter Series

SECTION 1

1. D	6. D	11. B	16. B	21. E
2. A	7. E	12. B	17. C	22. A
3. D	8. E	13. A	18. B	23. A
4. E	9. D	14. D	19. E	24. D
5. E	10. E	15. A	20. B	25. C

SECTION 2

1. E	6. D	11. A	16. C	21. C
2. A	7. C	12. A	17. B	22. E
3. A	8. A	13. C	18. C	23. D
4. A	9. C	14. E	19. A	24. D
5. B	10. B	15. B	20. E	25. B

SECTION 3

1. C	6. A	11. B	16. D	21. A
2. B	7. D	12. E	17. C	22. B
3. A	8. B	13. E	18. A	23. E
4. B	9. B	14. C	19. D	24. D
5. D	10. A	15. D	20. C	25. E

Explanatory Answers—Letter Series

SECTION 1

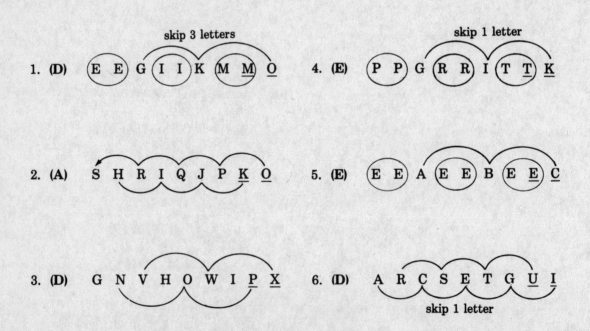

7. **(E)** Ⓐ V Ⓐ W Ⓐ X Ⓐ Y Ⓐ

8. **(E)** X C X D X C X <u>D</u> <u>X</u>

9. **(D)** skip 1 letter
T G H U E F V <u>C</u> <u>D</u>
skip 1 letter

10. **(E)** skip 3 letters
D J H N L R <u>P</u> V
skip 3 letters

11. **(B)** J M K N L O M P <u>P</u> <u>N</u>

12. **(B)** C F I L O R <u>U</u> <u>X</u>
skip 2 letters

13. **(A)** B D F H J L <u>N</u> P
skip 1 letter

14. **(D)** A B Z C D Y E <u>F</u> <u>X</u>
pair   pair   pair

15. **(A)** R L S M T N U <u>O</u> V

16. **(B)** L C D L E F L <u>G</u> <u>H</u>

17. **(C)** F G G F H H F <u>I</u> <u>I</u>

18. **(B)** M N O M N O M <u>N</u> <u>O</u>

19. **(E)**   C   F   I L
A B D E G H J <u>K</u> <u>M</u>

20. **(B)** R R S S T T U <u>U</u> V

21. **(E)** A B C B D F C F I D H L E <u>J</u> <u>O</u>
skip 0   skip 1   skip 2   skip 3   skip 4

22. **(A)** C D C E C F C G C <u>H</u> <u>C</u>

23. **(A)**
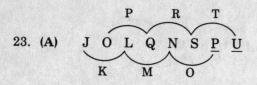

24. **(D)**

25. **(C)**

SECTION 2

1. **(E)**
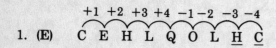

2. **(A)**

    F G D I B K L I N
    6 7 4 9 2 11 12 9 14
    +1 −3 +5 −7 +9 +1 −3 +5

3. **(A)**

    Z X U Q O L H F C
    skip 1 2 3 1 2 3 1 2

4. **(A)**

5. **(B)**

    C D F G J K O P U
    3 4 6 7 10 11 15 16 21
       5   8-9 12-13-14 17-18-19-20
    skip 1   skip 2   skip 3   skip 4

6. **(D)**

    A G L M L Q R Q V
    1 7 12 13 12 17 18 17 22
    +6 +5 +1 −1 +5 +1 −1 +5

7. **(C)**

    A C F H K M P R U
    1 3 6 8 11 13 16 18 21
    +2 +3 +2 +3 +2 +3 +2 +3

8. **(A)**

    M P N Q O R P S Q
    13 16 14 17 15 18 16 19 17
    +3 −2 +3 −2 +3 −2 +3 −2

9. **(C)**

    F R H T J V L X N
    6 18 8 20 10 22 12 24 14

10. **(B)**
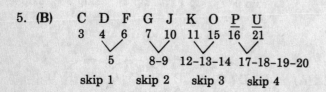

11. **(A)**   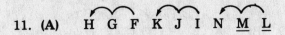 H G F K J I N M̲ L

19. **(A)**
A D F G J L M P̲ R̲
1 4 6 7 10 12 13 16̲ 18̲
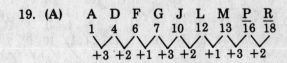
+3 +2 +1 +3 +2 +1 +3 +2

12. **(A)**   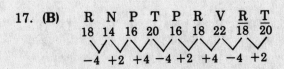

S H R I Q J P K̲ O̲

20. **(E)**
G I K H J L I K̲ M̲
7 9 11 8 10 12 9 11̲ 13̲
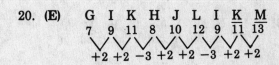
+2 +2 −3 +2 +2 −3 +2 +2

13. **(C)**
J H N L R P V T̲ Z̲
10 8 14 12 18 16 22 20̲ 26̲
2 6 2 6 2 6 2 6

21. **(C)**
B D C E G F H J̲ I̲
2 4 3 5 7 6 8 10̲ 9̲
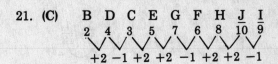
+2 −1 +2 +2 −1 +2 +2 −1

14. **(E)**
M K H E K I F C̲ I̲
13 11 8 5 11 9 6 3̲ 9̲
−2 −3 −3 +6 −2 −3 −3 +6

22. **(E)**
A B D E G H J K̲ M̲
1 2 4 5 7 8 10 11̲ 13̲
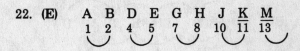

15. **(B)**
C E I O C F K R̲ C̲
3 5 9 15 3 6 11 18̲ 3̲
2 4 6   3 5 7

23. **(D)**
R P N L J H F D̲ B̲
18 16 14 12 10 8 6 4̲ 2̲

16. **(C)**
Y X V T S Q O N L J I G̲ E̲
25 24 22 20 19 17 15 14 12 10 9 7̲ 5̲
1 2 2 1 2 2 1 2 2 1 2 2

24. **(D)**
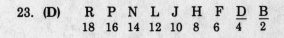
T G H U E F V C̲ D̲
20 7 8 21 5 6 22 3̲ 4̲

17. **(B)**
R N P T P R V R̲ T̲
18 14 16 20 16 18 22 18̲ 20̲
−4 +2 +4 −4 +2 +4 −4 +2

25. **(B)**
Q J R K S L T M̲ U̲

18. **(C)**
C D H F J H L J̲ N̲
3 4 8 6 10 8 12 10̲ 14̲
+1 +4 −2 +4 −2 +4 −2 +4

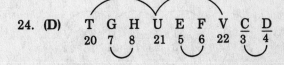
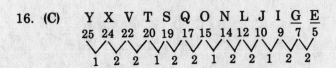
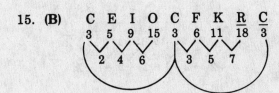

SECTION 3

1. (C) Y X V T S Q O N L J I G E
25 24 22 20 19 17 15 14 12 10 9 7 5
−1 −2 −2 −1 −2 −2 −1 −2 −2 −1 −2 −2

2. (B) E G T H J T K M T
5 7 20 8 10 20 11 13 20
2   2   2

3. (A) H G F K J I N M L
8 7 6 11 10 9 14 13 12

4. (B) Q G R I S K T M U
H   J   L

5. (D) A B Z C D Y E F X
1 2 26 3 4 25 5 6 24

6. (A) R L S M T N U O V
18 12 19 13 20 14 21 15 22

7. (D) L C D L C F L C H
12 3 4 12 3 6 12 3 8
skip 1   skip 1

8. (B) M N O M N O M N O

9. (B) A K B J C I D H E

10. (A) Y V W T U R S P Q
25 22 23 20 21 18 19 16 17

11. (B) M L N K O J P I Q
13 12 14 11 15 10 16 9 17

12. (E) F G I J L M O P R S
6 7 9 10 11 13 15 16 18 19
1 2 1 2 1 2 1 2 1

13. (E) G I K J L N M O
7 9 11 10 12 14 13 15
+2 +2 −1 +2 +2 −1 +2

14. (C) B C D E F G H I J
2 3 4 5 6 7 8 9 10

15. (D) R P N L J H F D B
18 16 14 12 10 8 6 4 2

16. (D) T G H U E F V C D
20 7 8 21 5 6 22 3 4

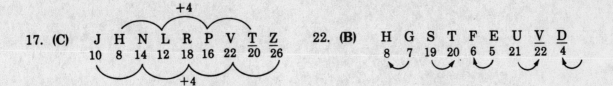

17. (C)   J H N L R P V T Z
          10 8 14 12 18 16 22 20 26

22. (B)   H G S T F E U V D
          8 7 19 20 6 5 21 22 4

18. (A)   S H R I Q J P K O
          19 8 18 9 17 10 16 11 15

23. (E)   Y Z X W U V T S Q
          25 26 24 23 21 22 20 19 17

19. (D)   H N V I O W J P X
          8 14 22 9 15 23 10 16 24

24. (D)   B Y X C D W V E F
          2 25 24 3 4 23 22 5 6

20. (C)   F G G F H H F I I
             7 7   8 8   9 9

25. (E)   R Y Z X Y W X V W
          18 25 26 24 25 23 24 22 23

21. (A)   A C D B E G H F I
          1 3 4 2 5 7 8 6 9

AIR TRAFFIC CONTROLLER EXAMINATION
Test 2   Part II
SYMBOL CLASSIFICATION

DIRECTIONS: *Each question consists of two sets of symbols that are analogous to each other. That means the sets share a common characteristic while they differ in a specific aspect of that characteristic. In each question, the first set contains three symbols and the second set contains two symbols and a question mark. Following the symbol sets are five alternatives labelled A, B,C, D and E. You must choose the one lettered symbol which can best be substituted for the question mark. The correct choice will have the characteristic common to both sets of symbols and yet maintain the same variation of that characteristic as the two symbols in the second set.*

Symbol Classification—Section 1

Time: 15 minutes

1.

(A)   (B)   (C)   (D)   (E)

2.

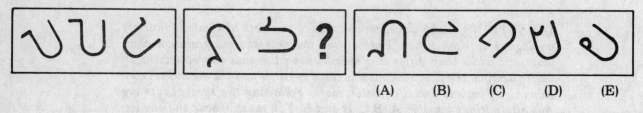

(A)   (B)   (C)   (D)   (E)

3.

(A)   (B)   (C)   (D)   (E)

4.

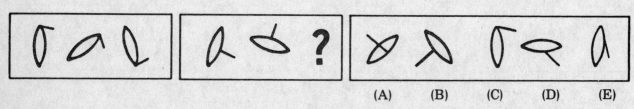

(A)   (B)   (C)   (D)   (E)

5.

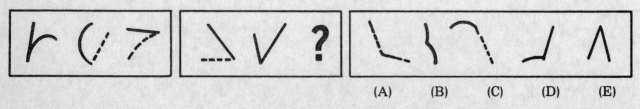

(A)   (B)   (C)   (D)   (E)

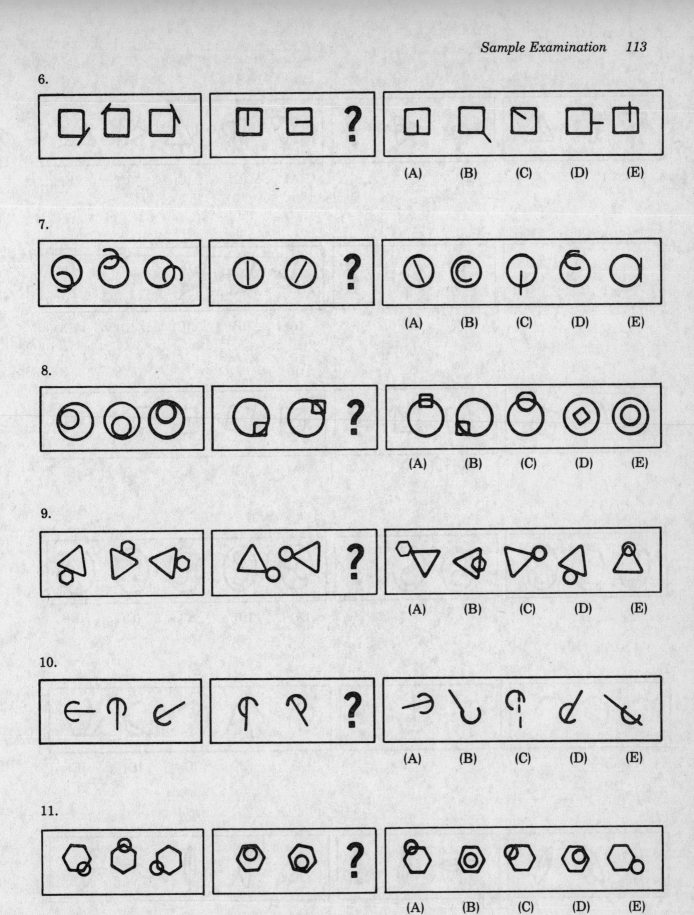

6.

7.

(A) (B) (C) (D) (E)

8.

(A) (B) (C) (D) (E)

9.

(A) (B) (C) (D) (E)

10.

(A) (B) (C) (D) (E)

11.

(A) (B) (C) (D) (E)

12.

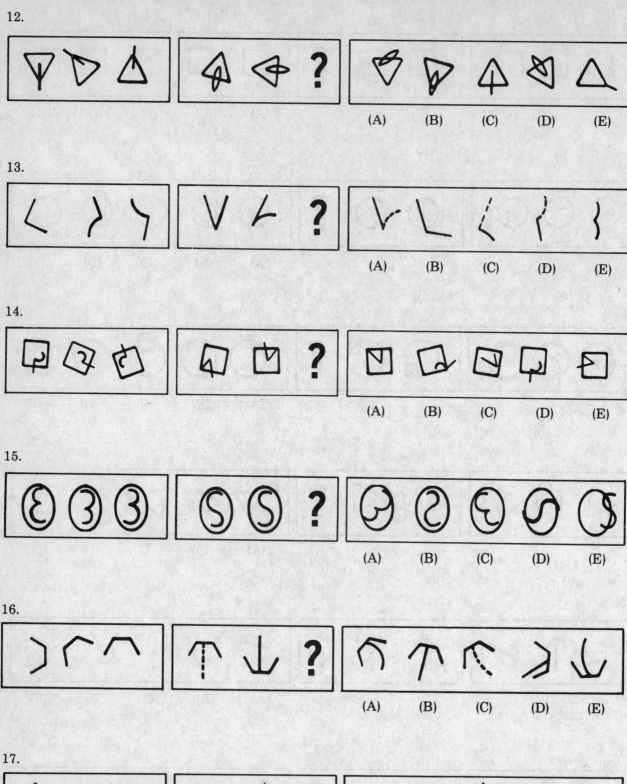

13.

14.

15.

16.

17.

18.

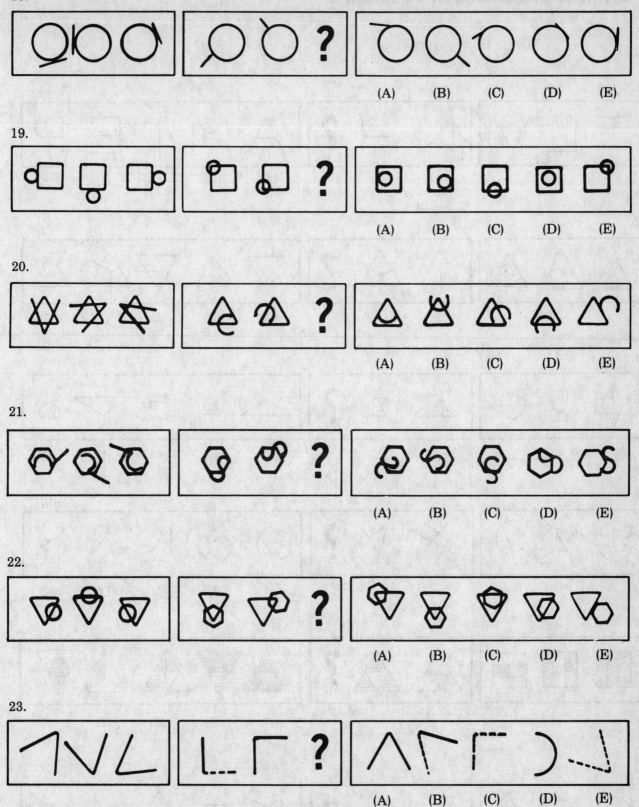

(A) (B) (C) (D) (E)

19.

(A) (B) (C) (D) (E)

20.

(A) (B) (C) (D) (E)

21.

(A) (B) (C) (D) (E)

22.

(A) (B) (C) (D) (E)

23.

(A) (B) (C) (D) (E)

END OF SECTION 1.
GO TO SECTION 2.

Symbol Classification—Section 2

Time: 15 minutes

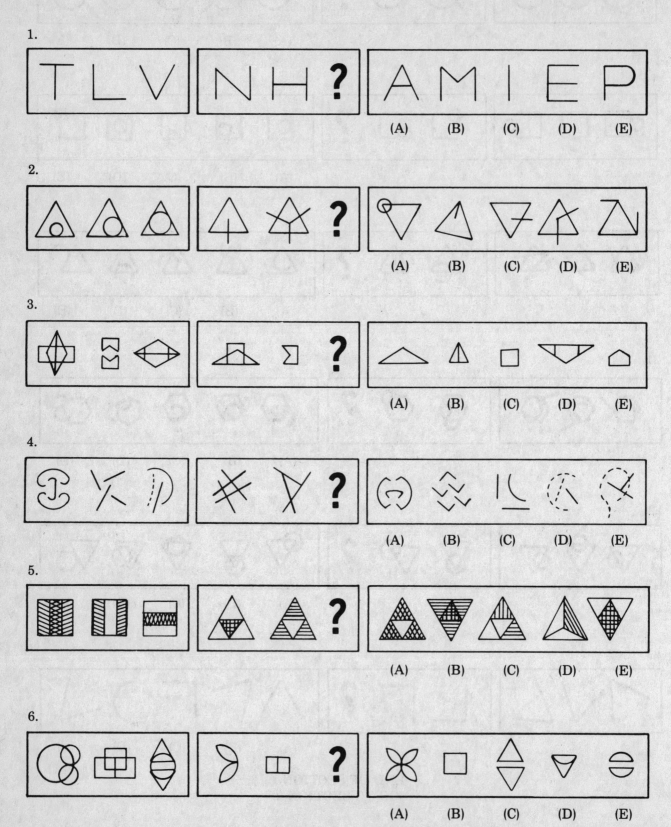

7.

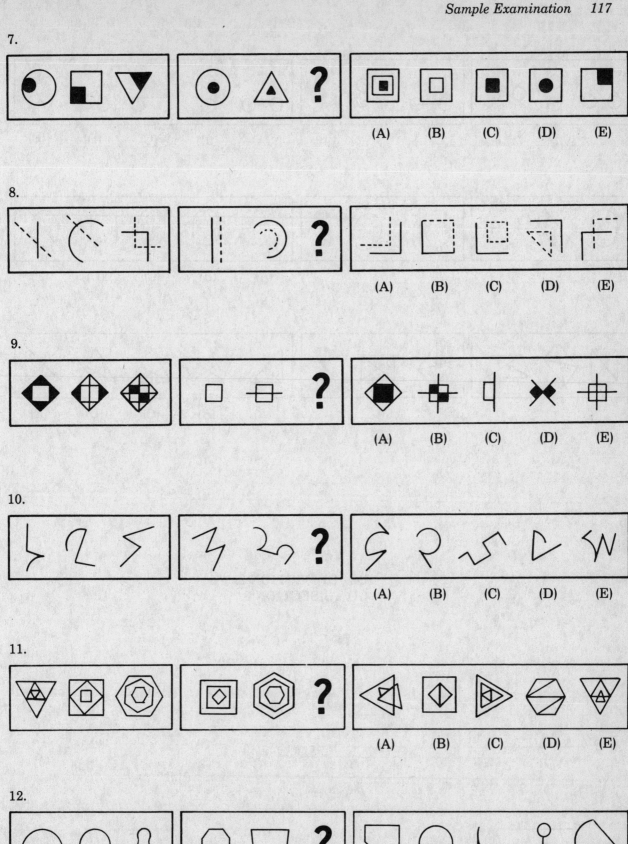

(A)   (B)   (C)   (D)   (E)

8.

(A)   (B)   (C)   (D)   (E)

9.

(A)   (B)   (C)   (D)   (E)

10.

(A)   (B)   (C)   (D)   (E)

11.

(A)   (B)   (C)   (D)   (E)

12.

(A)   (B)   (C)   (D)   (E)

13.

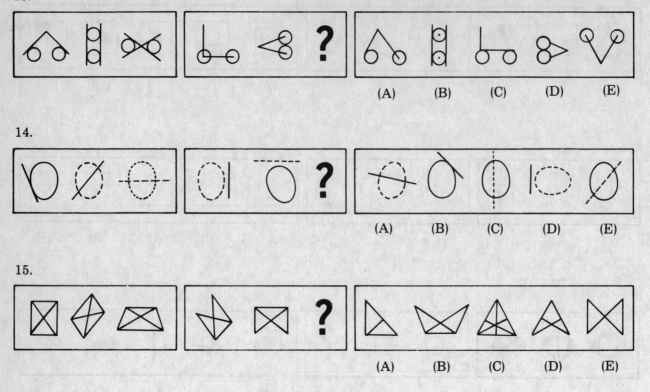

14.

15.

END OF SECTION 2.
GO TO SECTION 3.

Symbol Classification—Section 3

Time: 15 minutes

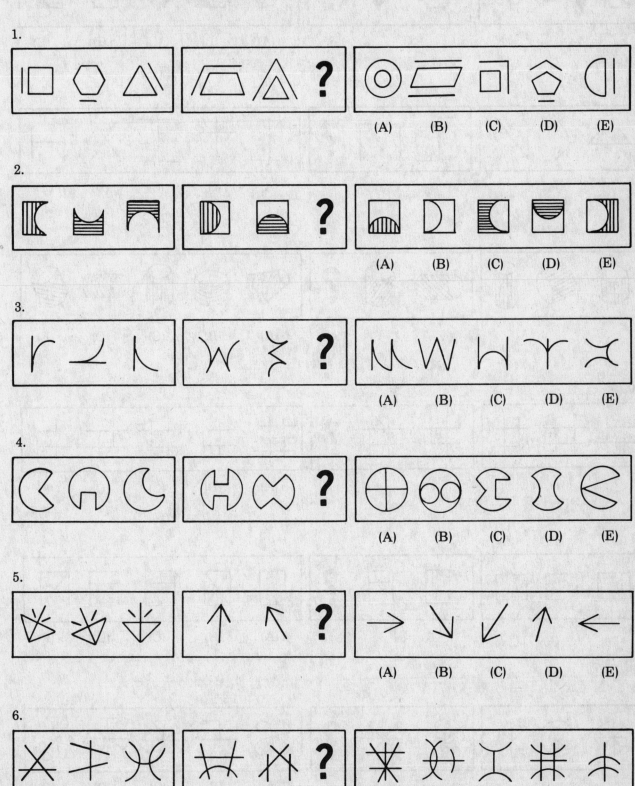

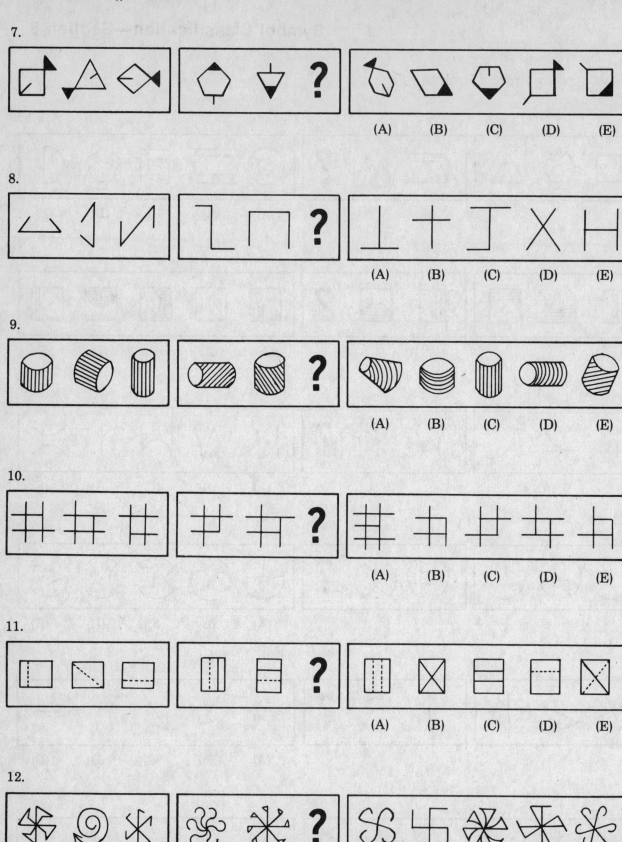

13.

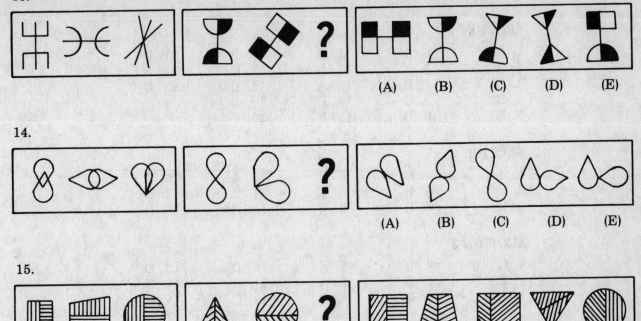

(A)   (B)   (C)   (D)   (E)

14.

(A)   (B)   (C)   (D)   (E)

15.

(A)   (B)   (C)   (D)   (E)

END OF TEST 2 PART II.

Answer Key—Symbol Classification

SECTION 1

1. E	6. A	11. D	16. B	21. D
2. A	7. A	12. D	17. C	22. A
3. C	8. B	13. A	18. B	23. C
4. B	9. C	14. E	19. E	
5. E	10. D	15. B	20. C	

SECTION 2

1. A	4. E	7. C	10. A	13. E
2. D	5. B	8. A	11. C	14. D
3. D	6. E	9. B	12. A	15. B

SECTION 3

1. C	4. D	7. E	10. D	13. D
2. D	5. D	8. A	11. E	14. C
3. A	6. B	9. E	12. C	15. B

Explanatory Answers—Symbol Classification

SECTION 1

1. **(E)** All the symbols in this set consist of hexagons intersected by straight lines. In the first set, two straight lines form an angle at one angle of each hexagon. In the second set, a straight line intersects one side of each hexagon to meet another line within the hexagon. Alternative D is incorrect because the line cuts through an angle of the hexagon, not through a side of the figure.

2. **(A)** Each symbol in this series consists of a U-shaped curve and a line adjoining one end of the U. In the first set, the adjoining line is a straight line which meets the U at a right angle. In the second set, the adjoining line is a curve which meets the U at an acute angle. Only alternative A depicts a curve which joins one side of the U to form an acute angle outside the U.

3. **(C)** The common feature of this series is that each symbol consists of a closed semi-circle which is intersected by some other figure. In the first set, one leg of an angle intersects the straight side of each semi-circle. In the second set, a figure S intersects the curved side of each semi-circle as in alternative C.

4. **(B)** Each symbol in this series consists of a closed figure and a short straight line that touches but does not pass through it. In the first set, the straight line touches at the point of each closed figure. In the second set, the straight line touches and is perpendicular to one side of each closed figure. Alternative D is incorrect because of the angle at which the line meets the closed figure.

5. **(E)** The similarity in this series is that all the lines meet to form acute angles. The difference is that in the first set, the angles are formed by one straight and one curved line, while in the second set, the angles are formed by straight lines only.

6. **(A)** The common feature of this series is squares with lines that touch them. The difference is in the placement of the lines. In the first set, the lines are tangent to one corner and outside each square. In the second set, the lines are perpendicular to one side and fall completely within each square as in alternative A.

7. **(A)** The first set consists of circles intersected by arcs. The second set consists of circles enclosing straight lines. Only alternative A continues the pattern of a line enclosed in a circle.

8. **(B)** In the first set, each circle encloses a smaller circle. In the second set, each circle is overlapped by a square in such a way that the edge of the circle passes through two corners of the square as in alternative B. Alternative A is incorrect because the edge of the circle does not pass through the corners of the square.

9. **(C)** The common feature of this set is triangles that touch another figure. The difference is the point at which the figures touch. In the first set, each triangle touches a hexagon so that the two figures share a common side. In the second set, each triangle touches a circle at one angle of the triangle. Alternative C is the only choice in which a circle touches the corner of a triangle.

10. **(D)** Each symbol in this series consists of a straight line and a curve. In the first set, each straight line is perpendicular to the midpoint of each curve. In the second set, the straight line extends from a point on the curve to meet one end of the curve without intersecting it as in alternative D. Alternative E is wrong because the straight line intersects the curve.

11. **(D)** All the figures in this series consist of hexagons and circles. In the first set, a circle overlaps one corner of each hexagon. In the second set, a circle is completely enclosed in each hexagon and touches one side of the hexagon. Only alternative D meets both these requirements.

12. **(D)** Each triangle in the first set is intersected by a line which passes through one angle of the triangle. Each triangle in the second set is intersected by an oval which passes through one side of the triangle and is perpendicular to the intersected side as in alternative D.

13. **(A)** The common feature of this series is that each symbol consists of two lines that form an angle. The difference is the size of the angle formed. The angles in the first set are all 90° or greater. The angles in the second set are all angles of much less than 90°. Only alternative A pictures two lines that meet to form an acute angle.

14. **(E)** Each symbol consists of a square which is intersected by another figure. In the first set, each square is intersected on one side by a straight line which joins a curve inside the square. In the second set, each square is intersected on one side by one leg of an angle whose other leg extends into a corner of the square as in alternative E.

15. **(B)** The common feature of this series is similar curves enclosed in ovals. In the first set, two of the enclosed figures face in the same direction and one is reversed. Since the second set contains two enclosed figures facing in the same

direction, the missing figure must be the reverse of the enclosed figure, which is alternative B.

16. **(B)** Each symbol in the first set consists of half a hexagon. The same figure is repeated in the second set with the addition of a straight line perpendicular to the middle side. Only alternative B maintains this pattern.

17. **(C)** Each symbol consists of an almond-shaped figure pierced by a line. In the first set, each almond-shaped figure is pierced by a curved line which intersects the figure twice on a single side. In the second set, each almond-shaped figure is pierced by a straight line which passes through the two pointed ends of the figure. Only alternative C maintains this pattern.

18. **(B)** Each of the symbols in this set consists of a circle and a line. In the first set, all of the lines are outside the circles and none could intersect the circle no matter how far it was extended. In the second set, each line, if extended, would bisect the circle. Only in alternative B could the line bisect the circle if extended.

19. **(E)** The common feature of this series is that each symbol is made up of a square and a circle. The difference is in the position of the circles. In the first set, the circles touch one side of each square but fall completely outside the squares. In the second set, the circles overlap the squares at one corner as in alternative E. Alternative C is incorrect because the circle overlaps the square on one side, not at the corner.

20. **(C)** In this series, each symbol consists of a triangle intersected by an open figure. In the first set, each triangle is intersected by the two legs of an angle which pass through the triangle at four points. In the second set, each triangle is intersected by a curved line which passes through the triangle at only one point as in alternative C. Alternative D is incorrect because the curve passes through the triangle at two points.

21. **(D)** Each symbol in this series consists of a hexagon which is overlapped by another figure. In each case, the overlapping figure is half in and half out of the hexagon. In the first set, the curved half of each figure falls within the hexagon and the straight half is outside the hexagon. In the second set, one curve falls within each hexagon and the other curve falls without. Additionally, each curve begins and ends at the point of intersection of two sides of the hexagon. Only alternative D meets both of these conditions.

22. **(A)** The common feature of this series is triangles overlapped by another figure. The difference is the position of the other figure. In the first set, one side of each triangle is overlapped by a circle. In the second set, one corner of each triangle is overlapped by one corner of a hexagon so that the figure formed by the overlapping area has four sides. Alternative B is wrong because the figure formed by the overlapping area has only three sides.

23. **(C)** The common feature of this series is that each symbol consists of two straight lines that meet to form an angle. The difference is the size of the angle formed. In the first set, the lines form acute angles, while in the second set, the lines form right angles. Only alternative C is made up of two lines which meet to form a right angle.

SECTION 2

1. **(A)** Each figure in this series is a letter made up of straight lines. In the first set, each letter consists of two straight lines. In the second set, each letter consists of three straight lines. The only letter which can complete this pattern is represented by alternative A.

2. **(D)** All of the figures in this series are triangles with some other shape that touches one or more sides of the triangle. In the first set, the circles touch first one, then two, then all three sides of the triangles. In the second set, the lines intersect first one and then three sides of the triangles. The missing figure, therefore, must be a triangle with lines intersecting two sides as in alternative D.

3. **(D)** The same figures appear in each set, but the figures in the second set are only one-half of the figures in the first set. In each set, the third figure represents the first figure minus the second figure. Only alternative D maintains this pattern.

4. **(E)** The figures in each set consist of lines, both straight and curved and both broken and solid. The distinguishing feature is that in the first set, none of the lines in any figure touches any other line in the figure, while in the second set all the figures are made up of lines that touch. Only alternative E maintains the pattern of touching lines.

5. **(B)** Both sets consist of closed figures which are divided into sections similar in shape to the larger figure. Additionally, some sections of each figure are shaded. When the outer sections of the figures are shaded, they are shaded by lines that are parallel to each other. When the center section is shaded, it is shaded by lines that cross each other. The only alternative which maintains this pattern is B, in which all the outer sections are shaded by parallel lines and the center section by lines that cross.

6. **(E)** The figures in the second set are all contained in the figures in the first set. The first set consists of figures made up of three overlapping shapes. The second set shows only the overlapping portions of the figures from the first set. The missing figure must, therefore, depict only the overlapping portions of the third figure in the first set as does alternative E.

7. **(C)** The common feature of this series is a larger shape completely enclosing a similar but smaller shape that is darkened. In the first set, the smaller shape touches at least one edge of the larger shape that encloses it. In the second set, the smaller shape is centered in the larger one. Only alternative C maintains the pattern of a small, dark shape centered in a larger yet similar shape.

8. **(A)** Each figure in this series consists of both dotted and solid lines. In the first set, the dotted and solid lines intersect, while in the second set, the dotted and solid lines are parallel with no point of intersection. Alternative A maintains this pattern. Alternative E is wrong because the lines intersect.

9. **(B)** All of the figures in this series are squares. In the first set, a square is enclosed within a larger square and divided first into halves and then into quarters with two of the quarters darkened. The second set repeats the enclosed figure from the first set. Therefore, the missing figure must be a square divided into quarters with two of the quarters darkened as in alternative B.

10. **(A)** The common feature of this series is that each figure consists of a number of segments. All of the figures in the first set have three segments and all of the figures in the second set have four segments. Therefore, alternative A, which is the only choice made up of four segments, is correct.

11. **(C)** Each figure in this series consists of three similar shapes, two of which are parallel. In the first set, the innermost and outermost shapes are parallel. In the second set, the two outer shapes are parallel. Alternative C is the only one that maintains the pattern of two outer shapes that are parallel.

12. **(A)** The common feature of this set is closed figures composed of a single type of line. In the first set, each figure is made up of curved lines only and in the second set of straight lines only. Alternative A, which is composed solely of straight lines, maintains this pattern.

13. **(E)** Each figure in this series consists of two circles and two straight lines. In the first set, the lines are tangent to the circles. In the second set, the lines radiate from the center of each circle. Only alternative E maintains the pattern of two lines that radiate from the centers of two circles.

14. **(D)** The common feature of this series is that each symbol consists of an oval and a straight line. In the first set, the lines touch one or more points on the oval. In the second set, the lines are all outside the ovals and do not touch at any point. Only alternative D satisfies these requirements.

15. **(B)** The figures in the second set are all contained within the figures in the first set. In the first set, each figure has four sides and contains two diagonals. The second set consists of the same figures except that one is now open. Since three-sided versions of the first two figures in the first set already appear in the second set, the missing figure must be a three-sided version of the third figure in the first set, which is represented by alternative B.

SECTION 3

1. **(C)** All of the symbols in this series consist of a closed shape and lines outside and parallel to the shape. In the first set, there is one line outside each shape and parallel to one side. In the second set, there are two adjoining lines outside each closed shape. These outside lines run parallel to two of the sides of each closed shape. Only figure C follows this pattern.

2. **(D)** Each figure consists of both straight and curved lines, and each is shaded. In the first set, the lines in the shaded area run parallel to the longest straight edge. In the second set, the lines in the shaded area run parallel to the diameter of the semi-circle. Only in alternative D is this pattern maintained.

3. **(A)** Each symbol in this series consists of two or more lines. In the first set, each figure has two lines—one straight and one curved. In the second set, each figure has four lines—two straight and two curved. Figure A is the only symbol that can complete the second set.

4. **(D)** All of the figures in this series consist of circles with some part cut out. In the first set there is first a triangle, then a square and then a curved cut-out

in the circles. In the second set, the cut-outs follow the same pattern, but here there are two cut-outs in each circle. Since the triangular and square cut-outs are shown, the missing figure in the second set must be a circle with two curved cut-outs as in alternative D.

5. **(D)** All of the figures in this series are essentially arrows, but they differ in the direction in which they point. All of the figures in the first set are pointing down and all of the figures in the second set are pointing up. Therefore, the missing arrow must be alternative D, the only one pointing in the right direction.

6. **(B)** All of the figures in this series are made up of lines, either straight or curved, or a combination of the two. However, each figure in the first set consists of three lines, while each figure in the second set consists of four lines. Only alternative B presents a figure made up of four lines, which is what is needed to complete the second set.

7. **(E)** Each symbol in this series consists of a closed shape, a small dark triangle and a short line. In the first set, the small dark triangle is outside the closed shape with the short line opposite and inside the figure. In the second set, the small dark triangle is inside each figure and the short line opposite and outside. Alternative E, which meets both these conditions, is the figure needed to complete the second set.

8. **(A)** All of the figures in this series consist of straight lines that form angles. In the first set, each group of lines forms two acute angles. In the second set, each group of lines forms two right angles. The only alternative which forms two right angles is A.

9. **(E)** The common feature of this series is that each symbol is a cylinder with lines on the outside surface. In the first set, the lines all run perpendicular to the base. In the second set, the lines all run diagonal to the base. Alternative E is the only one that correctly completes the set.

10. **(D)** Each figure in this series consists of four lines—some long and some short. All of the figures in the first set are made up of three long lines and one short line. All of the figures in the second set consist of two long lines and two short ones. Therefore, alternative D is the one that is needed to complete the set.

11. **(E)** The common feature of this series is that each symbol is a rectangle with lines inside it. In the first set, each rectangle has one broken line within it. In the second set, each rectangle contains one broken and one solid line. Such a figure is illustrated by alternative E.

12. **(C)** Each figure in this series represents rotation. In the first set, the figures indicate rotation in a clockwise direction, while in the second set, the figures indicate counterclockwise rotation. Figure C, which represents counterclockwise rotation, is the one that is needed to complete the set.

13. **(D)** The symbols in the first set are repeated in the second set except that in the second set, the ends are closed and opposite segments are shaded. Since the first two symbols from the first set already appear in the second set, it must be a variation of the third symbol which is needed to complete the set. Such a figure is provided by alternative D.

14. **(C)** All of the symbols in this series are teardrops. In the first set, the teardrops overlap. In the second set, the pointed ends touch. The missing figure must, therefore, be C, which consists of teardrop shapes with points touching.

15. **(B)** The common feature of these sets is that each symbol is a closed shape with lines in it. In the first set, the enclosed lines run at right angles to each other. In the second set, each shape is divided in half and the enclosed lines form a herringbone pattern as in alternative B.

AIR TRAFFIC CONTROLLER EXAMINATION
Test 3

Time: 50 minutes

DIRECTIONS: *This portion of the examination is designed to find out how much you already know about air traffic control. The questions deal with air traffic rules, air traffic procedures, in-flight traffic control procedures, communications, operating procedures, flight assistance service procedures, air navigation and aids to navigation, and aviation weather. Remember, you can receive additional points on your score by answering questions in Test 3 correctly, but your total score on the exam will not be affected if you answer any questions in Test 3 incorrectly.*

1. What runway is used when the wind is less than 5 knots?
   (A) Pilot choice   (B) Controller choice   (C) Calm wind   (D) Any

2. What runway is used when the wind is more than 5 knots?
   (A) Most nearly aligned with the wind   (B) Any
   (C) The one opposite the wind   (D) North runway

3. Instruct an aircraft if runway environments are not in sight to:
   (A) Continue approach   (B) Execute a missed approach
   (C) Check with FSS   (D) Check with weather man

4. For what type of approach will the controller provide recommended altitudes on final approach if requested by the pilot?
   (A) Straight-in   (B) Timed   (C) Contact   (D) Surveillance

5. Issue trend information as required, to indicate target position with respect to the _____ and elevation cursors.
   (A) Range   (B) ASR   (C) Azimuth   (D) PAR

6. Coordinate with the appropriate local controller or tower on an individual aircraft basis before issuing a clearance which would require flight within an airport traffic area, unless otherwise specified in a(n):
   (A) Letter of agreement   (B) 7110.60B   (C) Agency directive   (D) AIM

7. Separate an arriving aircraft from another aircraft using the same sealane by ensuring that the arriving aircraft does not cross the landing threshold until:
   (A) First aircraft in sight   (B) Cannot be done
   (C) Departing aircraft has started its takeoff roll
   (D) Departing aircraft has departed and crossed the end of the sealane or turned to avert any conflict

8. What is the VHF emergency frequency?
   (A) 121.35   (B) 121.95   (C) 121.15   (D) 121.5

9. What is the UHF emergency frequency?
   (A) 243.0   (B) 369.0   (C) 391.9   (D) 246.4

10. Transponder with no altitude encoding capability is:
    (A) /A   (B) /T   (C) /D   (D) /P

11. DME transponder with no altitude encoding capability is:
    (A) /A   (B) /B   (C) /T   (D) /D

12. DME transponder with altitude encoding capability is:
    (A) /C   (B) /T   (C) /A   (D) /G

13. Altitude expressed in feet measured from mean sea level is:
    (A) MSL   (B) Above sea level   (C) Below sea level   (D) Range

14. The track over the ground of an aircraft flying at a constant distance from a navigational aid by reference to distance measuring equipment is:
    (A) VOR   (B) Slant range   (C) ASR   (D) ARC

15. Pilots should discontinue position reporting over compulsory reporting points when informed by ATC that their aircraft is:
    (A) On the ground   (B) In radar contact
    (C) Above 14,000 feet   (D) In Class A airspace

16. Identify a primary or radar beacon target by observing a departing aircraft target within _____ .
    (A) Class D airspace   (B) 1½ miles of the takeoff runway end
    (C) 1 mile of the takeoff runway end   (D) 2 miles of the takeoff runway end

17. _____ need not be given when identification is established by position correlation.
    (A) Location   (B) Position information   (C) Time check   (D) Turns

18. When may an aircraft discontinue reporting over compulsory reporting points?
    (A) Never   (B) After the first fix
    (C) Any time   (D) After receiving the statement "radar contact" from ATC

19. Special VFR operations are conducted _____ .
    (A) In daylight hours   (B) In Class B, C, D, and E surface areas
    (C) Within one mile of airport   (D) Within uncontrolled airspace

20. For No Gyro procedures, the controller issues: the type of vector, direction of turn, and _____ .
    (A) When to stop turn   (B) How fast to go
    (C) What altitude to maintain   (D) When to expect a lower altitude

21. When using the broadband radar system, what is the separation minimum when less than 40 miles from the antenna?
    (A) 5 miles   (B) 10 miles   (C) 3 miles   (D) 2 miles

22. Do not request speed adjustment of aircraft cleared for approach, except when action is necessary to maintain or achieve desired or required spacing.
    (A) True   (B) False

23. What speed is assigned to aircraft operating between 10,000 feet and FL280?
(A) 230 knots   (B) Speed not more than 230 knots
(C) 250 knots   (D) Speed not less than 250 knots

24. Use the runway most nearly aligned with the wind when windspeed is
_____ .

(A) Less than five knots   (B) Five knots or more
(C) Three knots   (D) Three knots or more

25. What FAR requires a pilot to receive a clearance for a procedure turn when vectored to a final approach fix or position, conducting timed approach, or when the procedure specifies "No PT"?
(A) FAR 33.213   (B) FAR 91.116   (C) FAR 93.134   (D) FAR 33.440

26. Clear an aircraft for contact approach only if the following are met:
(A) Pilot requests it and ground visibility is at least 3 statute miles
(B) Ground visibility is at least 2 statute miles
(C) Pilot requests it and controller deems it
(D) Pilot requests it and ground visibility is at least 1 statute mile

27. When applying vertical separation, do not assign a fixed altitude but clear the aircraft at or below an altitude which is at least _____ feet below any IFR traffic but not below the minimum safe altitude prescribed in FAR 91.79.
(A) 3000   (B) 1500   (C) 1000   (D) 2000

28. FAR 121 permits landing or takeoff by domestic scheduled air carriers where a local surface restriction to visibility is not less than _____ , provided all turns after takeoff or before landing and all flights beyond _____ from the airport boundary can be accomplished above or outside the area so restricted.
(A) ½ statute mile, 1 statute mile   (B) 1½ statute miles, 1 statute mile
(C) 2 statute miles, 1 statute mile   (D) 5 statute miles, 3 statute miles

29. This question pertains to number 28. Who is responsible for determining the nature of the visibility restriction that will permit compliance with the provisions of FAR 121?
(A) Controller   (B) Airport manager   (C) Pilot   (D) Supervisor

30. When an aircraft reports a NAVAID malfunction, you should request a report from a second aircraft.
(A) True   (B) False

31. When may visual separation be authorized between an arriving and a departing aircraft?
(A) Tower has both aircraft in sight   (B) Tower has arriving aircraft in sight
(C) Tower has departing aircraft in sight   (D) Never

32. When, in your judgment, there is reason to believe that flight in VFR conditions may become impractical, issue a(n) _____ which will ensure separation from all other aircraft for which you have separation responsibility.
    (A) Clearance to maintain VFR   (B) Clearance back to departing airport
    (C) Clearance to another airport   (D) Alternative clearance

33. What is the phraseology for verification of an aircraft's altitude in level flight?
    (A) "Say altitude"   (B) "Verify assigned altitude"
    (C) "Say altitude at"   (D) "Verify at (altitude)"

34. When a position report affecting separation is not received, take action to obtain the report no later than _____ after the aircraft was estimated over the fix.
    (A) 5 minutes   (B) 3 minutes   (C) 8 minutes   (D) 10 minutes

35. Clear aircraft to hold over different fixes whose holding pattern airspace areas:
    (A) Do not touch
    (B) Do not overlap each other
    (C) Have at least seven miles between them
    (D) Have at least 10 miles between them

36. Include routes through Class G airspace only:
    (A) For separation of traffic   (B) Never
    (C) Above FL180   (D) When requested by the pilot

37. If no delay is expected, issue a clearance beyond the clearance limit as soon as possible and, whenever possible, at least _____ minutes before the aircraft reaches the fix.
    (A) 3   (B) 10   (C) 5   (D) 7

38. When a filed route will require minor revisions, state the phrase, "cleared to (destination) airport, as filed, _____ (amended route portion), maintain (altitude)."
    (A) Except change route to read   (B) Then
    (C) Nothing   (D) Except amend route

39. When the weather is below _____ feet or _____ miles, or the highest circling minimums, whichever is greater, issue current weather to aircraft executing an instrument approach if it changes from that on the ATIS.
    (A) 3,000, 3   (B) 2,000, 3   (C) 3,000, 2   (D) 1,000, 3

40. The flight path parallel to the landing runway in the direction of landing is:
    (A) Downwind   (B) Base   (C) Upwind   (D) Final

41. _____ is based on what a pilot in a moving aircraft should see looking down the runway.
    (A) RVV   (B) RVR   (C) VRV   (D) RRV

42. Who is responsible for classifying and disseminating Notices to Airmen?
    (A) ARTCC   (B) Towers   (C) FSS   (D) Operations

43. Air carrier aircraft identification may be abbreviated.
    (A) True   (B) False

44. Terminate interphone message with:
    (A) Operating initials   (B) A goodbye   (C) Your name   (D) SSN

45. How is altimeter 30.01 stated?
    (A) "Altimeter, thirty point zero one"   (B) "Altimeter, three zero point zero"
    (C) "Altimeter, thirty zero one"   (D) "Altimeter, three zero zero one"

46. State heading of 5 degrees as:
    (A) "Heading, five degrees"   (B) "Heading, zero zero five"
    (C) "Heading zero zero five degrees"   (D) "Heading zero five"

47. Runway 27R is stated how?
    (A) "Runway twenty seven right"   (B) "Runway twenty seven"
    (C) "Runway two seven right"   (D) "Runway two seven"

48. State airways or jet routes as _____ followed by the number of the airway or jet route in group form.
    (A) The letter "V" or "J"   (B) The word "Victor" or "Jet"
    (C) The letter "V" or the word "Jet"   (D) The word "Victor" or the letter "J"

49. When a second aircraft confirms a NAVAID malfunction, you should:
    (A) Fill out form 7230-4
    (B) Activate the standby equipment or request the monitor facility to activate
    (C) Check with FSS   (D) Consult with your supervisor

50. When can a contact approach be authorized?
    (A) Anytime
    (B) Between sunrise and sunset
    (C) When pilot requests it and ground visibility is at least one statute mile
    (D) When issued by controller

51. The effect of ground clutter is minimized by use of _____ circuits in the radar equipment, resulting in a radar presentation which displays only targets that are _____ .
    (A) PCA, not moving   (B) Target trail, above 10,000 feet
    (C) GAC, in motion   (D) Moving target indicator, in motion

52. A marker beacon that defines a point along the glide slope of an ILS normally located at or near the point of decision height is:
(A) Middle marker   (B) Outer marker
(C) Inner marker   (D) Final marker

53. A marker beacon at or near the glide slope intercept altitude of an ILS approach is:
(A) Inner marker   (B) Outer marker
(C) Final marker   (D) Middle marker

54. Precision approach radar (PAR) is used to detect and display azimuth, elevation, and range of aircraft on the _____ course to a runway.
(A) First approach   (B) Second approach
(C) Final approach   (D) Initial approach

55. Use a(n) _____ departure clearance to reduce verbiage when certain conditions are met.
(A) Authorized   (B) Preferred
(C) Confirmed   (D) Abbreviated

56. For a turbojet operating below 10,000 feet, speed should not be adjusted below _____ knots except within 20 miles of the airport of intended landing.
(A) 300   (B) 250   (C) 210   (D) 200

57. Propeller aircraft within 20 miles of the airport should not be assigned a speed less than _____ knots.
(A) 150   (B) 110   (C) 190   (D) 90

58. A departing turbojet should not be assigned a speed less than _____ knots.
(A) 300   (B) 120   (C) 190   (D) 250

59. If a VFR departure report has not been received within _____ of the proposed departure time and specific arrangements have not been made to activate the flight plan, cancel and file the proposed flight plan.
(A) 3 hours   (B) 1 hour   (C) 2 hours   (D) 5 hours

60. The area within ten miles of an airport without a control tower or where the tower is not in operation, and on which a flight service station is located, is a(n):
(A) Air Navigation facility   (B) Warning area
(C) Restricted area   (D) Airport advisory area

61. How many hours do you add to Central Standard Time to convert to Coordinated Universal Time (UTC)?
(A) 5   (B) 6   (C) 4   (D) 3

62. How are non-radar environment aircraft in a holding pattern separated?
(A) Vertically   (B) Longitudinally   (C) By 2 miles   (D) By 5 miles

63. One method of ensuring radar contact is identifying an aircraft when it is _____ from the end of takeoff runway.
(A) One mile   (B) Two miles   (C) Three miles   (D) Four miles

64. The ADF beacon needle in an aircraft points toward the radio beacon on the ground.
(A) True   (B) False

65. An aircraft descending from high altitude to low altitude can cancel its instrument flight plan leaving what altitude?
(A) 16,500   (B) 18,500   (C) 17,000   (D) 18,000

66. In DF the steers or heading to an airport are given in:
(A) Degrees   (B) Thousands of feet   (C) Magnetic headings   (D) Time

67. What is the phraseology for issuing a heading of thirty-two degrees?
(A) "Turn to heading of thirty-two degrees"   (B) "Fly thirty-two degrees"
(C) "Turn to heading zero three two"   (D) "Fly heading zero three two"

68. What is the emergency transponder code?
(A) 3100   (B) 7700   (C) 7600   (D) 3000

69. What is a SIGMET?
(A) Significant Meteorological Information   (B) Significant Maneuver Information   (D) Significant Altitude Information

70. DME stands for Distance Measuring Equipment.
(A) True   (B) False

71. When the localizer fails, an ILS approach is:
(A) Authorized   (B) Not authorized
(C) Authorized during daytime only   (D) Authorized to the outer marker

72. The middle marker indicates a position at which an aircraft is approximately _____ feet from the landing threshold.
(A) 100   (B) 1,000   (C) 3,000   (D) 3,500

73. What code is used to show descent below 24,000 feet?
    (A) 1200   (B) 7600   (C) 1000   (D) 1500

74. What does SID mean?
    (A) Safe Instrument Departure   (B) Special Instrument Departure
    (C) Standard Instrument Departure   (D) Standard Inspection Department

75. VOR airways system consists of airways designated from 1200 feet above the surface, but not including _____ .
    (A) 18,000 feet   (B) 17,500 feet   (C) 19,000 feet   (D) 17,000 feet

76. Service _____ handles flight movement and control messages.
    (A) C   (B) Z   (C) A   (D) B

77. Inverted lapse rate is a decrease of temperature with height.
    (A) True   (B) False

78. Non-DME aircraft in a non-radar environment are normally separated longitudinally or by:
    (A) 5 miles   (B) Reporting past a VOR   (C) 2 miles   (D) Units of time

79. What is a report over a known location as transmitted by an aircraft in flight?
    (A) SIGMET   (B) PIREP   (C) NABP   (D) IACOR

80. What is the international radio telephone distress signal?
    (A) Three dots and one dash   (B) Help
    (C) Dot, dash, dot, dot, dash   (D) Mayday

END OF TEST 3.

Answer Key—Test 3

1. C	17. B	33. D	49. B	65. D
2. A	18. D	34. A	50. C	66. C
3. B	19. B	35. B	51. D	67. D
4. D	20. A	36. D	52. A	68. B
5. C	21. C	37. C	53. B	69. A
6. A	22. A	38. A	54. C	70. A
7. D	23. D	39. A	55. D	71. B
8. D	24. B	40. C	56. B	72. D
9. A	25. B	41. B	57. A	73. D
10. B	26. D	42. C	58. D	74. C
11. B	27. C	43. B	59. B	75. A
12. C	28. A	44. A	60. D	76. D
13. A	29. C	45. D	61. B	77. A
14. D	30. A	46. B	62. A	78. D
15. B	31. B	47. C	63. A	79. B
16. C	32. D	48. D	64. A	80. D

Explanatory Answers

1. **(C)** When less than five knots, use the calm wind runway.

2. **(A)** Use the runway most nearly aligned with the wind when the wind is five knots or more.

3. **(B)** If runway environments are not in sight, instruct the aircraft to execute a missed approach.

4. **(D)** Surveillance approaches provide recommended altitudes on final approach if the pilot requests.

5. **(C)** Issue trend information as required, to indicate target position with respect to the azimuth and elevation cursors.

6. **(A)** Coordinate with the appropriate local controller or tower on an individual aircraft before issuing a clearance which would require flights within an airport traffic area, unless otherwise specified in a letter of agreement.

7. **(D)** Separate an arriving aircraft from another aircraft using the same sealane by ensuring that the arriving aircraft does not cross the landing threshold until the other aircraft has departed and crossed the end of the sealane or turned to avert any conflict.

8. **(D)** The VHF emergency frequency is 121.5.

9. **(A)** The UHF emergency frequency is 243.0.

10. **(B)** Transponder with no altitude encoding capability is /T.

11. **(B)** DME transponder with no altitude encoding capability is /B.

12. **(C)** DME transponder with altitude encoding capability is /A.

13. **(A)** MSL altitude is altitude expressed in feet measured from mean sea level.

14. **(D)** ARC is the track over the ground of an aircraft flying at a constant distance from a navigational aid by reference to distance measuring equipment (DME).

15. **(B)** Pilots should discontinue position reporting over compulsory reporting points when informed by ATC that their aircraft is "in radar contact."

16. **(C)** Identify a primary or radar beacon target by observing a departing aircraft target within one mile of the takeoff runway end.

17. **(B)** Position information need not be given when identification is established by position correlation or when a departing aircraft is identified within one mile of the takeoff runway.

18. **(D)** After an aircraft receives the statement "radar contact" from ATC, it discontinues reporting over compulsory reporting points.

19. **(B)** Special VFR operations are authorized only within Class B, C, D, or E surface areas.

20. **(A)** For No Gyro procedures, the controller issues the type of vector, direction of turn, and when to stop turn. The phraseology is "This will be a No Gyro vector," "Turn left/right," "Stop turn."

21. **(C)** When using the broadband radar system, the separation minimum is 3 miles when less than 40 miles from the antenna.

22. **(A)** Do not request speed adjustment for aircraft cleared for approach, except when action is necessary to maintain or achieve desired or required spacing. These procedures are preferable to S-turns or discontinuance of approach.

23. **(D)** To aircraft operating between 10,000 feet and FL280, assign a speed not less than 250 knots or the equivalent Mach number.

24. **(B)** Use the runway most nearly aligned with the wind when windspeed is five knots or more.

25. **(B)** FAR 91.116 requires a pilot to receive a clearance for a procedure turn when vectored to a final approach fix or position or when conducting a timed approach.

26. **(D)** Clear an aircraft for a contact approach only if the following conditions exist: the pilot requests it or the reported ground visibility is at least one statute mile.

27. **(C)** When applying vertical separation, do not assign a fixed altitude but clear the aircraft at or below an altitude which is at least 1000 feet below any IFR traffic but not below the minimum safe altitude prescribed in FAR 91.79.

28. **(A)** FAR 121 permits landing or takeoff by domestic scheduled air carriers where a local surface restriction to visibility is not less than one-half statute mile, pro-

vided all turns after takeoff or before landing and all flights beyond one statute mile from the airport boundary can be accomplished above or outside the area so restricted.

29. **(C)** The pilot is solely responsible for determining if the nature of the visibility restriction will permit compliance with the provisions of FAR 121.

30. **(A)** You should do this if possible. A second aircraft may confirm a malfunction or report normal operations.

31. **(B)** Visual separation may be authorized between an arriving and departing aircraft when the tower has the arrival in sight.

32. **(D)** When, in your judgment, there is reason to believe that flight in VFR conditions may become impractical, issue an alternative clearance.

33. **(D)** The phraseology for verification of an aircraft's altitude in level flight is "verify at (altitude)."

34. **(A)** When a position report affecting separation is not received, take action to obtain the report no later than five minutes after the aircraft was estimated over the fix.

35. **(B)** Clear aircraft to hold over different fixes whose holding pattern airspace areas do not overlap each other or other airspace to be protected.

36. **(D)** Include routes through Class G airspace only when requested by the pilot.

37. **(C)** If no delay is expected, issue a clearance beyond the clearance limit as soon as possible and, whenever possible, at least five minutes before the aircraft reaches the fix.

38. **(A)** When a filed route will require minor revisions, state the phrase: "cleared to (destination) airport, as filed, except change route to read (amended route portion), maintain (altitude)."

39. **(A)** When the weather is below 3000 feet or three miles, or the highest circling minimums, whichever is greater, issue current weather to aircraft executing an instrument approach if it changes from that on the ATIS or that previously forwarded to the Center/Approach Control.

40. **(C)** Upwind leg is the flight path parallel to the landing runway in the direction of landing.

41. **(B)** RVR is a measurement taken on a horizontal visual range, not a slant V range. It tells the pilot in an aircraft what he or she should see looking down the runway.

42. **(C)** FSS's are responsible for classifying and disseminating Notices to Airmen.

43. **(B)** Do not abbreviate similar sounding aircraft identifications or the identifications of an air carrier or civil aircraft having an FAA authorized call sign.

44. **(A)** Terminate interphone messages with your operating initials.

45. **(D)** State altimeter setting as the word "altimeter" followed by the separate digits of the altimeter setting (altimeter, three zero zero one).

46. **(B)** State heading as the word "heading" followed by the three separate digits of the number of degrees, omitting the word "degrees."

47. **(C)** State runway as the word "runway" followed by the separate digits of the runway's designation. For a parallel runway state the word "left," "right," or "center" if the letter "L," "R," or "C," is included in the designation (runway two seven right).

48. **(D)** State airways or jet routes as the word "Victor" or the letter "J" followed by the number of the airway or jet route in group form (J five thirty-three).

49. **(B)** When a second aircraft confirms a NAVAID malfunction, you should immediately activate standby equipment.

50. **(C)** Contact approach will only be authorized when requested by the pilot and the reported ground visibility at the destination is at least one statute mile.

51. **(D)** The effect of ground clutter is minimized by the use of moving target indicator (MTI) circuits in the radar equipment, resulting in a radar presentation which displays only targets that are in motion.

52. **(A)** Middle Marker (MM)—a marker beacon that defines a point along the glide slope of an ILS normally located at or near the point of decision height (ILS Category 1).

53. **(B)** Outer Marker (OM)—a marker beacon at or near the glide slope intercept altitude of an ILS approach.

54. **(C)** Precision Approach Radar (PAR) is used to detect and display azimuth, elevation, and range of aircraft on the final approach course to a runway.

55. **(D)** You can issue an abbreviated departure clearance if it reduces verbiage.

56. **(B)** FAR 7110.65D section #7 Para. 5-102.

57. **(A)** FAR 7110.65D section #7 Para. 5-102. For reciprocating engines, the speed should not be less than 150 knots.

58. **(D)** FAR 7110.65D section #7 Para. 5-102C. A speed of not less than 250 knots.

59. **(B)** A maximum of one hour is allowed for activation of flight plan.

60. **(D)** Airport advisory areas are defined as such.

61. **(B)** You add five hours to Eastern Standard Time to convert to Coordinated Universal Time and six hours to Central Standard Time.

62. **(A)** When radar is unavailable, aircraft are separated vertically.

63. **(A)** Radar contact is assured when aircraft are identified within one mile of the takeoff end of the runway.

64. **(A)** VOR direction-finding equipment points toward the radio beacon, allowing you to determine if you are tracking to or from the station.

65. **(D)** PCA or Positive Control Airspace exists between FL180 and including FL600.

66. **(C)** In direction finding or "DF Fix," the geographical location of an aircraft is obtained by one or more direction finders; aircraft are issued magnetic headings.

67. **(D)** To state heading, use the word "heading" followed by the three separate digits of the number of degrees, omitting the word "degrees."

68. **(B)** The emergency transponder code is 7700.

69. **(A)** SIGMETs contain significant meteorological condition reports.

70. **(A)** Distance Measuring Equipment (DME).

71. **(B)** When the localizer fails, an ILS approach is not authorized.

72. **(D)** The Middle Marker indicates a position at which an aircraft is approximately 3500 feet from the landing threshold.

73. **(D)** Below 24,000 feet, Code 1000 indicates descending.

74. **(C)** SID means Standard Instrument Departure.

75. **(A)** VOR Airways System consists of airways designated from 1200 feet above the surface up to but not including 18,000 feet.

76. **(D)** Service B handles flight movement and control messages.

77. **(A)** Inverted lapse rate is a decrease of temperature with height.

78. **(D)** Non-DME aircraft in a non-radar environment are normally separated longitudinally or by units of time.

79. **(B)** PIREP (Pilot Weather Reports)—a report over a known location as transmitted by an aircraft in flight.

80. **(D)** Mayday is the international radio telephone distress signal.

PART FOUR

Other Aviation Careers with the FAA and Other Government Agencies

FLIGHT SERVICE STATION (FSS) AIR TRAFFIC CONTROL SPECIALIST

About the Work

Flight Service personnel are a breed apart and are very hard-working employees. Air Traffic Control Specialists at Flight Service Stations render preflight, in-flight, and emergency assistance to all pilots on request. They give information about all actual weather conditions and forecasts for airports and flight paths, relay air traffic control instructions between controllers and pilots, assist pilots in emergency situations, and initiate searches for missing or overdue aircraft.

Working Conditions

Personnel use telephones, radios, teletypewriters, direction-finding and radar equipment. They work in office situations close to communications and computer equipment. The normal work week is forty hours, and shift work is necessary.

Job Locations

FAA Flight Service Stations are found at approximately 175 locations throughout the United States, the Virgin Islands, and Puerto Rico.

Salaries

The starting salary is normally GS-7. Trainees are paid while learning on the job. The highest grade for a Flight Service Station Specialist is GS-11.

Training

Trainees receive 16 weeks of instruction at the FAA Academy in Oklahoma City, Oklahoma. After completion of training, they are assigned to developmental positions for on-the-job training under close supervision until successful completion of training. However, those who fail to complete training are separated or reassigned from their positions.

The FAA conducts upgrading training programs for specialists continuously. Training in air traffic control continues long after the specialist reaches full performance level.

Advancement Opportunities

Excellent opportunities exist for employees who successfully progress to higher grade levels as they gain experience and as their responsibilities and complexity of duties increase.

Beginning as a trainee at a Flight Service Station, an employee may advance to an assistant chief of the facility. As a further upward step, a few positions at a higher grade level are available in FAA regional offices with administrative responsibilities over all Flight Service Stations within the area's jurisdiction.

Future Outlook

The number of specialists at Flight Service Stations is not expected to increase, as are the jobs in other areas of air traffic control employment. Flight Service Stations will serve larger areas through greater use of long distance telephone service and other communications devices. However, though job opportunities are not expected to increase, the jobs themselves will become more challenging as automation is introduced and thus can be stepping-stones to controller jobs in tower or center work.

ELECTRONIC TECHNICIAN

About the Work

FAA electronic technicians install and maintain electronic equipment required for aerial navigation, communications between aircraft and ground services, and control of aircraft movements to assure safety in the air and smooth flowing air traffic. This involves work with radar, radio, computers, wire communications systems, and other electronic devices at airports and along the network of federal airways. It includes preventive maintenance (inspection of equipment, meter reading, replacement of deteriorating parts, adjustments) and corrective maintenance (troubleshooting, repair, and replacement of malfunctioning equipment). Electronic technicians may also specialize in design, development and evaluation of new types of electronic equipment for the federal airways.

Working Conditions

Electronic technicians usually work out of an airways facilities sector field office with other technicians whose work is directed by a supervisor. The office is frequently located at an airport, and the equipment for which the office is responsible is within a 30- or 40-mile radius from the airport—in Control Towers, Air Traffic Control Centers, and Flight Service Stations, or in the open fields and even on remote mountain tops. Some of the work must be performed outdoors in all kinds of weather. The regular work week is 40 hours, with shift work and weekend work rotated.

Introduction To
Air Traffic Control Systems

Well over a million people board U.S. airliners every day. In the next two years, this number will reach nearly two million. In addition there will be 215,000 privately owned planes. And there will be over 74 million flight operations at tower-equipped airports. The safety of all these people and operations will depend in large part on the vigilance of the air traffic controllers who keep flight operations smooth and routine. When the unexpected does happen, the ability of the controller to assess the situation quickly and respond effectively is even more critical. In one dramatic incident in which a passenger jet suffered engine failure and had to be guided to Sioux City, Iowa, for an emergency landing, the captain praised the air traffic controllers involved for helping to save many lives. "There is nothing" he said, "like a calm, soothing voice talking to you, giving you the information you want."

In this section you will be introduced to the instruments and procedures that air traffic controllers and other aviation professionals must use in order to guide aircraft safely from departure to destination. Knowing this material could help you get a head start in your aviation career.

WHAT CONSTITUTES AN AIRCRAFT?

When is an aircraft an aircraft? An aircraft is any contrivance now known or here-after invented, used, or designed for navigation of flight in the air. In the broadest sense, an aircraft is any device that flies.

The FAA has developed detailed guidelines that assist in differentiating between the vast array of aircraft. One method of classification is based on the manner in which an aircraft sustains itself while airborne. Using this method, aircraft may be divided into four categories: lighter-than-air, gliders, rotorcraft, and airplanes.

Let's take a look at these four groups.

Lighter-Than-Air

Historically, balloons were the first aircraft to carry man into the atmosphere, enabling him to break the bonds that held him to earth. The balloon still survives primarily for sport. The highly inflammable gas hydrogen, which was previously used for lifting power, has now been replaced with nonflammable helium or with heated air.

The blimp is another variety of lighter-than-air. It generally has a rigid keel running along the bottom of a gas-filled envelope. Usually, a cabin or control car is attached to the keel and twin engines are attached to either side of the cabin or control car.

Another variety of lighter-than-air craft is the dirigible or zeppelin. These giant aircraft differ from blimps in that they have lightweight aluminum frames.

Gliders

The sailplane is probably the most popular glider today. This type of aircraft has excellent aerodynamic characteristics. It allows pilots to apply their knowledge of air currents and their skills in controlling the sailplane to achieve great altitudes and long-duration flights.

Rotorcraft

Rotorcraft can be divided into two categories: gyroplanes and helicopters. Gyro-planes attain their thrust with a pusher-type propeller and attain their lift with a free-wheeling rotor. Helicopters attain their lift with a powered rotor. The helicopter has evolved into an extremely versatile aircraft because of its ability to fly slowly, hover, and climb or descend vertically.

Airplanes

Airplanes are the most important type of aircraft in terms of numbers, economics, sociological impact, and national defense. Airplanes can be classified on the basis of landing gear, and on the location and configuration of their wings. There are four major types of airplanes: single-engine land, multi-engine land, single-engine sea, and multi-engine sea.

All aircraft flying today can fit into any one of the three main categories of aircraft designated by use. These three categories are: general aviation, commercial aviation (known as the air transport industry), and military aviation.

Today there are approximately 225,000 general aviation planes in operation throughout the United States. General aviation is a category that includes all civilian flying except that performed by the air transport industry. It includes a wide range of aircraft uses that can be grouped in five categories:

1. Personal flying—aircraft used for personal purposes not associated with a business or profession and not for hire.

2. Business flying—aircraft that are owned or leased by a company or individual to transport persons or property required by business.

3. Commercial flying—scheduled and non-scheduled taxi service and aerial application (agriculture).

4. Instructional flying—flight training.

5. Other flying—research and development, demonstration, sports, parachuting and ferrying flights, highway patrol, pipeline patrol, aerial photography, emergency and rescue operations.

Besides general aviation aircraft there is also the air transport industry, or commercial airlines, with more than 5,000 aircraft used for passenger service and freight.

VISUAL FLIGHT RULES (VFR)

A great percentage of the flying in the United States utilizes Visual Flight Rules (VFR). When flying was very young, there were no rules and all flight was done "by the seat of the pants," meaning that all flying was visual. Pilots followed certain familiar landmarks and features on the ground and somehow managed to get where they wanted to go. Clouds and fog were avoided and night flying was done only by the most experienced pilots, using the light of cities, towns and villages; some of the more adventurous navigated by the stars.

Visual flight has remained an important aspect of aviation and even today a large percentage of flying is done visually. However, even under the most ideal conditions, pilots flying VFR must abide by certain regulations and must be regulated in turn by air traffic control when entering or leaving any area of controlled airspace.

PILOT CERTIFICATION

Look at the "Pilot Ratings" table that follows. It shows what people have to do to obtain the status of pilot of any kind of aircraft. The specific written tests pilots must pass and the competencies they must prove are very carefully monitored by the FAA.

TABLE A. PILOT RATINGS

Airplane	Rotocraft	Glider	Lighter-Than-Air
Rating:	Rating:	Rating:	Rating:
Single-engine, land	Helicopter	Glider or Sailplane	Airship
Multi-engine, land	Gyroplane	Sailplane	Free Balloon
Single-engine, sea			
Multi-engine, sea			

NOTE: In addition to each of the pilot certificates issued, each pilot must be rating-qualified in order to operate the above various aircraft.

A pilot may also become an *instrument rated* pilot if he has 125 hours of flight time plus 40 hours of instrument time, and can pass practical and written tests in instrument flying.

Remember, VFR constitute a set of rules that apply to pilots even though the pilot may fly visually without contacting any control facility. The pilot must still follow certain rules designed primarily for the safety of all aircraft in any given airspace.

NEW AIRSPACE CLASSIFICATION

On September 16, 1993, a new system of airspace classification went into effect to enhance safety for all users. The new rules establish six class designations for U.S. airspace—A, B, C, D, E, and G. According to the FAA, the objectives of the airspace reorganization are to:

- simplify the airspace designations
- increase standardization of equipment and pilot requirements for operations in various classes of airspace
- promote pilot understanding of air traffic control services available, and
- achieve international commonality and satisfy our responsibilities as a member of ICAO (International Civil Aviation Organization)

Figures A and B diagram the new and old classification systems. The chart in Figure C provides a summary of the new airspace classifications by describing the former airspace equivalent, the appropriate pilot certification requirements, the visual flight rules (VFR), visibility and distance from cloud rules, and the air traffic services offered in each class of airspace.

FIGURE A. FORMER AIRSPACE CLASSIFICATIONS

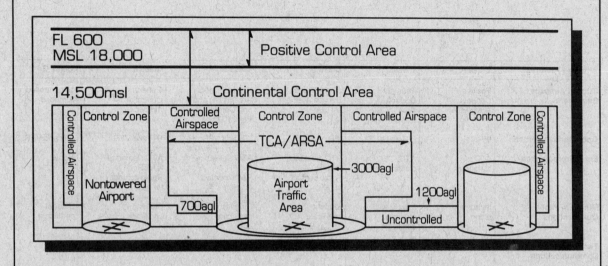

FIGURE B. NEW AIRSPACE CLASSIFICATIONS

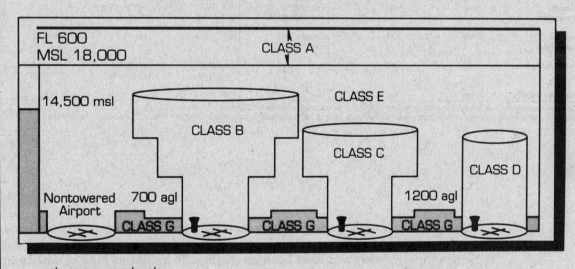

msl - mean sea level
agl - above ground level
FL - flight level

FIGURE C. AIRSPACE RECLASSIFICATION

Airspace Features	Class A	Class B	Class C	Class D	Class E	Class G
Current Airspace Equivalent	Positive Control Area (PCA)	Terminal Control Area (TCA)	Airport Radar Service Area (ARSA)	Airport Traffic Area (ATA) and and Control Zone (CZ)	General Controlled Airspace	Uncontrolled Airspace
Operations Permitted	IFR	IFR and VFR	IFR and VFR	IFR and VFR	IFR and VFR	IFR and VFR
Entry Prerequisites	ATC clearance	ATC clearance	ATC clearance for IFR. Radio contact for all.	ATC clearance for IFR. Radio contact for all.	ATC clearance for IFR. Radio contact for all IFR.	None
Minimum Pilot Qualifications	Instrument rating	Private or student certificate	Student certificate	Student certificate	Student certificate	Student certificate
Two-way Radio Communications	Yes	Yes	Yes	Yes	Yes for IFR	No
VFR Minimum Visibility	N/A	3 statute miles	3 statute miles	3 statute miles	*3 statute miles	**1 statute mile
VFR Minimum Distance from Clouds	N/A	Clear of clouds	500' below, 1,000' above, and 2,000' horizontal	500' below, 1,000' above, and 2,000' horizontal	*500' below, 1,000' above, and 2,000' horizontal	**500' below, 1,000' above, and 2,000' horizontal
Aircraft Separation	All	All	IFR, SVFR, and runway ops	IFR, SVFR, and runway ops	IFR and SVFR	None
Conflict Resolution	N/A	N/A	Between IFR and VFR ops	No	No	No
Traffic Advisories	N/A	N/A	Yes	Workload permitting	Workload permitting	Workload permitting
Safety Advisories	Yes	Yes	Yes	Yes	Yes	Yes

* Different visibility minima and distance cloud requirements exist for operations above 10,000' MSL
**Different visibility minima and distance from cloud requirements exist for night operations, operations above 10,000' MSL, and operations below 1,200' AGL

Unlike the land we travel on, the air is a three-dimensional medium. On the ground everyone travels at the same relative altitude—ground level. And as a result, we tend to bump into each other and have head-on crashes. To avoid this kind of mishap in the air, there are rules about what altitude to fly when you are going in a certain direction. Figure F (page 8A) shows how this system works.

Charts and VFR Flight

Although there are many types of aeronautical charts available to pilots, *sectional charts* are most commonly used for VFR flight. They provide significant topographical and aeronautical information. Understanding these charts is essential for navigating the airspace system. Figures D and E show a sectional legend and an extract from that sectional. Sectional charts are revised and issued every six months.

6A

FIGURE D. SECTIONAL CHART LEGEND

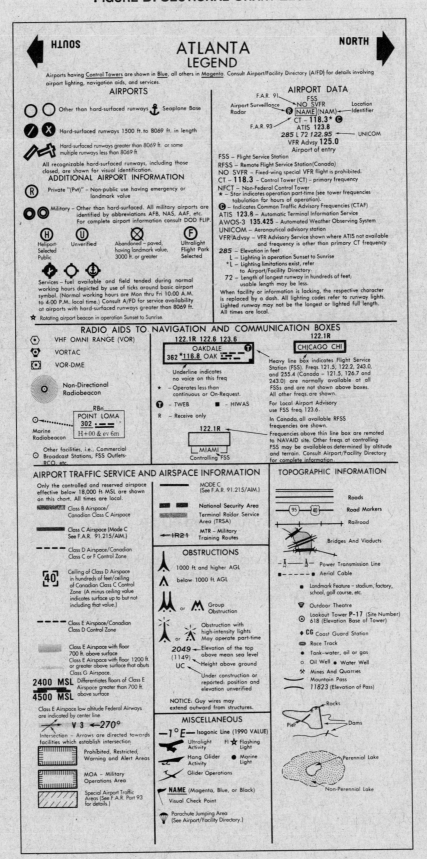

SOUTH ◀   **NORTH** ▶

ATLANTA
LEGEND

Airports having <u>Control Towers</u> are shown in <u>Blue</u>, all others in <u>Magenta</u>. Consult Airport/Facility Directory (A/FD) for details involving airport lighting, navigation aids, and services.

AIRPORTS

○ ○ Other than hard-surfaced runways ⚓ Seaplane Base

⊘ ⊗ Hard-surfaced runways 1500 ft. to 8069 ft. in length

Hard-surfaced runways greater than 8069 ft. or some multiple runways less than 8069 ft.

All recognizable hard-surfaced runways, including those closed, are shown for visual identification.

ADDITIONAL AIRPORT INFORMATION

Ⓡ Private "(Pvt)" – Non-public use having emergency or landmark value

◎ ◉ Military – Other than hard-surfaced. All military airports are identified by abbreviations AFB, NAS, AAF, etc. For complete airport information consult DOD FLIP.

Ⓗ Heliport-Selected Public   Ⓤ Unverified   ⊗ Abandoned – paved, having landmark value, 3000 ft. or greater   Ⓕ Ultralight Flight Park Selected

◆ ◇ ⚓ Services – fuel available and field tended during normal working hours depicted by use of ticks around basic airport symbol. (Normal working hours are Mon thru Fri 10:00 A.M. to 4:00 P.M. local time.) Consult A/FD for service availability at airports with hard-surfaced runways greater than 8069 ft.

☆ Rotating airport beacon in operation Sunset to Sunrise.

AIRPORT DATA

F.A.R. 91   FSS   NO SVFR
Airport Surveillance Radar   Ⓡ [NAME] (NAM)   Location Identifier
F.A.R. 93   CT – 118.3* Ⓒ
ATIS 123.8
285 L 72 122.95 ← UNICOM
VFR Advsy 125.0
Airport of entry

FSS – Flight Service Station
RFSS – Remote Flight Service Station(Canada)
NO SVFR – Fixed-wing special VFR flight is prohibited.
CT – **118.3** – Control Tower (CT) – primary frequency
NFCT – Non-Federal Control Tower
★ – Star indicates operation part-time (see tower frequencies tabulation for hours of operation).
Ⓒ – Indicates Common Traffic Advisory Frequencies (CTAF)
ATIS **123.8** – Automatic Terminal Information Service
AWOS-3 **135.425** – Automated Weather Observing System
UNICOM – Aeronautical advisory station
VFR Advsy – VFR Advisory Service shown where ATIS not available and frequency is other than primary CT frequency
285 – Elevation in feet
   L – Lighting in operation Sunset to Sunrise
   *L – Lighting limitations exist, refer to Airport/Facility Directory
   72 – Length of longest runway in hundreds of feet; usable length may be less.
When facility or information is lacking, the respective character is replaced by a dash. All lighting codes refer to runway lights. Lighted runway may not be the longest or lighted full length. All times are local.

RADIO AIDS TO NAVIGATION AND COMMUNICATION BOXES

⊙ VHF OMNI RANGE (VOR)
⬡ VORTAC
⬢ VOR-DME

◉ Non-Directional Radiobeacon

RBn
⊙— POINT LOMA
Marine Radiobeacon   302 ▪–▪ ▪▪▪
H+00 & ev 6m

⊙ Other facilities, i.e., Commercial Broadcast Stations, FSS Outlets- RCO, etc.

122.1R 122.6 123.6
OAKDALE
362 *116.8 OAK ▭▭▭ Ⓣ

Underline indicates no voice on this freq.
★ – Operates less than continuous or On-Request.
Ⓣ – TWEB   ▪ – HIWAS
R – Receive only

122.1R
MIAMI
Controlling FSS

122.1R
CHICAGO CHI

Heavy line box indicates Flight Service Station (FSS). Freqs. 121.5, 122.2, 243.0, and 255.4 (Canada – 121.5, 126.7 and 243.0) are normally available at all FSSs and are not shown above boxes. All other freqs. are shown.

For Local Airport Advisory use FSS freq. 123.6.

In Canada, all available RFSS frequencies are shown.

Frequencies above thin line box are remoted to NAVAID site. Other freqs. at controlling FSS may be available as determined by altitude and terrain. Consult Airport/Facility Directory for complete information.

AIRPORT TRAFFIC SERVICE AND AIRSPACE INFORMATION

Only the controlled and reserved airspace effective below 18,000 ft. MSL are shown on this chart. All times are local.

▨▨▨ Class B Airspace/ Canadian Class C Airspace

▬▬▬ Class C Airspace (Mode C See F.A.R. 91.215/AIM.)

– – – Class D Airspace/Canadian Class C or F Control Zone

[40] Ceiling of Class D Airspace in hundreds of feet/ceiling of Canadian Class C Control Zone (A minus ceiling value indicates surface up to but not including that value.)

- - - - Class E Airspace/Canadian Class D Control Zone

▨▨ Class E Airspace with floor 700 ft. above surface
Class E Airspace with floor 1200 ft. or greater above surface that abuts Class G Airspace.

2400 MSL
4500 MSL Differentiates floors of Class E Airspace greater than 700 ft. above surface

Class E Airspace low altitude Federal Airways are indicated by center line.

V 3 ←270°
Intersection – Arrows are directed towards facilities which establish intersection

▨▨▨ Prohibited, Restricted, Warning and Alert Areas

▨▨▨ MOA – Military Operations Area

▨▨▨ Special Airport Traffic Areas (See F.A.R. Part 93 for details.)

MODE C (See F.A.R. 91.215/AIM.)

National Security Area
Terminal Radar Service Area (TRSA)

← IR21 MTR – Military Training Routes

OBSTRUCTIONS

🗼 1000 ft. and higher AGL
🗼 below 1000 ft. AGL

🗼 or 🗼 Group Obstruction

🗼 or 🗼 Obstruction with high-intensity lights May operate part-time

2049 ← Elevation of the top above mean sea level
(1149) ← Height above ground
UC ← Under construction or reported; position and elevation unverified

NOTICE: Guy wires may extend outward from structures.

MISCELLANEOUS

–1°E– Isogonic Line (1990 VALUE)
✈ Ultralight Activity   Fl ☆ Flashing Light
✈ Hang Glider Activity   ● Marine Light
✈ Glider Operations

NAME (Magenta, Blue, or Black)
▷ Visual Check Point

☂ Parachute Jumping Area (See Airport/Facility Directory.)

TOPOGRAPHIC INFORMATION

▬▬▬ Roads
(95) (40) Road Markers
+++++ Railroad

Bridges And Viaducts

–A– –A– Power Transmission Line
▪–▪–▪ Aerial Cable

● Landmark Feature – stadium, factory, school, golf course, etc.
▽ Outdoor Theatre
⊙ Lookout Tower P-17 (Site Number) 618 (Elevation Base of Tower)
◆CG Coast Guard Station
⬭ Race Track
▪ Tank-water, oil or gas
○ Oil Well   ● Water Well
✹ Mines And Quarries
)(Mountain Pass
11823 (Elevation of Pass)

Rocks
Pier   Dams

Perennial Lake

Non-Perennial Lake

7A

FIGURE E. SECTIONAL CHART EXTRACT

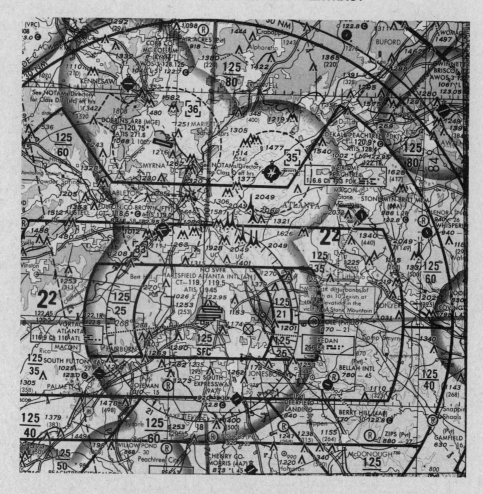

FIGURE F. ALTITUDES AND FLIGHT LEVELS

CONTROLLED AND UNCONTROLLED AIRSPACE VFR ALTITUDES AND FLIGHT LEVELS

IF YOUR MAGNETIC COURSE (GROUND TRACK) IS	MORE THAN 3000' ABOVE THE SURFACE BUT BELOW 18,000' MSL FLY	ABOVE 18,000' MSL TO FL 290 (EXCEPT WITHIN CLASS A AIRSPACE, FAR 71.193) FLY	ABOVE FL 290 (EXCEPT WITHIN CLASS A AIRSPACE, FAR 71.193) FLY 4000' INTERVALS
0° TO 179°	ODD THOUSANDS, MSL, PLUS 500' (3500, 5500, 7500, ETC)	ODD FLIGHT LEVELS PLUS 500' (FL 195, 215, 235, ETC)	BEGINNING AT FL 300 (FL 300, 340, 360, ETC)
180° TO 359°	EVEN THOUSANDS, MSL, PLUS 500' (4500, 6500, 8500, ETC)	EVEN FLIGHT LEVELS PLUS 500' (FL 185, 205, 225, ETC)	BEGINNING AT FL 320 (FL 320, 360, 400, ETC)

IFR ALTITUDES AND FLIGHT LEVELS

IF YOUR MAGNETIC COURSE (GROUND TRACK) IS	BELOW 18,000' MSL, FLY	AT OR ABOVE 18,000' MSL BUT BELOW FL 290, FLY	AT OR ABOVE FL 290, FLY 4000' INTERVALS
0° TO 179°	ODD THOUSANDS, MSL (3000, 5000, 7000, ETC)	ODD FLIGHT LEVELS (FL 190, 210, 230, ETC)	BEGINNING AT FL 290 (FL 290, 330, 370, ETC)
180° TO 359°	EVEN THOUSANDS, MSL, (2000, 4000, 6000, ETC)	EVEN FLIGHT LEVELS (FL 180, 200, 220, ETC)	BEGINNING AT FL 310 (FL 310, 350, 390, ETC)

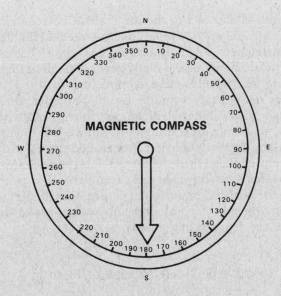

VHF Omnidirectional Range (VOR)

For many years, the VOR has been the basic radio aid to navigation. Transmitting frequencies of omnirange stations are in the VHF (very high frequency) band between 108 and 118 MHz. The word "omni" means *all,* and an omnirange is a VHF radio station that projects radials in all directions (360°) from the station, like spokes from the hub of a wheel. Each of these "spokes," or radials, is denoted by the outbound magnetic direction of the "spoke." A radial is defined as "a line of magnetic bearing extended *from* an omnidirectional range (VOR)." However, due to the features of VOR receivers it is possible to fly either *to* or *from* omnirange in any direction.

An important fact is that VOR signals, like other VHF transmissions, follow an approximate line of sight course. Therefore, reception distance increases with an increase in the airplane's altitude. Though new and improved types of electronic equipment are constantly being developed to make flying safer and easier, VOR and VORTAC (VOR-TACtical Air Navigation) are the basic VHF systems currently in use for radio navigation.

In addition to the bearing information obtained for the omnirange position of the VOR, a VORTAC supplies pilots of airplanes, which have Distance Measuring Equipment (DME), with the distance the airplane is from the VOR. Thus the pilot can determine the airplane's exact location, eliminating the need for taking cross-bearings on two or more stations.

VORs are assigned three-letter identifications. At most stations these identification letters are broadcast continuously in morse code. Some stations are also identified by voice recording (e.g., "Elizabeth V-O-R").

IFR—Instrument Flight Rules

Every IFR flight, regardless of weather, is a mission done cooperatively by the pilot and Air Traffic Control. The pilot must operate the craft within the parameters and constraints established by the Air Traffic Control and it is the responsibility of Air Traffic Control to provide separation between all flights under its jurisdiction.

IFR, or Instrument Flight Rules, are the key to basic air traffic safety for all commercial aviation flights and many general aviation flights.

The Air Traffic Control System, administered by the FAA, is an air traffic safety system set up nationwide, including Guam, Panama, and Puerto Rico. The system involves about 25,000 highly trained personnel, each with a mission designed to contribute to maximum air traffic safety. The system consists of 22 En Route Traffic Control Centers, some 400 Airport Towers and nearly 275 Flight Service Stations. Administration of these facilities requires tremendous cooperation and coordination—cooperation between pilots and controllers.

There are three basics, or universal phases, that all flights have in common. These three phases are: takeoff and climbout; en route; and descent/approach/landing. These phases are depicted in Figure G, below.

FIGURE G. THREE PHASES OF FLIGHT

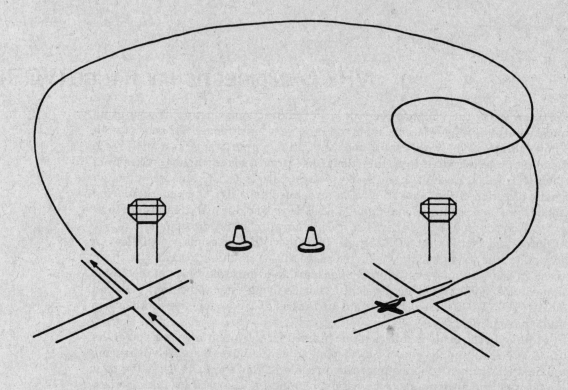

TAKEOFF AND CLIMBOUT   ENROUTE   DESCENT, APPROACH, AND LANDING

All IFR flights are continuously monitored by Air Traffic Control. (In Figure H on page 11A, an aircraft is being taxied onto the proper runway.)

Now look at Figure I on page 11A. This shows how the nation has been partitioned off into regions for the purpose of efficient and safe air traffic control. Many regions are divided by natural boundaries and by state or political boundaries. Each region has its own Air Route Traffic Control Center (ARTCC).

The Center is the "brains" of each air traffic control region. Within each center

FIGURE H. WASHINGTON NATIONAL AIRPORT AREA MAP

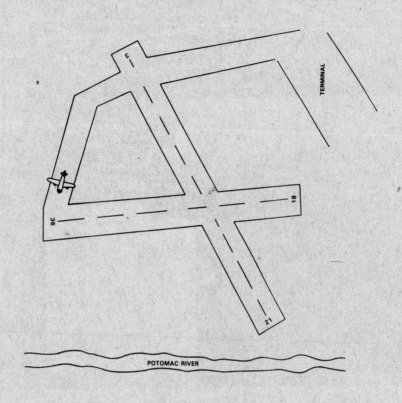

FIGURE I. FAA ARTCC BOUNDARIES (1981 SYSTEM ARTCC AND FLIGHT ADVISORY AREA)

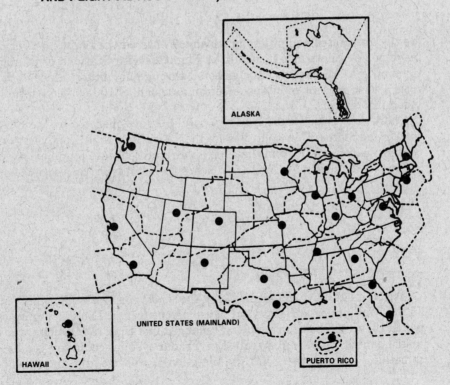

View of the TRACON computer area. The Automated Radar Tracking System IIIA (ARTS IIIA) equipment shown provides processed information for the alphanumeric displays. This latest state-of-the-art equipment provides the TRACON with data recording capability and redundancy.

are the automated computers in which are entered the flight plans that have been made out by pilots and turned in at Flight Service Stations or at military operations offices. All centers are connected through computer. Since each center controls a vast amount of airspace—often as much as 100,000 square miles—it is divided into sectors.

There are 21 Air Route Traffic Control Centers operated by the FAA throughout the United States. They control more than 30 million flights per year. These en route centers control traffic from the time an aircraft leaves the immediate vicinity of an airport (usually 25 miles) until it reaches the vicinity of the airport of destination.

RADAR

As you might have inferred by now, the whole Air Traffic Control System is based on one very important and vital development: radar. Look at Figure J (page 13A) which shows the basic principle of radar. At one time radar alone was the critical instrument for detecting aircraft. Early radar systems could tell you two things: (1) something was out there; (2) the direction it was moving and at approximately

Ra(dio) D(etection) a(nd) R(anging)

RADAR IS AN ELECTRONIC DEVICE THAT LOCATES OBJECTS BY BEAMING RADIO-FREQUENCY IMPULSES THAT ARE REFLECTED BACK FROM THE OBJECT, AND DETERMINES ITS DISTANCE BY A MEASUREMENT OF THE TIME ELAPSED BETWEEN TRANSMISSION AND RECEPTION OF THE IMPULSES.

ECHO BOUNCING BACK

RADIO WAVES

IF THE RADIATED SIGNAL IS IN THE FORM OF PULSES, THE TIME FROM THE EMISSION OF A PULSE TO THE RECEPTION OF ITS ECHO MEASURES THE DISTANCE OF THE REFLECTING OBJECT. THIS TECHNIQUE IS CALLED RADAR. BY MEANS OF THE REFLECTION OF A BEAM THAT IS PULSED, BOTH THE DIRECTION AND DISTANCE OF AN OBJECT CAN BE MEASURED.

what speed. The things that radar could not detect very accurately were the altitude and the identification of the aircraft. This had to be done by radio, and radio communication can be too time-consuming when perhaps seconds count in avoiding accidents. With the advent of more sophisticated technology, a tremendous improvement was made in radar detection of air traffic.

Figure K on page 15A shows the new system. In prior years, when an aircraft controller detected a blip or target on his or her radar screen, the controller had to identify the blip with a written tag that gave the aircraft identification number and altitude. Now when an aircraft is picked up on the radar screen, it can automatically give the controller information about itself. That information will show up right on the display screen, and a controller can instantly identify the aircraft (e.g., Delta flight 10, TWA 206), the altitude at which it is flying, and its apparent ground speed. The device that made this all possible is the *transponder.* Triggered by radar waves, the transponder instantly sends back the information coded into it to the Air Route Traffic Control Center. As shown in Figure L on page 15A, when police radar is beamed at your car, it triggers the radar detector in your car. You are being detected by radar and tracked. The transponder acts in the same way, except that it sends information back to the ARTCC computer.

As an aircraft in flight moves from one sector to another, the computer automatically prints a flight data strip for the next sector just before the flight enters that area of control. This same automatic process takes place when one controller is ready to hand off a flight to the next controller; thus the controllers are spared a time-consuming chore.

AIRPORT TERMINAL FACILITIES

Airport Terminal Facilities are vital in giving flight assistance to all VFR and IFR flights when necessary. Provided by the FAA, Airport Terminal Facilities are among the most important services any pilot can receive. The primary purposes of FAA facilities are to give information, advise on air traffic, provide traffic separation, and give weather information. Each piece of information a pilot can gather about his or her flight helps to make that flight safer and more fully ensures the safety of others.

Airport Terminal Facilities can be divided into specific areas based on the function of each facility. Basically, the facilities are:

- Automatic Terminal Information Service (ATIS)
- Control Tower or Local Controllers
- Approach and Departure Control
- Flight Service Stations (FSS's)

ATIS

Automatic Terminal Information Service (ATIS) is recorded information provided by the FAA at all major terminals. The recording is designed to give the pilot, both arriving and departing, advance information on active runways, weather conditions, communications frequencies, and any NOTAMS (notices to airmen) affecting the

FIGURE K. RADAR IDENTIFICATION THEN AND NOW

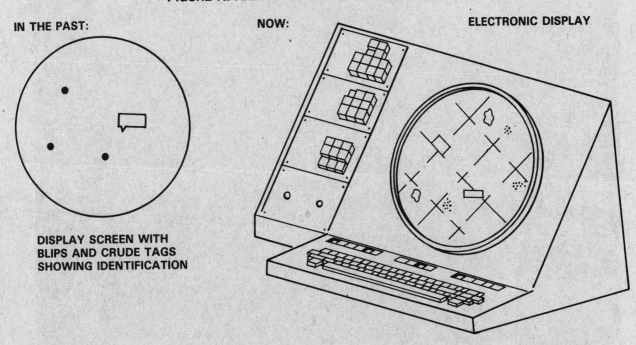

IN THE PAST:

DISPLAY SCREEN WITH
BLIPS AND CRUDE TAGS
SHOWING IDENTIFICATION

NOW:

ELECTRONIC DISPLAY

FIGURE L. TRANSPONDER PRINCIPLE

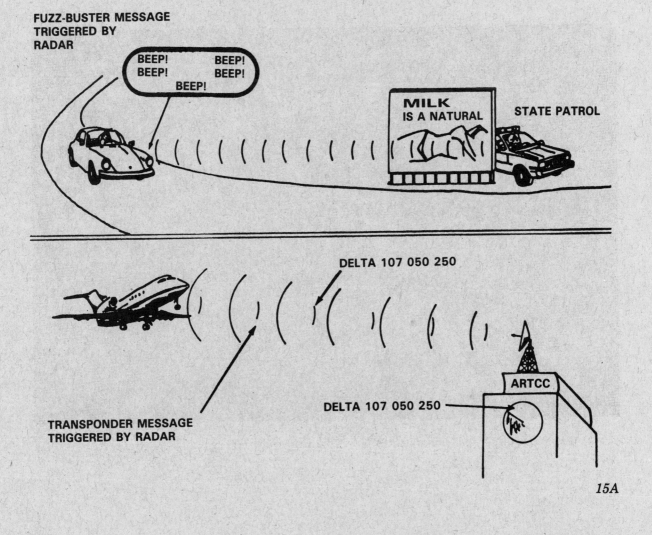

FUZZ-BUSTER MESSAGE
TRIGGERED BY
RADAR

BEEP!   BEEP!
BEEP!   BEEP!
   BEEP!

MILK
IS A NATURAL

STATE PATROL

DELTA 107 050 250

TRANSPONDER MESSAGE
TRIGGERED BY RADAR

DELTA 107 050 250

ARTCC

15A

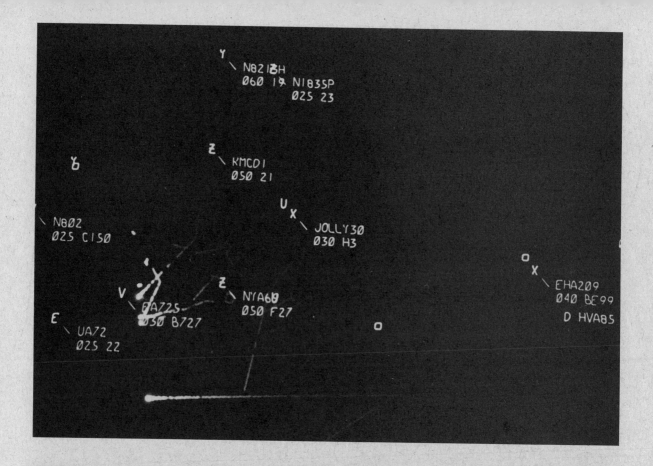

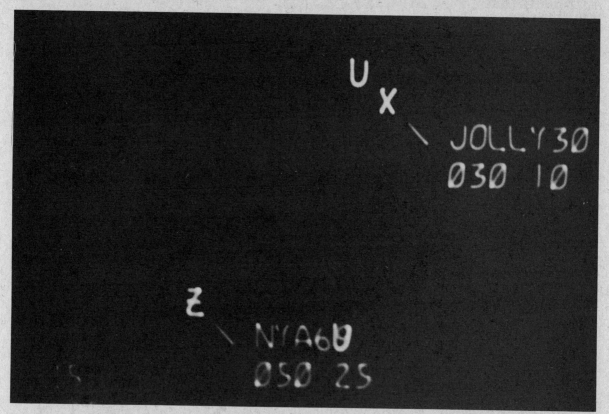

Two radar displays of aircraft in the New York metropolitan area.

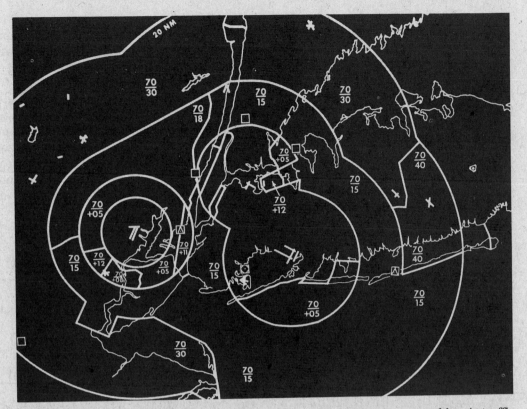

Static map mounted above radar screen displays the Class B airspace covered by air traffic controllers at the New York TRACON.

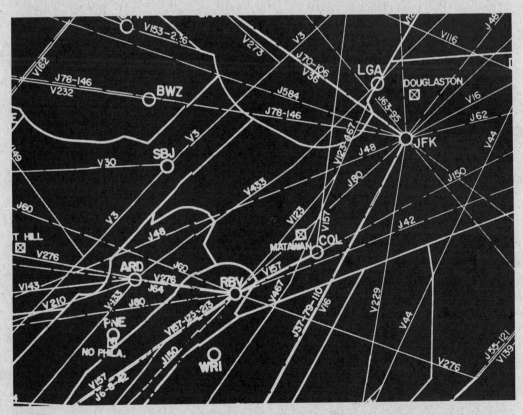

Static flight approach chart mounted above radar screen displays aircraft flight paths in the New York TRACON vicinity.

airport at a particular time. All this information is recorded on tape and transmitted continuously over a specified commonly used frequency at any airport area. As airport conditions change, such as wind direction and velocity, altimeter setting (barometric pressure), or active runways, a new recording is made.

The ATIS utilizes the International Phonetic Alphabet. This alphabet was adopted to eliminate the communications problems that could arise because of airplane travel. Planes travel thousands of miles in short time periods and can cross quite a number of international borders within a single day. Many nations therefore organized the International Civil Aviation Organization (ICAO) and adopted English as the international aviation communications language. The ICAO requires that the International Phonetic Alphabet be used during radio transmissions because many letters in the English language sound alike.

TABLE B. (ICAO) INTERNATIONAL PHONETIC ALPHABET

A •–	ALFA	(*AL*-FAH)	N –•	NOVEMBER	(NO-*VEM*-BER)
B –•••	BRAVO	(*BRAH*-VOH)	O –––	OSCAR	(*OSS*-CAH)
C –•–•	CHARLIE	(*CHAR*-LEE)	P •––•	PAPA	(PAH-*PAH*)
D –••	DELTA	(*DELL*-TAH)	Q ––•–	QUEBEC	(KEH-*BECK*)
E •	ECHO	(*ECK*-OH)	R •–•	ROMEO	(*ROW*-ME-OH)
F ••–•	FOXTROT	(*FOKS*-TROT)	S •••	SIERRA	(SEE-*AIR*-RAH)
G ––•	GOLF	(GOLF)	T –	TANGO	(*TANG*-GO)
H ••••	HOTEL	(HOH-*TELL*)	U ••–	UNIFORM	(*YOU*-NEE-FORM)
I ••	INDIA	(*IN*-DEE-AH)	V •••–	VICTOR	(*VIK*-TAH)
J •–––	JULIETT	(*JEW*-LEE-*ETT*)	W •––	WHISKEY	(*WISS*-KEY)
K –•–	KILO	(*KEY*-LOH)	X –••–	X RAY	(*ECKS*-RAY)
L •–••	LIMA	(*LEE*-MAH)	Y –•––	YANKEE	(*YANG*-KEY)
M ––	MIKE	(MIKE)	Z ––••	ZULU	(*ZOO*-LOO)

Time

The FAA uses Coordinated Universal Time (UTC) for all operations. The term "Zulu" is used when ATC procedures require a reference to UTC.

TABLE C. UTC CONVERSION TABLE*

Eastern Standard Time	Add 5 hours
Central Standard Time	Add 6 hours
Mountain Standard Time	Add 7 hours
Pacific Standard Time	Add 8 hours
Alaska Standard Time	Add 9 hours
Hawaii Standard Time	Add 10 hours

* For Daylight Time, subtract 1 hour.

The 24-hour clock system is used in radio-telephone transmissions. The hour is indicated by the first two figures and the minutes by the last two figures—e.g., 0920 should be stated as ZERO NINER TWO ZERO. Time may be stated in minutes only (two figures) in radio-telephone communications when no misunderstanding is likely to occur.

Current time in use at a station is stated in the nearest quarter minute in order that pilots may use this information for time checks. Fractions of a quarter minute less than 8 seconds are stated as the preceding quarter minute; fractions of a quarter minute of 8 seconds or more are stated as the succeeding quarter minute. For example:

0929:05 . . . . TIME, ZERO NINER TWO NINER
0929:10 . . . . TIME, ZERO NINER TWO NINER AND ONE QUARTER

The control tower or local controller is another part of the Air Terminal Facility. After the pilot has listened to the ATIS and completed the prelanding checklist, the radio transmitter and receiver are switched to the tower frequency. The pilot identifies his or her plane, gives his or her approximate location, and tells the tower that the approach is being made according to information "Alpha" (or whatever the current ATIS information is identified as). The controller will acknowledge and give any additional information the pilot needs to complete a safe landing.

Towers are usually responsible for the control of all airborne traffic within a specified area of the airport, if the traffic is either landing or taking off.

If VFR conditions exist, the tower is in control of all VFR traffic within the Airport Traffic Area. This is usually within a five-statute-mile radius from the center of the airport and includes all the airspace up to but not including 3000 feet above the airport. IFR traffic during this time may be controlled by departure control and approach control in the same area.

Figures M, N, and O (page 20A) help explain the Airport Traffic Area. Figure M shows the controlled area around most airports. Figure N shows the controlled area around major airports with heavy IFR and VFR traffic. Notice that the area is stacked similar to an upside-down wedding cake. This system allows the controller more flexibility during heavy traffic. Figure O shows how a Terminal Control Area (TCA) appears on an aeronautical sectional chart.

FIGURE M. AIRPORT CONTROLLED AREAS (COMMON TO MOST AIRPORTS)

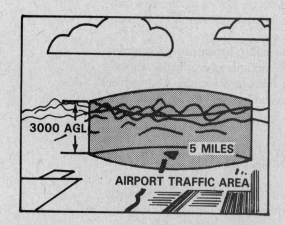

FIGURE N. AIRPORT CONTROLLED AREAS

TERMINAL CONTROL AREA

DESIGNED TO SEPARATE ALL ARRIVING TRAFFIC AT LARGE AIRPORTS (BOTH VFR AND IFR)

FIGURE O. SECTIONAL CHART REPRESENTATION OF TERMINAL CONTROL AREA

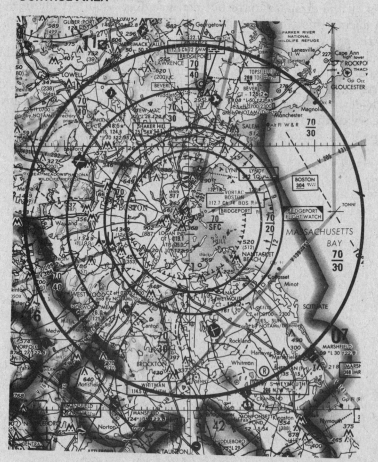

If radio communications should break down, every control tower has a powerful light gun that can beam an intense, narrow light—either red, green, or white—at the aircraft the tower is trying to contact. The light gun is equipped with a gun sight similar to that on a rifle; provided the pilot is looking in the direction of the control tower, the controller can send a limited amount of instructions. Table D shows the variety of visual signals that can be sent.

TABLE D. LIGHT GUN SIGNALS

Color and Type of Signal	On the Ground	In Flight
Steady Green	Clear for takeoff	Cleared to land
Flashing Green	Cleared to taxi	Return for landing (to be followed by steady green at proper time)
Steady Red	Stop	Give way to other aircraft and continue circling
Flashing Red	Taxi clear of landing area (runway in use)	Airport unsafe—do not land
Flashing White	Return to starting point on airport	(No Assigned Meaning)
Alternating Red and Green	General warning signal	Exercise extreme caution

Once a pilot lands, he or she will usually switch to ground control. The FAA Ground Controller is also located in the tower and that controller is responsible for the separation of traffic moving on the airport surface.

Ground control services may:

1. Provide the pilot with exact taxi instructions to the runway where the pilot will take off.
2. Point out all the hazards that might exist along the route across the airport.
3. Supply transient pilots with information about airport facilities:
   a. Where to tie down
   b. Maintenance service
   c. Ramp service
   d. Locations of many other facilities at the airport.

Approach and Departure Control

Approach and Departure Control, although sometimes located at the airport tower facility, may be located separately away from the tower. Approach and Departure Control utilizes radar to keep traffic separated, and this facility most commonly provides service to IFR traffic. VFR aircraft are urged to participate in using radar advisory surface whenever possible.

Airport surveillance radar (ASR) is a two-dimensional display (range and azimuth) with a range of approximately 60 miles. It is used by approach control to control traffic in an airport flight traffic pattern. The white bar on the top of the radar screen is a radar beacon which sends an identification request to a plane. ASRs are located at all major airports.

Flight Service Stations

There are approximately 175 FAA Flight Service Stations (FSS's) throughout the United States.

Flight Service Stations provide pilots with information on the station's particular area, including:

- terrain
- weather peculiarities
- preflight weather
- in-flight weather
- suggested routes

22A

- altitudes
- indications of turbulence
- icing
- airports

FSS's also initiate search and rescue when needed.

Automobile drivers have easy access to services on the road—road signs, service stations, roadside parks, information centers. Drivers use these services as needed and in an emergency can pull off the highway and evaluate the situation. Pilots obviously cannot pull off to the side of the road, but they can be in contact with Flight Service Stations before, during, and after flight.

Before flight, pilots gather complete weather information, not only about their local area but about weather along local routes. They may also obtain information about geologic peculiarities of that particular sector. Controllers or Flight Service Stations may suggest flight routes, altitudes, indications of turbulence, icing, or any other information important to the safety of a flight.

VFR pilots, after gathering all information, may want to file a flight plan with the Flight Service Station. The plan will include information about the flight and the aircraft. Figure P (pages 24A–25A) is a flight plan form with instructions for filling it out.

As a plane takes off, the FSS will "open" or activate the flight plan and notify the destination airport of the pilot's estimated time of arrival. It is the pilot's responsibility to "close" his or her flight plan within a half-hour after arrival. If the flight plan is not closed, the Flight Service Station will initiate a search for that plane and pilot, first by phone to airports along the way and eventually to a full-fledged search-and-rescue effort.

FIGURE P. FLIGHT SERVICE STATIONS

```
EACH YEAR
275 STATIONS
AND
4,000 CONTROLLERS

PROVIDE SERVICES TO 700,000 PILOTS (NON-AIRLINE)

WHO FLY 88,000 GENERAL AVIATION AIRCRAFT

15,000,000 MILES EACH YEAR
```

NOTE: The FAA is currently in the process of consolidating and automating the FSS system. When the project is complete, there will be fewer Service Stations, but each will serve a larger area and will be even more technologically advanced.

DEPARTMENT OF TRANSPORTATION— FEDERAL AVIATION ADMINISTRATION **FLIGHT PLAN**					Form Approved OMB No. 04-R0072	

FLIGHT PLAN FORM

- 1. TYPE: VFR / IFR / DVFR
- 2. AIRCRAFT IDENTIFICATION
- 3. AIRCRAFT TYPE/ SPECIAL EQUIPMENT
- 4. TRUE AIRSPEED ____ KTS
- 5. DEPARTURE POINT
- 6. DEPARTURE TIME — PROPOSED (Z) / ACTUAL (Z)
- 7. CRUISING ALTITUDE
- 8. ROUTE OF FLIGHT
- 9. DESTINATION (Name of airport and city)
- 10. EST. TIME ENROUTE — HOURS / MINUTES
- 11. REMARKS
- 12. FUEL ON BOARD — HOURS / MINUTES
- 13. ALTERNATE AIRPORT (S)
- 14. PILOT'S NAME, ADDRESS & TELEPHONE NUMBER & AIRCRAFT HOME BASE
- 15. NUMBER ABOARD
- 16. COLOR OF AIRCRAFT

CLOSE VFR FLIGHT PLAN WITH_____FSS ON ARRIVAL

FAA Form 7233-1 (5-72)

★ 1975-G.P.O.-1703-M/673-379/221

Explanation of Flight Plan Items

Block 1. Check the type flight plan. Check both the VFR and IFR blocks if composite VFR/IFR.

Block 2. Enter your complete aircraft identification including the prefix "N" if applicable.

Block 3. Enter the designator for the aircraft or, if unknown, the aircraft manufacturer's name (e.g., Cessna); followed by a slant (/) and the transponder or DME equipment code letter (e.g., C-182/U).

Block 4. Enter your computed true airspeed (TAS).
NOTE: If IFR and the average TAS changes plus or minus 5 percent or 10 knots, whichever is greater, advise ATC.

Block 5. Enter the departure airport identifier code (or the name if identifier is unknown).
NOTE: Use of identifier codes will expedite the processing of your flight plan.

Block 6. Enter the proposed departure time in Coordinated Universal Time (UTC) (Z). If airborne, specify the actual or proposed departure time as appropriate.

Block 7. If VFR, enter the appropriate VFR altitude (to assist the briefer in providing weather and wind information) and, if IFR, enter the requested enroute altitude or flight level.
NOTE: Enter only the initial requested altitude in this block. When more than one IFR altitude or flight level is desired along the route of flight, it is best to make a subsequent request direct to the controller.

Block 8. Define the route of flight by using NAVAID identifier codes (or names if the code is unknown), airways, jet routes, and waypoints (for RNAV).
NOTE: Use NAVAIDS or waypoints to define direct routes and radials/ bearings to define other unpublished routes.

Block 9. Enter the destination airport identifier code (or name if identifier is unknown).
NOTE: Include the city name (or even the state name) if needed for clarity.

Block 11. Enter only those remarks pertinent to ATC or to the clarification of other flight plan information. Items of a personnel nature are not accepted. Do not assume that remarks will be automatically transmitted to every controller. Specific ATC or Enroute requests should be made directly to the appropriate controller.

Block 12. Specify the fuel on board computed from the departure point.

Block 13. Specify an alternate airport if desired or required, but do not include routing to the alternate airport.

Block 14. Enter your complete name, address, and telephone number. Enter sufficient information to identify home base, airport, or operator.
NOTE: This information would be essential in the event of search and rescue operation.

Block 15. Enter the total number of persons on board including crew.

Block 16. Enter the predominant colors. Last Block. For VFR flight plans, record the FSS name for closing the flight plan. If the flight plan is closed with a different FSS or facility, state the recorded FSS name that would normally have closed your flight plan.
NOTE: Close IFR flight plans with tower, approach control, or ARTCC's, or if unable, with FSS. When landing at an airport with a functioning control tower, IFR flight plans are automatically cancelled.

The information transmitted to the destination FSS for VFR Flight Plans will consist only of flight plan blocks 2, 3, 9, and 10. Estimated time enroute (ETE) will be converted to the correct estimated time of arrival (ETA) for VFR flight plans.

The information transmitted to the ARTCC for IFR Flight Plans will consist of only flight plan blocks 2, 3, 4, 5, 6, 7, 8, 9, 10, and 11.

A description of the International Flight Plan Form is contained in the International Flight Information Manual.

PILOT/CONTROLLER ROLES AND RESPONSIBILITIES

This is how the Federal Aviation Administration defines the various roles of Pilot and Controller in safely guiding aircraft. It will give you a flavor of the kinds of manuals and documents that you will need to know. "FAR" refers to Federal Aviation Regulations.

Air Traffic Clearance

a. Pilot

(1) Acknowledge receipt and understanding of an ATC clearance.

(2) Request clarification or amendment, as appropriate, any time a clearance is not fully understood, or considered unacceptable from a safety standpoint.

(3) Promptly comply with air traffic clearance upon receipt except as necessary to cope with an emergency. If deviation is necessary, advise ATC as soon as possible and obtain an amended clearance.

b. Controller

(1) Issues appropriate clearances for the operation to be conducted, or being conducted, in accordance with established criteria.

(2) Assigns altitudes in IFR clearances that are at or above the minimum IFR altitudes in controlled airspace.

(3) Ensures acknowledgment by the pilot for issued information, clearance, or instructions.

(4) Ensures that readbacks by the pilot of altitude, heading, or other items are correct. If incorrect, distorted, or incomplete, makes corrections as appropriate.

Contact Approach

a. Pilot

(1) Approach must be requested by the pilot and is made in lieu of a standard or special instrument approach.

(2) By requesting the contact approach, the pilot indicates that the flight is operating clear of clouds, has at least one mile flight visibility, and can reasonably expect to continue to the destination airport in those conditions.

(3) Be aware that while conducting a contact approach, the pilot assumes responsibility for obstruction clearance.

(4) Advise ATC immediately if you are unable to continue the contact approach or if you encounter less than one mile flight visibility.

b. Controller

(1) Issues clearance for contact approach only when requested by the pilot. Does not solicit the use of this procedure.

(2) Before issuing clearance, ascertains that reported ground visibility at destination airport is at least one mile.

(3) Provides approved separation between aircraft cleared for contact approach and other IFR or special VFR aircraft. When using vertical separation, does not assign a fixed altitude but clears the aircraft at or below an altitude which is at least 1,000 feet below any IFR traffic but not below minimum safe altitudes prescribed in FAR—91.79.

(4) Issues alternative instructions if, in his/her judgment, weather conditions may make completion of the approach impracticable.

Instrument Approach

a. Pilot

(1) Be aware that the controller issues clearance for approach based only on known traffic.

(2) Follow the procedure as shown on the IAP, including all restrictive notations, such as:

    (a) Procedure not authorized at night;

    (b) Approach not authorized when local area altimeter not available;

    (c) Procedure not authorized when control tower not in operation;

    (d) Procedure not authorized when glide slope not used;

    (e) Straight-in minimums not authorized at night; etc.

    (f) Radar required; or

    (g) The circling minimums published on the instrument approach chart provide adequate obstruction clearance and the pilot should not descend below the circling altitude until the aircraft is in a position to make final descent for landing. Sound judgment and knowledge of his/her and the aircraft's capabilities are the criteria for a pilot to determine the exact maneuver in each instance since airport design and the aircraft position, altitude, and airspeed must all be considered.

(3) Upon receipt of an approach clearance while on an unpublished route or being radar vectored:

    (a) Comply with the minimum altitude for IFR, and

    (b) Maintain last assigned altitude until established on a segment of a published route or IAP, at which time published altitudes apply.

b. Controller

(1) Issues an approach clearance based on known traffic.

(2) Issues an IFR approach clearance only after the aircraft is established on a segment of published route or IAP, or assigns an appropriate altitude for the aircraft to maintain until so established.

Missed Approach

a. Pilot

(1) Execute a missed approach when one of the following conditions exist:

    (a) Arrival at the Missed Approach Point (MAP) or the Decision Height (DH) and visual reference to the runway environment is insufficient to complete the landing;

    (b) Determined that a safe landing is not possible; or

    (c) Instructed to do so by ATC.

(2) Advise ATC that a missed approach will be made. Include the reason for the missed approach unless the missed approach is initiated by ATC.

(3) Comply with the missed approach instructions for the IAP being executed unless other *missed approach* instructions are specified by ATC.

(4) If executing a missed approach prior to reaching the MAP or DH, fly the instrument procedure to the MAP at an altitude at or above the Minimum Descent Altitude (MDA) or DH before executing a turning maneuver.

(5) Radar vectors issued by ATC when informed that a missed approach is being executed supersedes the previous missed approach procedure.

(6) If making a missed approach from a radar approach, execute the missed approach procedure previously given or climb to the altitude and fly the heading specified by the controller.

(7) Following missed approach, request clearance for specific action; i.e., another approach, hold for improved conditions, proceed to an alternate airport, etc.

b. Controller

(1) Issues an approved alternative missed approach procedure if it is desired that the pilot execute a procedure other than as depicted on the instrument approach chart.

(2) May vector a radar identified aircraft executing a missed approach when operationally advantageous to the pilot or the controller.

(3) In response to the pilot's stated intentions, issues a clearance to an alternate airport, to a holding fix, or for reentry into the approach sequence, as traffic conditions permit.

Radar Vectors

a. Pilot

(1) Promptly comply with headings and altitudes assigned to you by the controller.

(2) Question any assigned heading or altitude believed to be incorrect.

(3) If operating VFR and compliance with any radar vector or altitude would cause a violation of any FAR, advise ATC and obtain a revised clearance or instruction.

b. Controller

(1) Vectors aircraft in controlled airspace:
   (a) For separation.
   (b) For noise abatement.
   (c) To obtain an operational advantage for the pilot or controller.

(2) Vectors aircraft in controlled and uncontrolled airspace when requested by the pilot.

(3) Vectors IFR aircraft at or above minimum vectoring altitudes.

(4) May vector VFR aircraft, not at an ATC assigned altitude, at any altitude. In these cases, terrain separation is the pilot's responsibility.

Safety Alert

a. Pilot

(1) Initiate appropriate action if a safety alert is received from ATC.

(2) Be aware that this service is not always available and that many factors affect the ability of the controller to be aware of a situation in which unsafe proximity to terrain, obstructions, or another aircraft may be developing.

b. Controller

(1) Issues a safety alert if he/she is aware an aircraft under his/her control is at an altitude which, in the controller's judgment, places the aircraft in unsafe proximity to terrain, obstructions, or another aircraft. Types of safety alerts are:

   (a) **Terrain or Obstruction Alert**—Immediately issued to an aircraft under his/her control if he/she is aware the aircraft is at an altitude believed to place the aircraft in unsafe proximity to terrain or obstructions.

   (b) **Aircraft Conflict Alert**—Immediately issued to an aircraft under his/her control if he/she is aware of an aircraft not under his/her control at an altitude believed to place the aircraft in unsafe proximity to each other. With the alert, he/she offers the pilot an alternative, if feasible.

(2) Discontinues further alerts if informed by the pilot that he/she is taking action to correct the situation or that he/she has the other aircraft in sight.

See and Avoid

a. Pilot

(1) When meteorological conditions permit, regardless of type of flight plan, whether or not under control of a radar facility, the pilot is responsible to see and avoid other traffic, terrain, or obstacles.

b. Controller

(1) Provides radar traffic information to radar identified aircraft operating outside positive control airspace on a workload permitting basis.

(2) Issues a safety alert to an aircraft under his/her control if he/she is aware the aircraft is at an altitude believed to place the aircraft in unsafe proximity to terrain, obstructions, or other aircraft.

Speed Adjustments

a. Pilot

(1) Advice ATC any time cruising airspeed varies plus or minus 5 percent, or 10 knots, whichever is greater, from that given in the flight plan.

(2) Comply with speed adjustments from ATC unless:

(a) The minimum or maximum safe airspeed for any particular operation is greater or less than the requested airspeed. In such cases, advise ATC.

(b) Operating at or above 10,000 feet MSL on an ATC assigned SPEED ADJUSTMENT of more than 250 knots IAS and subsequent clearance is received for descent below 10,000 feet MSL. In such cases, pilots are expected to comply with FAR—91.70(a).

(3) When complying with speed adjustments assignment, maintain an indicated airspeed within plus or minus 10 knots or .02 mach numbers of the specified speed.

b. Controller

(1) Assigns speed adjustments to aircraft when necessary but not as a substitute for good vectoring technique.

(2) Adheres to the restrictions published in the Controllers Handbook as to when speed adjustment procedures may be applied.

(3) Avoids speed adjustments requiring alternate decreases and increases.

(4) Assigns speed adjustments to a specified IAS (KNOTS)/mach number or to increase or decrease speed using increments of 10 knots or multiples thereof.

(5) Advises pilots to resume normal speed when speed adjustments are no longer required.

(6) Gives due consideration to aircraft capabilities to reduce speed while descending.

Traffic Advisories (Traffic Information)

a. Pilot

(1) Acknowledge receipt of traffic advisories.

(2) Inform controller if traffic is in sight.

(3) Advise ATC if a vector to avoid traffic is desired.

(4) Do not expect to receive radar traffic advisories on all traffic. Some aircraft may not appear on the radar display. Be aware that the controller may be occupied with higher priority duties and unable to issue traffic information for a variety of reasons.

(5) Advise controller if service is not desired.

b. Controller

(1) Issues radar traffic to the maximum extent consistent with higher priority duties except in positive controlled airspace.

(2) Provides vectors to assist aircraft to avoid observed traffic when requested by the pilot.

(3) Issues traffic information to aircraft in the airport traffic area for sequencing purposes.

Visual Approach

a. Pilot

(1) If a visual approach is not desired, advise ATC.

(2) Comply with controller's instructions for vectors toward the airport of intended landing or to a visual position behind a preceding aircraft.

(3) After being cleared for a visual approach, proceed to the airport in a normal manner or follow designated traffic and/or charted flight procedures as appropriate, remaining in VFR at all times.

(4) Acceptance of a visual approach clearance to visually follow a preceding aircraft is pilot acknowledgement that he/she will establish a safe landing interval behind the preceding aircraft, if so cleared, and that he/she accepts responsibility for his/her own wake turbulence separation.

(5) Advise ATC immediately if you are unable to continue following a designated aircraft or encounter less than basic VFR weather conditions.

(6) Be aware that radar service is automatically terminated without advising the pilot when the aircraft is instructed to contact the tower.

(7) Be aware that there may be other traffic in the traffic pattern and the landing sequence may differ from the traffic sequence assigned by the approach control or ARTCC.

b. Controller

(1) Does not vector an aircraft for a visual approach to an airport with weather reporting services unless the reported ceiling at the airport is 500 feet or more above the MVA and visibility is three miles or more.

(2) Informs the pilot when weather is not available for the destination airport and does not vector for a visual approach to those airports unless there is reasonable assurance that descent and flight to the airport can be made in VFR conditions.

(3) Does not clear an aircraft for a visual approach unless the aircraft is and can remain in VFR conditions.

(4) Issues visual approach clearance when the pilot reports sighting the airport or a preceding aircraft which is to be followed.

(5) Provides separation except when visual separation is being applied by the pilot of the aircraft executing the visual approach.

(6) Continues flight following and traffic information until the aircraft is instructed to contact the tower.

(7) Informs the pilot conducting the visual approach of the aircraft class when pertinent traffic is known to be a heavy aircraft.

Visual Separation

a. Pilot

(1) Acceptance of instructions to follow another aircraft to provide visual separation from it is an acknowledgement that the pilot will maneuver his/her aircraft as necessary to avoid the other aircraft or to maintain in-trail separation.

(2) If instructed by ATC to follow another aircraft or to provide visual separation from it, promptly notify the controller if you lose sight of that aircraft, are unable to maintain continued visual contact with it, or cannot accept the responsibility for your own separation for any reason.

(3) The pilot also accepts responsibility for wake turbulence separation under these conditions.

b. Controller

(1) Applies visual separation only within a terminal area when a controller has both aircraft in sight or by instructing a pilot who sees the other aircraft to maintain visual separation from it.

VFR-On Top

a. Pilot

(1) This clearance must be requested by the pilot on an IFR flight plan, and, if approved, permits the pilot to select an altitude or flight level of his/her choice (subject to any ATC restrictions) in lieu of an assigned altitude.

(2) By requesting a VFR-ON-TOP clearance, the pilot indicates that he/she is assuming the sole responsibility to be vigilant so as to see and avoid other aircraft and that he/she will:

(a) Fly at the appropriate VFR altitude as prescribed in FAR—91.109.

(b) Comply with the VFR visibility and distance from criteria in FAR—91.105 (Basic VFR Weather Minimums).

(c) Comply with instrument flight rules that are applicable to this flight (i.e., minimum IFR altitudes, position reporting, radio communications, course to be flown, adherence to ATC clearance, etc.).

(3) Should advise ATC prior to any altitude change to ensure the exchange of accurate traffic information.

b. Controller

(1) May clear an aircraft to maintain VFR-ON-TOP if the pilot on an aircraft on an IFR flight plan requests the clearance.

(2) Inform the pilot of an aircraft cleared to climb to VFR-ON-TOP; the reported height of the tops or that no top report is available; issues an alternate clearance if necessary; and once the aircraft reports reaching VFR-ON-TOP, reclears the aircraft to maintain VFR-ON-TOP.

(3) Before issuing clearance, ascertains that the aircraft is not in or will not enter positive control airspace.

Instrument Departures

a. Pilot

(1) Prior to departure: Consider the type of terrain and other obstructions on or in the vicinity of the departure airport.

(2) Determine if obstruction avoidance can be maintained visually or that the departure procedure should be followed.

(3) Determine whether a departure procedure and/or SID is available for obstruction avoidance.

(4) At airports where IAPs have not been published (hence no published departure procedure) determine what action will be necessary and take such action that will assure a safe departure.

b. Controller

(1) At locations with airport traffic control service, when necessary, specifies direction of takeoff, turn, or initial heading to be flown after takeoff.

(2) At locations without airport traffic control service, but within a control zone when necessary to specify direction of takeoff/turn or initial heading to be flown, obtains pilot's concurrence that the procedure will allow him/her to comply with local traffic patterns, terrain, and obstruction avoidance.

(3) Includes established departure procedures as part of the ATC clearance when pilot compliance is necessary to ensure separation.

Minimum Fuel Advisory

a. Pilot

(1) Advise ATC of your minimum fuel status when your fuel supply has reached a state where, upon reaching destination, you cannot accept any undue delay.

(2) Be aware that this is not an emergency situation but merely an advisory that indicates an emergency situation is possible should any undue delay occur.

(3) Be aware a minimum fuel advisory does not imply a need for traffic priority.

(4) If the remaining usable fuel supply suggests the need for traffic priority to ensure a safe landing you should declare an emergency, account low fuel, and report fuel remaining in minutes.

b. Controller

(1) When an aircraft declares a state of minimum fuel, relay this information to the facility to whom control jurisdiction is transferred.

(2) Be alert for any occurrence which might delay the aircraft.

A technician uses an oscilloscope to perform routine maintenance checks on TRACON's ARTS IIIA Sensor Receiver and Processor unit. The SRAP, produced by Sperry Univac, converts incoming radar signals from analog to digital format prior to processing by the ARTS IIIA digital computer.

Job Locations

The FAA employs thousands of electronic technicians. Most of them work in field offices or "sectors" scattered all over the country. Some work is located at the FAA's National Aviation Facilities Experimental Center, which is engaged in electronic research and development projects.

Salaries

Entry-level positions normally start at the GS–5 level.

Advancement Opportunities

Employees have opportunities to progress to higher-level grades depending on the complexity of their work duties, the degree of supervision received or exercised, and the growing knowledge and skills used in the performance of their work. Supervisory positions are available at sector, area, and regional offices. Promotion to managerial jobs at FAA headquarters is possible.

Job Requirements

Minimum age is 18. The electronics experience, education, or training required must include: knowledge of basic electronic theory and related mathematics, knowledge of transmitters and receivers, use of test equipment, techniques of troubleshooting and circuitry analysis, use of tools and installation practices. The greater the employee's degree of education or experience, the higher the employee's entrance level. Applicants must have a minimum experience of the kinds and amounts indicated in the following table for each grade. Excess "specialized" experience may be credited as "general" experience. Some types of civilian or military education, related to the option for which application is made, may be substituted for the specialized experience requirements.

TABLE 4. EXPERIENCE REQUIREMENTS FOR ELECTRONIC TECHNICIANS

Grade	General Experience (Years)	Specialized Experience (Years)	Total Experience (Years)
GS–5	3	0	3
GS–6	3	½	3½
GS–7	3	1	4
GS–8	3	1½	4½
GS–9	3	2	5
GS–11&12	3	3	6

In addition, applicants must show an ability to work without supervision and to write reports. They must be able to pass a physical examination and be free from color blindness. A technician may, in connection with performance of regular duties, be required to drive a government-owned automobile or truck.

Training

Basic training is available at technical and vocational schools offering courses in electronics. Upon assignment to an FAA sector office, new employees undergo a short period of on-the-job training to familiarize them with FAA equipment and procedures. Then they may receive several months of training at the FAA Academy at Oklahoma City, Oklahoma.

The Academy offers correspondence courses to support technical training efforts, and many of these correspondence courses are prerequisites to assignments for advanced courses at the Academy. Technicians receive regular salary and subsistence allowances while at the Academy. Basic training and experience for FAA employment may also be obtained during active duty in military service.

ELECTRONIC TECHNICIAN
(FAA AIRSPACE SYSTEM INSPECTION)

Technicians appointed for airborne technical/electronics duty are required to fly in government aircraft as a member of a crew with airspace system inspection pilots for data collection, evaluation and/or engineering purposes during the in-flight inspection of navigational aids. Applicants should indicate on their applications their willingness to fly. The requirements and salary scales are basically the same as for electronic technicians.

AVIATION SAFETY INSPECTOR
AVIATION SAFETY INSPECTOR (OPERATIONS)
AVIATION SAFETY INSPECTOR (AIRWORTHINESS)
AVIATION SAFETY INSPECTOR (MANUFACTURING)

Aviation safety inspectors develop, administer, and enforce regulations and standards concerning civil aviation safety, including the airworthiness of aircraft and aircraft systems; the competence of pilots, mechanics, and other aviation personnel; and safety aspects of aviation facilities, equipment and procedures. These positions require knowledge and skills in the operation, maintenance or manufacture of aircraft and aircraft systems.

Requirements to Enter These Jobs

Candidates must have experience as described on page 150. (Education may be substituted for general experience.)

TABLE 5. EXPERIENCE REQUIREMENTS FOR AVIATION
SAFETY INSPECTORS

Grade	General Experience (Years)	Specialized Experience (Years)	Total Experience (Years)
GS–9	3	2	5
GS–11–15	3	3	6

General Experience

General experience is that which has provided familiarity with aircraft operation or the aviation industry. The following are examples of qualifying general experience:

- pilot or crew member in civil or military aviation
- civilian or military air traffic controller
- aviation mechanic or repairperson
- avionics or electronics technician
- skilled machinist, assemblyperson, or inspector in production of aircraft, aircraft parts, or avionics equipment

Substitution of Education

For all positions in this series, successful completion of post-high-school education in related fields such as engineering, aeronautics, and air transportation may be substituted for the required general experience. Education may be substituted at the rate of one academic year of full-term study for nine months of general experience, up to the maximum of three years of general experience.

Specialized experience is that which has provided knowledge and skills for work in the specialty field, that is, in operations, airworthiness, or manufacturing. In addition, specialized experience must have provided a broad knowledge of the aviation industry, the general principles of aviation safety, and the federal laws, regulations and policies regulating aviation. Examples of qualifying specialized experience are described under the appropriate specialty area.

Level of Experience

Candidates for positions at grades GS–11 and below must have at least six months of specialized experience at a level of difficulty and responsibility comparable to that of the next lower grade in the federal service, or one year equivalent to the second lower grade. Candidates for grades GS–12 and above must have at least one year of specialized experience of difficulty and responsibility comparable to that of the next lower grade. For any grade, the required amount of experience and education will not itself be accepted as proof of qualification for a position. The candidate's total record of experience and education must demonstrate that he or she possesses the ability to perform the duties of the position.

Physical Requirements

Candidates must be physically able to perform efficiently the duties of the position. They must have good distant vision in each eye and be able to read without strain printed material the size of typewritten characters, glasses permitted. Ability to hear the conversational voice with or without a hearing aid is required. Any physical condition which would cause the applicant to be a hazard to him- or herself or others, or any condition which would interfere with his or her ability to fly as a passenger in a variety of airplanes, will disqualify the applicant for appointment. In addition, candidates for positions that require participation in the operation of aircraft must possess a current valid first-class medical certificate in accordance with the regulations of the FAA. Incumbents in these positions must pass recurrent medical examinations that may be prescribed by the FAA.

Basic Rating

No written examination is required. Candidates will be rated, on a scale of 100, on the extent and quality of their experience and training. Ratings will be based upon candidates' statements in the applications and upon additional information that may be obtained by the Office of Personnel Management. For positions that involve specialization in flight operations, the nature, amount and recency of flight time as a pilot or flight instructor will be given substantial weight in ranking candidates.

Interview

Before appointment, candidates may be required to appear for an interview. The purpose is to observe and evaluate certain personal characteristics to determine whether candidates possess the following essential qualities: ability to express ideas logically and accurately and to speak effectively and convincingly; and ability to operate successfully and easily in group situations.

Candidates should be evaluated on the basis of the extent to which their experience and training provide knowledge and skills necessary for positions for which they are being considered. The following are elements of aviation safety positions that a candidate's background should have provided:

- broad knowledge of specialization
- independence and responsibility
- skills in evaluation and fact-finding
- ability to advise and guide others
- skill in reading comprehension and report writing

Selective Placement

For positions that require particular knowledge and skills, consideration may be restricted to candidates whose background indicates that they possess such knowledge and skills. For example, an aviation safety inspector operational position may require the ability to operate a specific type of jet aircraft or helicopter, in which case consideration may be restricted to candidates who have ratings in that type of aircraft.

Working Conditions

The job may require considerable travel, as inspections, consultations and investigations must be made at various facilities and locations or at the scenes of accidents. Forty hours constitute a normal work week. Change of assignment from one duty station to another is required as staffing demands.

Job Locations

Inspectors operate out of Air Carrier District Offices, General Aviation District Offices and Flight Standards District Offices. These are located throughout the country. Five international field offices have the same functions as the FSDOs.

Opportunities for Advancement

Outstanding inspectors may be promoted to the next higher level, with increased responsibility and salary. An inspector demonstrating managerial ability may become a section or branch chief. She or he may also become an instructor at the FAA academy.

The recent recession and associated government hiring freeze has resulted in a net loss of inspectors, but concern over safety since the advent of economic deregulation of the airlines has put new emphasis on the need for more aviation safety inspectors.

AVIATION SAFETY INSPECTOR (OPERATIONS)

Nature of the Work

Persons appointed to these positions apply knowledge and skills acquired as airmen (pilots, navigators, flight instructors, etc.) to develop and administer the regulations and safety standards pertaining to the operation of aircraft. Their primary duties include:

1. Examining airmen for initial certification and continuing competence.
2. Evaluating airmen training programs, equipment and facilities.
3. Evaluating the operations aspect of programs of air carriers and other commercial operations.

Job Requirements

Examples of qualifying specialized experiences are:

1. Pilot (copilot) experience that provides comprehensive knowledge of operations requirements, facilities, practices, procedures and flight activities of scheduled or supplemental air carriers, commercial operators, executive operators, air taxis, air travel clubs, or other civilian or military activities.
2. Flight instructor in civilian or military training school.
3. Flight test pilot or flight instructor involved in enforcing regulations concerning the safe operation of aircraft.

Certificates and Ratings

GENERAL AVIATION OPERATIONS. Candidates for positions that require operation of aircraft in the general aviation field must hold a current commercial pilot certificate with single- and multi-engine land and instrument ratings.

AIR CARRIER OPERATIONS. Candidates for positions that require flight operation of aircraft in the air carrier field must hold either a current airline transport pilot certificate or a current commercial pilot certificate with multi-engine land and instrument ratings, and be eligible for an airline transport pilot certificate.

Training Opportunities

Flight training may be obtained in the military or at private or university-operated flight schools for a commercial pilot's license and for multi-engine or for instrument ratings. From time to time, retraining is required as new developments in aircraft engines and equipment appear.

AVIATION SAFETY INSPECTORS (AIRWORTHINESS)

About the Work

Persons appointed to these positions apply knowledge and skills acquired as repairpersons of aircraft and aircraft parts or avionics equipment to develop and administer regulations and safety standards pertaining to the airworthiness and maintenance of aircraft and related systems. Their primary duties include:

1. Evaluating mechanics and repair facilities for initial certification and continuing adequacy.
2. Evaluating mechanics training programs.
3. Inspecting aircraft and related systems for airworthiness.

4. Evaluating the maintenance aspects of programs of air carriers and other commercial operators including the adequacy of maintenance facilities, equipment and procedures, the competence of personnel, the adequacy of the program or schedule for periodic maintenance and overhauls, and the airworthiness of aircraft.

Job Requirements

Examples of qualifying experience are:

1. Experience involving technical supervision or management of the maintenance and repair of aircraft, aircraft engines, or aircraft electronics, communication, and navigation systems and equipment of aircraft with responsibility for airworthiness following federal aviation or military regulations and safety standards. This experience must demonstrate a broad and comprehensive knowledge of maintenance of aircraft or aircraft systems. It must also demonstrate an ability to gain cooperation at management levels in complying with and supporting proper maintenance standards.

2. Work as an aviation safety inspector or air safety investigator concerned with aircraft powerplants, structures, or systems.

3. Experience gained as a field service representative of a manufacturer of aircraft systems and equipment may be accepted up to a maximum of one year.

Certificates and Ratings

Candidates for positions at GS–9 and above are required to have knowledge and skills in the maintenance of aircraft (except positions that involve primarily avionics equipment) and must hold an FAA Mechanic Certificate with airframe and powerplant ratings.

Training Opportunities

Basic training as an aircraft mechanic or in electronics and communications systems repair in a technical or vocational school is a starting point. College level work in aeronautical engineering or aeronautical maintenance or electrical or electronic engineering is preferred. Occasionally, retraining is required as new developments in aircraft engines and equipment appear.

AVIATION SAFETY INSPECTOR (MANUFACTURING)

Nature of the Work

Persons appointed to these positions apply knowledge and skills pertaining to the design and production of aircraft, aircraft parts, and avionics equipment to develop and administer regulations and safety standards pertaining to the original airworthiness of aircraft, aircraft parts and avionics equipment. Their primary duties include:

1. Inspecting prototype or modified aircraft, aircraft parts, and avionics equipment for conformity with design specifications.

2. Inspecting production operations including equipment, facilities, techniques, and quality control programs for capability to produce the aircraft or parts in conformance with design specifications and safety standards.

3. Making original airworthiness determinations and issuing certificates for all civil aircraft including modified, import, export, military surplus, and amateur-built aircraft.

Job Requirements

Examples of qualifying specialized experience are:

1. Experience involving quality control of the manufacture of the aircraft, aircraft engines, propellers, or aircraft assemblies produced under the requirements of FAA regulations.

2. For grades GS–11 and above, this experience must demonstrate the ability to evaluate and provide technical guidance and direction to the quality control program of a manufacturer producing aircraft, aircraft engines, propellers or major aircraft assemblies. This experience may be acquired in such positions as quality control engineer, quality control supervisor or service representative with quality control supervisory experience.

Training Opportunities

A college degree in aeronautical, production, or industrial engineering is the best preparation for entry jobs at higher levels. Technical or vocational school training in various trades associated with aircraft manufacturing (drafting, sheet metal work, air conditioning, electrical systems, etc.) leading to jobs in aircraft manufacturing can give minimum background and experience. Occasionally, retraining is required as new developments in aircraft, engines, and equipment appear.

AIRSPACE SYSTEM INSPECTION PILOT (FAA)

About the Work

These pilots conduct in-flight inspections of ground-based air navigational facilities to determine if they are operating correctly. They pilot multi-engine high performance jet aircraft with specially installed ultra-sophisticated, computerized, and automated electronic equipment. This serves as a flying electronic laboratory on day and night flights, under both visual and instrument flight rules, recording and analyzing facility performance, and reporting potential hazards to air navigation for correction. The pilot assists in accident investigations by making special flight tests of any FAA navigational aids involved. While maintaining liaison with aviation interests regarding the installation, operation, and use of their navigational facilities, these pilots remain most involved with the FAA personnel who maintain the NAVAIDS.

Working Conditions

The job involves considerable travel, and flights cover navigational aids supporting federal airways and civil and military airports located throughout the entire country. The basic work week is forty hours.

Job Locations

Airspace System Inspection Pilots work out of one of seven flight inspection field offices within the contiguous 48 states. Upon reaching the journeyman level of proficiency, a pilot could, at his or her option, bid on a job in one of the flight inspection offices in Alaska, Hawaii, Tokyo, or Germany.

Salary

The entry level is at the GS–9 grade.

Training Opportunities

Employees enter as trainees, then advance to the job of second pilot on an in-flight inspection or at air navigation facilities. The next step is that of supervisory airplane pilot, who supervises the flight inspection crews and evaluates the report findings on navigation systems. The top jobs, located in field offices, are those of supervisors responsible for the overall program accomplishment of the field office. If assigned to a flight inspection field office, an employee can advance through second pilot to airspace and procedures specialist responsible for developing instrument approach, terminal, and enroute air traffic procedures, or he or she may move up to become senior flight inspector or aircraft commander, supervising flight crews and results of inspection missions. Managers of field offices have the top jobs.

Job Requirements

Experience as a pilot in general, air carrier or military aviation is required. Experience requirements are specified in terms of flying time, certificates and ratings rather than in number of years of experience. As a minimum, a pilot must hold a valid commercial pilot certificate with multi-engine and instrument ratings.

Flying time in any category may be as a pilot or copilot, except for the pilot-in-command hours specifically required. The instrument/night requirement must include at least 40 hours of actual instrument weather time. Experience as an air traffic controller, chief test pilot, chief pilot of an FAA certified flight school or designated pilot examiner may be substituted for not more than 50 hours of flying time required for the last 12 months. The pilot must have a valid first class FAA medical certificate and must requalify periodically in physical examinations to maintain employment in this job.

TABLE 6. EXPERIENCE REQUIREMENTS FOR AIRSPACE SYSTEM INSPECTION PILOTS

(in hours of flying time)

Grade	Total Time	Pilot in Command	Multi-Engine	Inst. Night	Minimum For Each 12 Mon. in this Job
GS–9	1200	250	100	100	100
GS–11	1500	250	500	150	100

Opportunities for Training

Flight instruction may be obtained from private or university-operated flight schools or from military services.

FLIGHT TEST PILOT (FAA)

Nature of the Work

The flight test pilot (FAA) checks the airworthiness of aircraft through inspection, flight testing, and evaluation of flight performance, engine operation and flight characteristics of either prototype aircraft or modifications of production aircraft components that are presented for FAA type certification. The flight test pilot supervises FAA-designated flight test representatives and participates in investigations of accidents and violations of the federal air regulations.

Working Conditions

This employee flies new types of aircraft under all kinds of conditions to test their performance. Considerable travel is required, and his or her duty station may be changed from time to time as circumstances require.

Where The Jobs Are

The jobs are located in areas where aircraft manufacturing plants are situated. They are chiefly in California, Washington, Missouri, Maryland, Texas, Kansas, Florida and New York.

Wages

The entry level of a flight test pilot is a grade of GS–9. Entry salary will vary with the degree of the applicant's experience and training.

Opportunities for Advancement

The flight test pilot may progress to branch chief positions in the engineering or manufacturing areas. An administration post with respect to all FAA flight test pilots at FAA headquarters, or perhaps an assignment with the FAA test center (the research and development arm of the FAA), may provide opportunities for an administrative flight test engineering job.

Requirements for the Job

Three years of general experience as a pilot or copilot in any civilian or military major aircraft operation is required. Also required is one to three years of special experience in the aircraft manufacturing industry or in the military or civil service of the federal government as a flight test pilot, aeronautical engineer or flight test engineer. The special experience must include engineering flight testing of experimental types of aircraft or the solution of technical engineering problems at a professional level. The pilot must have experience in obtaining and evaluating flight data related to flight performance, flight characteristics, engine operation, and other performance details of the prototype or modification of production aircraft. Experience as an instructor in engineering flight testing of aircraft is also required. The higher entry grades require completion of a flight test pilot course, such as a military flight test school or the FAA flight test pilot course. College study in aeronautical, electrical, electronics or mechanical engineering, mathematics or physics may be substituted for some of the general experience requirements. Physical exams at regular intervals are required to retain the job.

Opportunities for Training

Flight training with advanced training at a military flight school may be obtained in the military service. Flight training through commercial pilot's license with appropriate ratings may be obtained from private schools and institutes. A college degree in aeronautical engineering with flight training is preferred.

MAINTENANCE MECHANIC (FAA)

Nature of the Work

There are a number of employees classified under the federal wage system schedule. These employees perform jobs associated with the trades and crafts and are paid on an hourly basis. One example is the maintenance mechanic (FAA). They maintain aids to navigation such as the approach light systems serving airport runways. They also work on the structural, electrical, and mechanical devices that are major parts of other facilities. This includes maintenance and repair of heating, air conditioning and ventilating systems; electrical generating and power distribution systems; and the buildings and antenna structures that house a wide variety of FAA facilities. The job involves carpentry, painting, plumbing, electrical, and masonry construction, and installation, repair and maintenance of air conditioning, heating and power generating equipment.

Working Conditions

Work is indoors or outdoors as the jobs require. Work may be on outdoor structures of heights up to 300 feet. The basic work week is forty hours. The employee must be able to drive a truck to jobs in outlying areas.

Where The Jobs Are

Jobs are located in all areas of the U.S., Puerto Rico, the Virgin Islands, and anywhere the FAA air navigational aids and air traffic control towers and centers are situated.

Wages

Hourly wages vary according to experience and the prevailing rates paid where the jobs are located.

Requirements to Enter the Job

The employee must have four years of progressively responsible experience in two or more of the following occupational groups: machinist, machine repairperson, automobile mechanic, carpenter, woodworker, electrician, electric motor repairperson, painter, air conditioning and refrigeration repairperson, heating equipment and power generation repairperson. Training in a trade school may be substituted for some of the required experience. Candidates must have a driver's license.

ENGINEER

General Information

The FAA, as well as the National Aeronautics and Space Administration (NASA) and the Department of Defense, employs engineers of all specialties to work on research and development problems in aviation, such as STOL (very short takeoff and landing) aircraft, aircraft sound, sonic boom, hypersonic aircraft, and new equipment and devices to increase aviation safety. Engineers also provide guidance in airport design, construction, operation and maintenance.

Nature of the Work

The facilities, devices and machines needed by the FAA to carry on its work require the services of a number of engineering specialists.

Aerospace (aeronautical) engineers develop, interpret, and administer safety regulations relating to airworthiness of aircraft and their accessories. They analyze and evaluate manufacturers' designs, set up test procedures, observe tests, and furnish engineering advice to manufacturers. They deal with such problems as vibration, flutter, stability, control, weight and balance, and aerodynamic characteristics.

Electrical engineers deal with power supply, distribution and standby power generation required for the operation of air navigational aids. They are also involved in the design and evaluation of airport and runway lighting and electrical equipment aboard aircraft.

Electronic engineers are concerned with designing improved electronic navigational aids and communications systems. They may design, modify or oversee installation, calibration and maintenance of ground and airborne electronic equipment. They also recommend location of NAVAIDS.

Mechanical engineers are concerned with the design of gasoline and diesel powerplants for standby power generation in case of emergencies. They are also concerned with heating, ventilating, and air conditioning equipment at FAA installations. Some mechanical engineers check out such things as the performance of new types of aircraft engines, fuel systems, and fire detection devices.

Civil engineers involved in the airports program deal with a broad range of airport design, construction, and maintenance matters. FAA involvement in these matters is in the area of providing advice and guidance to civil airport developers, with particular emphasis on airports developed with federal grants in aid.

Working Conditions

The engineer works at a desk in an engineering laboratory or works outdoors conducting or observing tests of equipment during a forty-hour week. Travel must be required as the engineer consults with aircraft and engine manufacturers and with suppliers of all kinds of equipment related to the engineering specialty. Engineers may travel to consult with state and city officials who need federal funds for building or improving airports and to military bases where equipment is tested.

Where The Jobs Are

Engineering jobs are located at FAA headquarters, district and regional offices, at NASA headquarters and centers, and at certain military bases scattered throughout the nation.

Wages

GS–5 to GS–14 are beginning salaries, depending upon previous experience and educational background.

Opportunities for Advancement

Promotion is normally from within.

Requirements for the Job

A B.S. degree in engineering is required, or four years of technical engineering experience and training that provides technical knowledge equal to that possessed by a graduate engineer. From no experience to as much as three additional years of experience are required depending upon entry grade level.

Opportunities for Training

Engineering training may be obtained from colleges offering courses in the specialized engineering field.

ENGINEERING AID OR TECHNICIAN

Nature of the Work

Depending upon the specialty, the engineering aid or technician assists engineers by drafting engineering plans, conducting efficiency and performance tests, making calculations, setting up laboratory equipment and instruments, and preparing technical reports, specifications and estimates.

Working Conditions

The basic work week is forty hours. Travel may be required as the technician consults with aircraft and engine manufacturers and with suppliers of all kinds of equipment related to his or her engineering specialty. He or she may travel to consult with state or city officials who need federal funds for building or improving airports and to military bases where equipment is tested.

Where The Jobs Are

Jobs are located at FAA facilities and at the FAA Test Center at Atlantic City, New Jersey, at NASA headquarters and centers, and at certain military bases scattered throughout the nation.

Wages

Starting salaries for engineering aids are GS-1 to GS-3, and for engineering technicians GS-4 to GS-12 depending upon previous experience and educational background.

Requirements to Enter the Job

TABLE 7. EXPERIENCE REQUIREMENTS FOR ENGINEERING
AIDS/TECHNICIANS

Grade	General Experience (Years)	Specialized Experience (Years)	Total Experience (Years)
GS–1	0	0	0
GS–2	½	0	½
GS–3	1	0	1
GS–4	1½	½	2
GS–5	2	1	3
GS–6	2	2	4
GS–7	2	3	5
GS–8 & Above	2	4	6

Engineering technicians may be certified by the Institute for Certification of Engineering Technicians, an organization sponsored by the National Society of Professional Engineers. They may be certified as junior engineering technician, engineering technician, or senior engineering technician.

Opportunities for Training

The technician or aid may study his or her specialty at a vocational or technical school, junior or community college, or a four-year college.

OTHER PROFESSIONAL EMPLOYEES (FAA)

The FAA also requires the services of professional people other than engineers. Aviation medicine is an important discipline, and physicians who have chosen aviation medicine as a specialty beyond their general medical education are employed by the FAA in limited numbers. These physicians study such things as the effects of flying on the human body, the need for oxygen above certain altitudes, the effects of fatigue on pilot performance, vision and hearing standards, the tension and stress factors associated with the air traffic controller's job, and the standards of the various classes of medical examinations required for pilots and other members of flight crews. A wide scope of professionals are represented in the FAA. These include airport safety specialists, urban planners, economists, mathematicians, statisticians, program officers, management analysts, and budget analysts.

The FAA requires logistic support for all its programs, particularly in the area of establishment, operation and maintenance of air navigation and traffic control facilities. Personnel plan and manage programs for the establishment and installation of facilities, acquire real and personal property needed to establish, operate and maintain facilities, and provide all aspects of property and material management.

This work requires logistics specialists, inventory and supply managers, procurement analysts, contracting specialists, transportation officers, and purchasing clerks.

The FAA also employs lawyers to write federal aviation regulations, to interpret them, and to represent the FAA in legal controversies. It employs many other kinds of workers found in business and industry such as accountants, public information officers, librarians, photographers, and supporting personnel such as receptionists, secretaries, typists, office machine operators, mail clerks, and data computer programmers and operators. In addition, the FAA operates two federal commercial airports in the Washington, D.C. area and employs runway, building and ground maintenance personnel as well as an airport administrative staff.

WORK OUTSIDE OF THE FAA

The National Transportation Safety Board

The National Transportation Safety Board accident investigators interview accident survivors and witnesses and examine aircraft parts, instruments, and engines. They also review maintenance and flight records to determine the probable cause of airplane accidents. There are aviation-related engineering, medical and/or professional positions with this safety-related organization. Travel and field work typify the investigator's position. Salary and experience rankings are similar to those of the Department of Transportation.

U.S. Military Services

The U.S. Military Services are a large employer of civilians for jobs in aviation, such as aircraft mechanics, engineers, technicians, and general office workers like secretaries and typists. Civilian jobs come under the federal civil service, and employees do many of the same kinds of work and receive the same wages and benefits as their counterparts in the FAA or other federal government departments and agencies.

There are many aviation career opportunities in the military services for enlisted personnel and officers, both men and women. The air force, of course, offers the greatest number of training and employment opportunities to fly as a pilot or to work as an aircraft mechanic, air traffic controller, electronic technician, flight nurse, or meteorological technician, to name a few. Navy and marine aviation also have jobs that are counterparts to those in the air force. Army aviation is mostly connected with operation and maintenance of helicopters and subsonic light planes and requires flight crews and ground service people and weather specialists to support its aerial operations. Many of these military aviation jobs equip the service man or woman for similar jobs in civilian life, if he or she chooses to leave the service. For example, flying officers released by the military services, especially the air force, have constituted the major source of supply of airline pilots in recent years. An Air Transportation Association survey revealed that a high percentage of all airline pilots employed had their principal training in the military services.

Other Federal Government Departments and Agencies

Many other federal government departments, bureaus and agencies operate aircraft to carry on their work more effectively. For example, the Fish and Wildlife Service of the Department of the Interior uses airplanes to make wildlife census; the Department of Agriculture's Forest Service uses aircraft to check on aerial forest spraying contracted to commercial operators or to oversee forest firefighting procedures; the Immigration and Naturalization Service of the Department of Justice uses aircraft to detect people entering the U.S. illegally; and the Coast Guard operates aircraft for search and rescue purposes. Although pilot and mechanic jobs within these agencies are comparatively few in number, they are mentioned to complete the full picture of aviation career opportunities within the federal service. Pilots for these federal government agencies fly aircraft to transport office staff members and supplies, perform aerial surveys, make wildlife census, etc., as required by their particular government office. They fly in single- or multi-engine aircraft day or night, as required, and over all kinds of terrain in all kinds of flyable weather.

The jobs are based throughout the country wherever the department operations require. Pilots must have from 1,200 to 2,500 flying hours' experience, including extended cross-country flights over land and/or water during which they performed their own navigating. They must be able to pass a first class and second class FAA physical examination every six and twelve months, respectively. The annual salary ranges from GS–9 to GS–12, depending upon experience and educational background.

STATE AVIATION JOBS

Almost every state has an aeronautics department or commission that consists of a small number of aviation-minded men and women usually appointed by the governor to make policies about aviation activities within the state. Persons appointed may not be considered employees and may be paid only expenses connected with their attendance at meetings. If the state department or commission is well funded, it employs some employees who work in the area of airport design and operations, flight safety and promotion of aviation activities in the state.

Frequently, employees have dual responsibilities, especially when the staff is small. Qualifications and requirements for these various jobs are determined by law; however, the top level employees (safety officers, field service representatives and engineers) must have experience and training in their specialty. Most employees working under state civil service enjoy retirement plans, social security, low cost insurance, and medical service. In most cases, department employees work out of the department office in the state capital.

PART FIVE

A Real-Life Scenario—
Avianca Flight 052

COMMUNICATIONS AND SAFETY—AVIANCA FLIGHT 052*

As an air traffic controller, your job will be to ensure that aircraft do not get into dangerous situations. In the real world, most flights are uneventful. And your job is routine.

But never forget that things can go wrong. If an emergency arises, you must think quickly and act decisively to meet the situation. The following story of Avianca Flight 052 shows how critical your job is and why air traffic control work is so important.

OVERVIEW

On January 25, 1990, Avianca Airlines flight 052, a Colombian registered Boeing 707, crashed in a wooded residential area in Cove Neck, Long Island, New York. AVA 052 was a scheduled international passenger flight from Bogotá, Colombia, to John F. Kennedy Airport, New York, with an international stop at Cordova Airport, Colombia. Of the 158 persons aboard, 73 were fatally injured.

Because of poor weather in the northeastern part of the United States, the flightcrew was placed in holding three times by air traffic control for a total of about 1 hour and 17 minutes. During the third period of holding, the flightcrew reported that the airplane could not hold longer than 5 minutes, and that it was running out of fuel and could not reach its alternate airport, Boston-Logan Airport. Subsequently, the flightcrew executed a missed approach to JFK Airport. While trying to return to the airport, the airplane experienced a loss of power to all four engines and crashed approximately 16 miles from the airport.

The National Transportation Safety Board (NTSB) determined that the probable cause of the accident was the failure of the flightcrew to adequately manage the airplane's fuel load and their failure to communicate an emergency fuel situation to air traffic control before fuel exhaustion occurred. Contributing to the accident was the flightcrew's failure to use an airline operational dispatch system to assist them during the international flight into a high-density airport in poor weather. Also contributing to the accident was inadequate traffic flow management by the Federal Aviation Administration and the lack of standardized understandable terminology for pilot and controllers for minimum and emergency fuel states.

The safety board also determined that wind shear, crew fatigue, and stress were factors that led to the unsuccessful completion of the first approach and thus contributed to the accident. Here is a recap of the safety issues raised:

1. Pilot and dispatch responsibilities regarding planning, flight following, and fuel requirements
2. Pilot-controller communications regarding fuel states and special handling
3. ATC flow control procedures and responsibilities
4. Flightcrew coordination and English language proficiency

HISTORY OF THE FLIGHT

AVA 052 departed Bogotá Airport at 1310 and landed at Medellín at 1404. The flight refueled and departed Medellín at 1508. The flight plan was via an oceanic route over the Bahamas Islands, then northbound towards the U.S. east coast. As the flight proceeded northward, it was placed in holding three times: first over Norfolk

* From *National Transportation Safety Briefs,* Volume I/Issue 3, September/October 1992.

for 19 minutes, second near Atlantic City for 29 minutes, and a third time at CAMRN intersection 39 miles south of JFK for 29 minutes.

The cockpit voice recorder (CVR) revealed that the first officer was the only crewmember who spoke to ATC. He received instructions in English and repeated them in Spanish in the cockpit.

New York ATC (R67) at 2044:

R67: "Avianca 052 ah we just got off the line its ah indefinite hold at this time . . . hold at CAMRN . . . expect further clearance time 0205" (2105 est)

AVA052: "0205 ahhhh well I think we need priority we're passing (unintelligible)"

R67: "Avianca 052 heavy roger how long can you hold and ah what is your alternate"

AVA052: "Yes sir ah we'll be able to hold about five minutes that all we can do"

R67: "Avianca 052 heavy roger what is your alternate"

AVA052: "Ah we said Boston but ah it is ah full of traffic I think"

R67: "Avianca 052 say again your alternate airport"

AVA052: "It was Boston but we we can't do it now we, we don't, we run out of fuel now"

R67: "Avianca 052 ah just stand by"

A handoff controller, who was assisting the radar controller (R67) and was monitoring these radio transmissions, initiated a call on the land-line to approach control (TRACON) at 2046: "Avianca 052 just coming on CAMRN can only do 5 more minutes in the hold you going to be able to take him or I'll set him up for his alternate"

TRACON: "Slow him to one eighty and I'll take him"

The handoff controller later stated that he did not hear a portion of the transmission from AVA052 and therefore did not pass the information to tracon that the flight could no longer reach its alternate airport.

Avianca 052 was cleared to JFK airport and instructed to contact New York Approach (APP). AVA052 was then provided with routine radar service, including descents to lower altitudes and heading changes to sequence with other airplanes en route to JFK.

14* 2054; including cockpit voice recording, from Captain (CAP), First Officer (F/O), Second Officer (S/O), and Ground Proximity Warning System (GPWS).

APP: "Avianca 052 turn right right turn to heading 220 I'm gunna have to spin you sir"

AVA052: "Two twenty"

APP: "Avianca 052 I have wind shear for you ah at 15 a increase of ten knots at 1500 feet and then an increase of ten knots at 500 feet reported by 727"

AVA052: "Thank you very much Avianca 052"

CAP: "What is he saying windshear"

F/O: "He is advising us that a 727 reported a wind shear condition during approach at 500 feet exceeding the speed in ten knots"

15* At 2103 the flightcrew began to discuss the go-around procedure with 1,000 pounds or less of fuel in any tank.

S/O: "When we have—with thousand

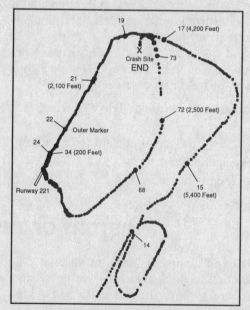

AVA 052 FLIGHT TRACK

* Refer to AVA 052 Flight Track.

pounds or less in any tank it is necessary to do . . . then the go around procedure is stating that the power be applied slowly . . . and to have a minimum of nose up attitude"

CAP: "To maintain what"

S/O: "Minimum minimum nose up attitude that means the less nose up attitude that one can hold"

17* 2109 cockpit conversation

S/O: "They got us they are already vectoring us"

F/O: "They accommodate us ahead of an—"

S/O: "They already know that we are in bad condition"

CAP: "No they are descending us"

F/O: "They are giving us priority"

19* At 2111, the final controller stated "you are one five miles from the outer marker maintain two thousand until established on the localizer cleared ILS two two left."

21* At 2115, the first officer contacted JFK Tower.

Tower: "Avianca 052 heavy Kennedy tower 22 left you're number three following 727 traffic on a ah niner mile final"

CAP: "Can I lower the landing gear yet"

F/O: "No I think it is too early. . ."

Tower: "Avianca 052 can you increase airspeed one zero knots"

AVA052: "Ah say again the speed"

Tower: "Can you increase you speed one zero knots"

AVA052: "Okay one zero knots increasing"

Tower: "Increase increase"

AVA05: "Increasing"

CAP: "What"

S/O: "Ten knots more"

F/O: "Ten little knots more"

CAP: "Tell me things louder because—I'm not hearing it"

The engine igniter sound starts and continues until the end of the tape.

22* At 2119, the captain said "mode selector approach landing checklist" and JFK tower called "Avianca 052 two two left wind one nine zero at two zero cleared to land."

23* At 2121, the first officer said "slightly below glide slope"

24* 2122, F/O: "Below glide slope"

26* F/O: "Glide slope . . . this is the wind shear"

S/O: "Glide slope"

28* thru 31*

GPWS: "Whoop whoop pull up"

S/O: "Sink rate"

S/O: "500 feet"

GPWS: "Whoop whoop pull up" repeated three times

32* Captain calls for "lights"

GPWS: "Whoop whoop pull up" four times

34* At 200 feet

CAP: "Where is the runway"

GPWS "Whoop whoop pull up" three times.

CAP: "The runway where is it"

F/O: "I don't see it I don't see it"

CAP: "Give me the landing gear up"

41* CAP: "Request another traffic pattern"

At 2123, the first officer radioed "executing a missed approach" and the JFK tower controller responded " . . . roger climb and maintain two thousand turn left heading 180."

CAP: "We don't have fue-" . . . "tell them we are in emergency"

AVA052: "That's right to one eight zero on the heading and ah we'll try one again we're running out of fuel"

Tower: "Okay"

CAP: "Advise him we are emergency . . . did you tell him"

F/O: "Yes sir . . . I already advised him"

TOWER: "Avianca 052 heavy contact approach. . ."

AVA052: "Avianca 05 ah 2 heavy we just missed a missed approach and ah we're maintaining two thousand and five oh th-"

APP: "Avianca 052 heavy New York good evening climb and maintain three thousand"

CAP: "Advise him we don't have fuel"

AVA052: "Climb and maintain three thousand and ah we're running out of fuel sir"

APP: "Okay fly heading zero eight zero"

CAP: "Did you already advise that we don't have fuel"

F/O: "Yes sir I already advise him and he's going to get us back"

CAP: "Okay"

APP: "Avianca 052 heavy ah I'm gunna bring you about 15 miles north east and then turn you back onto the approach is that fine with you and your fuel"

AVA052: "I guess so thank you very much"

CAP: "What did he say"

S/O: "The guy is angry"

F/O: "15 miles in order to get back to the localizer"

68* AVA052: "Ah can you give us a final now Avianca 052 heavy"

APP: "Avianca 052 affirmative sir turn left . . . climb and maintain 3,000"

AVA052: "Ah negative sir we just running out of fuel we okay three thousand now okay"

73* CVR momentary interruption

S/O: "Flame out flame out on engine number four"

CAP: "Flame out on it"

S/O: "Flame out on engine number three essential on number two on number one"

CAP: "Show me the runway"

AVA052: "Avianca 052 we just ah lost two engines and ah we need priority please"

APP: "Avianca 052 turn left heading 250 intercept the localizer"

Sound of engine spooling down

APP: "Avianca 052 heavy you're one five miles from the outer marker maintain 2000 . . . cleared for approach"

CAP: "Did you select the ILS"

F/O: "It is ready on two"

End of recording

FINDINGS

The captain possessed a U.S. ATP certificate and 16,787 flight hours, the first officer a U.S. Commercial certificate and 1,837 hours, and the second officer held a Colombian flight engineer certificate and had a total time of 10,134 hours.

All three were fatally injured at impact by blunt-force head and upper torso trauma. The pilots' seats had no shoulder harnesses installed. Toxicological samples were negative, and there was no evidence that any of the three were not rested prior to departure nor evidence of recent unusual stress.

The Avianca dispatcher held a Colombian dispatcher's certificate. Training records showed no instruction in navigation and meteorological information.

The evidence confirmed that this accident occurred when the engines lost power from fuel exhaustion. The investigation found no engine or fuel system malfunctions that could have caused premature fuel exhaustion.

AVA 052 had sufficient fuel to complete the scheduled flight and to meet IFR fuel requirements—e.g., to fly the scheduled route to JFK, execute a missed approach, and fly to Boston, the alternate airport. When AVA 052's flight plan was filed, Boston was forecast to be below IFR alternate minimums and the actual weather deteriorated further while the flight was en route.

The weather data provided to the flightcrew was 9 to 10 hours old and showed the JFK visibility forecast to be near or below that authorized to execute an approach. Avianca indicated that BOS was listed as an alternate because it was part of a computer-generated flight plan for all JFK flights regardless of weather.

Avianca Airlines had a contract with Dispatch Services, located in Miami. The dispatcher on duty stated that he received a telex from Avianca stating AVA 052 departed Medellín, but no departure time was given. He obtained the latest weather and air traffic information for JFK anticipating the flightcrew's contacting him in the vicinity of Miami. He did not receive a call from the flight nor was there any record of communication between other flight services such as VOLMET or EFAS. The NTSB was unable to determine why the flightcrew and the dispatcher did not communicate when they were clearly able to do so.

Weather, Fuel, and Communication Factors

The first indication that the crew had some concerns about the weather and fuel occurred when they requested information about Boston delays from the Washington controller after being in holding about 20 minutes. The NTSB concluded that the flightcrew had already exhausted its reserve fuel to reach its alternate by the time it asked for priority handling. Although the first officer radioed ". . . we'll be able to hold about 5 minutes. . . ," they did not have sufficient fuel to fly to the alternate. The airplane exhausted its fuel supply and crashed 47 minutes after they stated that there was not sufficient fuel to make it to the alternate.

A captain from Avianca testified that the use of the word "priority" rather than "emergency" may have resulted from Avianca training at Boeing. He stated that they received the impression from the training that the words *priority* and *emergency* conveyed the same meaning to ATC. Boeing bulletins stated "during any operations with very low fuel quantity, priority handling from ATC should be requested." However, when asked which phraseology that they would respond to, controllers replied that they would do their utmost to assist a flight that requested "priority" but that the word did not require a specific response.

Aircraft maintenance records indicated recurrent problems with the autopilot, including the altitude hold function. The captain who flew the aircraft just prior to the accident had some problems with the flight director in the approach mode. And the NTSB believed that the aircraft might have been flown manually from Medellín to JFK and that the ILS approach was flown using the raw data without the aid of a flight director. The Safety Board concluded that their inability to maintain a position on the glideslope was attributable to a combination of the windshear, fatigue, and stress concerning the remaining fuel.

The weather and air traffic conditions at JFK during the hours before the accident set the stage for the delays that led to the holding of the flight for more than 1 hour. The FAA Central Flow Control Facility (CFCF) had a program in place beginning at 1400 to prevent problems, but this program failed for several reasons.

The JFK program was implemented based upon forecast weather conditions that should have permitted the continuous use of the ILS approach to runway 22 left, which requires a visibility of ½ mile, and the limited use of 22 right, which requires ¾ of a mile. The visibility was expected to deteriorate to ½ mile. In fact, the visibility was ¼ mile as early as 1600. The investigation also revealed that the National Weather Service did not inform traffic management personnel of severe wind conditions that affected the controller's ability to provide appropriate separation. These winds and the deteriorating weather caused the missed approaches, compromising the CFCF program.

When CFCF implemented a ground stop for JFK traffic, the action was not sufficient or timely enough to abate the airborne holding that had already begun. Most long-distance traffic was already airborne; therefore, a ground stop was not effective for these flights. The NTSB believed that the forecast weather was inaccurate and that the CFCF personnel were neither accurate nor timely for JFK traffic.

SUMMARY

The NTSB believed that the two key factors leading to this accident were the crew's failure to notify ATC of their fuel situation and a breakdown in communications between the flightcrew and ATC and among themselves. Much of their failure to communicate effectively resulted from their inability to use the English language and their knowledge of ATC terminology. They did not communicate effectively among themselves in addressing the operational problems they encountered. Specifically, the captain did not make use of dispatch and other resources available to him, nor did the first officer and engineer provide the kind of active team support that was needed under the circumstances.

This Glossary includes those terms that are intended for pilot/controller communications. Those terms most frequently used in pilot/controller communications are printed in ***bold italics.*** The definitions are primarily defined in an operational sense applicable to both users and operators of the National Airspace System.

Because of the international nature of flying, terms used in the "Lexicon," published by the International Civil Aviation Organization (ICAO), are included when they differ from FAA definitions.

NOTE: The abbreviation FAR in the Glossary refers to the Federal Aviation Regulations.

AAI—(See ARRIVAL AIRCRAFT INTERVAL).

AAR—(See AIRPORT ACCEPTANCE RATE).

ABBREVIATED IFR FLIGHT PLANS—An authorization by ATC requiring pilots to submit only that information needed for the purpose of ATC. It includes only a small portion of the usual IFR flight plan information. In certain instances, this may be only aircraft identification, location, and pilot request. Other information may be requested if needed by ATC for separation/control purposes. It is frequently used by aircraft which are airborne and desire an instrument approach or by aircraft which are on the ground and desire a climb to VFR-ON-TOP).

(See VFR-ON-TOP).

ABEAM—An aircraft is "abeam" a fix, point, or object when that fix, point, or object is approximately 90 degrees to the right or left of the aircraft track. Abeam indicates a general position rather than a precise point.

ABORT—To terminate a preplanned aircraft maneuver; e.g., an aborted takeoff.

ACC [ICAO]—(See AREA CONTROL CENTER).

ACCELERATE-STOP DISTANCE AVAILABLE—The runway plus stopway length declared available and suitable for the acceleration and deceleration of an airplane aborting a takeoff.

ACCELERATE-STOP DISTANCE AVAILABLE [ICAO]—The length of the take-off run available plus the length of the stopway if provided.

ACDO—(See AIR CARRIER DISTRICT OFFICE).

ACKNOWLEDGE—Let me know that you have received my message.

(See ICAO term ACKNOWLEDGE).

ACKNOWLEDGE [ICAO]—Let me know that you have received and understood this message.

ACLS—(See AUTOMATIC CARRIER LANDING SYSTEM).

ACLT—(See ACTUAL CALCULATED LANDING TIME).

ACROBATIC FLIGHT—An intentional maneuver involving an abrupt change in an aircraft's attitude, an abnormal attitude, or abnormal acceleration not necessary for normal flight.

(See ICAO term ACROBATIC FLIGHT).

ACROBATIC FLIGHT [ICAO]—Maneuvers intentionally performed by an aircraft involving an abrupt change in its attitude, an abnormal attitude, or an abnormal variation in speed.

ACTIVE RUNWAY—(See RUNWAY IN USE/ACTIVE RUNWAY/DUTY RUNWAY).

ACTUAL CALCULATED LANDING TIME—ACLT is a flight's frozen calculated landing time. An actual time determined at freeze calculated landing time (FCLT) or meter list display interval (MLDI) for the adapted vertex for each arrival aircraft based upon runway configuration, airport acceptance rate, airport arrival delay period, and other metered arrival aircraft. This time is either the vertex time of arrival (VTA) of the aircraft or the tentative calculated landing time (TCLT)/ACLT of the previous aircraft plus the arrival aircraft interval (AAI), whichever is later. This time will not be updated in response to the aircraft's progress.

ADDITIONAL SERVICES—Advisory information provided by ATC which includes but is not limited to the following:

1. Traffic advisories.
2. Vectors, when requested by the pilot, to assist aircraft receiving traffic advisories to avoid observed traffic.

3. Altitude deviation information of 300 feet or more from an assigned altitude as observed on a verified (reading correctly) automatic altitude readout (Mode C).

4. Advisories that traffic is no longer a factor.

5. Weather and chaff information.

6. Weather assistance.

7. Bird activity information.

8. Holding pattern surveillance. Additional services are provided to the extent possible contingent only upon the controller's capability to fit them into the performance of higher priority duties and on the basis of limitations of the radar, volume of traffic, frequency congestion, and controller workload. The controller has complete discretion for determining if he is able to provide or continue to provide a service in a particular case. The controller's reason not to provide or continue to provide a service in a particular case is not subject to question by the pilot and need not be made known to him.

(See TRAFFIC ADVISORIES).

ADF—(See AUTOMATIC DIRECTION FINDER).

ADIZ—(See AIR DEFENSE IDENTIFICATION ZONE).

ADLY—(See ARRIVAL DELAY).

ADMINISTRATOR—The Federal Aviation Administrator or any person to whom he has delegated his authority in the matter concerned.

ADVISE INTENTIONS—Tell me what you plan to do.

ADVISORY—Advice and information provided to assist pilots in the safe conduct of flight and aircraft movement.

(See ADVISORY SERVICE).

ADVISORY FREQUENCY—The appropriate frequency to be used for Airport Advisory Service.

(See LOCAL AIRPORT ADVISORY). (See UNICOM).

ADVISORY SERVICE—Advice and information provided by a facility to assist pilots in the safe conduct of flight and aircraft movement.

(See LOCAL AIRPORT ADVISORY). (See TRAFFIC ADVISORIES). (See SAFETY ALERT). (See ADDITIONAL SERVICES). (See RADAR ADVISORY). (See EN ROUTE FLIGHT ADVISORY SERVICE).

AERIAL REFUELING—A procedure used by the military to transfer fuel from one aircraft to another during flight.

AERODROME—A defined area on land or water (including any buildings, installations and equipment) intended to be used either wholly or in part for the arrival, departure, and movement of aircraft.

AERODROME BEACON [ICAO]—Aeronautical beacon used to indicate the location of an aerodrome from the air.

AERODROME CONTROL SERVICE [ICAO]—Air traffic control service for aerodrome traffic.

AERODROME CONTROL TOWER [ICAO]—A unit established to provide air traffic control service to aerodrome traffic.

AERODROME ELEVATION [ICAO]—The elevation of the highest point of the landing area.

AERODROME TRAFFIC CIRCUIT [ICAO]—The specified path to be flown by aircraft operating in the vicinity of an aerodrome.

AERONAUTICAL BEACON—A visual NAVAID displaying flashes of white and/or colored light to indicate the location of an airport, a heliport, a landmark, a certain point of a Federal airway in mountainous terrain, or an obstruction.

(See AIRPORT ROTATING BEACON).

AERONAUTICAL CHART—A map used in air navigation containing all or part of the following: Topographic features, hazards and obstructions, navigation aids, navigation routes, designated airspace, and airports. Commonly used aeronautical charts are:

1. Sectional Aeronautical Charts (1:500,000). Designed for visual navigation of slow or medium speed aircraft. Topographic information on these charts features the portrayal of relief and a judicious selection of visual check points for VFR flight. Aeronautical information includes visual and radio aids to navigation, airports, controlled airspace, restricted areas, obstructions, and related data.

2. VFR Terminal Area Charts (1:250,000). Depict Class B airspace which provides for the control or segregation of all the aircraft within Class B airspace. The chart depicts topographic information and aeronautical information which includes visual and radio aids to navigation, airports, controlled airspace, restricted areas, obstructions, and related data.

3. World Aeronautical Charts (WAC) (1:1,000,000). Provide a standard series of aeronautical charts covering land areas of the world at a size and scale convenient for navigation by moderate speed aircraft. Topographic information includes cities and towns, principal roads, railroads, distinctive landmarks, drainage, and relief. Aeronautical information includes visual and radio aids to navigation, airports, airways, restricted areas, obstructions, and other pertinent data.

4. En Route Low Altitude Charts. Provide aeronautical information for en route instrument navigation (IFR) in the low al-

titude stratum. Information includes the portrayal of airways, limits of controlled airspace, position identification and frequencies of radio aids, selected airports, minimum en route and minimum obstruction clearance altitudes, airway distances, reporting points, restricted areas, and related data. Area charts, which are a part of this series, furnish terminal data at a larger scale in congested areas.

5. En Route High Altitude Charts. Provide aeronautical information for en route instrument navigation (IFR) in the high altitude stratum. Information includes the portrayal of jet routes, identification and frequencies of radio aids, selected airports, distances, time zones, special use airspace, and related information.

6. Instrument Approach Procedures (IAP) Charts. Portray the aeronautical data which is required to execute an instrument approach to an airport. These charts depict the procedures, including all related data, and the airport diagram. Each procedure is designated for use with a specific type of electronic navigation system including NDB, TACAN, VOR, ILS/MLS, and RNAV. These charts are identified by the type of navigational aid(s) which provide final approach guidance.

7. Standard Instrument Departure (SID) Charts. Designed to expedite clearance delivery and to facilitate transition between takeoff and en route operations. Each SID procedure is presented as a separate chart and may serve a single airport or more than one airport in a given geographical location.

8. Standard Terminal Arrival (STAR) Charts. Designed to expedite air traffic control arrival procedures and to facilitate transition between en route and instrument approach operations. Each STAR procedure is presented as a separate chart and may serve a single airport or more than one airport in a given geographical location.

9. Airport Taxi Charts. Designed to expedite the efficient and safe flow of ground traffic at an airport. These charts are identified by the official airport name; e.g., Washington National Airport.

(See ICAO term AERONAUTICAL CHART).

AERONAUTICAL CHART [ICAO]—A representation of a portion of the earth, its culture and relief, specifically designated to meet the requirements of air navigation.

AERONAUTICAL INFORMATION PUBLICATION [AIP] [ICAO]—A publication issued by or with the authority of a State and containing aeronautical information of a lasting character essential to air navigation.

A/FD—(See AIRPORT/FACILITY DIRECTORY).

***AFFIRMATIVE*—Yes.**

AIM—(See AIRMAN'S INFORMATION MANUAL).

AIP [ICAO]—(See AERONAUTICAL INFORMATION PUBLICATION).

AIRBORNE DELAY—Amount of delay to be encountered in airborne holding.

AIR CARRIER DISTRICT OFFICE—An FAA field office serving an assigned geographical area, staffed with Flight Standards personnel serving the aviation industry and the general public on matters related to the certification and operation of scheduled air carriers and other large aircraft operations.

AIRCRAFT—Device(s) that are used or intended to be used for flight in the air, and when used in air traffic control terminology, may include the flight crew.
(See ICAO term AIRCRAFT).

AIRCRAFT [ICAO]—Any machine that can derive support in the atmosphere from the reactions of the air other than the reactions of the air against the earth's surface.

AIRCRAFT APPROACH CATEGORY—A grouping of aircraft based on a speed of 1.3 times the stall speed in the landing configuration at maximum gross landing weight. An aircraft shall fit in only one category. If it is necessary to maneuver at speeds in excess of the upper limit of a speed range for a category, the minimums for the next higher category should be used. For example, an aircraft which falls in Category A, but is circling to land at a speed in excess of 91 knots, should use the approach Category B minimums when circling to land. The categories are as follows:

1. Category A. Speed less than 91 knots.
2. Category B. Speed 91 knots or more but less than 121 knots.
3. Category C. Speed 121 knots or more but less than 141 knots.
4. Category D. Speed 141 knots or more but less than 166 knots.
5. Category E. Speed 166 knots or more.

AIRCRAFT CLASSES—For the purposes of Wake Turbulence Separation Minima, ATC classifies aircraft as Heavy, Large, and Small as follows:

1. Heavy. Aircraft capable of takeoff weights of 300,000 pounds or more whether or not they are operating at this weight during a particular phase of flight.
2. Large. Aircraft of more than 12,500 pounds, maximum certificated takeoff weight, up to 300,000 pounds.
3. Small. Aircraft of 12,500 pounds or less maximum certificated takeoff weight.

AIRCRAFT SITUATION DISPLAY—ASD is a computer system that receives radar track data from all 20 CONUS ARTCC's, organizes this data into a mosaic display, and presents it on a computer screen. The display allows the traffic management coordinator multiple methods of selection and high-lighting of individual aircraft or groups of aircraft. The user has the option of superimposing these aircraft positions over any number of background displays. These background options include ARTCC boundaries, any stratum of en route sector boundaries, fixes, airways, military and other special use airspace, airports, and geopolitical boundaries. By using the ASD, a coordinator can monitor any number of traffic situations or the entire systemwide traffic flows.

AIRCRAFT SURGE LAUNCH AND RECOVERY—Procedures used at USAF bases to provide increased launch and recovery rates in instrument flight rules conditions. ASLAR is based on:

1. Reduced separation between aircraft which is based on time or distance. Standard arrival separation applies between participants including multiple flights until the DRAG point. The DRAG point is a published location on an ASLAR approach where aircraft landing second in a formation slows to a predetermined airspeed. The DRAG point is the reference point at which MARSA applies as expanding elements effect separation within a flight or between subsequent participating flights.

2. ASLAR procedures shall be covered in a Letter of Agreement between the responsible USAF military ATC facility and the concerned Federal Aviation Administration facility. Initial Approach Fix spacing requirements are normally addressed as a minimum.

AIR DEFENSE EMERGENCY—A military emergency condition declared by a designated authority. This condition exists when an attack upon the continental U.S., Alaska, Canada, or U.S. installations in Greenland by hostile aircraft or missiles is considered probable, is imminent, or is taking place.

AIR DEFENSE IDENTIFICATION ZONE—The area of airspace over land or water, extending upward from the surface, within which the ready identification, the location, and the control of aircraft are required in the interest of national security.

1. Domestic Air Defense Identification Zone. An ADIZ within the United States along an international boundary of the United States.

2. Coastal Air Defense Identification Zone. An ADIZ over the coastal waters of the United States.

3. Distant Early Warning Identification Zone (DEWIZ). An ADIZ over the coastal waters of the State of Alaska.

AIRMAN'S INFORMATION MANUAL—A primary FAA publication whose purpose is to instruct airmen about operating in the National Airspace System of the U.S. It provides basic flight information, ATC Procedures and general instructional information concerning health, medical facts, factors affecting flight safety, accident and hazard reporting, and types of aeronautical charts and their use.

AIRMAN'S METEOROLOGICAL INFORMATION—(See AIRMET).

AIRMET—In-flight weather advisories issued only to amend the area forecast concerning weather phenomena which are of operational interest to all aircraft and potentially hazardous to aircraft having limited capability because of lack of equipment, instrumentation, or pilot qualifications. AIRMET's concern weather of less severity than that covered by SIGMET's or Convective SIGMET's. AIRMET's cover moderate icing, moderate turbulence, sustained winds of 30 knots or more at the surface, widespread areas of ceilings less than 1,000 feet and/or visibility less than 3 miles, and extensive mountain obscurement.
(See AWW). (See SIGMET). (See CONVECTIVE SIGMET). (See CWA).

AIR NAVIGATION FACILITY—Any facility used in, available for use in, or designed for use in, aid of air navigation, including landing areas, lights, any apparatus or equipment for disseminating weather information, for signaling, for radio-directional finding, or for radio or other electrical communication, and any other structure or mechanism having a similar purpose for guiding or controlling flight in the air or the landing and take-off of aircraft.
(See NAVIGATIONAL AID).

AIRPORT—An area on land or water that is used or intended to be used for the landing and takeoff of aircraft and includes its buildings and facilities, if any.

AIRPORT ACCEPTANCE RATE—A dynamic input parameter specifying the number of arriving aircraft which an airport or airspace can accept from the ARTCC per hour. The AAR is used to calculate the desired interval between successive arrival aircraft.

AIRPORT ADVISORY AREA—The area within ten miles of an airport without a control tower or where the tower is not in operation, and on which a Flight Service Station is located.
(See LOCAL AIRPORT ADVISORY).

AIRPORT ELEVATION—The highest point of an airport's usable runways measured in feet from mean sea level.
(See TOUCHDOWN ZONE ELEVATION). (See ICAO term AERODROME ELEVATION).

AIRPORT/FACILITY DIRECTORY—A publication designed primarily as a pilot's operational manual containing all airports, seaplane bases, and heliports open to the public including communications data, navigational facilities, and certain special notices and procedures. This publication is issued in seven volumes according to geographical area.

AIRPORT INFORMATION AID—(See AIRPORT INFORMATION DESK).

AIRPORT INFORMATION DESK—An airport unmanned facility designed for pilot self-serving briefing, flight planning, and filing of flight plans.

AIRPORT LIGHTING—Various lighting aids that may be installed on an airport. Types of airport lighting include:

1. Approach Light System (ALS). An airport lighting facility which provides visual guidance to landing aircraft by radiating light beams in a directional pattern by which the pilot aligns the aircraft with the extended centerline of the runway on his final approach for landing. Condenser-Discharge Sequential Flashing Lights/Sequenced Flashing Lights may be installed in conjunction with the ALS at some airports. Types of Approach Light Systems are:

   a. ALSF–1.—Approach Light System with Sequenced Flashing Lights in ILS Cat-I configuration.

   b. ALSF–2.—Approach Light System with Sequenced Flashing Lights in ILS Cat-II configuration. The ALSF–2 may operate as an SSALR when weather conditions permit.

   c. SSALF.—Simplified Short Approach Light System with Sequenced Flashing Lights.

   d. SSALR.—Simplified Short Approach Light System with Runway Alignment Indicator Lights.

   e. MALSF.—Medium Intensity Approach Light System with Sequenced Flashing Lights.

   f. MALSR.—Medium Intensity Approach Light System with Runway Alignment Indicator Lights.

   g. LDIN.—Lead-in-light system: Consists of one or more series of flashing lights installed at or near ground level that provides positive visual guidance along an approach path, either curving or straight, where special problems exist with hazardous terrain, obstructions, or noise abatement procedures.

   h. RAIL.—Runway Alignment Indicator Lights (Sequenced Flashing Lights which are installed only in combination with other light systems).

   i. ODALS.—Omnidirectional Approach Lighting System consists of seven omnidirectional flashing lights located in the approach area of a nonprecision runway. Five lights are located on the runway centerline extended with the first light located 300 feet from the threshold and extending at equal intervals up to 1,500 feet from the threshold. The other two lights are located, one on each side of the runway threshold, at a lateral distance of 40 feet from the runway edge, or 75 feet from the runway edge when installed on a runway equipped with a VASI.

2. Runway Lights/Runway Edge Lights. Lights having a prescribed angle of emission used to define the lateral limits of a runway. Runway lights are uniformly spaced at intervals of approximately 200 feet, and the intensity may be controlled or preset.

3. Touchdown Zone Lighting. Two rows of transverse light bars located symmetrically about the runway centerline normally at 100 foot intervals. The basic system extends 3,000 feet along the runway.

4. Runway Centerline Lighting. Flush centerline lights spaced at 50–foot intervals beginning 75 feet from the landing threshold and extending to within 75 feet of the opposite end of the runway.

5. Threshold Lights. Fixed green lights arranged symmetrically left and right of the runway centerline, identifying the runway threshold.

6. Runway End Identifier Lights (REIL). Two synchronized flashing lights, one on each side of the runway threshold, which provide rapid and positive identification of the approach end of a particular runway.

7. Visual Approach Slope Indicator (VASI). An airport lighting facility providing vertical visual approach slope guidance to aircraft during approach to landing by radiating a directional pattern of high intensity red and white focused light beams which indicate to the pilot that he is "on path" if he sees red/white, "above path" if white/white, and "below path" if red/red. Some airports serving large aircraft have three-bar VASIs which provide two visual glide paths to the same runway.

8. Boundary Lights. Lights defining the perimeter of an airport or landing area.

AIRPORT MARKING AIDS—Markings used on runway and taxiway surfaces to identify a specific runway, a runway threshold, a centerline, a hold line, etc. A runway should be marked in accordance with its present usage such as:

1. Visual.

2. Nonprecision instrument.

3. Precision instrument.

AIRPORT RESERVATION OFFICE—Office responsible for monitoring the operation of the high-density rule. Receives and processes requests for IFR operations at high density traffic airports.

AIRPORT ROTATING BEACON—A visual NAVAID operated at many airports. At civil airports, alternating white and green flashes indicate the location of the airport. At military airports, the beacons flash alternately white and green, but are differentiated from civil beacons by dualpeaked (two quick) white flashes between the green flashes.

(See SPECIAL VFR OPERATIONS). (See INSTRUMENT FLIGHT RULES). (See ICAO term AERODROME BEACON).

AIRPORT SURFACE DETECTION EQUIPMENT—Radar equipment specifically designed to detect all principal features on the surface of an airport, including aircraft and vehicular traffic, and to present the entire image on a radar indicator console in the control tower. Used to augment visual observation by tower personnel of aircraft and/or vehicular movements on runways and taxiways.

AIRPORT SURVEILLANCE RADAR—Approach control radar used to detect and display an aircraft's position in the terminal area. ASR provides range and azimuth information but does not provide elevation data. Coverage of the ASR can extend up to 60 miles.

AIRPORT TAXI CHARTS—(See AERONAUTICAL CHART).

AIRPORT TRAFFIC CONTROL SERVICE—A service provided by a control tower for aircraft operating on the movement area and in the vicinity of an airport.

(See MOVEMENT AREA). (See TOWER). (See ICAO term AERODROME CONTROL SERVICE).

AIRPORT TRAFFIC CONTROL TOWER—(See TOWER).

AIR ROUTE SURVEILLANCE RADAR—Air route traffic control center (ARTCC) radar used primarily to detect and display an aircraft's position while en route between terminal areas. The ARSR enables controllers to provide radar air traffic control service when aircraft are within the ARSR coverage. In some instances, ARSR may enable an ARTCC to provide terminal radar services similar to but usually more limited than those provided by a radar approach control.

AIR ROUTE TRAFFIC CONTROL CENTER—A facility established to provide air traffic control service to aircraft operating on IFR flight plans within controlled airspace and principally during the en route phase of flight. When equipment capabilities and controller workload permit, certain advisory/assistance services may be provided to VFR aircraft.

(See NAS STAGE A). (See EN ROUTE AIR TRAFFIC CONTROL SERVICES).

AIRSPACE HIERARCHY—Within the airspace classes, there is a hierarchy and, in the event of an overlap of airspace: Class A preempts Class B, Class B preempts Class C, Class C preempts Class D, Class D preempts Class E, and Class E preempts Class G.

AIRSPEED—The speed of an aircraft relative to its surrounding air mass. The unqualified term "airspeed" means one of the following:

1. Indicated Airspeed. The speed shown on the aircraft airspeed indicator. This is the speed used in pilot/controller communications under the general term "airspeed."
2. True Airspeed. The airspeed of an aircraft relative to undisturbed air. Used primarily in flight planning and en route portion of flight. When used in pilot/controller communications, it is referred to as "true airspeed" and not shortened to "airspeed."

AIRSTART—The starting of an aircraft engine while the aircraft is airborne, preceded by engine shutdown during training flights or by actual engine failure.

AIR TAXI—Used to describe a helicopter/VTOL aircraft movement conducted above the surface but normally not above 100 feet AGL. The aircraft may proceed either via hover taxi or flight at speeds more than 20 knots. The pilot is solely responsible for selecting a safe airspeed/altitude for the operation being conducted.

(See HOVER TAXI).

AIR TRAFFIC—Aircraft operating in the air or on an airport surface, exclusive of loading ramps and parking areas.

(See ICAO term AIR TRAFFIC).

AIR TRAFFIC [ICAO]—All aircraft in flight or operating on the manoeuvreing area of an aerodrome.

AIR TRAFFIC CLEARANCE—An authorization by air traffic control, for the purpose of preventing collision between known aircraft, for an aircraft to proceed under specified traffic conditions within controlled airspace. The pilot-in-command of an aircraft may not deviate from the provisions of a visual flight rules (VFR) or instrument flight rules (IFR) air traffic clearance unless an amended clearance has been obtained. Additionally, the pilot may request a different clearance from that which has been issued by air traffic control (ATC) if information available to the pilot makes another course of action more practicable or if aircraft equipment limitations or company procedures forbid compliance with the clearance issued. Pilots may also request clarification or amendment, as appropriate, any time a clearance is not fully understood, or considered unacceptable because of safety of flight. Controllers

should, in such instances and to the extent of operational practicality and safety, honor the pilot's request. FAR 91.3(a) states: "The pilot-in-command of an aircraft is directly responsible for, and is the final authority as to, the operation of that aircraft." THE PILOT IS RESPONSIBLE TO REQUEST AN AMENDED CLEARANCE if ATC issues a clearance that would cause a pilot to deviate from a rule or regulation, or in the pilot's opinion, would place the aircraft in jeopardy.
(See ATC INSTRUCTIONS). (See ICAO term AIR TRAFFIC CONTROL CLEARANCE).

AIR TRAFFIC CONTROL—A service operated by appropriate authority to promote the safe, orderly and expeditious flow of air traffic.
(See ICAO term AIR TRAFFIC CONTROL SERVICE).

AIR TRAFFIC CONTROL CLEARANCE [ICAO]—Authorization for an aircraft to proceed under conditions specified by an air traffic control unit.

Note 1: For convenience, the term air traffic control clearance is frequently abbreviated to clearance when used in appropriate contexts.

Note 2: The abbreviated term clearance may be prefixed by the words taxi, takeoff, departure, en route, approach or landing to indicate the particular portion of flight to which the air traffic control clearance relates.

AIR TRAFFIC CONTROL SERVICE—(See AIR TRAFFIC CONTROL).

AIR TRAFFIC CONTROL SERVICE [ICAO]—A service provided for the purpose of:

1. Preventing collisions:
   a. Between aircraft; and
   b. On the maneuvering area between aircraft and obstructions; and
2. Expediting and maintaining an orderly flow of air traffic.

AIR TRAFFIC CONTROL SPECIALIST—A person authorized to provide air traffic control service.
(See AIR TRAFFIC CONTROL). (See FLIGHT SERVICE STATION). (See ICAO term CONTROLLER).

AIR TRAFFIC CONTROL SYSTEM COMMAND CENTER—An Air Traffic Operations Service facility consisting of four operational units.

1. Central Flow Control Function (CFCF). Responsible for coordination and approval of all major intercenter flow control restrictions on a system basis in order to obtain maximum utilization of the airspace.
(See QUOTA FLOW CONTROL).
2. Central Altitude Reservation Function (CARF). Responsible for coordinating, planning, and approving special user requirements under the Altitude Reservation (ALTRV) concept.

(See ALTITUDE RESERVATION).
3. Airport Reservation Office (ARO). Responsible for approving IFR flights at designated high density traffic airports (John F. Kennedy, LaGuardia, O'Hare, and Washington National) during specified hours.
4. ATC Contingency Command Post. A facility which enables the FAA to manage the ATC system when significant portions of the system's capabilities have been lost or are threatened.

AIR TRAFFIC SERVICE—A generic term meaning:

1. Flight Information Service:
2. Alerting Service:
3. Air Traffic Advisory Service:
4. Air Traffic Control Service:
   a. Area Control Service,
   b. Approach Control Service, or
   c. Airport Control Service.

AIRWAY—A Class E airspace area established in the form of a corridor, the centerline of which is defined by radio navigational aids.
(See FEDERAL AIRWAYS). (See ICAO term AIRWAY).

AIRWAY [ICAO]—A control area or portion thereof established in the form of corridor equipped with radio navigational aids.

AIRWAY BEACON—Used to mark airway segments in remote mountain areas. The light flashes Morse Code to identify the beacon site.

AIT—(See AUTOMATED INFORMATION TRANSFER).

ALERFA (Alert Phase) [ICAO]—A situation wherein apprehension exists as to the safety of an aircraft and its occupants.

ALERT AREA—(See SPECIAL USE AIRSPACE).

ALERT NOTICE—A request originated by a flight service station (FSS) or an air route traffic control center (ARTCC) for an extensive communication search for overdue, unreported, or missing aircraft.

ALERTING SERVICE—A service provided to notify appropriate organizations regarding aircraft in need of search and rescue aid and assist such organizations as required.

ALNOT—(See ALERT NOTICE).

ALPHANUMERIC DISPLAY—Letters and numerals used to show identification, altitude, beacon code, and other information concerning a target on a radar display.
(See AUTOMATED RADAR TERMINAL SYSTEMS). (See NAS STAGE A).

ALTERNATE AERODROME [ICAO]—An aerodrome to which an aircraft may proceed when it becomes either impossible or inadvisable to proceed to or to land at the aerodrome of intended landing.

Note: The aerodrome from which a flight departs may also be an en-route or a destination alternate aerodrome for the flight.

ALTERNATE AIRPORT—An airport at which an aircraft may land if a landing at the intended airport becomes inadvisable.

(See FAA term ICAO term ALTERNATE AERODROME).

ALTIMETER SETTING—The barometric pressure reading used to adjust a pressure altimeter for variations in existing atmospheric pressure or to the standard altimeter setting (29.92).

ALTITUDE—The height of a level, point, or object measured in feet Above Ground Level (AGL) or from Mean Sea Level (MSL).

(See FLIGHT LEVEL).

1. MSL Altitude. Altitude expressed in feet measured from mean sea level.

2. AGL Altitude. Altitude expressed in feet measured above ground level.

3. Indicated Altitude. The altitude as shown by an altimeter. On a pressure or barometric altimeter it is altitude as shown uncorrected for instrument error and uncompensated for variation from standard atmospheric conditions.

(See ICAO term ALTITUDE).

ALTITUDE [ICAO]—The vertical distance of a level, a point or an object considered as a point, measured from mean sea level (MSL).

ALTITUDE READOUT—An aircraft's altitude, transmitted via the Mode C transponder feature, that is visually displayed in 100–foot increments on a radar scope having readout capability.

(See AUTOMATED RADAR TERMINAL SYSTEMS). (See NAS STAGE A). (See ALPHANUMERIC DISPLAY).

ALTITUDE RESERVATION—Airspace utilization under prescribed conditions normally employed for the mass movement of aircraft or other special user requirements which cannot otherwise be accomplished. ALTRVs are approved by the appropriate FAA facility.

(See AIR TRAFFIC CONTROL SYSTEM COMMAND CENTER).

ALTITUDE RESTRICTION—An altitude or altitudes, stated in the order flown, which are to be maintained until reaching a specific point or time. Altitude restrictions may be issued by ATC due to traffic, terrain, or other airspace considerations.

ALTITUDE RESTRICTIONS ARE CANCELLED—Adherence to previously imposed altitude restrictions is no longer required during a climb or descent.

ALTRV—(See ALTITUDE RESERVATION).

AMVER—(See AUTOMATED MUTUAL–ASSISTANCE VESSEL RESCUE SYSTEM).

APPROACH CLEARANCE—Authorization by ATC for a pilot to conduct an instrument approach. The type of instrument approach for which a clearance and other pertinent information is provided in the approach clearance when required.

(See INSTRUMENT APPROACH PROCEDURE). (See CLEARED APPROACH).

APPROACH CONTROL FACILITY—A terminal ATC facility that provides approach control service in a terminal area.

(See APPROACH CONTROL SERVICE). (See RADAR APPROACH CONTROL FACILITY).

APPROACH CONTROL SERVICE—Air traffic control service provided by an approach control facility for arriving and departing VFR/IFR aircraft and, on occasion, en route aircraft. At some airports not served by an approach control facility, the ARTCC provides limited approach control service.

(See ICAO term APPROACH CONTROL SERVICE).

APPROACH CONTROL SERVICE [ICAO]—Air traffic control service for arriving or departing controlled flights.

APPROACH GATE—An imaginary point used within ATC as a basis for vectoring aircraft to the final approach course. The gate will be established along the final approach course 1 mile from the outer marker (or the fix used in lieu of the outer marker) on the side away from the airport for precision approaches and 1 mile from the final approach fix on the side away from the airport for nonprecision approaches. In either case when measured along the final approach course, the gate will be no closer than 5 miles from the landing threshold.

APPROACH LIGHT SYSTEM—(See AIRPORT LIGHTING).

APPROACH SEQUENCE—The order in which aircraft are positioned while on approach or awaiting approach clearance.

(See LANDING SEQUENCE). (See ICAO term APPROACH SEQUENCE).

APPROACH SEQUENCE [ICAO]—The order in which two or more aircraft are cleared to approach to land at the aerodrome.

APPROACH SPEED—The recommended speed contained in aircraft manuals used by pilots when making an approach to landing. This speed will vary for different segments of an approach as well as the aircraft weight and configuration.

APPROPRIATE ATS AUTHORITY [ICAO]—The relevant authority designated by the State responsible for providing air traffic services in the airspace concerned. In the United States, the "appropriate ATS authority" is the Director,

Office of Air Traffic System Management, ATM–1.

APPROPRIATE AUTHORITY—

1. Regarding flight over the high seas: the relevant authority is the State of Registry.
2. Regarding flight over other than the high seas: the relevant authority is the State having sovereignty over the territory being overflown.

APPROPRIATE OBSTACLE CLEARANCE MINIMUM ALTITUDE—Any of the following: *(See Minimum IFR Altitude MIA). (See Minimum En Route Altitude MEA). (See Minimum Obstruction Clearance Altitude MOCA). (See Minimum Vectoring Altitude MVA).*

APRON—A defined area on an airport or heliport intended to accommodate aircraft for purposes of loading or unloading passengers or cargo, refueling, parking, or maintenance. With regard to seaplanes, a ramp is used for access to the apron from the water. *(See ICAO term APRON).*

APRON [ICAO]—A defined area, on a land aerodrome, intended to accommodate aircraft for purposes of loading or unloading passengers, mail or cargo, refueling, parking or maintenance.

ARC—The track over the ground of an aircraft flying at a constant distance from a navigational aid by reference to distance measuring equipment (DME).

AREA CONTROL CENTER [ICAO]—An ICAO term for an air traffic control facility primarily responsible for ATC services being provided IFR aircraft during the en route phase of flight. The U.S. equivalent facility is an air route traffic control center (ARTCC).

AREA NAVIGATION—A method of navigation that permits aircraft operation on any desired course within the coverage of station-referenced navigation signals or within the limits of a self-contained system capability. Random area navigation routes are direct routes, based on area navigation capability, between waypoints defined in terms of latitude/longitude coordinates, degree/distance fixes, or offsets from published or established routes/airways at a specified distance and direction. The major types of equipment are:

1. VORTAC referenced or Course Line Computer (CLC) systems, which account for the greatest number of RNAV units in use. To function, the CLC must be within the service range of a VORTAC.
2. OMEGA/VLF, although two separate systems, can be considered as one operationally. A long-range navigation system based upon Very Low Frequency radio signals transmitted from a total of 17 stations worldwide.
3. Inertial (INS) systems, which are totally self-contained and require no information from external references. They provide aircraft position and navigation information in response to signals resulting from inertial effects on components within the system.
4. MLS Area Navigation (MLS/RNAV), which provides area navigation with reference to an MLS ground facility.
5. LORAN-C is a long-range radio navigation system that uses ground waves transmitted at low frequency to provide user position information at ranges of up to 600 to 1,200 nautical miles at both en route and approach altitudes. The usable signal coverage areas are determined by the signal-to-noise ratio, the envelope-to-cycle difference, and the geometric relationship between the positions of the user and the transmitting stations.

(See ICAO term AREA NAVIGATION).

AREA NAVIGATION [ICAO]—A method of navigation which permits aircraft operation on any desired flight path within the coverage of station-referenced navigation aids or within the limits of the capability of self-contained aids, or a combination of these.

ARINC—An acronym for Aeronautical Radio, Inc., a corporation largely owned by a group of airlines. ARINC is licensed by the FCC as an aeronautical station and contracted by the FAA to provide communications support for air traffic control and meteorological services in portions of international airspace.

ARMY AVIATION FLIGHT INFORMATION BULLETIN—A bulletin that provides air operation data covering Army, National Guard, and Army Reserve aviation activities.

ARO—(See AIRPORT RESERVATION OFFICE).

ARRESTING SYSTEM—A system device consisting of two major components, namely, engaging or catching devices and energy absorption devices for the purpose of arresting both tailhook and/or nontailhook-equipped runways when the aircraft cannot be stopped after landing or during aborted takeoff. Arresting systems have various names; e.g., arresting gear, hook device, wire barrier cable. *(See ABORT).*

ARRIVAL AIRCRAFT INTERVAL—An internally generated program in hundredths of minutes based upon the AAR. AAI is the desired optimum interval between successive arrival aircraft over the vertex.

ARRIVAL CENTER—The ARTCC having jurisdiction for the impacted airport.

ARRIVAL DELAY—A parameter which specifies a period of time in which no aircraft will be metered for arrival at the specified airport.

ARRIVAL SECTOR—An operational control sector containing one or more meter fixes.

ARRIVAL SECTOR ADVISORY LIST—An ordered list of data on arrivals displayed at the PVD of the sector which controls the meter fix.

ARRIVAL SEQUENCING PROGRAM—The automated program designed to assist in sequencing aircraft destined for the same airport.

ARRIVAL TIME—The time an aircraft touches down on arrival.

ARSR—(See AIR ROUTE SURVEILLANCE RADAR).

ARTCC—(See AIR ROUTE TRAFFIC CONTROL CENTER).

ARTS—(See AUTOMATED RADAR TERMINAL SYSTEMS).

ASD—(See AIRCRAFT SITUATION DISPLAY).

ASDA—(See ACCELERATE–STOP DISTANCE AVAILABLE).

ASDA [ICAO]—(See ICAO Term ACCELERATE–STOP DISTANCE AVAILABLE).

ASDE—(See AIRPORT SURFACE DETECTION EQUIPMENT).

ASLAR—(See AIRCRAFT SURGE LAUNCH AND RECOVERY).

ASP—(See ARRIVAL SEQUENCING PROGRAM).

ASR—(See AIRPORT SURVEILLANCE RADAR).

ASR APPROACH—(See SURVEILLANCE APPROACH).

ATC—(See AIR TRAFFIC CONTROL).

ATCAA—(See ATC ASSIGNED AIRSPACE).

ATC ADVISES—Used to prefix a message of noncontrol information when it is relayed to an aircraft by other than an air traffic controller.

ATC ASSIGNED AIRSPACE—Airspace of defined vertical/lateral limits, assigned by ATC, for the purpose of providing air traffic segregation between the specified activities being conducted within the assigned airspace and other IFR air traffic.

(See SPECIAL USE AIRSPACE).

ATC CLEARANCE—(See AIR TRAFFIC CLEARANCE).

ATC CLEARS—Used to prefix an ATC clearance when it is relayed to an aircraft by other than an air traffic controller.

ATC INSTRUCTIONS—Directives issued by air traffic control for the purpose of requiring a pilot to take specific actions; e.g., "Turn left heading two five zero," "Go around," "Clear the runway."

ATCRBS—(See RADAR).

ATC REQUESTS—Used to prefix an ATC request when it is relayed to an aircraft by other than an air traffic controller.

ATCSCC—(See AIR TRAFFIC CONTROL SYSTEM COMMAND CENTER).

ATCSCC DELAY FACTOR—The amount of delay calculated to be assigned prior to departure.

ATCT—(See TOWER).

ATIS—(See AUTOMATIC TERMINAL INFORMATION SERVICE).

ATIS [ICAO]—(See ICAO Term AUTOMATIC TERMINAL INFORMATION SERVICE).

ATS Route [ICAO]—A specified route designed for channelling the flow of traffic as necessary for the provision of air traffic services.

Note: The term "ATS Route" is used to mean variously, airway, advisory route, controlled or uncontrolled route, arrival or departure, etc.

AUTOLAND APPROACH—An autoland approach is a precision instrument approach to touchdown and, in some cases, through the landing rollout. An autoland approach is performed by the aircraft autopilot which is receiving position information and/or steering commands from onboard navigation equipment (See COUPLED APPROACH).

Note: Autoland and coupled approaches are flown in VFR and IFR. It is common for carriers to require their crews to fly coupled approaches and autoland approaches (if certified) when the weather conditions are less than approximately 4,000 RVR.

AUTOMATED INFORMATION TRANSFER—A precoordinated process, specifically defined in facility directives, during which a transfer of altitude control and/or radar identification is accomplished without verbal coordination between controllers using information communicated in a full data block.

AUTOMATED MUTUAL–ASSISTANCE VESSEL RESCUE SYSTEM—A facility which can deliver, in a matter of minutes, a surface picture (SURPIC) of vessels in the area of a potential or actual search and rescue incident, including their predicted positions and their characteristics.

AUTOMATED RADAR TERMINAL SYSTEMS—The generic term for the ultimate in functional capability afforded by several automation systems. Each differs in functional capabilities and equipment. ARTS plus a suffix roman numeral denotes a specific system. A following letter indicates a major modification to that system. In general, an ARTS displays for the terminal controller aircraft identification, flight plan data, other flight associated information; e.g., altitude, speed, and aircraft position symbols in conjunction with his radar presentation. Normal radar co-exists with the alphanumeric display. In addition to enhancing visualization of the air traffic situation, ARTS facilitate intra/inter-facility transfer and coordination of flight information. These capabilities are enabled by specially designed computers and subsystems tailored to the radar and communications equipments and operational requirements of each automated facility. Modular design permits adoption of improvements in computer software and electronic technologies as they become available while retaining the characteristics unique to each system.

1. ARTS II. A programmable nontracking, computer-aided display subsystem capable of modular expansion. ARTSII systems provide a level of automated air traffic control capability at terminals having low to medium activity. Flight identification and altitude may be associated with the display of secondary radar targets. The system has the capability of communicating with ARTCC's and other ATRS II, IIA, III, and IIIA facilities.

2. ARTS IIA. A programmable radar-tracking computer subsystem capable of modular expansion. The ARTS IIA detects, tracks, and predicts secondary radar targets. The targets are displayed by means of computer-generated symbols, ground speed, and flight plan data. Although it does not track primary radar targets, they are displayed coincident with the secondary radar as well as the symbols and alphanumerics. The system has the capability of communicating with ARTCC's and other ARTS II, IIA, III, and IIIA facilities.

3. ARTS III. The Beacon Tracking Level of the modular programmable automated radar terminal system in use at medium to high activity terminals. ARTS III detects, tracks, and predicts secondary radar-derived aircraft targets. These are displayed by means of computer-generated symbols and alphanumeric characters depicting flight identification, aircraft altitude, ground speed, and flight plan data. Although it does not track primary targets, they are displayed coincident with the secondary radar as well as the symbols and alphanumerics. The system has the capability of communicating with ARTCC's and other ARTS III facilities.

4. ARTS IIIA. The Radar Tracking and Beacon Tracking Level (RT&BTL) of the modular, programmable automated radar terminal system. ARTS IIIA detects, tracks, and predicts primary as well as secondary radar-derived aircraft targets. This more sophisticated computer-driven system upgrades the existing ARTS III system by providing improved tracking, continuous data recording, and fail-soft capabilities.

AUTOMATIC ALTITUDE REPORT—(See ALTITUDE READOUT).

AUTOMATIC ALTITUDE REPORTING—That function of a transponder which responds to Mode C interrogations by transmitting the aircraft's altitude in 100–foot increments.

AUTOMATIC CARRIER LANDING SYSTEM—U.S. Navy final approach equipment consisting of precision tracking radar coupled to a computer data link to provide continuous information to the aircraft, monitoring capability to the pilot, and a backup approach system.

AUTOMATIC DIRECTION FINDER—An aircraft radio navigation system which senses and indicates the direction to a L/MF nondirectional radio beacon (NDB) ground transmitter. Direction is indicated to the pilot as a magnetic bearing or as a relative bearing to the longitudinal axis of the aircraft depending on the type of indicator installed in the aircraft. In certain applications, such as military, ADF operations may be based on airborne and ground transmitters in the VHF/UHF frequency spectrum.

(See BEARING). (See NONDIRECTIONAL BEACON).

AUTOMATIC TERMINAL INFORMATION SERVICE—The continuous broadcast of recorded noncontrol information in selected terminal areas. Its purpose is to improve controller effectiveness and to relieve frequency congestion by automating the repetitive transmission of essential but routine information; e.g., "Los Angeles information Alfa. One three zero zero Coordinated Universal Time. Weather, measured ceiling two thousand overcast, visibility three, haze, smoke, temperature seven one, dew point five seven, wind two five zero at five, altimeter two niner niner six. I-L-S Runway Two Five Left approach in use, Runway Two Five Right closed, advise you have Alfa."

(See ICAO term AUTOMATIC TERMINAL INFORMATION SERVICE).

AUTOMATIC TERMINAL INFORMATION SERVICE [ICAO]—The provision of current, routine information to arriving and departing aircraft by means of continuous and repetitive broadcasts throughout the day or a specified portion of the day.

AUTOROTATION—A rotocraft flight condition in which the lifting rotor is driven entirely by action of the air when the rotocraft is in motion.

1. Autorotative Landing/Touchdown Autorotation. Used by a pilot to indicate that he will be landing without applying power to the rotor.

2. Low Level Autorotation. Commences at an altitude well below the traffic pattern,

usually below 100 feet AGL and is used primarily for tactical military training.

3. 180 degrees Autorotation. Initiated from a downwind heading and is commenced well inside the normal traffic pattern. "Go around" may not be possible during the latter part of this maneuver.

AVIATION WEATHER SERVICE—A service provided by the National Weather Service (NWS) and FAA which collects and disseminates pertinent weather information for pilots, aircraft operators, and ATC. Available aviation weather reports and forecasts are displayed at each NWS office and FAA FSS.
(See EN ROUTE FLIGHT ADVISORY SERVICE). (See TRANSCRIBED WEATHER BROADCAST). (See WEATHER ADVISORY). (See PILOTS AUTOMATIC TELEPHONE WEATHER ANSWERING SERVICE).

AWW—(See SEVERE WEATHER FORECAST ALERTS).

AZIMUTH (MLS)—A magnetic bearing extending from an MLS navigation facility.
Note: azimuth bearings are described as magnetic and are referred to as "azimuth" in radio telephone communications.

BASE LEG—(See TRAFFIC PATTERN).

BEACON—(See RADAR).
(See NONDIRECTIONAL BEACON). (See MARKER BEACON). (See AIRPORT ROTATING BEACON). (See AERONAUTICAL BEACON). (See AIRWAY BEACON).

BEARING—The horizontal direction to or from any point, usually measured clockwise from true north, magnetic north, or some other reference point through 360 degrees.
(See NONDIRECTION BEACON).

BELOW MINIMUMS—Weather conditions below the minimums prescribed by regulation for the particular action involved; e.g., landing minimums, takeoff minimums.

BLAST FENCE—A barrier that is used to divert or dissipate jet or propeller blast.

BLIND SPEED—The rate of departure or closing of a target relative to the radar antenna at which cancellation of the primary radar target by moving target indicator (MTI) circuits in the radar equipment causes a reduction or complete loss of signal.
(See ICAO term BLIND VELOCITY).

BLIND SPOT—An area from which radio transmissions and/or radar echoes cannot be received. The term is also used to describe portions of the airport not visible from the control tower.

BLIND TRANSMISSION—(See TRANSMITTING IN THE BLIND).

BLIND VELOCITY [ICAO]—The radial velocity of a moving target such that the target is not seen on primary radars fitted with certain forms of fixed echo suppression.

BLIND ZONE—(See BLIND SPOT).

BLOCKED—Phraseology used to indicate that a radio transmission has been distorted or interrupted due to multiple simultaneous radio transmissions.

BOUNDARY LIGHTS—(See AIRPORT LIGHTING).

BRAKING ACTION (GOOD, FAIR, POOR, OR NIL)—A report of conditions on the airport movement area providing a pilot with a degree/quality of braking that he might expect. Braking action is reported in terms of good, fair, poor, or nil.
(See RUNWAY CONDITION READING).

BRAKING ACTION ADVISORIES—When tower controllers have received runway braking action reports which include the terms "poor" or "nil," or whenever weather conditions are conducive to deteriorating or rapidly changing runway braking conditions, the tower will include on the ATIS broadcast the statement, "BRAKING ACTION ADVISORIES ARE IN EFFECT." During the time Braking Action Advisories are in effect, ATC will issue the latest braking action report for the runway in use to each arriving and departing aircraft. Pilots should be prepared for deteriorating braking conditions and should request current runway condition information if not volunteered by controllers. Pilots should also be prepared to provide a descriptive runway condition report to controllers after landing.

BROADCAST—Transmission of information for which an acknowledgement is not expected.
(See ICAO term BROADCAST).

BROADCAST [ICAO]—A transmission of information relating to air navigation that is not addressed to a specific station or stations.

CALCULATED LANDING TIME—A term that may be used in place of tentative or actual calculated landing time, whichever applies.

CALL UP—Initial voice contact between a facility and an aircraft, using the identification of the unit being called and the unit initiating the call.

CALL FOR RELEASE—Wherein the overlying ARTCC requires a terminal facility to initiate verbal coordination to secure ARTCC approval for release of a departure into the en route environment.

CANADIAN MINIMUM NAVIGATION PERFORMANCE SPECIFICATION AIRSPACE—That portion of Canadian domestic airspace within which MNPS separation may be applied.

CARDINAL ALTITUDES—"Odd" or "Even" thousand-foot altitudes or flight levels; e.g., 5,000, 6,000, 7,000, FL 250, FL 260, FL 270.

(See ALTITUDE). (See FLIGHT LEVEL).

CARDINAL FLIGHT LEVELS—(See CARDINAL ALTITUDES).

CAT—(See CLEAR-AIR TURBULENCE).

CDT PROGRAMS—(See CONTROLLED DEPARTURE TIME PROGRAMS).

CEILING—The heights above the earth's surface of the lowest layer of clouds or obscuring phenomena that is reported as "broken," "overcast," or "obscuration," and not classified as "thin" or "partial".
(See ICAO term CEILING).

CEILING [ICAO]—The height above the ground or water of the base of the lowest layer of cloud below 6,000 metres (20,000 feet) covering more than half the sky.

CENTRAP—(See CENTER RADAR ARTS PRESENTATION/PROCESSING).

CENTRAP–PLUS—(See CENTER RADAR ARTS PRESENTATION/PROCESSING–PLUS).

CENTER—(See AIR ROUTE TRAFFIC CONTROL CENTER).

CENTER'S AREA—The specified airspace within which an air route traffic control center (ARTCC) provides air traffic control and advisory service.
(See AIR ROUTE TRAFFIC CONTROL CENTER).

CENTER RADAR ARTS PRESENTATION/PROCESSING—A computer program developed to provide a back-up system for airport surveillance radar in the event of a failure or malfunction. The program uses air route traffic control center radar for the processing and presentation of data on the ARTS IIA or IIIA displays.

CENTER RADAR ARTS PRESENTATION/PROCESSING-PLUS—A computer program developed to provide a back-up system for airport surveillance radar in the event of a terminal secondary radar system failure. The program uses a combination of Air Route Traffic Control Center Radar and terminal airport surveillance radar primary targets displayed simultaneously for the processing and presentation of data on the ARTS IIA or IIIA displays.

CENTER WEATHER ADVISORY—An unscheduled weather advisory issued by Center Weather Service Unit meteorologists for ATC use to alert pilots of existing or anticipated adverse weather conditions within the next 2 hours. A CWA may modify or redefine a SIGMET.
(See AWW). (See SIGMET). (See CONVECTIVE SIGMET). (See AIRMET).

CENTRAL EAST PACIFIC—An organized route system between the U.S. West Coast and Hawaii.

CEP—(See CENTRAL EAST PACIFIC).

CERAP—(See COMBINED CENTER-RAPCON).

CFR—(See CALL FOR RELEASE).

CHAFF—Thin, narrow metallic reflectors of various lengths and frequency responses, used to reflect radar energy. These reflectors when dropped from aircraft and allowed to drift downward result in large targets on the radar display.

CHARTED VFR FLYWAYS—Charted VFR Flyways are flight paths recommended for use to bypass areas heavily traversed by large turbine-powered aircraft. Pilot compliance with recommended flyways and associated altitudes is strictly voluntary. VFR Flyway Planning charts are published on the back of existing VFR Terminal Area charts.

CHARTED VISUAL FLIGHT PROCEDURE APPROACH—An approach wherein a radar-controlled aircraft on an IFR flight plan, operating in VFR conditions and having an ATC authorization, may proceed to the airport of intended landing via visual landmarks and altitudes depicted on a charted visual flight procedure.

CHASE—An aircraft flown in proximity to another aircraft normally to observe its performance during training or testing.

CHASE AIRCRAFT—(See CHASE).

CIRCLE-TO-LAND MANEUVER—A maneuver initiated by the pilot to align the aircraft with a runway for landing when a straight-in landing from an instrument approach is not possible or is not desirable. This maneuver is made only after ATC authorization has been obtained and the pilot has established required visual reference to the airport.
(See CIRCLE TO RUNWAY). (See LANDING MINIMUMS).

CIRCLE TO RUNWAY (RUNWAY NUMBER)—Used by ATC to inform the pilot that he must circle to land because the runway in use is other than the runway aligned with the instrument approach procedure. When the direction of the circling maneuver in relation to the airport/runway is required, the controller will state the direction (eight cardinal compass points) and specify a left or right downwind or base leg as appropriate; e.g., "Cleared VOR Runway Three Six Approach circle to Runway Two Two," or "Circle northwest of the airport for a right downwind to Runway Two Two."
(See CIRCLE-TO-CIRCLE MANEUVER). (See LANDING MINIMUMS).

CIRCLING APPROACH—(See CIRCLE-TO-LAND MANEUVER).

CIRCLING MANEUVER—(See CIRCLE-TO-LAND MANEUVER).

CIRCLING MINIMA—(See LANDING MINIMUMS).

CLASS A AIRSPACE—(See Controlled Airspace)

CLASS B AIRSPACE—(See Controlled Airspace)

CLASS C AIRSPACE—(See Controlled Airspace)

CLASS D AIRSPACE—(See Controlled Airspace)

CLASS E AIRSPACE—(See Controlled Airspace)

CLASS G AIRSPACE—That airspace not designated as Class A, B, C, D or E.

CLEAR-AIR TURBULENCE—Turbulence encountered in air where no clouds are present. This term is commonly applied to high-level turbulence associated with wind shear. CAT is often encountered in the vicinity of the jet stream.
(See WIND SHEAR). (See JET STREAM).

CLEAR OF THE RUNWAY—
1. A taxiing aircraft, which is approaching a runway, is clear of the runway when all parts of the aircraft are held short of the applicable holding position marking.
2. A pilot or controller may consider an aircraft, which is exiting or crossing a runway, to be clear of the runway when all parts of the aircraft are beyond the runway edge and there is no ATC restriction to its continued movement beyond the applicable holding position marking.
3. Pilots and controllers shall exercise good judgement to ensure that adequate separation exists between all aircraft on runways and taxiways at airports with inadequate runway edge lines or holding position markings.

CLEARANCE—(See AIR TRAFFIC CLEARANCE).

CLEARANCE LIMIT—The fix, point, or location to which an aircraft is cleared when issued an air traffic clearance.
(See ICAO term CLEARANCE LIMIT).

CLEARANCE LIMIT [ICAO]—The point of which an aircraft is granted an air traffic control clearance.

CLEARANCE VOID IF NOT OFF BY (TIME)—Used by ATC to advise an aircraft that the departure clearance is automatically canceled if takeoff is not made prior to a specified time. The pilot must obtain a new clearance or cancel his IFR flight plan if not off by the specified time.
(See ICAO term CLEARANCE VOID TIME).

CLEARANCE VOID TIME [ICAO]—A time specified by an air traffic control unit at which a clearance ceases to be valid unless the aircraft concerned has already taken action to comply therewith.

CLEARED AS FILED—Means the aircraft is cleared to proceed in accordance with the route of flight filed in the flight plan. This clearance does not include the altitude, SID, or SID Transition.
(See REQUEST FULL ROUTE CLEARANCE).

CLEARED (Type Of) APPROACH—ATC authorization for an aircraft to execute a specific instrument approach procedure to an airport; e.g., "Cleared ILS Runway Three Six Approach."
(See INSTRUMENT APPROACH PROCEDURE). (See APPROACH CLEARANCE).

CLEARED APPROACH—ATC authorization for an aircraft to execute any standard or special instrument approach procedure for that airport. Normally, an aircraft will be cleared for a specific instrument approach procedure.
(See INSTRUMENT APPROACH PROCEDURE). (See CLEARED (TYPE OF) APPROACH).

CLEARED FOR TAKEOFF—ATC authorization for an aircraft to depart. It is predicated on known traffic and known physical airport conditions.

CLEARED FOR THE OPTION—ATC authorization for an aircraft to make a touch-and-go, low approach, missed approach, stop and go, or full stop landing at the discretion of the pilot. It is normally used in training so that an instructor can evaluate a student's performance under changing situations.
(See OPTION APPROACH). (Refer to AIM).

CLEARED THROUGH—ATC authorization for an aircraft to make intermediate stops at specified airports without refiling a flight plan while en route to the clearance limit.

CLEARED TO LAND—ATC authorization for an aircraft to land. It is predicated on known traffic and known physical airport conditions.

CLEARWAY—An area beyond the takeoff runway under the control of airport authorities within which terrain or fixed obstacles may not extend above specified limits. These areas may be required for certain turbine-powered operations and the size and upward slope of the clearway will differ depending on when the aircraft was certified.

CLEARWAY—That portion of flight operation between takeoff and the initial cruising altitude.

CLIMB TO VFR—ATC authorization for an aircraft to climb to VFR conditions within Class B, C, D, and E surface areas when the only weather limitation is restricted visibility. The aircraft must remain clear of clouds while climbing to VFR.
(See Special VFR).

CLOSED RUNWAY—A runway that is unusable for aircraft operations. Only the airport management/military operations office can close a runway.

CLOSED TRAFFIC—Successive operations involving takeoffs and landings or low approaches where the aircraft does not exit the traffic pattern.

CLT—(See CALCULATED LANDING TIME).

CLUTTER—In radar operations, clutter refers to the reception and visual display of radar returns caused by precipitation, chaff, terrain, numerous aircraft targets, or other phenomena. Such returns may limit or preclude ATC from providing services based on radar.
(See GROUND CLUTTER). (See CHAFF). (See PRECIPITATION). (See TARGET). (See ICAO term Radar Clutter).

CMNPS—(See CANADIAN MINIMUM NAVIGATION PERFORMANCE SPECIFICATION AIRSPACE).

COASTAL FIX—A navigation aid or intersection where an aircraft transitions between the domestic route structure and the oceanic route structure.

CODES—The number assigned to a particular multiple pulse reply signal transmitted by a transponder.
(See DISCRETE CODE).

COMBINED CENTER-RAPCON—An air traffic facility which combines the functions of an ARTCC and a radar approach control facility.
(See AIR ROUTE TRAFFIC CONTROL CENTER). (See RADAR APPROACH CONTROL FACILITY).

COMMON POINT—A *significant point* over which two or more aircraft will report passing or have reported passing before proceeding on the same or diverging tracks. To establish/maintain longitudinal separation, a controller may determine a common point not originally in the aircraft's flight plan and then clear the aircraft to fly over the point. See significant point.

COMMON PORTION—(See COMMON ROUTE).

COMMON ROUTE—That segment of a North American Route between the inland navigation facility and the coastal fix.

COMMON TRAFFIC ADVISORY FREQUENCY—A frequency designed for the purpose of carrying out airport advisory practices while operating to or from an uncontrolled airport. The CTAF may be a UNICOM, Multicom, FSS, or tower frequency and is identified in appropriate aeronautical publications.

COMPASS LOCATOR—A low power, low or medium frequency (L/MF) radio beacon installed at the site of the outer or middle marker of an instrument landing system (ILS). It can be used for navigation at distances of approximately 15 miles or as authorized in the approach procedure.
1. Outer Compass Locator (LOM). A compass locator installed at the site of the outer marker of an instrument landing system.
(See OUTER MARKER).
2. Middle Compass Locator (LMM). A compass locator installed at the site of the middle marker of an instrument landing system.
(See MIDDLE MARKER). (See ICAO term LOCATOR).

COMPASS ROSE—A circle, graduated in degrees, printed on some charts or marked on the ground at an airport. It is used as a reference to either true or magnetic direction.

COMPOSITE FLIGHT PLAN—A flight plan which specifies VFR operation for one portion of flight and IFR for another portion. It is used primarily in military operations.

COMPOSITE ROUTE SYSTEM—An organized oceanic route structure, incorporating reduced lateral spacing between routes, in which composite separation is authorized.

COMPOSITE SEPARATION—A method of separating aircraft in a composite route system where, by management of route and altitude assignments, a combination of half the lateral minimum specified for the area concerned and half the vertical minimum is applied.

COMPULSORY REPORTING POINTS—Reporting points which must be reported to ATC. They are designated on aeronautical charts by solid triangles or filed in a flight plan as fixes selected to define direct routes. These points are geographical locations which are defined by navigation aids/fixes. Pilots should discontinue position reporting over compulsory reporting points when informed by ATC that their aircraft is in "radar contact."

CONFLICT ALERT—A function of certain air traffic control automated systems designed to alert radar controllers to existing or pending situations between tracked targets (known IFR or VFR aircraft) that require his immediate attention/action.
(See MODE C INTRUDER ALERT).

CONFLICT RESOLUTION—The resolution of potential conflictions between aircraft that are radar identified and in communication with ATC by ensuring that radar targets do not touch. Pertinent traffic advisories shall be issued when this procedure is applied.

Note: This procedure shall not be provided utilizing mosaic radar systems.

CONSOLAN—A low frequency, long-distance NAVAID used principally for transoceanic navigations.

CONTACT
1. Establish communication with (followed by the name of the facility and, if appropriate, the frequency to be used).
2. A flight condition wherein the pilot ascertains the attitude of his aircraft and

navigates by visual references to the surface.
(See CONTACT APPROACH). (See RADAR CONTACT).

CONTACT APPROACH—An approach wherein an aircraft on an IFR flight plan, having an air traffic control authorization, operating clear of clouds with at least 1 mile flight visibility and a reasonable expectation of continuing to the destination airport in those conditions, may deviate from the instrument approach procedure and proceed to the destination airport by visual reference to the surface. This approach will only be authorized when requested by the pilot and the reported ground visibility at the destination airport is at least 1 statute mile.

CONTERMINOUS U.S.—The 48 adjoining States and the District of Columbia.

CONTINENTAL UNITED STATES—The 49 States located on the continent of North America and the District of Columbia.

CONTROL AREA [ICAO]—A controlled airspace extending upwards from a specified limit above the earth.

CONTROLLED AIRSPACE—An airspace of defined dimensions within which air traffic control service is provided to IFR flights and to VFR flights in accordance with the airspace classification.

Note 1—Controlled airspace is a generic term that covers Class A, Class B, Class C, Class D, and Class E airspace.

Note 2—Controlled airspace is also that airspace within which all aircraft operators are subject to certain pilot qualifications, operating rules, and equipment requirements in FAR Part 91 (for specific operating requirements, please refer to FAR Part 91). For IFR operations in any class of controlled airspace, a pilot must file an IFR flight plan and receive an appropriate ATC clearance. Each Class B, Class C, and Class D airspace area designated for an airport contains at least one primary airport around which the airspace is designated (for specific designations and descriptions of the airspace classes, please refer to FAR Part 71). Controlled airspace in the United States is designated as follows:

1. CLASS A: Generally, that airspace from 18,000 feet MSL up to and including FL600, including the airspace overlying the waters within 12 nautical miles of the coast of the 48 contiguous States and Alaska. Unless otherwise authorized, all persons must operate their aircraft under IFR.

2. CLASS B: Generally, that airspace from the surface to 10,000 feet MSL surrounding the nation's busiest airports in terms of airport operations or passenger enplanements. The configuration of each Class B airspace area is individually tailored and consists of a surface area and two or more layers (some Class B airspaces areas resemble upside–down wedding cakes), and is designed to contain all published instrument procedures once an aircraft enters the airspace. An ATC clearance is required for all aircraft to operate in the area, and all aircraft that are so cleared receive separation services within the airspace. The cloud clearance requirement for VFR operations is "clear of clouds."

3. CLASS C: Generally, that airspace from the surface to 4,000 feet above the airport elevation (charted in MSL) surrounding those airports that have an operational control tower, are serviced by a radar approach control, and that have a certain number of IFR operations or passenger enplanements. Although the configuration of each Class C airspace area is individually tailored, the airspace usually consists of a surface area with a 5 nm radius, and an outer area with a 10 nm radius that extends from 1,200 feet to 4,000 feet above the airport elevation. Each person must establish two–way radio communications with the ATC facility providing air traffic services prior to entering the airspace and thereafter maintain those communications while within the airspace. VFR aircraft are only separated from IFR aircraft within the airspace.

4. CLASS D: Generally, that airspace from the surface to 2,500 feet above the airport elevation (charted in MSL) surrounding those airports that have an operational control tower. The configuration of each Class D airspace area is individually tailored and when instrument procedures are published, the airspace will normally be designed to contain the procedures. Arrival extensions for instrument approach procedures may be Class D or Class E airspace. Unless otherwise authorized, each person must establish two–way radio communications with the ATC facility providing air traffic services prior to entering the airspace and thereafter maintain those communications while in the airspace. No separation services are provided to VFR aircraft.

5. CLASS E: Generally, if the airspace is not Class A, Class B, Class C, or Class D, and it is controlled airspace, it is Class E airspace. Class E airspace extends upward from either the surface or a designated altitude to the overlying or adjacent controlled airspace. When designated as a surface area, the airspace will be configured to contain all instrument procedures. Also in this class are Federal airways, airspace beginning at either 700 or 1,200 feet AGL

used to transition to/from the terminal or enroute environment, enroute domestic, and offshore airspace areas designated below 18,000 feet MSL. Unless designated at a lower altitude, Class E airspace begins at 14,500 MSL over the United States, including that airspace overlying the waters within 12 nautical miles of the coast of the 48 contiguous States and Alaska. Class E airspace does not include the airspace 18,000 MSL or above.

CONTROLLED AIRSPACE [ICAO]—An airspace of defined dimensions within which air traffic control service is provided to IFR flights and to VFR flights in accordance with the airspace classification. *Note*-Controlled airspace is a generic term which covers ATS airspace Classes A, B, C, D, and E.

CONTROLLED DEPARTURE TIME PROGRAMS—These programs are the flow control process whereby aircraft are held on the ground at the departure airport when delays are projected to occur in either the en route system or the terminal of intended landing. The purpose of these programs is to reduce congestion in the air traffic system or to limit the duration of airborne holding in the arrival center or terminal area. A CDT is a specific departure slot shown on the flight plan as an expected departure clearance time (EDCT).

CONTROLLED TIME OF ARRIVAL—The original estimated time of arrival adjusted by the ATCSCC ground delay factor.

CONTROLLER [ICAO]—A person authorized to provide air traffic control services.

CONTROL SECTOR—An airspace area defined horizontal and vertical dimensions for which a controller or group of controllers has air traffic control responsibility, normally within an air route traffic control center or an approach control facility. Sectors are established based on predominant traffic flows, altitude strata, and controller workload. Pilot-communications during operations within a sector are normally maintained on discrete frequencies assigned to the sector.

(See DISCRETE FREQUENCY).

CONTROL SLASH—A radar beacon slash representing the actual position of the associated aircraft. Normally, the control slash is the one closest to the interrogating radar beacon site. When ARTCC radar is operating in narrowband (digitized) mode, the control slash is converted to a target symbol.

CONVECTIVE SIGMET—A weather advisory concerning convective weather significant to the safety of all aircraft. Convective SIGMET's are issued for tornadoes, lines of thunderstorms, embedded thunderstorms of any intensity level, areas of thunderstorms greater than or equal to

VIP level 4 with an area coverage of 4/10 (40%) or more, and hail 3/4 inch or greater.

(See AWW). (See SIGMET). (See CWA). (See AIRMET).

CONVECTIVE SIGNIFICANT METEOROLOGICAL INFORMATION—(See CONVECTIVE SIGMET).

COORDINATES—The intersection of lines of reference, usually expressed in degrees/minutes/seconds of latitude and longitude, used to determine position or location.

COORDINATION FIX—The fix in relation to which facilities will handoff, transfer control of an aircraft, or coordinate flight progress data. For terminal facilities, it may also serve as a clearance for arriving aircraft.

COPTER—(See HELICOPTER).

CORRECTION—An error has been made in the transmission and the correct version follows.

COUPLED APPROACH—A coupled approach is an instrument approach performed by the aircraft autopilot which is receiving position information and/or steering commands from onboard navigation equipment. In general, coupled nonprecision approaches must be discontinued and flown manually at altitudes lower than 50 feet below the minimum descent altitudes, and coupled precision approaches must be flown manually below 50 feet ALG.

(See AUTOLAND APPROACH).

Note: Coupled and autoland approaches are flown in VFR and IFR. It is common for carriers to require their crews to fly coupled approaches and autoland approaches (if certified) when the weather conditions are less than approximately 4,000 RVR.

COURSE—

1. The intended direction of flight in the horizontal plan measured in degrees from north.
2. The ILS localizer signal pattern usually specified as the front course or the back course.
3. The intended track along a straight, curved, or segmented MLS path.

(See BEARING). (See RADIAL). (See INSTRUMENT LANDING SYSTEM). (See MICROWAVE LANDING SYSTEM).

CPL [ICAO]—(See CURRENT FLIGHT PLAN).

CRITICAL ENGINE—The engine which, upon failure, would most adversely affect the performance or handling qualities of an aircraft.

CROSS (FIX) AT (ALTITUDE)—Used by ATC when a specific altitude restriction at a specified fix is required.

CROSS (FIX) AT OR ABOVE (ALTITUDE)—Used by ATC when an altitude restriction at a specified fix is required. It does not prohibit the aircraft from crossing the fix at a higher altitude than specified; however, the higher altitude may

not be one that will violate a succeeding altitude restriction or altitude assignment.
(See ALTITUDE RESTRICTION).

CROSS (FIX) AT OR BELOW (ALTITUDE)—Used by ATC when a maximum crossing altitude at a specific fix is required. It does not prohibit the aircraft from crossing the fix at a lower altitude; however, it must be at or above the minimum IFR altitude.
(See MINIMUM IFR ALTITUDES). (See ALTITUDE RESTRICTION).

CROSSWIND—

1. When used concerning the traffic pattern, the word means "crosswind leg."

(See TRAFFIC PATTERN).

2. When used concerning wind conditions, the word means a wind not parallel to the runway or the path of an aircraft.

(See CROSSWIND COMPONENT).

CROSSWIND COMPONENT—The wind component measured in knots at 90 degrees to the longitudinal axis of the runway.

CRUISE—Used in an ATC clearance to authorize a pilot to conduct flight at any altitude from the minimum IFR altitude up to and including the altitude specified in the clearance. The pilot may level off at any intermediate altitude within this block of airspace. Climb/descent within the block is to be made at the discretion of the pilot. However, once the pilot starts descent and verbally reports leaving an altitude in the block, he may not return to that altitude without additional ATC clearance. Further, it is approval for the pilot to proceed to and make an approach at destination airport and can be used in conjunction with:

1. An airport clearance limit at locations with standard/special instrument approach procedure. The FAR's require that if an instrument letdown to an airport is necessary, the pilot shall make the letdown in accordance with a standard/special instrument approach procedure for the airport, or

2. An airport clearance limit at locations that are within/below/outside controlled airspace and without a standard/special instrument approach procedure. Such clearance is NOT AUTHORIZATION for the pilot to descend under IFR conditions below the applicable minimum IFR altitude nor does it imply that ATC is exercising control over aircraft in Class G airspace; however, it provides a means for the aircraft to proceed to destination airport, descend, and land in accordance with applicable FAR's governing VFR flight operations. Also, this provides search and rescue protection until such time as the IFR flight plan is closed.

(See INSTRUMENT APPROACH PROCEDURE).

CRUISING ALTITUDE—An altitude or flight level maintained during en route level flight. This is a constant altitude and should not be confused with a cruise clearance.
(See ALTITUDE). (See ICAO term CRUISING LEVEL).

CRUISING LEVEL [ICAO]—A level maintained during a significant portion of a flight.

CRUISE CLIMB—A climb technique employed by aircraft, usually at a constant power setting, resulting in an increase of altitude as the aircraft weight decreases.

CRUISING LEVEL—(See CRUISING ALTITUDE).

CT MESSAGE—An EDCT time generated by the ATCSCC to regulate traffic at arrival airports. Normally, a CT message is automatically transferred from the Traffic Management System computer to the NAS en route computer and appears as an EDCT. In the event of a communication failure between the TMS and the NAS, the CT message can be manually entered by the TMC at the en route facility.

CTA—(See CONTROLLED TIME OF ARRIVAL).

CTA—(See CONTROL AREA [ICAO]).

CTAF—(See COMMON TRAFFIC ADVISORY FREQUENCY).

CURRENT FLIGHT PLAN [ICAO]—The flight plan, including changes, if any, brought about by subsequent clearances.

CVFP APPROACH—(See CHARTED VISUAL FLIGHT PROCEDURE APPROACH).

CWA—(See CENTER WEATHER ADVISORY). *(See WEATHER ADVISORY).*

DA [ICAO]—(See ICAO Term DECISION ALTITUDE/DECISION HEIGHT).

DAIR—(See DIRECT ALTITUDE AND IDENTITY READOUT).

DANGER AREA [ICAO]—An airspace of defined dimensions within which activities dangerous to the flight of aircraft may exist at specified times.
Note: The term "Danger Area" is not used in reference to areas within the United States or any of its possessions or territories.

DATA BLOCK—(See ALPHANUMERIC DISPLAY).

DEAD RECKONING—Dead reckoning, as applied to flying, is the navigation of an airplane solely by means of computations based on airspeed, course, heading, wind direction, and speed, groundspeed, and elapsed time.

DECISION ALTITUDE/DECISION HEIGHT [ICAO]—A specified altitude or height (A/H) in the precision approach at which a missed approach must be initiated if the required visual reference to continue the approach has not been established.

Note 1: Decision altitude [DA] is referenced to mean sea level [MSL] and decision height [DH] is referenced to the threshold elevation.

Note 2: The required visual reference means that section of the visual aids or of the approach area which should have been in view for sufficient time for the pilot to have made an assessment of the aircraft position and rate of change of position, in relation to the desired flight path.

DECISION HEIGHT—With respect to the operation of aircraft, means the height at which a decision must be made during an ILS, MLS, or PAR instrument approach to either continue the approach or to execute a missed approach.
(See ICAO term DECISION ALTITUDE/DECISION HEIGHT).

DECODER—The device used to decipher signals received from ATCRBS transponders to effect their display as select codes.
(See CODES). (See RADAR).

DEFENSE VISUAL FLIGHT RULES—Rules applicable to flights within an ADIZ conducted under the visual flight rules in Part 91.
(See AIR DEFENSE IDENTIFICATION ZONE).

DELAY INDEFINITE (REASON KNOWN) EXPECT FURTHER CLEARANCE (TIME)—Used by ATC to inform a pilot when an accurate estimate of the delay time and the reason for the delay cannot immediately be determined; e.g., a disabled aircraft on the runway, terminal or center area saturation, weather below landing minimums, etc.
(See EXPECT FURTHER CLEARANCE (TIME)).

DELAY TIME—The amount of time that the arrival must lose to cross the meter fix at the assigned meter fix time. This is the difference between ACLT and VTA.

DEPARTURE CENTER—The ARTCC having jurisdiction for the airspace that generates a flight to the impacted airport.

DEPARTURE CONTROL—A function of an approach control facility providing air traffic control service for departing IFR and, under certain conditions, VFR aircraft.
(See APPROACH CONTROL FACILITY).

DEPARTURE SEQUENCING PROGRAM—A program designed to assist in achieving a specified interval over a common point for departures.

DEPARTURE TIME—The time an aircraft becomes airborne.

DESCENT SPEED ADJUSTMENTS—Speed deceleration calculations made to determine an accurate VTA. These calculations start at the transition point and use arrival speed segments to the vertex.

DETRESFA (DISTRESS PHASE) [ICAO]—The code word used to designate an emergency phase wherein there is reasonable certainty that an aircraft and its occupants are threatened by grave and imminent danger or require immediate assistance.

DEVIATIONS—
1. A departure from a current clearance, such as an off course maneuver to avoid weather or turbulence.
2. Where specifically authorized in the FAR's and requested by the pilot, ATC may permit pilots to deviate from certain regulations.

DF—(See DIRECTION FINDER).

DF APPROACH PROCEDURE—Used under emergency conditions where another instrument approach procedure cannot be executed. DF guidance for an instrument approach is given by ATC facilities with DF capability.
(See DF GUIDANCE). (See DIRECTION FINDER).

DF FIX—The geographical location of an aircraft obtained by one or more direction finders.
(See DIRECTION FINDER).

DF GUIDANCE—Headings provided to aircraft by facilities equipped with direction finding equipment. These headings, if followed, will lead the aircraft to a predetermined point such as the DF station or an airport. DF guidance is given to aircraft in distress or to other aircraft which request the service. Practice DF guidance is provided when workload permits.
(See DIRECTION FINDER). (See DF FIX).

DF STEER—(See DF GUIDANCE).

DH—(See DECISION HEIGHT).

DH [ICAO]—(See ICAO Term DECISION ALTITUDE/DECISION HEIGHT).

DIRECT—Straight line flight between two navigational aids, fixes, points, or any combination thereof. When used by pilots in describing off-airway routes, points defining direct route segments become compulsory reporting points unless the aircraft is under radar contact.

DIRECT ALTITUDE AND IDENTITY READOUT—The DAIR System is a modification to the AN/TPX–42 Interrogator System. The Navy has two adaptations of the DAIR System-Carrier Air Traffic Control Direct Altitude and Identification Readout System for Aircraft Carriers and Radar Air Traffic Control Facility Direct Altitude and Identity Readout System for land-based terminal operations. The DAIR detects, tracks, and predicts secondary radar aircraft targets. Targets are displayed by means of computer-generated symbols and alphanumeric characters depicting flight identification, altitude, ground speed, and flight plan data. The DAIR System is capable of interfacing with ARTCC's.

DIRECTION FINDER—A radio receiver equipped with a directional sensing antenna used to take bearings on a radio transmitter. Specialized radio direction finders are used in aircraft as air navigation aids. Others are ground-based, primarily to obtain a "fix" on a pilot requesting orientation assistance or to locate downed aircraft. A location "fix" is established by the intersection of two or more bearing lines plotted on a navigational chart using either two separately located Direction Finders to obtain a fix on an aircraft or by a pilot plotting the bearing indications of his DF on two separately located ground-based transmitters, both of which can be identified on his chart. UDF's receive signals in the ultra high frequency radio broadcast band; VDF's in the very high frequency band; and UVDF's in both bands. ATC provides DF service at those air traffic control towers and flight service stations listed in the Airport/Facility Directory and the DOD FLIP IFR En Route Supplement.
(See DF GUIDANCE). (See DF FIX).

DISCRETE BEACON CODE—(See DIS-CRETE CODE).

DISCRETE CODE—As used in the Air Traffic Control Radar Beacon System (ATCRBS), any one of the 4096 selectable Mode 3/A aircraft transponder codes except those ending in zero zero; e.g., discrete codes: 0010, 1201, 2317, 7777; nondiscrete codes: 0100, 1200, 7700. Nondiscrete codes are normally reserved for radar facilities that are not equipped with discrete decoding capability and for other purposes such as emergencies (7700), VFR aircraft (1200), etc.
(See RADAR).

DISCRETE FREQUENCY—A separate radio frequency for use in direct pilot-controller communications in air traffic control which reduces frequency congestion by controlling the number of aircraft operating on a particular frequency at one time. Discrete frequencies are normally designated for each control sector in en route/terminal ATC facilities. Discrete frequencies are listed in the Airport/Facility Directory and the DOD FLIP IFR En Route Supplement.
(See CONTROL SECTOR).

DISPLACED THRESHOLD—A threshold that is located at a point on the runway other than the designated beginning of the runway.
(See THRESHOLD).

DISTANCE MEASURING EQUIPMENT—Equipment (airborne and ground) used to measure, in nautical miles, the slant range distance of an aircraft from the DME navigational aid.
(See TACAN). (See VORTAC). (See MICROWAVE LANDING SYSTEM).

DISTRESS—A condition of being threatened by serious and/or imminent danger and of requiring immediate assistance.

DIVE BRAKES—(See SPEED BRAKES).

DIVERSE VECTOR AREA—In a radar environment, that area in which a prescribed departure route is not required as the only suitable route to avoid obstacles. The area in which random radar vectors below the MVA/MIA, established in accordance with the TERPS criteria for diverse departures obstacles and terrain avoidance, may be issued to departing aircraft.

DME—(See DISTANCE MEASURING EQUIPMENT).

DME FIX—A geographical position determined by reference to a navigational aid which provides distance and azimuth information. It is defined by a specific distance in nautical miles and a radial, azimuth, or course (i.e., localizer) in degrees magnetic from that aid.
(See DISTANCE MEASURING EQUIPMENT). (See FIX). (See MICROWAVE LANDING SYSTEM).

DME SEPARATION—Spacing of aircraft in terms of distances (nautical miles) determined by reference to distance measuring equipment (DME).
(See DISTANCE MEASURING EQUIPMENT).

DOD FLIP—Department of Defense Flight Information Publications used for flight planning, en route, and terminal operations. FLIP is produced by the Defense Mapping Agency for world-wide use. United States Government Flight Information Publications (en route charts and instrument approach procedure charts) are incorporated in DOD FLIP for use in the National Airspace System (NAS).

DOMESTIC AIRSPACE—Airspace which overlies the continental land mass of the United States plus Hawaii and U.S. possessions. Domestic airspace extends to 12 miles offshore.

DOWNBURST—A strong downdraft which induces an outburst of damaging winds on or near the ground. Damaging winds, either straight or curved, are highly divergent. The sizes of downbursts vary from 1/2 mile or less to more than 10 miles. An intense down burst often causes widespread damage. Damaging winds, lasting 5 to 30 minutes, could reach speeds as high as 120 knots.

DOWNWIND LEG—(See TRAFFIC PATTERN).

DRAG CHUTE—A parachute device installed on certain aircraft which is deployed on landing roll to assist in deceleration of the aircraft.

DSP—(See DEPARTURE SEQUENCING PROGRAM).

DT—(See DELAY TIME).

DUE REGARD—A phase of flight wherein an aircraft commander of a State-operated aircraft assumes responsibility to separate his aircraft from all other aircraft.

DUTY RUNWAY—(See RUNWAY IN USE/ACTIVE RUNWAY/DUTY RUNWAY).

DVA—(See DIVERSE VECTOR AREA).

DVFR—(See DEFENSE VISUAL FLIGHT RULES).

DVFR FLIGHT PLAN—A flight plan filed for a VFR aircraft which intends to operate in airspace within which the ready identification, location, and control of aircraft are required in the interest of national security.

DYNAMIC—Continuous review, evaluation, and change to meet demands.

DYNAMIC RESTRICTIONS—Those restrictions imposed by the local facility on an "as needed" basis to manage unpredictable fluctuations in traffic demands.

EARTS—(See EN ROUTE AUTOMATED RADAR TRACKING SYSTEM).

EDCT—(See EXPECTED DEPARTURE CLEARANCE TIME).

EFC—(See EXPECT FURTHER CLEARANCE (TIME)).

ELT—(See EMERGENCY LOCATOR TRANSMITTER).

EMERGENCY—A *distress* or an *urgency* condition.

EMERGENCY LOCATOR TRANSMITTER—A radio transmitter attached to the aircraft structure which operates from its own power source on 121.5 mHz and 243.0 mHz. It aids in locating downed aircraft by radiating a downward sweeping audio tone, 2–4 times per second. It is designed to function without human action after an accident.

EMERGENCY SAFE ALTITUDE—(See MINIMUM SAFE ALTITUDE).

E-MSAW—(See EN ROUTE MINIMUM SAFE ALTITUDE WARNING).

ENTRY POINT—The point at which an aircraft transitions from an offshore control area to oceanic airspace.

ENGINEERED PERFORMANCE STANDARDS—A mathematically derived runway capacity standard. EPS's are calculated for each airport on an individual basis and reflect that airport's aircraft mix, operating procedures, runway layout, and specific weather conditions. EPS's do not give consideration to staffing, experience levels, equipment outages, and in-trail restrictions as does the AAR.

EN ROUTE AIR TRAFFIC CONTROL SERVICES—Air traffic control service provided aircraft on IFR flight plans, generally by centers, when these aircraft are operating between departure and destination terminal areas. When equipment, capabilities, and controller workload permit, certain advisory/assistance services may be provided to VFR aircraft. *(See NAS STAGE A). (See AIR ROUTE TRAFFIC CONTROL CENTER).*

EN ROUTE AUTOMATED RADAR TRACKING SYSTEM—An automated radar and radar beacon tracking system. Its functional capabilities and design are essentially the same as the terminal ARTS IIIA system except for the EARTS capability of employing both short-range (ASR) and long-range (ARSR) radars, use of full digital radar displays, and fail-safe design. *(See AUTOMATED RADAR TERMINAL SYSTEMS).*

EN ROUTE CHARTS—(See AERONAUTICAL CHART).

EN ROUTE DESCENT—Descent from the en route cruising altitude which takes place along the route of flight.

EN ROUTE FLIGHT ADVISORY SERVICE—A service specifically designed to provide, upon pilot request, timely weather information pertinent to his type of flight, intended route of flight, and altitude. The FSS's providing this service are listed in the Airport/Facility Directory. *(See FLIGHT WATCH).*

EN ROUTE HIGH ALTITUDE CHARTS—(See AERONAUTICAL CHART).

EN ROUTE LOW ALTITUDE CHARTS—(See AERONAUTICAL CHART).

EN ROUTE MINIMUM SAFE ALTITUDE WARNING—A function of the NAS Stage A en route computer that aids the controller by alerting him when a tracked aircraft is below or predicted by the computer to go below a predetermined minimum IFR altitude (MIA).

EN ROUTE SPACING PROGRAM—A program designed to assist the exit sector in achieving the required in-trail spacing.

EPS—(See ENGINEERED PERFORMANCE STANDARDS).

ESP—(See EN ROUTE SPACING PROGRAM).

ESTIMATED ELAPSED TIME [ICAO]—The estimated time required to proceed from one significant point to another. (See ICAO Term TOTAL ESTIMATED ELAPSED TIME).

ESTIMATED OFF-BLOCK TIME [ICAO]—The estimated time at which the aircraft will commence movement associated with departure.

ESTIMATED TIME OF ARRIVAL—The time the flight is estimated to arrive at the gate (scheduled operators) or the actual runway on times for nonscheduled operators.

ESTIMATED TIME EN ROUTE—The estimated flying time from departure point to destination (lift-off to touchdown).

ETA—(See ESTIMATED TIME OF ARRIVAL).

ETE—(See ESTIMATED TIME EN ROUTE).

EXECUTE MISSED APPROACH—Instructions issued to a pilot making an instrument approach which means continue inbound to the missed approach point and execute the missed approach procedure as described on the Instrument Approach Procedure Chart or as previously assigned by ATC. The pilot may climb immediately to the altitude specified in the missed approach procedure upon making a missed approach. No turns should be initiated prior to reaching the missed approach point. When conducting an ASR or PAR approach, execute the assigned missed approach procedure immediately upon receiving instructions to "execute missed approach."

EXPECT (ALTITUDE) AT (TIME) or (FIX)— Used under certain conditions to provide a pilot with an altitude to be used in the event of two-way communications failure. It also provides altitude information to assist the pilot in planning.

EXPECTED DEPARTURE CLEARANCE TIME—The runway release time assigned to an aircraft in a controlled departure time program and shown on the flight progress strip as an EDCT.

EXPECT FURTHER CLEARANCE (TIME)— The time a pilot can expect to receive clearance beyond a clearance limit.

EXPECT FURTHER CLEARANCE VIA (AIRWAYS, ROUTES OR FIXES)—Used to inform a pilot of the routing he can expect if any part of the route beyond a short range clearance limit differs from that filed.

EXPEDITE—Used by ATC when prompt compliance is required to avoid the development of an imminent situation.

FAF—(See FINAL APPROACH FIX).

FA MESSAGE—The data entered into the ARTCC computers that activates delay processing for an impacted airport. The FA data includes the delay factor for flight plans that have not been assigned delays under CT message processing. The delay factor appears on flight progress strips in the form of an EDCT (e.g., EDCT 1820). FA processing assigns delays in 15–minute time blocks. FA's control numbers of aircraft within a specified time block but do not spread aircraft out evenly throughout the time block.

FAP—(See FINAL APPROACH POINT).

FAST FILE—A system whereby a pilot files a flight plan via telephone that is tape recorded and then transcribed for transmission to the appropriate air traffic facility. Locations having a fast file capability are contained in the Airport/Facility Directory.

FCLT—(See FREEZE CALCULATED LANDING TIME).

FEATHERED PROPELLER—A propeller whose blades have been rotated so that the leading and trailing edges are nearly parallel with the aircraft flight path to stop or minimize drag and engine rotation. Normally used to indicate shutdown of a reciprocating or turboprop engine due to malfunction.

FEDERAL AIRWAYS—(See LOW ALTITUDE AIRWAY STRUCTURE).

FEEDER FIX—The fix depicted on Instrument Approach Procedure Charts which establishes the starting point of the feeder route.

FEEDER ROUTE—A route depicted on instrument approach procedure charts to designate routes for aircraft to proceed from the en route structure to the initial approach fix (IAF). *(See INSTRUMENT APPROACH PROCEDURE).*

FERRY FLIGHT—A flight for the purpose of:

1. Returning an aircraft to base.
2. Delivering an aircraft from one location to another.
3. Moving an aircraft to and from a maintenance base.—Ferry flights, under certain conditions, may be conducted under terms of a special flight permit.

FIELD ELEVATION—(See AIRPORT ELEVATION).

FILED—Normally used in conjunction with flight plans, meaning a flight plan has been submitted to ATC.

FILED EN ROUTE DELAY—Any of the following preplanned delays at points/areas along the route of flight which require special flight plan filing and handling techniques.

1. Terminal Area Delay. A delay within a terminal area for touch-and-go, low approach, or other terminal area activity.
2. Special Use Airspace Delay. A delay within a Military Operating Area, Restricted Area, Warning Area, or ATC Assigned Airspace.
3. Aerial Refueling Delay. A delay within an Aerial Refueling Track or Anchor.

FIELD FLIGHT PLAN—The flight plan as filed with an ATS unit by the pilot or his designated representative without any subsequent changes or clearances.

FINAL—Commonly used to mean that an aircraft is on the final approach course or is aligned with a landing area. *(See FINAL APPROACH COURSE). (See FINAL APPROACH-IFR). (See TRAFFIC PATTERN). (See SEGMENTS OF AN INSTRUMENT APPROACH PROCEDURE).*

FINAL APPROACH [ICAO]—That part of an instrument approach procedure which commences at the specified final approach fix or point, or where such a fix or point is not specified,

1. At the end of the last procedure turn, base turn or inbound turn of a racetrack procedure, if specified; or
2. At the point of interception of the last track specified in the approach procedure; and ends at a point in the vicinity of an aerodrome from which:

   a. A landing can be made; or

b. A missed approach procedure is initiated.

FINAL APPROACH COURSE—A published MLS course, a straight line extension of a localizer, a final approach radial/bearing, or a runway centerline all without regard to distance.
(See FINAL APPROACH-IFR). (See TRAFFIC PATTERN).

FINAL APPROACH FIX—The fix from which the final approach (IFR) to an airport is executed and which identifies the beginning of the final approach segment. It is designated on Government charts by the Maltese Cross symbol for nonprecision approaches and the lighting bold symbol for precision approaches; or when ATC directs a lower-than-published Glideslope/path Intercept Altitude, it is the resultant actual point of the glideslope/path intercept.
(See FINAL APPROACH POINT). (See GLIDESLOPE INTERCEPT ALTITUDE). (See SEGMENTS OF AN INSTRUMENT APPROACH PROCEDURE).

FINAL APPROACH-IFR—The flight path of an aircraft which is inbound to an airport on a final instrument approach course, beginning at the final approach fix or point and extending to the airport or the point where a circle-to-land maneuver or a missed approach is executed.
(See SEGMENTS OF AN INSTRUMENT APPROACH PROCEDURE). (See FINAL APPROACH FIX). (See FINAL APPROACH COURSE). (See FINAL APPROACH POINT). (See ICAO term FINAL APPROACH).

FINAL APPROACH POINT—The point, applicable only to a nonprecision approach with no depicted FAF (such as an on-airport VOR), where the aircraft is established inbound on the final approach course from the procedure turn and where the final approach descent may be commenced. The FAP serves as the FAF and identifies the beginning of the final approach segment.
(See FINAL APPROACH FIX). (See SEGMENTS OF AN INSTRUMENT APPROACH PROCEDURE).

FINAL APPROACH SEGMENT—(See SEGMENTS OF AN INSTRUMENT APPROACH PROCEDURE).

FINAL APPROACH SEGMENT [ICAO]—That segment of an instrument approach procedure in which alignment and descent for landing are accomplished.

FINAL APPROACH-VFR—(See TRAFFIC PATTERN).

FINAL CONTROLLER—The controller providing information and final approach guidance during PAR and ASR approaches utilizing radar equipment.
(See RADAR APPROACH).

FINAL MONITOR AID—A high resolution color display that is equipped with the controller alert system hardware/software which is used in the precision runway monitor (PRM) system. The display includes alert algorithms providing the target predictors, a color change alert when a target penetrates or is predicted to penetrate the no transgression zone (NTZ), a color change alert if the aircraft transponder becomes inoperative, synthesized voice alerts, digital mapping, and like features contained in the PRM system.
(See RADAR APPROACH).

FIR—(See FLIGHT INFORMATION REGION).

FIRST TIER CENTER—The ARTCC immediately adjacent to the impacted center.

FIX—A geographical position determined by visual reference to the surface, by reference to one or more radio NAVAIDs, by celestial plotting, or by another navigational device.

FIX BALANCING—A process whereby aircraft are evenly distributed over several available arrival fixes reducing delays and controller workload.

FLAG—A warning device incorporated in certain airborne navigation and flight instruments indicating that:

1. Instruments are inoperative or otherwise not operating satisfactorily, or
2. Signal strength or quality of the received signal falls below acceptable values.

FLAG ALARM—(See FLAG).

FLAMEOUT—Unintended loss of combustion in turbine engines resulting in the loss of engine power.

FLIGHT CHECK—A call-sign prefix used by FAA aircraft engaged in flight inspection/certification of navigational aids and flight procedures. The word "recorded" may be added as a suffix; e.g., "Flight Check 320 recorded" to indicate that an automated flight inspection is in progress in terminal areas.
(See FLIGHT INSPECTION).

FLIGHT FOLLOWING—(See TRAFFIC ADVISORIES).

FLIGHT INFORMATION REGION—An airspace of defined dimensions within which Flight Information Service and Alerting Service are provided.

1. Flight Information Service. A service provide for the purpose of giving advice and information useful for the safe and efficient conduct of flights.
2. Alerting Service. A service provided to notify appropriate organizations regarding aircraft in need of search and rescue aid and to assist such organizations as required.

FLIGHT INFORMATION SERVICE—A service provided for the purpose of giving advice and information useful for the safe and efficient conduct of flights.

FLIGHT INSPECTION—Inflight investigation and evaluation of a navigational aid to determine whether it meets established tolerances. *(See NAVIGATIONAL AID). (See FLIGHT CHECK).*

FLIGHT LEVEL—A level of constant atmospheric pressure related to a reference datum of 29.92 inches of mercury. Each is stated in three digits that represent hundreds of feet. For example, flight level 250 represents a barometric altimeter indication of 25,000 feet; flight level 255, an indication of 25,500 feet. *(See ICAO term FLIGHT LEVEL).*

FLIGHT LEVEL [ICAO]—A surface of constant atmospheric pressure which is related to a specific pressure datum, 1013.2 hPa (1013.2 mb), and is separated from other such surfaces by specific pressure intervals.

Note 1: A pressure type altimeter calibrated in accordance with the standard atmosphere:

1. When set to a QNH altimeter setting, will indicate altitude;
2. When set to a QFE altimeter setting, will indicate height above the QFE reference datum; and
3. When set to a pressure of 1013.2 hPa (1013.2 mb), may be used to indicate flight levels.

Note 2: The terms "height" and "altitude", used in Note 1 above, indicate altimetric rather than geometric heights and altitudes.

FLIGHT LINE—A term used to describe the precise movement of a civil photogrammetric aircraft along a predetermined course(s) at a predetermined altitude during the actual photographic run.

FLIGHT MANAGEMENT SYSTEMS—A computer system that uses a large data base to allow routes to be programmed and fed into the system by means of a data loader. The system is constantly updated with respect to position accuracy by reference to conventional navigation aids. The sophisticated program and its associated data base insures that the most appropriate aids are automatically selected during the information update cycle.

FLIGHT PATH—A line, course, or track along which an aircraft is flying or intended to be flown. *(See TRACK). (See COURSE).*

FLIGHT PLAN—Specified information relating to the intended flight of an aircraft that is filed orally or in writing with an FSS or an ATC facility. *(See FAST FILE). (See FILED).*

FLIGHT PLAN AREA—The geographical area assigned by regional air traffic divisions to a flight service station for the purpose of search and rescue for VFR aircraft, issuance of notams, pilot briefing, in-flight services, broadcast, emergency services, flight data processing, international operations, and aviation weather services. Three letter identifiers are assigned to every flight service station and are annotated in AFD's and Order 7350.6 as tie-in-facilities. *(See FAST FILE). (See FILED).*

FLIGHT RECORDER—A general term applied to any instrument or device that records information about the performance of an aircraft in flight or about conditions encountered in flight. Flight recorders may make records of airspeed, outside air temperature, vertical acceleration, engine RPM, manifold pressure, and other pertinent variables for a given flight. *(See ICAO term FLIGHT RECORDER).*

FLIGHT RECORDER [ICAO]—Any type of recorder installed in the aircraft for the purpose of complementing accident/incident investigation.

FLIGHT SERVICE STATION—Air traffic facilities which provide pilot briefing, en route communications and VFR search and rescue services, assist lost aircraft and aircraft in emergency situations, relay ATC clearances, originate Notices to Airmen, broadcast aviation weather and NAS information, receive and process IFR flight plans, and monitor NAVAID's. In addition, at selected locations, FSS's provide Enroute Flight Advisory Service (Flight Watch), take weather observations, issue airport advisories, and advise Customs and Immigration of transborder flights.

FLIGHT STANDARDS DISTRICT OFFICE—An FAA field office serving an assigned geographical area and staffed with Flight Standards personnel who serve the aviation industry and the general public on matters relating to the certification and operation of air carrier and general aviation aircraft. Activities include general surveillance of operational safety, certification of airmen and aircraft, accident prevention, investigation, enforcement, etc.

FLIGHT TEST—A flight for the purpose of:

1. Investigating the operation/flight characteristics of an aircraft or aircraft component.
2. Evaluation an applicant for a pilot certificate or rating.

FLIGHT VISIBILITY—(See VISIBILITY).

FLIGHT WATCH—A shortened term for use in air-ground contacts to identify the flight service station providing En Route Flight Advisory Service; e.g., "Oakland Flight Watch." *(See EN ROUTE FLIGHT ADVISORY SERVICE).*

FLIP—(See DOD FLIP).

FLOW CONTROL—Measures designed to adjust the flow of traffic into a given airspace,

along a given route, or bound for a given aerodrome (airport) so as to ensure the most effective utilization of the airspace.
(See QUOTA FLOW CONTROL).

FLY HEADING (DEGREES)—Informs the pilot of the heading he should fly. The pilot may have to turn to, or continue on, a specific compass direction in order to comply with the instructions. The pilot is expected to turn in the shorter direction to the heading unless otherwise instructed by ATC.

FMA—(See FINAL MONITOR AID).

FMS—(See FLIGHT MANAGEMENT SYSTEM).

FORMATION FLIGHT—More than one aircraft which, by prior arrangement between the pilots, operate as a single aircraft with regard to navigation and position reporting. Separation between aircraft within the formation is the responsibility of the flight leader and the pilots of the other aircraft in the flight. This includes transition periods when aircraft within the formation are maneuvering to attain separation from each other to effect individual control and during join-up and breakaway.

1. A standard formation is one in which a proximity of no more than 1 mile laterally or longitudinally and within 100 feet vertically from the flight leader is maintained by each wingman.
2. Nonstanding formations are those operating under any of the following conditions:
   a. When the flight leader has requested and ATC has approved other than standard formation dimensions.
   b. When operating within an authorized altitude reservation (ALTRV) or under the provisions of a letter of agreement.
   c. When the operations are conducted in airspace specifically designed for a special activity.

(See ALTITUDE RESERVATION).

FRC—(See REQUEST FULL ROUTE CLEARANCE).

FREEZE/FROZEN—Terms used in referring to arrivals which have been assigned ACLT's and to the lists in which they are displayed.

FREEZE CALCULATED LANDING TIME—A dynamic parameter number of minutes prior to the meter fix calculated time of arrival for each aircraft when the TCLT is frozen and becomes an ACLT (i.e., the VTA is updated and consequently the TCLT is modified as appropriate until FCLT minutes prior to meter fix calculated time of arrival, at which time updating is suspended and an ACLT and a frozen meter fix crossing time (MFT) is assigned).

FREEZE SPEED PARAMETER—A speed adapted for each aircraft to determine fast and slow aircraft. Fast aircraft freeze on parameter FCLT and slow aircraft freeze on parameter MLDI.

FSDO—(See FLIGHT STANDARDS DISTRICT OFFICE).

FSPD—(See FREEZE SPEED PARAMETER).

FSS—(See FLIGHT SERVICE STATION).

FUEL DUMPING—Airborne release of usable fuel. This does not include the dropping of fuel tanks.
(See JETTISONING OF EXTERNAL STORES).

FUEL REMAINING—A phrase used by either pilots or controllers when relating to the fuel remaining on board until actual fuel exhaustion. When transmitting such information in response to either a controller question or pilot initiated cautionary advisory to air traffic control, pilots will state the APPROXIMATE NUMBER OF MINUTES the flight can continue with the fuel remaining. All reserve fuel SHOULD BE INCLUDED in the time stated, as should an allowance for established fuel gauge systems error.

FUEL SIPHONING—Unintentional release of fuel caused by overflow, puncture, loose cap, etc.

FUEL VENTING—(See FUEL SIPHONING).

GADO—(See GENERAL AVIATION DISTRICT OFFICE).

GATE HOLD PROCEDURES—Procedures at selected airports to hold aircraft at the gate or other ground location whenever departure delays exceed or are anticipated to exceed 15 minutes. The sequence for departure will be maintained in accordance with initial call-up unless modified by flow control restrictions. Pilots should monitor the ground control/clearance delivery frequency for engine start/taxi advisories or new proposed start/taxi time if the delay changes.
(See FLOW CONTROL).

GCA—(See GROUND CONTROLLED APPROACH).

GENERAL AVIATION—That portion of civil aviation which encompasses all facets of aviation except air carriers holding a certificate of public convenience and necessity from the Civil Aeronautics Board and large aircraft commercial operators.
(See ICAO term GENERAL AVIATION).

GENERAL AVIATION [ICAO]—All civil aviation operations other than scheduled air services and nonscheduled air transport operations for remuneration or hire.

GENERAL AVIATION DISTRICT OFFICE—An FAA field office serving a designated geographical area and staffed with Flight Standards personnel who have the responsibility for serving the aviation industry and the general public on all matters relating to the certification and operation of general aviation aircraft.

GEO MAP—The digitized map markings associated with the ASR–9 Radar System.

GLIDEPATH—(See GLIDESLOPE).

GLIDEPATH INTERCEPT ALTITUDE—(See GLIDESLOPE INTERCEPT ALTITUDE).

GLIDESLOPE—Provides vertical guidance for aircraft during approach and landing. The glideslope/glidepath is based on the following:

1. Electronic components emitting signals which provide vertical guidance by reference to airborne instruments during instrument approaches such as ILS/MLS, or

2. Visual ground aids, such as VASI, which provide vertical guidance for a VFR approach or for the visual portion of an instrument approach and landing.

3. PAR. Used by ATC to inform an aircraft making a PAR approach of its vertical position (elevation) relative to the descent profile.

(See ICAO term GLIDEPATH).

GLIDEPATH [ICAO]—A descent profile determined for vertical guidance during a final approach.

GLIDESLOPE INTERCEPT ALTITUDE—The minimum altitude to intercept the glideslope/path on a precision approach. The intersection of the published intercept altitude with the glideslope/path, designated on Government charts by the lightning bolt symbol, is the precision FAF; however, when ATC directs a lower altitude, the resultant lower intercept position is then the FAF.

(See FINAL APPROACH FIX). (See SEGMENTS OF AN INSTRUMENT APPROACH PROCEDURE).

GLOBAL POSITIONING SYSTEM—A space-base radio positioning, navigation, and time-transfer system being developed by Department of Defense. When fully deployed, the system is intended to provide highly accurate position and velocity information, and precise time, on a continuous global basis, to an unlimited number of properly equipped users. The system will be unaffected by weather, and will provide a worldwide common grid reference system. The GPS concept is predicated upon accurate and continuous knowledge of the spatial position of each satellite in the system with respect to time and distance from a transmitting satellite to the user. The GPS receiver automatically selects appropriate signals from the satellites in view and translates these into a three-dimensional position, velocity, and time. Predictable system accuracy for civil users is projected to be 100 meters horizontally. Performance standards and certification criteria have not yet been established.

GO AHEAD—Proceed with your message. Not to be used for any other purpose.

GO AROUND—Instructions for a pilot to abandon his approach to landing. Additional instructions may follow. Unless otherwise advised by ATC, a VFR aircraft or an aircraft conducting visual approach should overfly the runway while climbing to traffic pattern altitude and enter the traffic pattern via the crosswind leg. A pilot on an IFR flight plan making an instrument approach should execute the published missed approach procedure or proceed as instructed by ATC; e.g., "Go around" (additional instructions if required).
(See LOW APPROACH). (See MISSED APPROACH).

GPS—(See Global Positioning System)

GROUND CLUTTER—A pattern produced on the radar scope by ground returns which may degrade other radar returns in the affected area. The effect of ground clutter is minimized by the use of moving target indicator (MTI) circuits in the radar equipment resulting in a radar presentation which displays only targets which are in motion.
(See CLUTTER).

GROUND CONTROLLED APPROACH—A radar approach system operated from the ground by air traffic control personnel transmitting instructions to the pilot by radio. The approach may be conducted with surveillance radar (ASR) only or with both surveillance and precision approach radar (PAR). Usage of the term "GCA" by pilots is discouraged except when referring to a GCA facility. Pilots should specifically request a "PAR" approach when a precision radar approach is desired or request an "ASR" or "surveillance" approach when a nonprecision radar approach is desired.
(See RADAR APPROACH).

GROUND DELAY—The amount of delay attributed to ATC, encountered prior to departure, usually associated with a CDT program.

GROUND SPEED—The speed of an aircraft relative to the surface of the earth.

GROUND STOP—Normally, the last initiative to be utilized; this method mandates that the terminal facility will not allow any departures to enter the ARTCC airspace until further notified.

GROUND VISIBILITY—(See VISIBILITY).

HAA—(See HEIGHT ABOVE AIRPORT).

HAL—(See HEIGHT ABOVE LANDING).

HANDOFF—An action taken to transfer the radar identification of an aircraft from one controller to another if the aircraft will enter the receiving controller's airspace and radio communications with the aircraft will be transferred.

HAT—(See HEIGHT ABOVE TOUCHDOWN).

HAVE NUMBERS—Used by pilots to inform ATC that they have received runway, wind, and altimeter information only.

HAZARDOUS INFLIGHT WEATHER ADVISORY SERVICE—Continuous recorded hazardous inflight weather forecasts broadcasted to airborne pilots over the selected VOR outlets defined as an HIWAS BROADCAST AREA.

HAZARDOUS WEATHER INFORMATION—Summary of significant meteorological information (SIGMET/WS), convective significant meteorological information (convective SIGMET/WST), urgent pilot weather reports (urgent PIREP/UUA), center weather advisories (CWA), airmen's meteorological information (AIRMET/WA) and any other weather such as isolated thunderstorms that are rapidly developing and increasing in intensity, or low ceilings and visibilities that are becoming widespread which is considered significant and are not included in a current hazardous weather advisory.

HEAVY (AIRCRAFT)—(See AIRCRAFT CLASSES).

HEIGHT ABOVE AIRPORT—The height of the Minimum Descent Altitude above the published airport elevation. This is published in conjunction with circling minimums.
(See MINIMUM DESCENT ALTITUDE).

HEIGHT ABOVE LANDING—The height above a designated helicopter landing area used for helicopter instrument approach procedures.

HEIGHT ABOVE TOUCHDOWN—The height of the Decision Height or Minimum Descent Altitude above the highest runway elevation in the touchdown zone (first 3,000 feet of the runway). HAT is published on instrument approach charts in conjunction with all straight-in minimums.
(See DECISION HEIGHT). (See MINIMUM DESCENT ALTITUDE).

HELICOPTER—Rotocraft that, for its horizontal motion, depends principally on its engine-driven rotors.
(See ICAO term HELICOPTER).

HELICOPTER [ICAO]—A heavier-than-air aircraft supported in flight chiefly by the reactions of the air on one or more power-driven rotors on substantially vertical axes.

HELIPAD—A small, designated area, usually with a prepared surface, on a heliport, airport, landing/takeoff area, apron/ramp, or movement area used for takeoff, landing, or parking of helicopters.

HELIPORT—An area of land, water, or structure used or intended to be used for the landing and takeoff of helicopters and includes its buildings and facilities if any.

HERTZ—The standard radio equivalent of frequency in cycles per second of an electromagnetic wave. Kilohertz (kHz) is a frequency of one thousand cycles per second. Megahertz (mHz) is a frequency of one million cycles per second.

HF—(See HIGH FREQUENCY).

HF COMMUNICATIONS—(See HIGH FREQUENCY COMMUNICATIONS).

HIGH FREQUENCY—The frequency band between 3 and 30 mHz.
(See HIGH FREQUENCY COMMUNICATIONS).

HIGH FREQUENCY COMMUNICATIONS—High radio frequencies (HF) between 3 and 30 mHz used for air-to-ground voice communications in overseas operations.

HIGH SPEED EXIT—(See HIGH SPEED TAXIWAY).

HIGH SPEED TAXIWAY—A long radius taxiway designed and provided with lighting or marking to define the path of aircraft, traveling at high speed (up to 60 knots), from the runway center to a point on the center of a taxiway. Also referred to as long radius exit or turn-off taxiway. The high speed taxiway is designed to expedite aircraft turning off the runway after landing, thus reducing runway occupancy time.

HIGH SPEED TURNOFF—(See HIGH SPEED TAXIWAY).

HIWAS—(See HAZARDOUS INFLIGHT WEATHER ADVISORY SERVICE).

HIWAS AREA—(See HAZARDOUS INFLIGHT WEATHER ADVISORY SERVICE).

HIWAS BROADCAST AREA—A geographical area of responsibility including one or more HIWAS outlet areas assigned to an AFSS/FSS for hazardous weather advisory broadcasting.

HIWAS OUTLET AREA—An area defined as a 150 NM radius of a HIWAS outlet, expanded as necessary to provide coverage.

HOLDING PROCEDURE—(See HOLD PROCEDURE).

HOLD PROCEDURE—A predetermined maneuver which keeps aircraft within a specified airspace while awaiting further clearance from air traffic control. Also used during ground operations to keep aircraft within a specified area or at a specified point while awaiting further clearance from air traffic control.
(See HOLDING FIX).

HOLDING FIX—A specified fix identifiable to a pilot by NAVAID's or visual reference to the ground used as a reference point in establishing and maintaining the position of an aircraft while holding.
(See FIX). (See VISUAL HOLDING).

HOLDING POINT [ICAO]—A specified location, identified by visual or other means, in the vicinity of which the position of an aircraft in flight is maintained in accordance with air traffic control clearances.

HOLD FOR RELEASE—Used by ATC to delay an aircraft for traffic management reasons; i.e., weather, traffic volume, etc. Hold for release instructions (including departure delay information) are used to inform a pilot or a controller (either directly or through an authorized relay) that a departure clearance is not valid until a release time or additional instructions have been received.
(See ICAO term HOLDING POINT).

HOMING—Flight toward a NAVAID, without correcting for wind, by adjusting the aircraft heading to maintain a relative bearing of zero degrees.
(See BEARING). (See ICAO term HOMING).

HOMING [ICAO]—The procedure of using the direction-finding equipment of one radio station with the emission of another radio station, where at least one of the stations is mobile, and whereby the mobile station proceeds continuously towards the other station.

HOVER CHECK—Used to describe when a helicopter/VTOL aircraft requires a stabilized hover to conduct a performance/power check prior to hover taxi, air taxi, or takeoff. Altitude of the hover will vary based on the purpose of the check.

HOVER TAXI—Used to describe a helicopter/VTOL aircraft movement conducted above the surface and in ground effect at airspeeds less than approximately 20 knots. The actual height may vary, and some helicopters may require hover taxi above 25 feet AGL to reduce ground effect turbulence or provide clearance for cargo slingloads.
(See AIR TAXI). (See HOVER CHECK).

HOW DO YOU HEAR ME?—A question relating to the quality of the transmission or to determine how well the transmission is being received.

HZ—(See HERTZ).

IAF—(See INITIAL APPROACH FIX).

IAP—(See INSTRUMENT APPROACH PROCEDURE).

ICAO—(See INTERNATIONAL CIVIL AVIATION ORGANIZATION).

ICAO [ICAO]—(See ICAO Term INTERNATIONAL CIVIL AVIATION ORGANIZATION).

IDENT—A request for a pilot to activate the aircraft transponder identification feature. This will help the controller to confirm an aircraft identity or to identify an aircraft.

IDENT FEATURE—The special feature in the Air Traffic Control Radar Beacon System (ARCRBS) equipment. It is used to immediately distinguish one displayed beacon target from other beacon targets.

(See IDENT).

IF—(See INTERMEDIATE FIX).

IFIM—(See INTERNATIONAL FLIGHT INFORMATION MANUAL).

IF NO TRANSMISSION RECEIVED FOR (TIME)—Used by ATC in radar approaches to prefix procedures which should be followed by the pilot in the event of lost communications.
(See LOST COMMUNICATIONS).

IFR—(See INSTRUMENT FLIGHT RULES).

IFR AIRCRAFT—An aircraft conducting flight in accordance with instrument flight rules.

IFR CONDITIONS—Weather conditions below the minimum for flight under visual flight rules.
(See INSTRUMENT METEOROLOGICAL CONDITIONS).

IFR DEPARTURE PROCEDURE—(See IFR TAKEOFF MINIMUMS AND DEPARTURE PROCEDURES).

IFR FLIGHT—(See IFR AIRCRAFT).

IFR LANDING MINIMUMS—(See LANDING MINIMUMS).

IFR MILITARY TRAINING ROUTES (IR)—Routes used by the Department of Defense and associated Reserve and Air Guard units for the purpose of conducting low-altitude navigation and tactical training in both IFR and VFR weather conditions below 10,000 feet MSL at airspeeds in excess of 250 knots IAS.

IFR TAKEOFF MINIMUMS AND DEPARTURE PROCEDURES—Federal Aviation Regulations, Part 91, prescribes standard takeoff rules for certain civil users. At some airports, obstructions or other factors require the establishment of nonstandard takeoff minimums, departure procedures, or both to assist pilots in avoiding obstacles during climb to the minimum en route altitude. Those airports are listed in NOS/DOD Instrument Approach Charts (IAP's) under a section entitled "IFR Takeoff Minimums and Departure Procedures." The NOS/DOD IAP chart legend illustrates the symbol used to alert the pilot to nonstandard takeoff minimums and departure procedures. When departing IFR from such airports or from any airports where there are no departure procedures, SID's, or ATC facilities available, pilots should advise ATC of any departure limitations. Controllers may query a pilot to determine acceptable departure directions, turns, or headings after takeoff. Pilots should be familiar with the departure procedures and must assure that their aircraft can meet or exceed any specified climb gradients.

ILS—(See INSTRUMENT LANDING SYSTEM).

ILS CATEGORIES—1. ILS Category I. An ILS approach procedure which provides for approach to a height above touchdown of not less than 200 feet and with runway visual range of not less than 1,800 feet.—2. ILS Category II. An ILS approach procedure which provides for approach to a height above touchdown of not less than 100 feet and with runway visual range of not less than 1,200 feet.—3. Category III:

1. IIIA.—An ILS approach procedure which provides for approach without a decision height minimum and with runway visual range of not less than 700 feet.

2. IIIB.—An ILS approach procedure which provides for approach without a decision height minimum and with runway visual range of not less than 150 feet.

3. IIIC.—An ILS approach procedure which provides for approach without a decision height minimum and without runway visual range minimum.

IM—(See INNER MARKER).

IMC—(See INSTRUMENT METEOROLOGICAL CONDITIONS).

IMMEDIATELY—Used by ATC when such action compliance is required to avoid an imminent situation.

INCERFA (Uncertainty Phase) [ICAO]—A situation wherein uncertainty exists as to the safety of an aircraft and its occupants.

INCREASE SPEED TO (SPEED)—(See SPEED ADJUSTMENT).

INERTIAL NAVIGATION SYSTEM—An RNAV system which is a form of self-contained navigation.
(See Area Navigation/RNAV).

INFLIGHT REFUELING—(See AERIAL REFUELING).

INFLIGHT WEATHER ADVISORY—(See WEATHER ADVISORY).

INFORMATION REQUEST—A request originated by an FSS for information concerning an overdue VFR aircraft.

INITIAL APPROACH FIX—The fixes depicted on instrument approach procedure charts that identify the beginning of the initial approach segment(s).
(See FIX). (See SEGMENTS OF AN INSTRUMENT APPROACH PROCEDURE).

INITIAL APPROACH SEGMENT—(See SEGMENTS OF AN INSTRUMENT APPROACH PROCEDURE).

INITIAL APPROACH SEGMENT [ICAO]—That segment of an instrument approach procedure between the initial approach fix and the intermediate approach fix or, where applicable, the final approach fix or point.

INLAND NAVIGATION FACILITY—A navigation aid on a North American Route at which the common route and/or the noncommon route begins or ends.

INNER MARKER—A marker beacon used with an ILS (CAT II) precision approach located between the middle marker and the end of the ILS runway, transmitting a radiation pattern keyed at six dots per second and indicating to the pilot, both aurally and visually, that he is at the designated decision height (DH), normally 100 feet above the touchdown zone elevation, on the ILS CAT II approach. It also marks progress during a CAT II approach.
(See INSTRUMENT LANDING SYSTEM).

INNER MARKER BEACON—(See INNER MARKER).

INREQ—(See INFORMATION REQUEST).

INS—(See INERTIAL NAVIGATION SYSTEM).

INSTRUMENT APPROACH—(See INSTRUMENT APPROACH PROCEDURE).

INSTRUMENT APPROACH PROCEDURE—A series of predetermined maneuvers for the orderly transfer of an aircraft under instrument flight conditions from the beginning of the initial approach to a landing or to a point from which a landing may be made visually. It is prescribed and approved for a specific airport by competent authority.
(See SEGMENTS OF AN INSTRUMENT APPROACH PROCEDURE).

1. U.S. civil standard instrument approach procedures are approved by the FAA as prescribed under Part 97 and are available for public use.

2. U.S. military standard instrument approach procedures are approved and published by the Department of Defense.

3. Special instrument approach procedures are approved by the FAA for individual operators but are not published in Part 97 for public use.
(See ICAO term INSTRUMENT APPROACH PROCEDURE).

INSTRUMENT APPROACH PROCEDURE [ICAO]—A series of predetermined manoeuvres by reference to flight instruments with specified protection from obstacles from the initial approach fix, or where applicable, from the beginning of a defined arrival route to a point from which a landing can be completed and thereafter, if a landing is not completed, to a position at which holding or en route obstacle clearance criteria apply.

INSTRUMENT APPROACH PROCEDURES CHARTS—(See AERONAUTICAL CHART).

INSTRUMENT FLIGHT RULES—Rules governing the procedures for conducting instrument flight. Also a term used by pilots and controllers to indicate type of flight plan.
(See VISUAL FLIGHT RULES). (See INSTRUMENT METEOROLOGICAL CONDITIONS). (See VISUAL METEOROLOGICAL CONDITIONS).

(Refer to AIM). (See ICAO term INSTRUMENT FLIGHT RULES).

INSTRUMENT FLIGHT RULES [ICAO]—A set of rules governing the conduct of flight under instrument meteorological conditions.

INSTRUMENT LANDING SYSTEM—A precision instrument approach system which normally consists of the following electronic components and visual aids:

1. Localizer.
(See LOCALIZER).
2. Glideslope.
(See GLIDESLOPE).
3. Outer Marker.
(See OUTER MARKER).
4. Middle Marker.
(See MIDDLE MARKER).
5. Approach Lights.
(See AIRPORT LIGHTING).

INSTRUMENT METEOROLOGICAL CONDITIONS—Meteorological conditions expressed in terms of visibility, distance from cloud, and ceiling less than the minima specified for visual meteorological conditions.
(See VISUAL METEOROLOGICAL CONDITIONS). (See INSTRUMENT FLIGHT RULES). (See VISUAL FLIGHT RULES).

INSTRUMENT RUNWAY—A runway equipped with electronic and visual navigation aids for which a precision or nonprecision approach procedure having straight-in landing minimums has been approved.
(See ICAO term INSTRUMENT RUNWAY).

INSTRUMENT RUNWAY [ICAO]—One of the following types of runways intended for the operation of aircraft using instrument approach procedures:

1. *Nonprecision Approach Runway*—An instrument runway served by visual aids and a nonvisual aid providing at least directional guidance adequate for a straight-in approach.
2. *Precision Approach Runway, Category I*—An instrument runway served by ILS and visual aids intended for operations down to 60 m (200 feet) decision height and down to an RVR of the order of 800 m.
3. *Precision Approach Runway, Category II*—An instrument runway served by ILS and visual aids intended for operations down to 30 m (100 feet) decision height and down to an RVR of the order of 400 m.
4. *Precision Approach Runway, Category III—An instrument runway served by ILS to and along the surface of the runway and:*
   a. Intended for operations down to an RVR of the order of 200 m (no decision height being applicable) using visual aids during the final phase of landing;
   b. Intended for operations down to an RVR of the order of 50 m (no decision height being applicable) using visual aids for taxiing;
   c. Intended for operations without reliance on visual reference for landing or taxiing.

Note 1: See Annex 10 Volume I, Part I Chapter 3, for related ILS specifications.

Note 2: Visual aids need not necessarily be matched to the scale of nonvisual aids provided. The criterion for the selection of visual aids is the conditions in which operations are intended to be conducted.

INTERMEDIATE APPROACH SEGMENT—(See SEGMENTS OF AN INSTRUMENT APPROACH PROCEDURE).

INTERMEDIATE APPROACH SEGMENT [ICAO]—That segment of an instrument approach procedure between either the intermediate approach fix and the final approach fix or point, or between the end of a reversal, race track or dead reckoning track procedure and the final approach fix or point, as appropriate.

INTERMEDIATE FIX—The fix that identifies the beginning of the intermediate approach segment of an instrument approach procedure. The fix is not normally identified on the instrument approach chart as an intermediate fix (IF).
(See SEGMENTS OF AN INSTRUMENT APPROACH PROCEDURE).

INTERMEDIATE LANDING—On the rare occasion that this option is requested, it should be approved. The departure center, however, must advise the ATCSCC so that the appropriate delay is carried over and assigned at the intermediate airport. An intermediate landing airport within the arrival center will not be accepted without coordination with and the approval of the ATCSCC.

INTERNATIONAL AIRPORT—Relating to international flight, it means:

1. An airport of entry which has been designated by the Secretary of Treasury or Commissioner of Customs as an international airport for customs service.
2. A landing rights airport at which specific permission to land must be obtained from customs authorities in advance of contemplated use.
3. Airports designated under the Convention on International Civil Aviation as an airport for use by international commercial air transport and/or international general aviation.

(Refer to AIRPORT/FACILITY DIRECTORY). (Refer to IFIM). (See ICAO term INTERNATIONAL AIRPORT).

INTERNATIONAL AIRPORT [ICAO]—Any airport designated by the Contracting State in whose territory it is situated as an airport of entry and departure for international air traffic, where the formalities incident to customs, immigration, public health, animal and plant quarantine and similar procedures are carried out.

INTERNATIONAL CIVIL AVIATION ORGANIZATION [ICAO]—A specialized agency of the United Nations whose objective is to develop the principles and techniques of international air navigation and to foster planning and development of international civil air transport. ICAO Regions include:

AFI African-Indian Ocean Region

CAR Caribbean Region

EUR European Region

MID/ASIA Middle East/Asia Region

NAM North American Region

NAT North Atlantic Region

PAC Pacific Region

SAM South American Region

INTERNATIONAL FLIGHT INFORMATION MANUAL—A publication designed primarily as a pilot's preflight planning guide for flights into foreign airspace and for flights returning to the U.S. from foreign locations.

INTERROGATOR—The ground-based surveillance radar beacon transmitter-receiver, which normally scans in synchronism with a primary radar, transmitting discrete radio signals which repetitiously request all transponders on the mode being used to reply. The replies received are mixed with the primary radar returns and displayed on the same plan position indicator (radar scope). Also, applied to the airborne element of the TACAN/DME system.

(See TRANSPONDER).

INTERSECTING RUNWAYS—Two or more runways which cross or meet within their lengths.

(See INTERSECTION).

INTERSECTION—

1. A point defined by any combination of courses, radials, or bearings of two or more navigational aids.
2. Used to describe the point where two runways, a runway and a taxiway, or two taxiways cross or meet.

INTERSECTION DEPARTURE—A departure from any runway intersection except the end of the runway. (See INTERSECTION).

INTERSECTION TAKEOFF—(See INTERSECTION DEPARTURE).

IR—(See IFR MILITARY TRAINING ROUTES).

I SAY AGAIN—The message will be repeated.

JAMMING—Electronic or mechanical interference which may disrupt the display of aircraft on radar or the transmission/reception of radio communications/ navigation.

JET BLAST—Jet engine exhaust (thrust stream turbulence).

(See WAKE TURBULENCE).

JET ROUTE—A route designed to serve aircraft operations from 18,000 feet MSL up to and including flight level 450. The routes are referred to as "J" routes with numbering to identify the designated route; e.g., J105.

(See Class A airspace).

JET STREAM—A migrating stream of high-speed winds present at high altitudes.

JETTISONING OF EXTERNAL STORES—Airborne release of external stores; e.g., tiptanks, ordnance.

(See FUEL DUMPING).

JOINT USE RESTRICTED AREA—(See RESTRICTED AREA).

KNOWN TRAFFIC—With respect to ATC clearances, means aircraft whose altitude, position, and intentions are known to ATC.

LAA—(See LOCAL AIRPORT ADVISORY).

LAAS—(See LOW ALTITUDE ALERT SYSTEM).

LANDING AREA—Any locality either on land, water, or structures, including airports/ heliports and intermediate landing fields, which is used, or intended to be used, for the landing and takeoff of aircraft whether or not facilities are provided for the shelter, servicing, or for receiving or discharging passengers or cargo.

(See ICAO term LANDING AREA).

LANDING AREA [ICAO]—That part of a movement area intended for the landing or takeoff of aircraft.

LANDING DIRECTION INDICATOR—A device which visually indicates the direction in which landings and takeoffs should be made.

(See TETRAHEDRON).

LANDING DISTANCE AVAILABLE [ICAO]—The length of runway which is declared available and suitable for the ground run of an aeroplane landing.

LANDING MINIMUMS—The minimum visibility prescribed for landing a civil aircraft while using an instrument approach procedure. The minimum applies with other limitations set forth in Part 91 with respect to the Minimum Descent Altitude (MDA) or Decision Height (DH) prescribed in the instrument approach procedures as follows:

1. Straight-in landing minimums. A statement of MDA and visibility, or DH and visibility, required for a straight-in landing on a specified runway, or

2. Circling minimums. A statement of MDA and visibility required for the circle-to-land maneuver.

Descent below the established MDA or DH is not authorized during an approach unless the aircraft is in a position from which a normal approach to the runway of intended landing can be made and adequate visual reference to required visual cues is maintained.

(See STRAIGHT-IN LANDING). (See CIRCLE-TO-LAND MANEUVER). (See DECISION HEIGHT). (See MINIMUM DESCENT ALTITUDE). (See VISIBILITY). (See INSTRUMENT APPROACH PROCEDURE).

LANDING ROLL—The distance from the point of touchdown to the point where the aircraft can be brought to a stop or exit the runway.

LANDING SEQUENCE—The order in which aircraft are positioned for landing.
(See APPROACH SEQUENCE).

LAST ASSIGNED ALTITUDE—The last altitude/flight level assigned by ATC and acknowledged by the pilot.
(See MAINTAIN).

LATERAL SEPARATION—The lateral spacing of aircraft at the same altitude by requiring operation on different routes or in different geographical locations.
(See SEPARATION).

LDA—(See LOCALIZER TYPE DIRECTIONAL AID).

LDA [ICAO]—(See ICAO Term LANDING DISTANCE AVAILABLE).

LF—(See LOW FREQUENCY).

LIGHTED AIRPORT—An airport where runway and obstruction lighting is available.
(See AIRPORT LIGHTING).

LIGHT GUN—A handheld directional light signaling device which emits a brilliant narrow beam of white, green, or red light as selected by the tower controller. The color and type of light transmitted can be used to approve or disapprove anticipated pilot actions where radio communication is not available. The light gun is used for controlling traffic operating in the vicinity of the airport and on the airport movement area.
(Refer to AIM).

LOCALIZER—The component of an ILS which provides course guidance to the runway.
(See INSTRUMENT LANDING SYSTEM). (See ICAO term LOCALIZER COURSE).

LOCALIZER COURSE [ICAO]—The locus of points, in any given horizontal plane, at which the DDM (difference in depth of modulation) is zero.

LOCALIZER TYPE DIRECTIONAL AID—A NAVAID used for nonprecision instrument approaches with utility and accuracy comparable to a localizer but which is not a part of a complete ILS and is not aligned with the runway.

LOCALIZER USABLE DISTANCE—The maximum distance from the localizer transmitter at a specified altitude, as verified by flight inspection, at which reliable course information is continuously received.

LOCAL AIRPORT ADVISORY [LAA]—A service provided by flight service stations or the military at airports not serviced by an operating control tower. This service consists of providing information to arriving and departing aircraft concerning wind direction and speed, favored runway, altimeter setting, pertinent known traffic, pertinent known field conditions, airport taxi routes and traffic patterns, and authorized instrument approach procedures. This information is advisory in nature and does not constitute an ATC clearance.
(See AIRPORT ADVISORY AREA).

LOCAL TRAFFIC—Aircraft operating in the traffic pattern or within sight of the tower, or aircraft known to be departing or arriving from flight in local practice areas, or aircraft executing practice instrument approaches at the airport.
(See TRAFFIC PATTERN).

LOCATOR [ICAO]—An LM/MF NDB used as an aid to final approach.
Note: A locator usually has an average radius of rated coverage of between 18.5 and 46.3 km (10 and 25 NM).

LONGITUDINAL SEPARATION—The longitudinal spacing of aircraft at the same altitude by a minimum distance expressed in units of time or miles.
(See SEPARATION).

LONG RANGE NAVIGATION—(See LORAN).

LORAN—An electronic navigational system by which hyperbolic lines of position are determined by measuring the difference in the time of reception of synchronized pulse signals from two fixed transmitters. Loran A operates in the 1750–1950 kHz frequency band. Loran C and D operate in the 100–110 kHz frequency band.

LOST COMMUNICATIONS—Loss of the ability to communicate by radio. Aircraft are sometimes referred to as NORDO (No Radio). Standard pilot procedures are specified in Part 91. Radar controllers issue procedures for pilots to follow in the event of lost communications during a radar approach when weather reports indicate that an aircraft will likely encounter IFR weather conditions during the approach.

LOW ALTITUDE AIRWAY STRUCTURE—The network of airways serving aircraft operations up to but not including 18,000 feet MSL.
(See AIRWAY).

LOW ALTITUDE ALERT, CHECK YOUR ALTITUDE IMMEDIATELY—(See SAFETY ALERT).

LOW ALTITUDE ALERT SYSTEM—An automated function of the TPX-42 that alerts the controller when a Mode C transponder-equipped aircraft on an IFR flight plan is below a predetermined minimum safe altitude. If requested by the pilot, LAAS monitoring is also available to VFR Mode C transponder-equipped aircraft.

LOW APPROACH—An approach over an airport or runway following an instrument approach or a VFR approach including the go-around maneuver where the pilot intentionally does not make contact with the runway.

LOW FREQUENCY—The frequency band between 30 and 300 kHz.

MAA—(See MAXIMUM AUTHORIZED ALTITUDE).

MACH NUMBER—The ratio of true airspeed to the speed of sound; e.g., MACH .82, MACH 1.6.
(See AIRSPEED).

MACH TECHNIQUE [ICAO]—Describes a control technique used by air traffic control whereby turbojet aircraft operating successively along suitable routes are cleared to maintain appropriate MACH numbers for a relevant portion of the en route phase of flight. The principle objective is to achieve improved utilization of the airspace and to ensure that separation between successive aircraft does not decrease below the established minima.

MAINTAIN—
1. Concerning altitude/flight level, the term means to remain at the altitude/flight level specified. The phrase "climb and" or "descend and" normally precedes "maintain" and the altitude assignment; e.g., "descend and maintain 5,000."
2. Concerning other ATC instructions, the term is used in its literal sense; e.g., maintain VFR.

*MAKE SHORT APPROACH—*Used by ATC to inform a pilot to alter his traffic pattern so as to make a short final approach.
(See TRAFFIC PATTERN).

MANDATORY ALTITUDE—An altitude depicted on an instrument Approach Procedure Chart requiring the aircraft to maintain altitude at the depicted value.

MAP—(See MISSED APPROACH POINT).

MAKER BEACON—An electronic navigation facility transmitting a 75 mHz vertical fan or boneshaped radiation pattern. Marker beacons are identified by their modulation frequency and keying code, and when received by compatible airborne equipment, indicate to the pilot, both aurally and visually, that he is passing over the facility.
(See OUTER MARKER). (See MIDDLE MARKER). (See INNER MARKER).

MARSA—(See MILITARY AUTHORITY ASSUMES RESPONSIBILITY FOR SEPARATION OF AIRCRAFT).

MAXIMUM AUTHORIZED ALTITUDE—A published altitude representing the maximum usable altitude or flight level for an airspace structure or route segment. It is the highest altitude on a Federal airway, jet route, area navigation low or high route, or other direct route for which an MEA is designated in Part 95 at which adequate reception or navigation aid signals is assured.

*MAYDAY—*The international radiotelephony distress signal. When repeated three times, it indicates imminent and grave danger and that immediate assistance is requested.
(See PAN-PAN).

MCA—(See MINIMUM CROSSING ALTITUDE).

MDA—(See MINIMUM DESCENT ALTITUDE).

MEA—(See MINIMUM EN ROUTE IFR ALTITUDE).

METEOROLOGICAL IMPACT STATEMENT—An unscheduled planning forecast describing conditions expected to begin within 4 to 12 hours which may impact the flow of air traffic in a specific center's (ARTCC) area.

METER FIX TIME/SLOT TIME—A calculated time to depart the meter fix in order to cross the vertex at the ACLT. This time reflects descent speed adjustment and any applicable time that must be absorbed prior to crossing the meter fix.

METER LIST DISPLAY INTERVAL—A dynamic parameter which controls the number of minutes prior to the flight plan calculated time of arrival at the meter fix for each aircraft, at which time the TCLT is frozen and becomes an ACLT; i.e., the VTA is updated and consequently the TCLT modified as appropriate until frozen at which time updating is suspended and an ACLT is assigned. When frozen, the flight entry is inserted into the arrival sector's meter list for display on the sector PVD. MLDI is used if filed true airspeed is less than or equal to freeze speed parameters (FSPD).

METERING—A method of time-regulating arrival traffic flow into a terminal area so as not to exceed a predetermined terminal acceptance rate.

METERING AIRPORTS—Airports adapted for metering and for which optimum flight paths are defined. A maximum of 15 airports may be adapted.

METERING FIX—A fix along an established route from over which aircraft will be metered prior to entering terminal airspace. Normally, this fix should be established at a distance from the airport which will facilitate a profile descent 10,000 feet above airport elevation [AAE] or above.

METERING POSITION(S)—Adapted PVD's and associated "D" positions eligible for display of a metering position list. A maximum of four PVD's may be adapted.

METERING POSITION LIST—An ordered list of data on arrivals for a selected metering airport displayed on a metering position PVD.

MFT—(See METER FIX TIME/SLOT TIME).

MHA—(See MINIMUM HOLDING ALTITUDE).

MIA—(See MINIMUM IFR ALTITUDES).

MICROBURST—A small downburst with outbursts of damaging winds extending 2.5 miles or less. In spite of its small horizontal scale, an intense microburst could induce wind speeds as high as 150 knots.

MICROWAVE LANDING SYSTEM—A precision instrument approach system operating in the microwave spectrum which normally consists of the following components:

1. Azimuth Station.
2. Elevation Station.
3. Precision Distance Measuring Equipment.

(See MLS CATEGORIES).

MIDDLE COMPASS LOCATOR—(See COMPASS LOCATION).

MIDDLE MARKER—A marker beacon that defines a point along the glideslope of an ILS normally located at or near the point of decision height (ILS Category I). It is keyed to transmit alternate dots and dashes, with the alternate dots and dashes keyed at the rate of 95 dot/dash combinations per minute on a 1300 Hz tone, which is received aurally and visually by compatible airborne equipment.

(See MARKER BEACON). (See INSTRUMENT LANDING SYSTEM).

MID RVR—(See VISIBILITY).

MILES-IN-TRAIL—A specified distance between aircraft, normally, in the same stratum associated with the same destination or route of flight.

MILITARY AUTHORITY ASSUMES RESPONSIBILITY FOR SEPARATION OF AIRCRAFT—A condition whereby the military services involved assume responsibility for separation between participating military aircraft in the ATC system. It is used only for required IFR operations which are specified in letters of agreement or other appropriate FAA or military documents.

MILITARY OPERATIONS AREA—(See SPECIAL USE AIRSPACE).

MILITARY TRAINING ROUTES—Airspace defined vertical and lateral dimensions established for the conduct of military flight training at airspeeds in excess of 250 knots IAS.

(See IFR MILITARY TRAINING ROUTES). (See VFR MILITARY TRAINING ROUTES).

MINIMA—(See MINIMUMS).

MINIMUM CROSSING ALTITUDE—The lowest altitude at certain fixes at which an aircraft must cross when proceeding in the direction of a higher minimum en route IFR altitude (MEA).

(See MINIMUM EN ROUTE IFR ALTITUDE).

MINIMUM DESCENT ALTITUDE—The lowest altitude, expressed in feet above mean sea level, to which descent is authorized on final approach or during circle-to-land maneuvering in execution of a standard instrument approach procedure where no electronic glideslope is provided.

(See NONPRECISION APPROACH PROCEDURE).

MINIMUM EN ROUTE IFR ALTITUDE—The lowest published altitude between radio fixes which assures acceptable navigational signal coverage and meets obstacle clearance requirements between those fixes. The MEA prescribed for a Federal airway or segment thereof, area navigation low or high route, or other direct route applies to the entire width of the airway, segment, or route between the radio fixes defining the airway, segment, or route.

MINIMUM FUEL—Indicates that an aircraft's fuel supply has reached a state where, upon reaching the destination, it can accept little or no delay. This is not an emergency situation but merely indicates an emergency situation is possible should any undue delay occur.

MINIMUM HOLDING ALTITUDE—The lowest altitude prescribed for a holding pattern which assures navigational signal coverage, communications, and meets obstacle clearance requirements.

MINIMUM IFR ALTITUDES—Minimum altitudes for IFR operations as prescribed in Part 91. These altitudes are published on aeronautical charts and prescribed in Part 95 for airways and routes, and in Part 97 for standard instrument approach procedures. If no applicable minimum altitude is prescribed in FAR 95 or FAR 97, the following minimum IFR altitude applies:

1. In designated mountainous area, 2,000 feet above the highest obstacle within a horizontal distance of 4 nautical miles from the course to be flown; or
2. Other than mountainous areas, 1,000 feet above the highest obstacle within a horizontal distance of 4 nautical miles from the course to be flown; or

3. As otherwise authorized by the Administrator or assigned by ATC.
(See MINIMUM EN ROUTE IFR ALTITUDE).
(See MINIMUM OBSTRUCTION CLEARANCE ALTITUDE). (See MINIMUM CROSSING ALTITUDE). (See MINIMUM SAFE ALTITUDE). (See MINIMUM VECTORING ALTITUDE).

MINIMUM OBSTRUCTION CLEARANCE ALTITUDE—The lowest published altitude in effect between radio fixes on VOR airways, off-airway routes, or route segments which meets obstacle clearance requirements for the entire route segment and which assures acceptable navigational signal coverage only within 25 statute (22 nautical) miles of a VOR.

MINIMUM NAVIGATION PERFORMANCE SPECIFICATION—A set of standards which require aircraft to have a minimum navigation performance capability in order to operate in MNPS designated airspace. In addition, aircraft must be certified by their State of Registry for MNPS operation.

MINIMUM NAVIGATION PERFORMANCE SPECIFICATIONS AIRSPACE—Designated airspace in which MNPS procedures are applied between MNPS certified and equipped aircraft. Under certain conditions, non-MNPS aircraft can operate in MNPSA. However, standard oceanic separation minima is provided between the non-MNPS aircraft and other traffic. Currently, the only designated MNPSA is described as follows:

1. Between FL 275 and FL 400;
2. Between latitudes 27– N and the North Pole;
3. In the east, the eastern boundaries of the CTA's Santa Maria Oceanic, Shanwick Oceanic, and Reykjavik;
4. In the west, the western boundaries of CTA's Reykjavik and Gander Oceanic and New York Oceanic excluding the area west of 60– W and south of 38–30' N.

MINIMUM RECEPTION ALTITUDE—The lowest altitude at which an intersection can be determined.

MINIMUM SAFE ALTITUDE—

1. The minimum altitude specified in Part 91 for various aircraft operations.
2. Altitudes depicted on approach charts which provide at least 1,000 feet of obstacle clearance for emergency use within a specified distance from the navigation facility upon which a procedure is predicated. These altitudes will be identified as Minimum Sector Altitudes or Emergency Safe Altitudes and are established as follows:
   a. Minimum Sector Altitudes. Altitudes depicted on approach charts which provide at least 1,000 feet of obstacle clearance within a 25–mile radius of the navigation facility upon which the procedure is predicated. Sectors depicted on approach charts must be at least 90 degrees in scope. These altitudes are for emergency use only and do not necessarily assure acceptable navigational signal coverage.
   (See ICAO term Minimum Sector Altitude).
   b. Emergency Safe Altitudes. Altitudes depicted on approach charts which provide at least 1,000 feet of obstacle clearance in nonmountainous areas and 2,000 feet of obstacle clearance in designated mountainous areas within a 100–mile radius of the navigation facility upon which the procedure is predicated and normally used only in military procedures. These altitudes are identified on published procedures as "Emergency Safe Altitudes."

MINIMUM SAFE ALTITUDE WARNING—A function of the ARTS III computer that aids the controller by alerting him when a tracked Mode C—equipped aircraft is below or is predicted by the computer to go below the predetermined minimum safe altitude.

MINIMUM SECTOR ALTITUDE [ICAO]—The lowest altitude which may be used under emergency conditions which will provide a minimum clearance of 300 m (1,000 feet) above all obstacles located in an area contained within a sector of a circle of 46 km (25 NM) radius centered on a radio aid to navigation.

MINIMUMS—Weather condition requirements established for a particular operation or type of operation; e.g., IFR takeoff or landing, alternate airport for IFR flight plans, VFR flight, etc.
(See LANDING MINIMUMS). (See IFR TAKEOFF MINIMUMS AND DEPARTURE PROCEDURES). (See VFR CONDITIONS). (See IFR CONDITIONS).

MINIMUM VECTORING ALTITUDE—The lowest MSL altitude at which an IFR aircraft will be vectored by a radar controller, except as otherwise authorized for radar approaches, departures, and missed approaches. The altitude meets IFR obstacle clearance criteria. It may be lower than the published MEA along an airway or J-route segment. It may be utilized for radar vectoring only upon the controller's determination that an adequate radar return is being received from the aircraft being controlled. Charts depicting minimum vectoring altitudes are normally available only to the controllers and not to pilots.
(Refer to AIM).

MINUTES-IN-TRAIL—A specified interval between aircraft expressed in time. This method would more likely be utilized regardless of altitude.

MIS—(See METEOROLOGICAL IMPACT STATEMENT).

MISSED APPROACH—

1. A maneuver conducted by a pilot when an instrument approach cannot be completed to a landing. The route of flight and altitude are shown on instrument approach procedure charts. A pilot executing a missed approach prior to the Missed Approach Point (MAP) must continue along the final approach to the MAP. The pilot may climb immediately to the altitude specified in the missed approach procedure.

2. A term used by the pilot to inform ATC that he is executing the missed approach.

3. At locations where ATC radar service is provided, the pilot should conform to radar vectors when provided by ATC in lieu of the published missed approach procedure.

(See Missed Approach Point).

MISSED APPROACH POINT—A point prescribed in each instrument approach procedure at which a missed approach procedure shall be executed if the required visual reference does not exist.

(See MISSED APPROACH). (See SEGMENTS OF AN INSTRUMENT APPROACH PROCEDURE).

MISSED APPROACH PROCEDURE [ICAO]— The procedure to be followed if the approach cannot be continued.

MISSED APPROACH SEGMENT—(See SEGMENTS OF AN INSTRUMENT APPROACH PROCEDURE).

MLDI—(See METER LIST DISPLAY INTERVAL).

MLS—(See MICROWAVE LANDING SYSTEM).

MLS CATEGORIES—

1. MLS Category I. An MLS approach procedure which provides for an approach to a height above touchdown of not less than 200 feet and a runway visual range of not less than 1,800 feet.

2. MLS Category II. Undefined until data gathering/analysis completion.

3. MLS Category III. Undefined until data gathering/analysis completion.

MM—(See MIDDLE MARKER).

MNPS—(See MINIMUM PERFORMANCE SPECIFICATIONS).

MNPSA—(See MINIMUM PERFORMANCE SPECIFICATIONS AIRSPACE).

MOA—(See MILITARY OPERATIONS AREA).

MOCA—(See MINIMUM OBSTRUCTION CLEARANCE ALTITUDE).

MODE—The letter or number assigned to a specific pulse spacing of radio signals transmitted or received by ground interrogator or airborne transponder components of the Air Traffic Control Radar Beacon System (ATCRBS). Mode A (military Mode 3) and Mode C (altitude reporting) are used in air traffic control.

(See TRANSPONDER). (See INTERROGATOR). (See RADAR). (See ICAO term MODE).

MODE (SSR MODE) [ICAO]—The letter or number assigned to a specific pulse spacing of the interrogation signals transmitted by an interrogator. There are 4 modes, A, B, C and D specified in Annex 10, corresponding to four different interrogation pulse spacings.

MODE C INTRUDER ALERT—A function of certain air traffic control automated systems designed to alert radar controllers to existing or pending situations between a tracked target (known IFR or VFR aircraft) and an untracked target (unknown IFR or VFR aircraft) that requires immediate attention/action.

(See CONFLICT ALERT).

MONITOR—(When used with communication transfer) listen on a specific frequency and stand by for instructions. Under normal circumstances do not establish communications.

MOVEMENT AREA—The runways, taxiways, and other areas of an airport/heliport which are utilized for taxiing/hover taxiing, air taxiing, takeoff, and landing of aircraft, exclusive of loading ramps and parking areas. At those airports/heliports with a tower, specific approval for entry onto the movement area must be obtained from ATC.

(See ICAO term MOVEMENT AREA).

MOVEMENT AREA [ICAO]—That part of an aerodrome to be used for the takeoff, landing and taxiing of aircraft, consisting of the manoeuvreing area and the apron(s).

MOVING TARGET INDICATOR—An electronic device which will permit radar scope presentation only from targets which are in motion. A partial remedy for ground clutter.

MRA—(See MINIMUM RECEPTION ALTITUDE).

MSA—(See MINIMUM SAFE ALTITUDE).

MSAW—(See MINIMUM SAFE ALTITUDE WARNING).

MTI—(See MOVING TARGET INDICATOR).

MTR—(See MILITARY TRAINING ROUTES).

MULTICOM—A mobile service not open to public correspondence used to provide communications essential to conduct the activities being performed by or directed from private aircraft.

MULTIPLE RUNWAYS—The utilization of a dedicated arrival runway(s) for departures and a dedicated departure runway(s) for arrivals when feasible to reduce delays and enhance capacity.

MVA—(See MINIMUM VECTORING ALTITUDE).

NAS—(See NATIONAL AIRSPACE SYSTEM).

NAS STAGE A—The en route ATC system's radar, computers and computer programs, controller plan view displays (PVDs/Radar Scopes), input/output devices, and the related communications equipment which are integrated to form the heart of the automated IFR air traffic control system. This equipment performs Flight Data Processing (FDP) and Radar Data Processing (RDP). It interfaces with automated terminal systems and is used in the control of en route IFR aircraft.

NATIONAL AIRSPACE SYSTEM—The common network of U.S. airspace; air navigation facilities, equipment and services, airports or landing areas; aeronautical charts, information and services; rules, regulations and procedures, technical information, and manpower and material. Included are system components shared jointly with the military.

NATIONAL BEACON CODE ALLOCATION PLAN AIRSPACE—Airspace over United States territory located within the North American continent between Canada and Mexico, including adjacent territorial waters outward to about boundaries of oceanic control areas (CTA)/Flight Information Regions (FIR).
(See FLIGHT INFORMATION REGION).

NATIONAL FLIGHT DATA CENTER—A facility in Washington D.C., established by FAA to operate a central aeronautical information service for the collection, validation, and dissemination of aeronautical data in support of the activities of government, industry, and the aviation community. The information is published in the National Flight Data Digest.
(See NATIONAL FLIGHT DATA DIGEST).

NATIONAL FLIGHT DATA DIGEST—A daily (except weekends and Federal holidays) publication of flight information appropriate to aeronautical charts, aeronautical publications, Notices to Airmen, or other media serving the purpose of providing operational flight data essential to safe and efficient aircraft operations.

NATIONAL SEARCH AND RESCUE PLAN—An interagency agreement which provides for the effective utilization of all available facilities in all types of search and rescue missions.

NAVAID—(See NAVIGATIONAL AID).

NAVAID CLASSES—VOR, VORTAC, and TACAN aids are classed according to their operational use. The three classes of NAVAID's are:

   T-Terminal.
   L-Low altitude.
   H-High altitude.

The normal service range for T, L, and H class aids is found in the AIM. Certain operational requirements make it necessary to use some of these aids at greater service ranges than specified. Extended range is made possible through flight inspection determinations. Some aids also have lesser service range due to location, terrain, frequency protection, etc. Restrictions to service range are listed in Airport/Facility Directory.

NAVIGABLE AIRSPACE—Airspace at and above the minimum flight altitudes prescribed in the FAR's including airspace needed for safe takeoff and landing.

NAVIGATIONAL AID—Any visual or electronic device airborne or on the surface which provides point-to-point guidance information or position data to aircraft in flight.
(See AIR NAVIGATION FACILITY).

NBCAP AIRSPACE—(See NATIONAL BEACON CODE ALLOCATION PLAN AIRSPACE).

NDP—(See NONDIRECTIONAL BEACON).

NEGATIVE—"No," or "permission not granted," or "that is not correct."

NEGATIVE CONTACT—Used by pilots to inform ATC that:

1. Previously issued traffic is not in sight. It may be followed by the pilot's request for the controller to provide assistance in avoiding the traffic.

2. They were unable to contact ATC on a particular frequency.

NFDC—(See NATIONAL FLIGHT DATA CENTER).

NFDD—(See NATIONAL FLIGHT DATA DIGEST).

NIGHT—The time between the end of evening civil twilight and the beginning of morning civil twilight, as published in the American Air Almanac, converted to local time.
(See ICAO term NIGHT).

NIGHT [ICAO]—The hours between the end of evening civil twilight and the beginning of morning civil twilight or such other period between sunset and sunrise as may be specified by the appropriate authority.

Note: Civil twilight ends in the evening when the centre of the sun's disk is 6 degrees below the horizon and begins in the morning when the centre of the sun's disk is 6 degrees below the horizon.

NO GYRO APPROACH—A radar approach/vector provided in case of a malfunctioning gyro-compass or directional gyro. Instead of providing the pilot with headings to be flown, the controller observes the radar track and issues control instructions "turn right/left" or "stop turn" as appropriate.

NO GYRO VECTOR—(See NO GYRO APPROACH).

NONAPPROACH CONTROL TOWER—Authorizes aircraft to land or takeoff at the airport controlled by the tower or to transit the

Class D airspace. The primary function of a nonapproach control tower is the sequencing of aircraft in the traffic pattern and on the landing area. Nonapproach control towers also separate aircraft operating under instrument flight rules clearances from approach controls and centers. They provide ground control services to aircraft, vehicles, personnel, and equipment on the airport movement area.

NONCOMMON ROUTE/PORTION—That segment of a North American Route between the inland navigation facility and a designated North American terminal.

NONCOMPOSITE SEPARATION—Separation in accordance with minima other than the composite separation minimum specified for the area concerned.

NONDIRECTIONAL BEACON—An L/MF or UHF radio beacon transmitting nondirectional signals whereby the pilot of an aircraft equipped with direction finding equipment can determine his bearing to or from the radio beacon and "home" on or track to or from the station. When the radio beacon is installed in conjunction with the Instrument Landing System marker, it is normally called a Compass Locator.
(See COMPASS LOCATOR). (See AUTOMATIC DIRECTION FINDER).

NONMOVEMENT AREAS—Taxiways and apron (ramp) areas not under the control of air traffic.

NONPRECISION APPROACH—(See NONPRECISION APPROACH PROCEDURE).

NONPRECISION APPROACH PROCEDURE—A standard instrument approach procedure in which no electronic glideslope is provided; e.g., VOR, TACAN, NDB, LOC, ASR, LDA, OR SDF approaches.

NONRADAR—Precedes other terms and generally means without the use of radar, such as:

1. Nonradar Approach. Used to describe instrument approaches for which course guidance on final approach is not provided by ground-based precision or surveillance radar. Radar vectors to the final approach course may or may not be provided by ATC. Examples of nonradar approaches are VOR, NDB, TACAN, and ILS/MLS approaches.
(See FINAL APPROACH-IFR). (See FINAL APPROACH COURSE). (See RADAR APPROACH). (See INSTRUMENT APPROACH PROCEDURE).

2. Nonradar Approach Control. An ATC facility providing approach control service without the use of radar.
(See APPROACH CONTROL FACILITY). (See APPROACH CONTROL SERVICE).

3. Nonradar Arrival. An aircraft arriving at an airport without radar service or at an airport served by a radar facility and radar contact has not been established or has been terminated due to a lack of radar service to the airport.
(See RADAR ARRIVAL). (See RADAR SERVICE).

4. Nonradar Route. A flight path or route over which the pilot is performing his own navigation. The pilot may be receiving radar separation, radar monitoring, or other ATC services while on a nonradar route.
(See RADAR ROUTE).

5. Nonradar Separation. The spacing of aircraft in accordance with established minima without the use of radar; e.g., vertical, lateral, or longitudinal separation.
(See RADAR SEPARATION). (See ICAO term NONRADAR SEPARATION).

NONRADAR SEPARATION [ICAO]—The separation used when aircraft position information is derived from sources other than radar.

NOPAC—(See NORTH PACIFIC).

NORDO—(See LOST COMMUNICATIONS).

NORTH AMERICAN ROUTE—A numerically coded route preplanned over existing airway and route systems to and from specific coastal fixes serving the North Atlantic. North American Routes consist of the following:

1. Common Route/Portion. That segment of a North American Route between the inland navigation facility and the coastal fix.

2. NonCommon Route/Portion. That segment of a North American Route between the inland navigation facility and a designated North American terminal.

3. Inland Navigation Facility. A navigation aid on a North American Route at which the common route and/or the noncommon route begins or ends.

4. Coastal Fix. A navigation aid or intersection where an aircraft transitions between the domestic route structure and the oceanic route structure.

NORTH MARK—A beacon data block sent by the host computer to be displayed by the ARTS on a 360 degree bearing at a locally selected radar azimuth and distance. The North Mark is used to ensure correct range/azimuth orientation during periods of CENRAP.

NORTH PACIFIC—An organized route system between the Alaskan west coast and Japan.

NOTAM—(See NOTICE TO AIRMEN).

NOTICE TO AIRMEN—A notice containing information (not known sufficiently in advance to publicize by other means) concerning the establishment, condition, or change in any component (facility, service, or procedure of, or hazard in the National Airspace System) the timely knowledge of which is essential to personnel concerned with flight operations.

1. NOTAM(D). A NOTAM given (in addition to local dissemination) distant dissemination beyond the area of responsibility of the Flight Service Station. These NOTAM's will be stored and available until canceled.

2. NOTAM(L). A NOTAM given local dissemination by voice and other means, such as telautograph and telephone, to satisfy local user requirements.

3. FDC NOTAM. A NOTAM regulatory in nature, transmitted by USNOF and given system wide dissemination.

(See ICAO term NOTAM).

NOTAM [ICAO]—A notice containing information concerning the establishment, condition or change in any aeronautical facility, service, procedure or hazard, the timely knowledge of which is essential to personnel concerned with flight operations.

Class I Distribution—Distribution by means of telecommunication.

Class II Distribution—Distribution by means other than telecommunications.

NOTICE TO AIRMEN PUBLICATION—A publication issued every 14 days, designed primarily for the pilot, which contains current NOTAM information considered essential to the safety of flight as well as supplemental data to other aeronautical publications. The contraction NTAP is used in NOTAM text.

(See NOTICE TO AIRMEN).

NTAP—(See NOTICE TO AIRMEN PUBLICATION).

NUMEROUS TARGETS VICINITY (LOCATION)—A traffic advisory issued by ATC to advise pilots that targets on the radar scope are too numerous to issue individually.

(See TRAFFIC ADVISORIES).

OALT—(See OPERATIONAL ACCEPTABLE LEVEL OF TRAFFIC).

OBSTACLE—An existing object, object of natural growth, or terrain at a fixed geographical location or which may be expected at a fixed location within a prescribed area with reference to which vertical clearance is or must be provided during flight operation.

OBSTACLE FREE ZONE—The OFZ is a three dimensional volume of airspace which protects for the transition of aircraft to and from the runway. The OFZ clearing standard precludes taxiing and parked airplanes and object penetrations, except for frangible NAVAID locations that are fixed by function. Additionally, vehicles, equipment, and personnel may be authorized by air traffic control to enter the area using the provisions of Order 7110.65, Air Traffic Control, paragraph 3–5. The runway OFZ and when applicable, the inner–approach OFZ, and the inner–transitional OFZ, comprise the OFZ.

1. Runway OFZ. The runway OFZ is a defined volume of airspace centered above the runway. The runway OFZ is the airspace above the surface whose elevation at any point is the same as the elevation of the nearest point on the runway centerline. The runway OFZ extends 200 feet beyond each end of the runway. The width is as follows:

a. For runways serving large airplanes, the greater of:

(1) 400 feet, or

(2) 180 feet, plus the wingspan of the most demanding airplane, plus 20 feet per 1,000 feet of airport elevation.

b. For runways serving only small airplanes:

(1) 300 feet for precision instrument runways.

(2) 250 feet for other runways serving small airplanes with approach speeds of 50 knots, or more.

(3) 120 feet for other runways serving small airplanes with approach speeds of less than 50 knots.

2. Inner–approach OFZ. The inner–approach OFZ is a defined volume of airspace centered on the approach area. The inner–approach OFZ applies only to runways with an approach lighting system. The inner–approach OFZ begins 200 feet from the runway threshold at the same elevation as the runway threshold and extends 200 feet beyond the last light unit in the approach lighting system. The width of the inner–approach OFZ is the same as the runway OFZ and rises at a slope of 50 (horizontal) to 1 (vertical) from the beginning.

3. Inner–transitional OFZ. The inner transitional surface OFZ is a defined volume of airspace along the sides of the runway and inner–approach OFZ and applies only to precision instrument runways. The inner–transitional surface OFZ slopes 3 (horizontal) to 1 (vertical) out from the edges of the runway OFZ and inner–approach OFZ to a height of 150 feet above the established airport elevation.

OBSTRUCTION—Any object/obstacle exceeding the obstruction standards specified by Part 77, Subpart C.

OBSTRUCTION LIGHT—A light or one of a group of lights, usually red or white, frequently mounted on a surface structure or natural terrain to warn pilots of the presence of an obstruction.

OCEANIC AIRSPACE—Airspace over the oceans of the world, considered international airspace, where oceanic separation and procedures per the International Civil Aviation Organization are applied. Responsibility for the provisions of air traffic control service in this airspace is delegated to various countries, based generally upon geographic proximity and the availability of the required resources.

OCEANIC DISPLAY AND PLANNING SYSTEM—An automated digital display system which provides flight data processing, conflict probe, and situation display for oceanic air traffic control.

OCEANIC NAVIGATIONAL ERROR REPORT—A report filed when an aircraft exiting oceanic airspace has been observed by radar to be off course. ONER reporting parameters and procedures are contained in Order 7110.82, Monitoring of Navigational Performance In Oceanic Areas.

OCEANIC PUBLISHED ROUTE—A route established in international airspace and charted or described in flight information publications, such as Route Charts, DOD Enroute Charts,. Chart Supplements, NOTAM's, and Track Messages.

OCEANIC TRANSITION ROUTE—An ATS route established for the purpose of transitioning aircraft to/from an organized track system.

ODAPS—(See OCEANIC DISPLAY AND PLANNING SYSTEM).

OFF COURSE—A term used to describe a situation where an aircraft has reported a position fix or is observed on radar at a point not on the ATC-approved route of flight.

OFFSHORE CONTROL AREA—That portion of airspace between the U.S. 12–mile limit and the oceanic CTA/FIR boundary within which air traffic control is exercised. These areas are established to permit the application of domestic procedures in the provision of air traffic control services. Offshore control area is generally synonymous with Federal Aviation Regulations, Part 71, Subpart E, "Control Areas and Control Area Extensions."

OFF-ROUTE VECTOR—A vector by ATC which takes an aircraft off a previously assigned route. Altitudes assigned by ATC during such vectors provide required obstacle clearance.

OFFSET PARALLEL RUNWAYS—Staggered runways having centerlines which are parallel.

OFT—(See OUTER FIX TIME).

OM—(See OUTER MARKER).

OMEGA—An RNAV system designed for long-range navigation based upon ground-based electronic navigational aid signals.

ONER—(See OCEANIC NAVIGATIONAL ERROR REPORT).

OPERATIONAL—(See DUE REGARD).

ON COURSE—

1. Used to indicate that an aircraft is established on the route centerline.

2. Used by ATC to advise a pilot making a radar approach that his aircraft is lined up on the final approach course.
(See ON-COURSE INDICATION).

ON-COURSE INDICATION—An indication on an instrument, which provides the pilot a visual means of determining that the aircraft is located on the centerline of a given navigational track, or an indication on a radar scope that an aircraft is on a given track.

OPERATIONAL ACCEPTABLE LEVEL OF TRAFFIC—An air traffic activity level associated with the designed capacity for a sector or airport. The OALT considers dynamic changes in staffing, personnel experience levels, equipment outages, operational configurations, weather, traffic complexity, aircraft performance mixtures, transitioning flights, adjacent airspace, handoff/point-out responsibilities, and other factors that may affect an air traffic operational position or system element. The OALT is normally considered to be the total number of aircraft that any air traffic functional position can accommodate for a defined period of time under a given set of circumstances.

OPPOSITE DIRECTION AIRCRAFT—Aircraft are operating in opposite directions when:

1. They are following the same track in reciprocal directions; or
2. Their tracks are parallel and the aircraft are flying in reciprocal directions; or
3. Their tracks intersect at an angle of more than 135°.

OPTION APPROACH—An approach requested and conducted by a pilot which will result in either a touch-and-go, missed approach, low approach, stop-and-go, or full stop landing.
(See CLEARED FOR THE OPTION).

ORGANIZED TRACK SYSTEM—A movable system of oceanic tracks that traverses the North Atlantic between Europe and North America the physical position of which is determined twice daily taking the best advantage of the winds aloft.

ORGANIZED TRACK SYSTEM—A series of ATS routes which are fixed and charted; i.e., CEP, NOPAC, or flexible and described by NOTAM; i.e., NAT TRACK MESSAGE.

OTR—(See OCEANIC TRANSITION ROUTE).

OTS—(See ORGANIZED TRACK SYSTEM).

OUT—The conversation is ended and no response is expected.

OUTER AREA (associated with Class C airspace)—Nonregulatory airspace surrounding designated Class C airspace airports wherein ATC provides radar vectoring and sequencing on a full-time basis for all IFR and participating VFR aircraft. The service provided in the outer area is called Class C service which includes: IFR/IFR-standard IFR separation; IFR/VFR-traffic advisories and conflict resolution; and VFR/VFR-traffic advisories and, as appropriate, safety alerts. The normal radius will be 20 nautical miles with some variations based on site-specific requirements. The outer area extends outward from the primary Class C airspace airport and extends from the lower limits of radar/radio coverage up to the ceiling of the approach control's delegated airspace excluding the Class C charted area and other airspace as appropriate.

(See CONTROLLED AIRSPACE). (See CONFLICT RESOLUTION).

OUTER COMPASS LOCATOR—(See COMPASS LOCATOR).

OUTER FIX—A general term used within ATC to describe fixes in the terminal area, other than the final approach fix. Aircraft are normally cleared to these fixes by an Air Route Traffic Control Center or an Approach Control Facility. Aircraft are normally cleared from these fixes to the final approach fix or final approach course.

OUTER FIX—An adapted fix along the converted route of flight, prior to the meter fix, for which crossing times are calculated and displayed in the metering position list.

OUTER FIX TIME—A calculated time to depart the outer fix in order to cross the vertex at the ACLT. The time reflects descent speed adjustments and any applicable delay time that must be absorbed prior to crossing the meter fix.

OUTER MARKER—A marker beacon at or near the glideslope intercept altitude of an ILS approach. It is keyed to transmit two dashes per second on a 400 Hz tone, which is received aurally and visually by compatible airborne equipment. The OM is normally located four to seven miles from the runway threshold on the extended centerline of the runway.

(See MARKER BEACON). (See INSTRUMENT LANDING SYSTEM).

OVER—My transmission is ended; I expect a response.

OVERHEAD MANEUVER—A series of predetermined maneuvers prescribed for aircraft (often in formation) for entry into the VFR traffic pattern and to proceed to a landing. An overhead maneuver is not an IFR approach procedure. These aircraft shall be considered VFR and the IFR flight plan is cancelled when the aircraft crosses the landing threshold on the initial approach portion of the maneuver. The pattern usually specifies the following:

1. The radio contact required of the pilot.
2. The speed to be maintained.
3. An initial approach 3 to 5 miles in length.
4. An elliptical pattern consisting of two 180 degree turns.
5. A break point at which the first 180 degree turn is started.
6. The direction of turns.
7. Altitude (at least 500 feet above the conventional pattern).
8. A "Roll-out" on final approach not less than 1/4 mile from the landing threshold and not less than 300 feet above the ground.

OVERLYING CENTER—The ARTCC facility that is responsible for arrival/departure operations at a specific terminal.

P TIME—(See PROPOSED DEPARTURE TIME).

PAN-PAN—The international radio-telephony urgency signal. When repeated three times, indicates uncertainty or alert followed by the nature of the urgency.

(See MAYDAY).

PAR—(See PRECISION APPROACH RADAR).

PAR [ICAO]—(See ICAO Term PRECISION APPROACH RADAR).

PARALLEL ILS APPROACHES—Approaches to parallel runways by IFR aircraft which, when established inbound toward the airport on the adjacent final approach courses, are radar-separated by at least 2 miles.

(See FINAL APPROACH COURSE). (See SIMULTANEOUS ILS APPROACHES).

PARALLEL MLS APPROACHES—(See PARALLEL ILS APPROACHES).

PARALLEL OFFSET ROUTE—A parallel track to the left or right of the designated or established airway/route. Normally associated with Area Navigation (RNAV) operations.

(See AREA NAVIGATION).

PARALLEL RUNWAYS—Two or more runways at the same airport whose centerlines are parallel. In addition to runway number, parallel runways are designated as L (left) and R (right) or, if three parallel runways exist, L (left), C (center), and R (right).

PATWAS—(See PILOTS AUTOMATIC TELEPHONE WEATHER ANSWERING SERVICE).

PBCT—(See PROPOSED BOUNDARY CROSSING TIME).

PERMANENT ECHO—Radar signals reflected from fixed objects on the earth's surface; e.g., buildings, towers, terrain. Permanent echoes are distinguished from "ground clutter" by being definable locations rather than large areas. Under certain conditions they may be used to check radar alignment.

PHOTO RECONNAISSANCE—Military activity that requires locating individual photo targets and navigating to the targets at a preplanned angle and altitude. The activity normally requires a lateral route width of 16 NM and altitude range of 1,500 feet to 10,000 feet AGL.

PIDP—(See PROGRAMMABLE INDICATOR DATA PROCESSOR).

PILOT BRIEFING—A service provided by the FSS to assist pilots in flight planning. Briefing items may include weather information, NOTAMS, military activities, flow control information, and other items as requested.

PILOT IN COMMAND—The pilot responsible for the operation and safety of an aircraft during flight time.

PILOTS AUTOMATIC TELEPHONE WEATHER ANSWERING SERVICE—A continuous telephone recording containing current and forecast weather information for pilots.
(See FLIGHT SERVICE STATION).

PILOT'S DISCRETION—When used in conjunction with altitude assignments, means that ATC has offered the pilot the option of starting climb or descent whenever he wishes and conducting the climb or descent at any rate he wishes. He may temporarily level off at any intermediate altitude. However, once he has vacated an altitude, he may not return to that altitude.

PILOT WEATHER REPORT—A report of meteorological phenomena encountered by aircraft in flight.

PIREP—(See PILOT WEATHER REPORT).

POINT OUT—(See RADAR POINT OUT).

POLAR TRACK STRUCTURE—A system of organized routes between Iceland and Alaska which overlie Canadian MNPS Airspace.

POSITION REPORT—A report over a known location as transmitted by an aircraft to ATC.
(Refer to AIM).

POSITION SYMBOL—A computer-generated indication shown on a radar display to indicate the mode of tracking.

POSITIVE CONTROL—The separation of all air traffic within designated airspace by air traffic control.

PRACTICE INSTRUMENT APPROACH—An instrument approach procedure conducted by a VFR or an IFR aircraft for the purpose of pilot training or proficiency demonstrations.

PREARRANGED COORDINATION—A standardized procedure which permits an air traffic controller to enter the airspace assigned to another air traffic controller without verbal coordination. The procedures are defined in a facility directive which ensures standard separation between aircraft.

PRECIPITATION—Any or all forms of water particles (rain, sleet, hail, or snow) that fall from the atmosphere and reach the surface.

PRECISION APPROACH—(See PRECISION APPROACH PROCEDURE).

PRECISION APPROACH PROCEDURE—A standard instrument approach procedure in which an electronic glideslope/glidepath is provided; e.g., ILS/MLS and PAR.
(See INSTRUMENT LANDING SYSTEM). (See MICROWAVE LANDING SYSTEM). (See PRECISION APPROACH RADAR).

PRECISION APPROACH RADAR—Radar equipment in some ATC facilities operated by the FAA and/or the military services at joint-use civil/military locations and separate military installations to detect and display azimuth, elevation, and range of aircraft on the final approach course to a runway. This equipment may be used to monitor certain nonradar approaches, but is primarily used to conduct a precision instrument approach (PAR) wherein the controller issues guidance instructions to the pilot based on the aircraft's position in relation to the final approach course (azimuth), the glidepath (elevation), and the distance (range) from the touchdown point on the runway as displayed on the radar scope.
(See GLIDEPATH). (See PAR).—The abbreviation "PAR" is also used to denote preferential arrival routes in ARTCC computers.
(See PREFERENTIAL ROUTES). (See ICAO term PRECISION APPROACH RADAR).

PRECISION APPROACH RADAR [ICAO]—Primary radar equipment used to determine the position of an aircraft during final approach, in terms of lateral and vertical deviations relative to a nominal approach path, and in range relative to touchdown.

Note: Precision approach radars are designed to enable pilots of aircraft to be given guidance by radio communication during the final stages of the approach to land.

PRECISION RUNWAY MONITOR—Provides air traffic controllers with high precision secondary surveillance data for aircraft on final approach to closely spaced parallel runways. High resolution color monitoring displays (FMA) are required to present surveillance track data to controllers along with detailed maps depicting approaches and no transgression zone.

PREFERENTIAL ROUTES—Preferential routes (PDR's, PAR's, and PDAR's) are adapted in ARTCC computers to accomplish inter/intrafacility controller coordination and to assure that flight data is posted at the proper control positions. Locations having a need for these specific inbound and outbound routes normally publish such routes in local facility bulletins, and their use by pilots minimizes flight plan route amendments. When the workload or traffic situation permits, controllers normally provide radar vectors or assign requested routes to minimize circuitous routing. Preferential routes are usually confined to one ARTCC's area and are referred to by the following names or acronyms:

1. Preferential Departure Route (PDR). A specific departure route from an airport or terminal area to an en route point where there is no further need for flow control. It may be included in a Standard Instrument Departure (SID) or a Preferred IFR Route.

2. Preferential Arrival Route (PAR). A specific arrival route from an appropriate en route point to an airport or terminal area. It may be included in a Standard Terminal Arrival (STAR) or a Preferred IFR Route. The abbreviation "PAR" is used primarily within the ARTCC and should not be confused with the abbreviation for Precision Approach Radar.

3. Preferential Departure and Arrival Route (PDAR). A route between two terminals which are within or immediately adjacent to one ARTCC's area. PDAR's are not synonymous with Preferred IFR Routes but may be listed as such as they do accomplish essentially the same purpose.

(See PREFERRED IFR ROUTES). (See NAS STAGE A).

PREFERRED IFR ROUTES—Routes established between busier airports to increase system efficiency and capacity. They normally extend through one or more ARTCC areas and are designed to achieve balanced traffic flows among high density terminals. IFR clearances are issued on the basis of these routes except when severe weather avoidance procedures or other factors dictate otherwise. Preferred IFR Routes are listed in the Airport/Facility Directory. If a flight is planned to or from an area having such routes but the departure or arrival point is not listed in the Airport/Facility Directory, pilots may use that part of a Preferred IFR Route which is appropriate for the departure or arrival point that is listed. Preferred IFR Routes are correlated with SID's and STAR's and may be defined by airways, jet routes, direct routes between NAVAID's, Waypoints, NAVAID radials/DME, or any combination thereof.

(See STANDARD INSTRUMENT DEPARTURE). (See STANDARD TERMINAL ARRIVAL). (See PREFERENTIAL ROUTES). (See CENTER'S AREA).

PRE-FLIGHT PILOT BRIEFING—(See PILOT BRIEFING).

PREVAILING VISIBILITY—(See VISIBILITY).

PRM—(See PRECISION RUNWAY MONITOR).

PROCEDURE TURN—The maneuver prescribed when it is necessary to reverse direction to establish an aircraft on the intermediate approach segment or final approach course. The outbound course, direction of turn, distance within which the turn must be completed, and minimum altitude are specified in the procedure. However, unless otherwise restricted, the point at which the turn may be commenced and the type and rate of turn are left to the discretion of the pilot.

(See ICAO term PROCEDURE TURN).

PROCEDURE TURN [ICAO]—A manoeuvre in which a turn is made away from a designated track followed by a turn in the opposite direction to permit the aircraft to intercept and proceed along the reciprocal of the designated track.

Note 1: Procedure turns are designated "left" or "right" according to the direction of the initial turn.

Note 2: Procedure turns may be designated as being made either in level flight or while descending, according to the circumstances of each individual approach procedure.

PROCEDURE TURN INBOUND—That point of a procedure turn maneuver where course reversal has been completed and an aircraft is established inbound on the intermediate approach segment or final approach course. A report of "procedure turn inbound" is normally used by ATC as a position report for separation purposes.

(See FINAL APPROACH COURSE). (See PROCEDURE TURN). (See SEGMENTS OF AN INSTRUMENT APPROACH PROCEDURE).

PROFILE DESCENT—An uninterrupted descent (except where level flight is required for speed adjustment; e.g., 250 knots at 10,000 feet MSL) from cruising altitude/level to interception of a glideslope or to a minimum altitude specified for the initial or intermediate approach segment of a nonprecision instrument approach. The profile descent normally terminates at the approach gate or where the glideslope or other appropriate minimum altitude is intercepted.

PROGRAMMABLE INDICATOR DATA PROCESSOR—The PIDP is a modification to the AN/TPX–42 interrogator system currently installed in fixed RAPCON's. The PIDP detects, tracks, and predicts secondary radar aircraft targets. These are displayed by means of computer-generated symbols and alphanumeric characters depicting flight identification, aircraft altitude, ground speed, and flight plan data. Although primary radar targets are not tracked, they are displayed coincident with the secondary radar targets as well as with the other symbols and alphanumerics. The system has the capability of interfacing with ARTCC's.

PROGRESS REPORT—(See POSITION REPORT).

PROGRESSIVE TAXI—Precise taxi instructions given to a pilot unfamiliar with the airport or issued in stages as the aircraft proceeds along the taxi route.

PROHIBITED AREA—(See SPECIAL USE AIRSPACE).

(See ICAO term PROHIBITED AREA).

PROHIBITED AREA [ICAO]—An airspace of defined dimensions, above the land areas or territorial waters of a State, within which the flight of aircraft is prohibited.

PROPOSED BOUNDARY CROSSING TIME—Each center has a PBCT parameter for each internal airport. Proposed internal flight plans are transmitted to the adjacent center if the flight time along the proposed route from the departure airport to the center boundary is less than or equal to the value of PBCT or if airport adaptation specifies transmission regardless of PBCT.

PROPOSED DEPARTURE TIME—The time a scheduled flight will depart the gate (scheduled operators) or the actual runway off time for nonscheduled operators. For EDCT purposes, the ATCSCC adjusts the "P" time for scheduled operators to reflect the runway off times.

PROTECTED AIRSPACE—The airspace on either side of an oceanic route/track that is equal to one-half the lateral separation minimum except where reduction of protected airspace has been authorized.

PT—(See PROCEDURE TURN).

PTS—(See POLAR TRACK STRUCTURE).

PUBLISHED ROUTE—A route for which an IFR altitude has been established and published; e.g., Federal Airways, Jet Routes, Area Navigation Routes, Specified Direct Routes.

QUEUING—(See STAGING/QUEUING).

QNE—The barometric pressure used for the standard altimeter setting (29.92 inches Hg.).

QNH—The barometric pressure as reported by a particular station.

QUADRANT—A quarter part of a circle, centered on a NAVAID, oriented clockwise from magnetic north as follows: NE quadrant 000-089, SE quadrant 090-179, SW quadrant 180-269, NW quadrant 270-359.

QUICK LOOK—A feature of NAS Stage A and ARTS which provides the controller the capability to display full data blocks of tracked aircraft from other control positions.

QUOTA FLOW CONTROL—A flow control procedure by which the Central Flow Control Function (CFCF) restricts traffic to the ARTC Center area having an impacted airport, thereby avoiding sector/area saturation.

(See AIR TRAFFIC CONTROL SYSTEM COMMAND CENTER).

RADAR—A device which, by measuring the time interval between transmission and reception of radio pulses and correlating the angular orientation of the radiated antenna beam or beams in azimuth and/or elevation, provides information on range, azimuth, and/or elevation of objects in the path of the transmitted pulses.

1. Primary Radar. A radar system in which a minute portion of a radio pulse transmitted from a site is reflected by an object and then received back at that site for processing and display at an air traffic control facility.

2. Secondary Radar/Radar Beacon (ATCRBS). A radar system in which the object to be detected is fitted with cooperative equipment in the form of a radio receiver/transmitter (transponder). Radar pulses transmitted from the searching transmitter/receiver (interrogator) site are received in the cooperative equipment and used to trigger a distinctive transmission from the transponder. This reply transmission, rather than a reflected signal, is then received back at the transmitter/receiver site for processing and display at an air traffic control facility.

(See TRANSPONDER). (See INTERROGATOR). (See ICAO term RADAR). (See ICAO term PRIMARY RADAR). (See ICAO term SECONDARY RADAR).

RADAR [ICAO]—A radio detection device which provides information on range, azimuth and/or elevation of objects.

Primary Radar.—Radar system which uses reflected radio signals.

Secondary Radar.—Radar system wherein a radio signal transmitted from a radar station initiates the transmission of a radio signal from another station.

RADAR ADVISORY—The provision of advice and information based on radar observations.
(See ADVISORY SERVICE).

RADAR ALTIMETER—(See RADIO ALTIMETER).

RADAR APPROACH—An instrument approach procedure which utilizes Precision Approach Radar (PAR) or Airport Surveillance Radar (ASR).

(See SURVEILLANCE APPROACH). (See AIRPORT SURVEILLANCE RADAR). (See PRECISION APPROACH RADAR). (See INSTRUMENT APPROACH PROCEDURE). (See ICAO term RADAR APPROACH).

RADAR APPROACH [ICAO]—An approach, executed by an aircraft, under the direction of a radar controller.

RADAR APPROACH CONTROL FACILITY—A terminal ATC facility that uses radar and nonradar capabilities to provide approach control services to aircraft arriving, departing, or transiting airspace controlled by the facility. Provides radar ATC services to aircraft operating in the vicinity of one or more civil and/or military airports in a terminal area. The facility may provide services of a ground controlled approach (GCA); i.e., ASR and PAR approaches. A radar approach control facility may be operated by FAA, USAF, US Army, USN, USMC, or jointly by FAA and a military service. Specific facility nomenclatures are used for administrative purposes only and are related to the physical location of the facility and the operating service generally as follows:

Army Radar Approach Control (ARAC) (Army).

Radar Air Traffic Control Facility (RATCF) (Navy/FAA).

Radar Approach Control (RAPCON) (Air Force/FAA).

Terminal Radar Approach Control (TRACON) (FAA).

Tower/Airport Traffic Control Tower (ATCT) (FAA). (Only those towers delegated approach control authority.)

RADAR ARRIVAL—An aircraft arriving at an airport served by a radar facility and in radar contact with the facility.
(See NONRADAR).

RADAR BEACON—(See RADAR).

RADAR CONTACT—

1. Used by ATC to inform an aircraft that it is identified on the radar display and radar flight following will be provided until radar identification is terminated. Radar service may also be provided within the limits of necessity and capability. When a pilot is informed of "radar contact," he automatically discontinues reporting over compulsory reporting points.
(See RADAR FLIGHT FOLLOWING). (See RADAR CONTACT LOST). (See RADAR SERVICE). (See RADAR SERVICE TERMINATED).

2. The term used to inform the controller that the aircraft is identified and approval is granted for the aircraft to enter the receiving controllers airspace.
(See ICAO term RADAR CONTACT).

RADAR CONTACT LOST—Used by ATC to inform a pilot that radar data used to determine the aircraft's position is no longer being received, or is no longer reliable and radar service is no longer being provided. The loss may be attributed to several factors including the aircraft merging with weather or ground clutter, the aircraft operating below radar line of sight coverage, the aircraft entering an area of poor radar return, failure of the aircraft transponder, or failure of the ground radar equipment. (See Clutter). (See Radar Contact).
(See CLUTTER). (See RADAR CONTACT).

RADAR CLUTTER [ICAO]—The visual indication on a radar display of unwanted signals.

RADAR CONTACT [ICAO]—The situation which exists when the radar blip or radar position symbol of a particular aircraft is seen and identified on a radar display.

RADAR ENVIRONMENT—An area in which radar service may be provided.

(See RADAR CONTACT). (See RADAR SERVICE). (See ADDITIONAL SERVICES). (See TRAFFIC ADVISORIES).

RADAR FLIGHT FOLLOWING—The observation of the progress of radar identified aircraft, whose primary navigation is being provided by the pilot, wherein the controller retains and correlates the aircraft identity with the appropriate target or target symbol displayed on the radar scope.
(See RADAR CONTACT). (See RADAR SERVICE).

RADAR IDENTIFICATION—The process of ascertaining that an observed radar target is the radar return from a particular aircraft.
(See RADAR CONTACT). (See RADAR SERVICE). (See ICAO term RADAR IDENTIFICATION).

RADAR IDENTIFICATION [ICAO]—The process of correlating a particular radar blip or radar position symbol with a specific aircraft.

RADAR IDENTIFIED AIRCRAFT—An aircraft, the position of which has been correlated with an observed target or symbol on the radar display.
(See RADAR CONTACT). (See RADAR CONTACT LOST).

RADAR MONITORING—(See RADAR SERVICE).

RADAR NAVIGATIONAL GUIDANCE—(See RADAR SERVICE).

RADAR POINT OUT—An action taken by a controller to transfer the radar identification of an aircraft to another controller if the aircraft will or may enter the airspace or protected airspace of another controller and radio communications will not be transferred.

RADAR REQUIRED—A term displayed on charts and approach plates and included in FDC Notams to alert pilots that segments of either an instrument approach procedure or a route are not navigable because of either the absence or unusability of a NAVAID. The pilot can expect to be provided radar navigational guidance while transiting segments labeled with this term.
(See RADAR ROUTE). (See RADAR SERVICE).

RADAR ROUTE—A flight path or route over which an aircraft is vectored. Navigational guidance and altitude assignments are provided by ATC.
(See FLIGHT PATH). (See ROUTE).

RADAR SEPARATION—(See RADAR SERVICE).

RADAR SERVICE—A term which encompasses one or more of the following services based on the use of radar which can be provided by a controller to a pilot of a radar identified aircraft.

1. Radar Monitoring. The radar flight-following of aircraft, whose primary navigation is being performed by the pilot, to observe and note deviations from its authorized

flight path, airway, or route. When being applied specifically to radar monitoring of instrument approaches; i.e., with precision approach radar (PAR) or radar monitoring of simultaneous ILS/MLS approaches, it includes advice and instructions whenever an aircraft nears or exceeds the prescribed PAR safety limit or simultaneous ILS/MLS no transgression zone.

(See ADDITIONAL SERVICES). (See TRAFFIC ADVISORIES).

2. Radar Navigational Guidance. Vectoring aircraft to provide course guidance.

3. Radar Separation. Radar spacing of aircraft in accordance with established minima.

(See ICAO term RADAR SERVICE).

RADAR SERVICE [ICAO]—Term used to indicate a service provided directly by means of radar.

Radar Monitoring.—The use of radar for the purpose of providing aircraft with information and advice relative to significant deviations from nominal flight path.

Radar Separation.—The separation used when aircraft position information is derived from radar sources.

RADAR SERVICE TERMINATED—Used by ATC to inform a pilot that he will no longer be provided any of the services that could be received while in radar contact. Radar service is automatically terminated, and the pilot is not advised in the following cases:

1. An aircraft cancels its IFR flight plan, except within Class B airspace, Class C airspace, a TRSA, or where Basic Radar service is provided.

2. An aircraft conducting an instrument, visual, or contact approach has landed or has been instructed to change to advisory frequency.

3. An arriving VFR aircraft, receiving radar service to a tower-controlled airport within Class B airspace, Class C airspace, a TRSA, or where Basic Radar service is provided, has landed; or to all other airports, is instructed to change to tower or advisory frequency.

4. An aircraft completes a radar approach.

RADAR SURVEILLANCE—The radar observation of a given geographical area for the purpose of performing some radar function.

RADAR TRAFFIC ADVISORIES—Advisories issued to alert pilots to known or observed radar traffic which may affect the intended route of flight of their aircraft.

(See TRAFFIC ADVISORIES).

RADAR TRAFFIC INFORMATION SERVICE—(See TRAFFIC ADVISORIES).

RADAR VECTORING [ICAO]—Provision of navigational guidance to aircraft in the form of specific headings, based on the use of radar.

RADAR WEATHER ECHO INTENSITY LEVELS—Existing radar systems cannot detect turbulence. However, there is a direct correlation between the degree of turbulence and other weather features associated with thunderstorms and the radar weather echo intensity. The National Weather Service has categorized radar weather echo intensity for precipitation into six levels. These levels are sometimes expressed during communications as "VIP LEVEL" 1 through 6 (derived from the component of the radar that produces the information-Video Integrator and Processor). The following list gives the "VIP LEVELS" in relation to the precipitation intensity within a thunderstorm:

Level 1. WEAK
Level 2. MODERATE
Level 3. STRONG
Level 4. VERY STRONG
Level 5. INTENSE
Level 6. EXTREME

RADIAL—A magnetic bearing extending from a VOR/VORTAC/TACAN navigation facility.

RADIO—

1. A device used for communication.

2. Used to refer to a flight service station; e.g., "Seattle Radio" is used to call Seattle FSS.

RADIO ALTIMETER—Aircraft equipment which makes use of the reflection of radio waves from the ground to determine the height of the aircraft above the surface.

RADIO BEACON—(See NONDIRECTIONAL BEACON).

RADIO DETECTION AND RANGING—(See RADAR).

RADIO MAGNETIC INDICATOR—An aircraft navigational instrument coupled with a gyro compass or similar compass that indicates the direction of a selected NAVAID and indicates bearing with respect to the heading of the aircraft.

RAMP—(See APRON).

RANDOM ALTITUDE—An altitude inappropriate for direction of flight and/or not in accordance with paragraph 4–40.

RANDOM ROUTE—Any route not established or charted/published or not otherwise available to all users.

RC—(See ROAD RECONNAISSANCE).

RCAG—(See REMOTE COMMUNICATIONS AIR/GROUND FACILITY).

RCC—(See RESCUE COORDINATION CENTER).

RCO—(See REMOTE COMMUNICATIONS OUTLET).

RCR—(See RUNWAY CONDITION READING).

READ BACK—Repeat my message back to me.

RECEIVING CONTROLLER—A controller/facility receiving control of an aircraft from another controller/facility.

RECEIVING FACILITY—(See RECEIVING CONTROLLER).

REDUCE SPEED TO (SPEED)—(See SPEED ADJUSTMENT).

REIL—(See RUNWAY END IDENTIFIER LIGHTS).

RELEASE TIME—A departure time restriction issued to a pilot by ATC (either directly or through an authorized relay) when necessary to separate a departing aircraft from other traffic.

(See ICAO term RELEASE TIME).

RELEASE TIME [ICAO]—Time prior to which an aircraft should be given further clearance or prior to which it should not proceed in case of radio failure.

REMOTE COMMUNICATIONS AIR/GROUND FACILITY—An unmanned VHF/UHF transmitter/receiver facility which is used to expand ARTCC air/ground communications coverage and to facilitate direct contact between pilots and controllers. RCAG facilities are sometimes not equipped with emergency frequencies 121.5 mHz and 243.0 mHz.

REMOTE COMMUNICATIONS OUTLET—An unmanned communications facility remotely controlled by air traffic personnel. RCO's serve FSS's. RTR's serve terminal ATC facilities. An RCO or RTR may be UHF or VHF and will extend the communication range of the air traffic facility. There are several classes of RCO's and RTR's. The class is determined by the number of transmitters or receivers. Classes A through G are used primarily for air/ground purposes. RCO and RTR class O facilities are nonprotected outlets subject to undetected and prolonged outages. RCO (O's) and RTR (O's) were established for the express purpose of providing ground-to-ground communications between air traffic control specialists and pilots located at a satellite airport for delivering en route clearances, issuing departure authorizations, and acknowledging instrument flight rules cancellations or departure/landing times. As a secondary function, they may be used for advisory purposes whenever the aircraft is below the coverage of the primary air/ground frequency.

REMOTE TRANSMITTER/RECEIVER—(See REMOTE COMMUNICATIONS OUTLET).

REPORT—Used to instruct pilots to advise ATC of specified information; e.g., "Report passing Hamilton VOR."

REPORTING POINT—A geographical location in relation to which the position of an aircraft is reported.

(See COMPULSORY REPORTING POINTS). (See ICAO term REPORTING POINT).

REPORTING POINT [ICAO]—A specified geographical location in relation to which the position of an aircraft can be reported.

REQUEST FULL ROUTE CLEARANCE—Used by pilots to request that the entire route of flight be read verbatim in an ATC clearance. Such request should be made to preclude receiving an ATC clearance based on the original filed flight plan when a filed IFR flight plan has been revised by the pilot, company, or operations prior to departure.

RESCUE COORDINATION CENTER—A search and rescue (SAR) facility equipped and manned to coordinate and control SAR operations in an area designated by the SAR plan. The U.S. Coast Guard and the U.S. Air Force have responsibility for the operation of RCC's.

(See ICAO term RESCUE CO-ORDINATION CENTRE).

RESCUE CO-ORDINATION CENTRE [ICAO]—A unit responsible for promoting efficient organization of search and rescue service and for co-ordinating the conduct of search and rescue operations within a search and rescue region.

RESTRICTED AREA—(See SPECIAL USE AIRSPACE).

(See ICAO term RESTRICTED AREA).

RESTRICTED AREA [ICAO]—An airspace of defined dimensions, above the land areas or territorial waters of a State, within which the flight of aircraft is restricted in accordance with certain specified conditions.

RESUME OWN NAVIGATION—Used by ATC to advise a pilot to resume his own navigational responsibility. It is issued after completion of a radar vector or when radar contact is lost while the aircraft is being radar vectored.

(See RADAR CONTACT LOST). (See RADAR SERVICE TERMINATED).

RMI—(See RADIO MAGNETIC INDICATOR).

RNAV—(See AREA NAVIGATION).

RNAV [ICAO]—(See ICAO Term AREA NAVIGATION).

RNAV APPROACH—An instrument approach procedure which relies on aircraft area navigation equipment for navigational guidance.

(See INSTRUMENT APPROACH PROCEDURE). (See AREA NAVIGATION).

ROAD RECONNAISSANCE—Military activity requiring navigation along roads, railroads, and rivers. Reconnaissance route/route segments are seldom along a straight line and normally require a lateral route width of 10 NM to 30 NM and an altitude range of 500 feet to 10,000 feet AGL.

ROGER—I have received all of your last transmission. It should not be used to answer a question requiring a yes or a no answer.
(See AFFIRMATIVE). (See NEGATIVE).

ROLLOUT RVR—(See VISIBILITY).

ROUTE—A defined path, consisting of one or more courses in a horizontal plane, which aircraft traverse over the surface of the earth.
(See AIRWAY). (See JET ROUTE). (See PUBLISHED ROUTE). (See UNPUBLISHED ROUTE).

ROUTE SEGMENT—As used in Air Traffic Control, a part of a route that can be defined by two navigational fixes, two NAVAID's, or a fix and a NAVAID.
(See FIX). (See ROUTE). (See ICAO term ROUTE SEGMENT).

ROUTE SEGMENT [ICAO]—A portion of a route to be flown, as defined by two consecutive significant points specified in a flight plan.

RSA—(See RUNWAY SAFETY AREA).

RTR—(See REMOTE TRANSMITTER/RECEIVER).

RUNWAY—A defined rectangular area on a land airport prepared for the landing and takeoff run of aircraft along its length. Runways are normally numbered in relation to their magnetic direction rounded off to the nearest 10 degrees; e.g., Runway 01, Runway 25.
(See PARALLEL RUNWAYS). (See ICAO term RUNWAY).

RUNWAY [ICAO]—A defined rectangular area on a land aerodrome prepared for the landing and takeoff of aircraft.

RUNWAY CENTERLINE LIGHTING—(See AIRPORT LIGHTING).

RUNWAY CONDITION READING—Numerical decelerometer readings relayed by air traffic controllers at USAF and certain civil bases for use by the pilot in determining runway braking action. These readings are routinely relayed only to USAF and Air National Guard Aircraft.
(See BRAKING ACTION).

RUNWAY END IDENTIFIER LIGHTS—(See AIRPORT LIGHTING).

RUNWAY GRADIENT—The average slope, measured in percent, between two ends or points on a runway. Runway gradient is depicted on Government aerodrome sketches when total runway gradient exceeds 0.3%.

RUNWAY HEADING—The magnetic direction that corresponds with the runway centerline extended, not the painted runway number. When cleared to "fly or maintain runway heading," pilots are expected to fly or maintain the heading that corresponds with the extended centerline of the departure runway. Drift correction shall not be applied; e.g., Runway 4, actual magnetic heading of the runway centerline 044, fly 044.

RUNWAY IN USE/ACTIVE RUNWAY/DUTY RUNWAY—Any runway or runways currently being used for takeoff or landing. When multiple runways are used, they are all considered active runways. In the metering sense, a selectable adapted item which specifies the landing runway configuration or direction of traffic flow. The adapted optimum flight plan from each transition fix to the vertex is determined by the runway configuration for arrival metering processing purposes.

RUNWAY LIGHTS—(See AIRPORT LIGHTING).

RUNWAY MARKINGS—(See AIRPORT MARKING AIDS).

RUNWAY OVERRUN—In military aviation exclusively, a stabilized or paved area beyond the end of a runway, of the same width as the runway plus shoulders, centered on the extended runway centerline.

RUNWAY PROFILE DESCENT—An instrument flight rules (IFR) air traffic control arrival procedure to a runway published for pilot use in graphic and/or textual form and may be associated with a STAR. Runway Profile Descents provide routing and may depict crossing altitudes, speed restrictions, and headings to be flown from the en route structure to the point where the pilot will receive clearance for and execute an instrument approach procedure. A Runway Profile Descent may apply to more than one runway if so stated on the chart.

RUNWAY SAFETY AREA—A defined surface surrounding the runway prepared, or suitable, for reducing the risk of damage to airplanes in the event of an undershoot, overshoot, or excursion from the runway. The dimensions of the RSA vary and can be determined by using the criteria contained within Advisory Circular 150/5300–13, Chapter 3. Figure 3–1 in Advisory Circular 150/5300–13 depicts the RSA. The design standards dictate that the RSA shall be:

1. Cleared, graded, and have no potentially hazardous ruts, humps, depressions, or other surface variations;

2. Drained by grading or storm sewers to prevent water accumulation;

3. Capable, under dry conditions, of supporting snow removal equipment, aircraft rescue and firefighting equipment, and the occasional passage of aircraft without causing structural damage to the aircraft; and,

4. Free of objects, except for objects that need to be located in the runway safety area because of their function. These objects

shall be constructed on low impact resistant supports (frangible mounted structures) to the lowest practical height with the frangible point no higher than 3 inches above grade.

RUNWAY USE PROGRAM—A noise abatement runway selection plan designed to enhance noise abatement efforts with regard to airport communities for arriving and departing aircraft. These plans are developed into runway use programs and apply to all turbojet aircraft 12,500 pounds or heavier; turbojet aircraft less than 12,500 pounds are included only if the airport proprietor determines that the aircraft creates a noise problem. Runway use programs are coordinated with FAA offices, and safety criteria used in these programs are developed by the Office of Flight Operations. Runway use programs are administered by the Air Traffic Service as "Formal" or "Informal" programs.

1. Formal Runway Use Program. An approved noise abatement program which is defined and acknowledged in a Letter of Understanding between Flight Operations, Air Traffic Service, the airport proprietor, and the users. Once established, participation in the program is mandatory for aircraft operators and pilots as provided for in FAR 91.129.

2. Informal Runway Use Program. An approved noise abatement program which does not require a Letter of Understanding, and participation in the program is voluntary for aircraft operators/pilots.

RUNWAY VISIBILITY VALUE—(See VISIBILITY).

RUNWAY VISUAL RANGE—(See VISIBILITY).

SAFETY ALERT—A safety alert issued by ATC to aircraft under their control if ATC is aware the aircraft is at an altitude which, in the controller's judgement, places the aircraft in unsafe proximity to terrain, obstructions, or other aircraft. The controller may discontinue the issuance of further alerts if the pilot advises he is taking action to correct the situation or has the other aircraft in sight.

1. Terrain/Obstruction Alert. A safety alert issued by ATC to aircraft under their control if ATC is aware the aircraft is at an altitude which, in the controller's judgment, places the aircraft in unsafe proximity to terrain/obstructions; e.g., "Low Altitude Alert, check your altitude immediately."

2. Aircraft Conflict Alert. A safety alert issued by ATC to aircraft under their control if ATC is aware of an aircraft that is not under their control at an altitude which, in the controller's judgment, places both aircraft in unsafe proximity to each other. With the alert, ATC will offer the pilot an alternate course of action when feasible; e.g., "Traffic Alert, advise you turn right heading zero niner zero or climb to eight thousand immediately."

The issuance of a safety alert is contingent upon the capability of the controller to have an awareness of an unsafe condition. The course of action provided will be predicated on the other traffic under ATC control. Once the alert is issued, it is solely the pilot's prerogative to determine what course of action, if any, he will take.

SAIL BACK—A maneuver during high wind conditions (usually with power off) where float plane movement is controlled by water rudders/opening and closing cabin doors.

SAME DIRECTION AIRCRAFT—Aircraft are operating in the same direction when:

1. They are following the same track in the same direction; or

2. Their tracks are parallel and the aircraft are flying in the same direction; or

3. Their tracks intersect at an angle of less than 45 degrees.

SAR—(See SEARCH AND RESCUE).

SAY AGAIN—Used to request a repeat of the last transmission. Usually specifies transmission or portion thereof not understood or received; e.g., "Say again all after ABRAM VOR."

SAY ALTITUDE—Used by ATC to ascertain an aircraft's specific altitude/flight level. When the aircraft is climbing or descending, the pilot should state the indicated altitude rounded to the nearest 100 feet.

SAY HEADING—Used by ATC to request an aircraft heading. The pilot should state the actual heading of the aircraft.

SDF—(See SIMPLIFIED DIRECTIONAL FACILITY).

SEA LANE—A designated portion of water outlined by visual surface markers for and intended to be used by aircraft designed to operate on water.

SEARCH AND RESCUE—A service which seeks missing aircraft and assists those found to be in need of assistance. It is a cooperative effort using the facilities and services of available Federal, state and local agencies. The U.S. Coast Guard is responsible for coordination of search and rescue for the Maritime Region, and the U.S. Air Force is responsible for search and rescue for the Inland Region. Information pertinent to search and rescue should be passed through any air traffic facility or be transmitted directly to the Rescue Coordination Center by telephone.

(See FLIGHT SERVICE STATION). (See RESCUE COORDINATION CENTER).

SEARCH AND RESCUE FACILITY—A facility responsible for maintaining and operating a search and rescue (SAR) service to render aid to persons and property in distress. It is any SAR unit, station, NET, or other operational activity which can be usefully employed during an SAR Mission; e.g., a Civil Air Patrol Wing, or a Coast Guard Station.
(See SEARCH AND RESCUE).

SECTIONAL AERONAUTICAL CHARTS—
(See AERONAUTICAL CHART).

SECTOR LIST DROP INTERVAL—A parameter number of minutes after the meter fix time when arrival aircraft will be deleted from the arrival sector list.

SEE AND AVOID—A visual procedure wherein pilots of aircraft flying in visual meteorological conditions (VMC), regardless of type of flight plan, are charged with the responsibility to observe the presence of other aircraft and to maneuver their aircraft as required to avoid the other aircraft. Right-of-way rules are contained in FAR 91.
(See INSTRUMENT FLIGHT RULES). (See VISUAL FLIGHT RULES). (See VISUAL METEOROLOGICAL CONDITIONS). (See INSTRUMENT METEOROLOGICAL CONDITIONS).

SEGMENTED CIRCLE—A system of visual indicators designed to provide traffic pattern information at airports without operating control towers.

SEGMENTS OF AN INSTRUMENT APPROACH PROCEDURE—An instrument approach procedure may have as many as four separate segments depending on how the approach procedure is structured.

1. Initial Approach. The segment between the initial approach fix and the intermediate fix or the point where the aircraft is established on the intermediate course or final approach course.
(See ICAO term INITIAL APPROACH SEGMENT).

2. Intermediate Approach. The segment between the intermediate fix or point and the final approach fix.
(See ICAO term INTERMEDIATE APPROACH SEGMENT).

3. Final Approach. The segment between the final approach fix or point and the runway, airport, or missed approach point.
(See ICAO term FINAL APPROACH SEGMENT).

4. Missed Approach. The segment between the missed approach point or the point of arrival at decision height and the missed approach fix at the prescribed altitude.
(See ICAO term MISSED APPROACH PROCEDURE).

SELECTED GROUND DELAYS—A traffic management procedure whereby selected flights are issued ground delays to better regulate traffic flows over a particular fix or area.

SEPARATION—In air traffic control, the spacing of aircraft to achieve their safe and orderly movement in flight and while landing and taking off.

SEPARATION [ICAO]—Spacing between aircraft, levels or tracks.

SEPARATION MINIMA—The minimum longitudinal, lateral, or vertical distances by which aircraft are spaced through the application of air traffic control procedures.
(See SEPARATION).

SERVICE—A generic term that designates functions or assistance available from or rendered by air traffic control. For example, Class C service would denote the ATC services provided within a Class C airspace area.

SEVERE WEATHER AVOIDANCE PLAN—An approved plan to minimize the affect of severe weather on traffic flows in impacted terminal and/or ARTCC areas. SWAP is normally implemented to provide the least disruption to the ATC system when flight through portions of airspace is difficult or impossible due to severe weather.

SEVERE WEATHER FORECAST ALERTS—Preliminary messages issued in order to alert users that a Severe Weather Watch Bulletin (WW) is being issued. These messages define areas of possible severe thunderstorms or tornado activity. The messages are unscheduled and issued as required by the National Severe Storm Forecast Center at Kansas City, Missouri.
(See SIGMET). (See CONVECTIVE SIGMET). (See CWA). (See AIRMET).

SFA—(See SINGLE FREQUENCY APPROACH).

SFO—(See SIMULATED FLAMEOUT).

SHF—(See SUPER HIGH FREQUENCY).

SHORT RANGE CLEARANCE—A clearance issued to a departing IFR flight which authorizes IFR flight to a specific fix short of the destination while air traffic control facilities are coordinating and obtaining the complete clearance.

SHORT TAKEOFF AND LANDING AIRCRAFT—An aircraft which, at some weight within its approved operating weight, is capable of operating from a STOL runway in compliance with the applicable STOL characteristics, airworthiness, operations, noise, and pollution standards.
(See VERTICAL TAKEOFF AND LANDING AIRCRAFT).

SIAP—(See STANDARD INSTRUMENT APPROACH PROCEDURE).

SIDESTEP MANEUVER—A visual maneuver accomplished by a pilot at the completion of an instrument approach to permit a straight-in landing on a parallel runway not more than 1,200 feet to either side of the runway to which the instrument approach was conducted.

SIGMET—A weather advisory issued concerning weather significant to the safety of all aircraft. SIGMET advisories cover severe and extreme turbulence, severe icing, and widespread dust or sandstorms that reduce visibility to less than 3 miles.
(See AWW). (See CONVECTIVE SIGMET). (See CWA). (See AIRMET). (See ICAO term SIGMET INFORMATION).

SIGMET INFORMATION [ICAO]—Information issued by a meteorological watch office concerning the occurrence or expected occurrence of specified en-route weather phenomena which may affect the safety of aircraft operations.

SIGNIFICANT METEOROLOGICAL INFORMATION—(See SIGMET).

SIGNIFICANT POINT—A point, whether a named intersection, a NAVAID, a fix derived from a NAVAID(s), or geographical coordinate expressed in degrees of latitude and longitude, which is established for the purpose of providing separation, as a reporting point, or to delineate a route of flight.

SIMPLIFIED DIRECTIONAL FACILITY—A NAVAID used for nonprecision instrument approaches. The final approach course is similar to that of an ILS localizer except that the SDF course may be offset from the runway, generally not more than 3 degrees, and the course may be wider than the localizer, resulting in a lower degree of accuracy.

SIMULATED FLAMEOUT—A practice approach by a jet aircraft (normally military) at idle thrust to a runway. The approach may start at a relatively high altitude over a runway (high key) and may continue on a relatively high and wide downwind leg with a high rate of descent and a continuous turn to final. It terminates in a landing or low approach. The purpose of this approach is to simulate a flameout.
(See FLAMEOUT).

SIMULTANEOUS ILS APPROACHES—An approach system permitting simultaneous ILS/MLS approaches to airports having parallel runways separated by at least 4,300 feet between centerlines. Integral parts of a total system are ILS/MLS, radar, communications, ATC procedures, and appropriate airborne equipment.
(See PARALLEL RUNWAYS).

SIMULTANEOUS MLS APPROACHES—(See SIMULTANEOUS ILS APPROACHES).

SIMULTANEOUS OPERATIONS ON INTERSECTING RUNWAYS—Operations which include simultaneous takeoffs and landings and/or simultaneous landings when a landing aircraft is able and is instructed by the controller to hold short of the intersecting runway or designated hold short point. Pilots are expected to promptly inform the controller if the hold short clearance cannot be accepted.
(See PARALLEL RUNWAYS).

SINGLE DIRECTION ROUTES—Preferred IFR Routes which are sometimes depicted on high altitude en route charts and which are normally flown in one direction only.
(See PREFERRED IFR ROUTES). (Refer to AIRPORT/FACILITY DIRECTORY).

SINGLE FREQUENCY APPROACH—A service provided under a letter of agreement to military single-piloted turbojet aircraft which permits use of a single UHF frequency during approach for landing. Pilots will not normally be required to change frequency from the beginning of the approach to touchdown except that pilots conducting an en route descent are required to change frequency when control is transferred from the air route traffic control center to the terminal facility. The abbreviation "SFA" in the DOD FLIP IFR Supplement under "Communications" indicates this service is available at an aerodrome.

SINGLE-PILOTED AIRCRAFT—A military turbojet aircraft possessing one set of flight controls, tandem cockpits, or two sets of flight controls but operated by one pilot is considered single-piloted by ATC when determining the appropriate air traffic service to be applied.
(See SINGLE FREQUENCY APPROACH).

SLASH—A radar beacon reply displayed as an elongated target.

SLDI—(See SECTOR LIST DROP INTERVAL).

SLOT TIME—(See METER FIX TIME/SLOT TIME).

SLOW TAXI—To taxi a float plane at low power or low RPM.

SN—(See SYSTEM STRATEGIC NAVIGATION).

SPEAK SLOWER—Used in verbal communications as a request to reduce speech rate.

SPECIAL EMERGENCY—A condition of air piracy or other hostile act by a person(s) aboard an aircraft which threatens the safety of the aircraft or its passengers.

SPECIAL INSTRUMENT APPROACH PROCEDURE—(See INSTRUMENT APPROACH PROCEDURE).

SPECIAL USE AIRSPACE—Airspace of defined dimensions identified by an area on the surface of the earth wherein activities must be confined because of their nature and/or wherein limitations may be imposed upon aircraft operations that are not a part of those activities. Types of special use airspace are:

1. Alert Area. Airspace which may contain a high volume of pilot training activities or an unusual type of aerial activity, neither

of which is hazardous to aircraft. Alert Areas are depicted on aeronautical charts for the information of nonparticipating pilots. All activities within an Alert Area are conducted in accordance with Federal Aviation Regulations, and pilots of participating aircraft as well as pilots transiting the area are equally responsible for collision avoidance.

2. Controlled Firing Area. Airspace wherein activities are conducted under conditions so controlled as to eliminate hazards to nonparticipating aircraft and to ensure the safety of persons and property on the ground.

3. Military Operations Area (MOA). An MOA is an airspace assignment of defined vertical and lateral dimensions established outside Class A airspace to separate/segregate certain military activities from IFR traffic and to identify for VFR traffic where these activities are conducted.

(Refer to Aim).

4. Prohibited Area. Designated airspace within which the flight of aircraft is prohibited.

5. Restricted Area. Airspace designated under Part 73, within which the flight of aircraft, while not wholly prohibited, is subject to restriction. Most restricted areas are designated joint use and IFR/VFR operations in the area may be authorized by the controlling ATC facility when it is not being utilized by the using agency. Restricted areas are depicted on en route charts. Where joint use is authorized, the name of the ATC controlling facility is also shown.

6. Warning Area. Airspace which may contain hazards to nonparticipating aircraft in international airspace.

SPECIAL VFR CONDITIONS—Meteorological conditions that are less than those required for basic VFR flight in Class B, C, D, or E surface areas and in which some aircraft are permitted flight under visual flight rules.
(See SPECIAL VFR OPERATIONS).

SPECIAL VFR FLIGHT [ICAO]—A VFR flight cleared by air traffic control to operate within Class B, C, D, and E surface areas in meteorological conditions below VMC.

SPECIAL VFR OPERATIONS—Aircraft operating in accordance with clearances within Class B, C, D, and E surface areas in weather conditions less than the basic VFR weather minima. Such operations must be requested by the pilot and approved by ATC.
(See SPECIAL VFR CONDITIONS). (See ICAO term SPECIAL VFR FLIGHT).

SPEED—(See AIRSPEED).
(See GROUND SPEED).

SPEED ADJUSTMENT—An ATC procedure used to request pilots to adjust aircraft speed to a specific value for the purpose of providing desired spacing. Pilots are expected to maintain a speed of plus or minus 10 knots or 0.02 mach number of the specified speed. Examples of speed adjustments are:

1. "Increase/reduce speed to mach point (number)."

2. "Increase/reduce speed to (speed in knots)" or "Increase/reduce speed (number of knots) knots."

SPEED BRAKES—Moveable aerodynamic devices on aircraft that reduce airspeed during descent and landing.

SPEED SEGMENTS—Portions of the arrival route between the transition point and the vertex along the optimum flight path for which speeds and altitudes are specified. There is one set of arrival speed segments adapted from each transition point to each vertex. Each set may contain up to six segments.

SQUAWK (Mode, Code, Function)—Activate specific modes/codes/functions on the aircraft transponder; e.g., "Squawk three/alpha, two one zero five, low."
(See TRANSPONDER).

STAGING/QUEUING—The placement, integration, and segregation of departure aircraft in designated movement areas of an airport by departure fix, EDCT, and/or restriction.

STANDARD INSTRUMENT APPROACH PROCEDURE—(See INSTRUMENT APPROACH PROCEDURE).

STANDARD INSTRUMENT DEPARTURE—A preplanned instrument flight rule (IFR) air traffic control departure procedure printed for pilot use in graphic and/or textual form. SID's provide transition from the terminal to the appropriate en route structure.
(See IFR TAKEOFF MINIMUMS AND DEPARTURE PROCEDURES).

STANDARD INSTRUMENT DEPARTURE CHARTS—(See AERONAUTICAL CHART).

STANDARD RATE TURN—A turn of three degrees per second.

STANDARD TERMINAL ARRIVAL—A preplanned instrument flight rule (IFR) air traffic control arrival procedure published for pilot use in graphic and/or textual form. STAR's provide transition from the en route structure to an outer fix or an instrument approach fix/arrival waypoint in the terminal area.

STANDARD TERMINAL ARRIVAL CHARTS—(See AERONAUTICAL CHART).

STAND BY—Means the controller or pilot must pause for a few seconds, usually to attend to other duties of a higher priority. Also means to wait as in "stand by for clearance." The caller should reestablish contact if a delay is lengthy. "Stand by" is not an approval or denial.

STAR—(See STANDARD TERMINAL ARRIVAL).

STATE AIRCRAFT—Aircraft used in military, customs and police service, in the exclusive service of any government, or of any political subdivision, thereof including the government of any state, territory, or possession of the United States or the District of Columbia, but not including any government-owned aircraft engaged in carrying persons or property for commercial purposes.

STATIC RESTRICTIONS—Those restrictions that are usually not subject to change, fixed, in place, and/or published.

STATIONARY RESERVATIONS—Altitude reservations which encompass activities in a fixed area. Stationary reservations may include activities, such as special tests of weapons systems or equipment, certain U.S. Navy carrier, fleet, and anti-submarine operations, rocket, missile and drone operations, and certain aerial refueling or similar operations.

STEPDOWN FIX—A fix permitting additional descent within a segment of an instrument approach procedure by identifying a point at which a controlling obstacle has been safely overflown.

STEP TAXI—To taxi a float plane at full power or high RPM.

STEP TURN—A maneuver used to put a float plane in a planing configuration prior to entering an active sea lane for takeoff. The STEP TURN maneuver should only be used upon pilot request.

STEREO ROUTE—A routinely used route of flight established by users and ARTCC's identified by a coded name; e.g., ALPHA 2. These routes minimize flight plan handling and communications.

STOL AIRCRAFT—(See SHORT TAKEOFF AND LANDING AIRCRAFT).

STOP ALTITUDE SQUAWK—Used by ATC to inform an aircraft to turn-off the automatic altitude reporting feature of its transponder. It is issued when the verbally reported altitude varies 300 feet or more from the automatic altitude report.
(See ALTITUDE READOUT). (See TRANSPONDER).

STOP AND GO—A procedure wherein an aircraft will land, make a complete stop on the runway, and then commence a takeoff from that point.
(See LOW APPROACH). (See OPTION APPROACH).

STOP BURST—(See STOP STREAM).

STOP BUZZER—(See STOP STREAM).

STOPOVER FLIGHT PLAN—A flight plan format which permits in a single submission the filing of a sequence of flight plans through interim full-stop destinations to a final destination.

STOP SQUAWK (Mode or Code)—Used by ATC to tell the pilot to turn specified functions of the aircraft transponder off.
(See STOP ALTITUDE SQUAWK). (See TRANSPONDER).

STOP STREAM—Used by ATC to request a pilot to suspend electronic countermeasure activity.
(See JAMMING).

STOPWAY—An area beyond the takeoff runway no less wide than the runway and centered upon the extended centerline of the runway, able to support the airplane during an aborted takeoff, without causing structural damage to the airplane, and designated by the airport authorities for use in decelerating the airplane during an aborted takeoff.

STRAIGHT-IN APPROACH-IFR—An instrument approach wherein final approach is begun without first having executed a procedure turn, not necessarily completed with a straight-in landing or made to straight-in landing minimums.
(See STRAIGHT-IN LANDING). (See LANDING MINIMUMS). (See STRAIGHT-IN APPROACH-VFR).

STRAIGHT-IN APPROACH-VFR—Entry into the traffic pattern by interception of the extended runway centerline (final approach course) without executing any other portion of the traffic pattern.
(See TRAFFIC PATTERN).

STRAIGHT-IN LANDING—A landing made on a runway aligned within 30° of the final approach course following completion of an instrument approach.
(See STRAIGHT-IN APPROACH-IFR).

STRAIGHT-IN MINIMUMS—
(See STRAIGHT-IN LANDING MINIMUMS).

SUBSTITUTIONS—Users are permitted to exchange CTA's. Normally, the airline dispatcher will contact the ATCSCC with this request. The ATCSCC shall forward approved substitutions to the TMU's who will notify the appropriate terminals. Permissible swapping must not change the traffic load for any given hour of an EQF program.

SUBSTITUTE ROUTE—A route assigned to pilots when any part of an airway or route is unusable because of NAVAID status. These routes consist of:

1. Substitute routes which are shown on U.S. Government charts.
2. Routes defined by ATC as specific NAVAID radials or courses.
3. Routes defined by ATC as direct to or between NAVAID's.

SUNSET AND SUNRISE—The mean solar times of sunset and sunrise as published in the Nautical Almanac, converted to local standard time for the locality concerned. Within Alaska, the end of evening civil twilight and the beginning of morning civil twilight, as defined for each locality.

SUPER HIGH FREQUENCY—The frequency band between 3 and 30 gigahertz (gHz). The elevation and azimuth stations of the microwave landing system operate from 5031 mHz to 5091 in this spectrum.

SUPPLEMENTAL WEATHER SERVICE LOCATION—Airport facilities staffed with contract personnel who take weather observations and provide current local weather to pilots via telephone or radio. (All other services are provided by the parent FSS).

SUPPS—Refers to ICAO Document 7030 Regional Supplementary Procedures. SUPPS contain procedures for each ICAO Region which are unique to that Region and are not covered in the worldwide provisions identified in the ICAO Air Navigation Plan. Procedures contained in chapter 8 are based in part on those published in SUPPS.

SURFACE AREA—The airspace contained by the lateral boundary of the Class B, C, D, or E airspace designated for an airport that begins at the surface and extends upward.

SURPIC—A description of surface vessels in the area of a Search and Rescue incident including their predicted positions and their characteristics.

SURVEILLANCE APPROACH—An instrument approach wherein the air traffic controller issues instructions, for pilot compliance, based on aircraft position in relation to the final approach course (azimuth), and the distance (range) from the end of the runway as displayed on the controller's radar scope. The controller will provide recommended altitudes on final approach if requested by the pilot.

SWAP—(See SEVERE WEATHER AVOIDANCE PLAN).

SWSL—(See SUPPLEMENTAL WEATHER SERVICE LOCATION).

SYSTEM STRATEGIC NAVIGATION—Military activity accomplished by navigating along a preplanned route using internal aircraft systems to maintain a desired track. This activity normally requires a lateral route width of 10 NM and altitude range of 1,000 feet to 6,000 feet AGL with some route segments that permit terrain following.

TACAN—(See TACTICAL AIR NAVIGATION).

TACAN-ONLY AIRCRAFT—An aircraft, normally military, possessing TACAN with DME but no VOR navigational system capability.

Clearances must specify TACAN or VORTAC fixes and approaches.

TACTICAL AIR NAVIGATION—An ultra-high frequency electronic rho-theta air navigation aid which provides suitably equipped aircraft a continuous indication of bearing and distance to the TACAN station.
(See VORTAC).

TAILWIND—Any wind more than 90 degrees to the longitudinal axis of the runway. The magnetic heading of the runway shall be used as the basis for determining the longitudinal axis.

TAKEOFF AREA—(See LANDING AREA).

TAKE–OFF DISTANCE AVAILABLE [ICAO]—The length of the take–off run available plus the length of the clearway, if provided.

TAKE–OFF RUN AVAILABLE [ICAO]—The length of runway declared available and suitable for the ground run of an aeroplane take–off.

TARGET—The indication shown on a radar display resulting from a primary radar return or a radar beacon reply.
(See RADAR). (See TARGET SYMBOL). (See ICAO term TARGET).

TARGET [ICAO]—In radar:
1. Generally, any discrete object which reflects or retransmits energy back to the radar equipment.
2. Specifically, an object of radar search or surveillance.

TARGET RESOLUTION—A process to ensure that correlated radar targets do not touch. Target resolution shall be applied as follows:
1. Between the edges of two primary targets or the edges of the ASR–9 primary target symbol.
2. Between the end of the beacon control slash and the edge of a primary target.
3. Between the ends of two beacon control slashes.— MANDATORY TRAFFIC ADVISORIES AND SAFETY ALERTS SHALL BE ISSUED WHEN THIS PROCEDURE IS USED.

Note: This procedure shall not be provided utilizing mosaic radar systems.

TARGET SYMBOL—A computer-generated indication shown on a radar display resulting from a primary radar return or a radar beacon reply.

TAXI—The movement of an airplane under its own power on the surface of an airport (Part 135.100–Note). Also, it describers the surface movement of helicopters equipped with wheels.
(See AIR TAXI). (See HOVER TAXI).

TAXI INTO POSITION AND HOLD—Used by ATC to inform a pilot to taxi onto the departure runway in takeoff position and hold. It is not authorization for takeoff. It is used when takeoff clearance cannot immediately be issued because of traffic or other reasons.

(See CLEARED FOR TAKEOFF).

TAXI PATTERNS—Patterns established to illustrate the desired flow of ground traffic for the different runways or airport areas available for use.

TCAS—(See TRAFFIC ALERT AND COLLISION AVOIDANCE SYSTEM).

TCH—(See THRESHOLD CROSSING HEIGHT).

TCLT—(See TENTATIVE CALCULATED LANDING TIME).

TDZE—(See TOUCHDOWN ZONE ELEVATION).

TELEPHONE INFORMATION BRIEFING SERVICE—A continuous telephone recording of meteorological and/or aeronautical information.

TENTATIVE CALCULATED LANDING TIME—A projected time calculated for adapted vertex for each arrival aircraft based upon runway configuration, airport acceptance rate, airport arrival delay period, and other metered arrival aircraft. This time is either the VTA of the aircraft or the TCLT/ACLT of the previous aircraft plus the AAI, whichever is later. This time will be updated in response to an aircraft's progress and its current relationship to other arrivals.

TERMINAL AREA—A general term used to describe airspace in which approach control service or airport traffic control service is provided.

TERMINAL AREA FACILITY—A facility providing air traffic control service for arriving and departing IFR, VFR, Special VFR, and on occasion en route aircraft.

(See APPROACH CONTROL FACILITY). (See TOWER).

TERMINAL VFR RADAR SERVICE—A national program instituted to extend the terminal radar services provided IFR aircraft to VFR aircraft. Pilot participation in the program is urged but is not mandatory. The program is divided into two parts and referred to as Stage II and Stage III. The Stage service provided at a particular location is contained in the Airport/Facility Directory. A national program instituted to extend the terminal radar services provided instrument flight rules (IFR) aircraft to visual flight rules (VFR) aircraft. The program is divided into four types service referred to as basic radar service, terminal radar service area (TRSA) service, Class B service and Class C service. The type of service provided at a particular location is contained in the Airport/Facility Directory.

1. Basic Radar Service: These services are provided for VFR aircraft by all commissioned terminal radar facilities. Basic radar service includes safety alerts, traffic advisories, limited radar vectoring when requested by the pilot, and sequencing at locations where procedures have been established for this purpose and/or when covered by a letter of agreement. The purpose of this service is to adjust the flow of arriving IFR and VFR aircraft into the traffic pattern in a safe and orderly manner and to provide traffic advisories to departing VFR aircraft.

2. TRSA Service: This service provides, in addition to basic radar service, sequencing of all IFR and participating VFR aircraft to the primary airport and separation between all participating VFR aircraft. The purpose of this service is to provide separation between all participating VFR aircraft and all IFR aircraft operating within the area defined as a TRSA.

3. Class C Service: This service provides, in addition to basic radar service, approved separation between IFR and VFR aircraft, and sequencing of VFR aircraft, and sequencing of VFR arrivals to the primary airport.

4. Class B Service: This service provides, in addition to basic radar service, approved separation of aircraft based on IFR, VFR, and/or weight, and sequencing of VFR arrivals to the primary airport(s).

(See CONTROLLED AIRSPACE). (See TERMINAL RADAR SERVICE AREA).

TERMINAL RADAR SERVICE AREA—Airspace surrounding designated airports wherein ATC provides radar vectoring, sequencing, and separation on a full-time basis for all IFR and participating VFR aircraft. Service provided in a TRSA is called Stage III Service. The AIM contains an explanation of TRSA. TRSA's are depicted on VFR aeronautical charts. Pilot participation is urged but is not mandatory.

(See TERMINAL RADAR PROGRAM).

TERMINAL-VERY HIGH FREQUENCY OMNIDIRECTIONAL RANGE STATION—A very high frequency terminal omnirange station located on or near an airport and used as an approach aid.

(See NAVIGATIONAL AID). (See VOR).

TERRAIN FOLLOWING—The flight of a military aircraft maintaining a constant AGL altitude above the terrain or the highest obstruction. The altitude of the aircraft will constantly change with the varying terrain and/or obstruction.

TETRAHEDRON—A device normally located on uncontrolled airports and used as a landing direction indicator. The small end of a tetrahedron points in the direction of landing. At controlled airports, the tetrahedron, if in-

stalled, should be disregarded because tower instructions supersede the indicator.
(See SEGMENTED CIRCLE).

TF—(See TERRAIN FOLLOWING).

THAT IS CORRECT—The understanding you have is right.

360 OVERHEAD—(See OVERHEAD APPROACH).

THRESHOLD—The beginning of that portion of the runway usable for landing.
(See AIRPORT LIGHTING). (See DISPLACED THRESHOLD).

THRESHOLD CROSSING HEIGHT—The theoretical height above the runway threshold at which the aircraft's glideslope antenna would be if the aircraft maintains the trajectory established by the mean ILS glideslope or MLS glidepath.
(See GLIDESLOPE). (See THRESHOLD).

THRESHOLD LIGHTS—(See AIRPORT LIGHTING).

TIBS—(See TELEPHONE INFORMATION BRIEFING SERVICE).

TIME GROUP—Four digits representing the hour and minutes from the 24–hour clock. Time groups without time zone indicators are understood to be UTC (Coordinated Universal Time); e.g., "0205." The term"Zulu" is used when ATC procedures require a reference to UTC. A time zone designator is used to indicate local time; e.g., "0205M." The end and the beginning of the day are shown by "2400" and "0000," respectively.

TMPA—(See TRAFFIC MANAGEMENT PROGRAM ALERT).

TMU—(See TRAFFIC MANAGEMENT UNIT).

TODA [ICAO]—(See ICAO Term TAKE–OFF DISTANCE AVAILABLE).

TORA [ICAO]—(See ICAO Term TAKE-OFF RUN AVAILABLE).

TORCHING—The burning of fuel at the end of an exhaust pipe or stack of a reciprocating aircraft engine, the result of an excessive richness in the fuel air mixture.

TOTAL ESTIMATED ELAPSED TIME [ICAO]—For IFR flights, the estimated time required from take-off to arrive over that designated point, defined by reference to navigation aids, from which it is intended that an instrument approach procedure will be commenced, or, if no navigation aid is associated with the destination aerodrome, to arrive over the destination aerodrome. For VFR flights, the estimated time required from takeoff to arrive over the destination aerodrome.
(See ESTIMATED ELAPSED TIME).

TOUCH-AND-GO—An operation by an aircraft that lands and departs on a runway without stopping or exiting the runway.

TOUCHING-AND-GO LANDING—(See TOUCH-AND-GO).

TOUCHDOWN—

1. The point at which an aircraft first makes contact with the landing surface.
2. Concerning a precision radar approach (PAR), it is the point where the glide path intercepts the landing surface.

(See ICAO term TOUCHDOWN).

TOUCHDOWN [ICAO]—The point where the nominal glide path intercepts the runway.
Note: Touchdown as defined above is only a datum and is not necessarily the actual point at which the aircraft will touch the runway.

TOUCHDOWN RVR—(See VISIBILITY).

TOUCHDOWN ZONE—The first 3,000 feet of the runway beginning at the threshold. The area is used for determination of Touchdown Zone Elevation in the development of straight-in landing minimum for instrument approaches.
(See ICAO term TOUCHDOWN ZONE).

TOUCHDOWN ZONE [ICAO]—The portion of a runway, beyond the threshold, where it is intended landing aircraft first contact the runway.

TOUCHDOWN ZONE ELEVATION—The highest elevation in the first 3,000 feet of the landing surface. TDZE is indicated on the instrument approach procedure chart when straight-in landing minimums are authorized.
(See TOUCHDOWN ZONE).

TOUCHDOWN ZONE LIGHTING—(See AIRPORT LIGHTING).

TOWER—A terminal facility that uses air/ground communications, visual signaling, and other devices to provide ATC services to aircraft operating in the vicinity of an airport or on the movement area. Authorizes aircraft to land or takeoff at the airport controlled by the tower or to transit the Class D airspace area regardless of flight plan or weather conditions (IFR or VFR). A tower may also provide approach control services (radar or nonradar).
(See AIRPORT TRAFFIC CONTROL SERVICE). (See APPROACH CONTROL FACILITY). (See APPROACH CONTROL SERVICE). (See MOVEMENT AREA). (See TOWER EN ROUTE CONTROL SERVICE). (See ICAO term AERODROME CONTROL TOWER).

TOWER EN ROUTE CONTROL SERVICE—The control of IFR en route traffic within delegated airspace between two or more adjacent approach control facilities. This service is designed to expedite traffic and reduce control and pilot communication requirements.

TOWER TO TOWER—(See TOWER EN ROUTE CONTROL SERVICE).

TPX–42—A numeric beacon decoder equipment/system. It is designed to be added to terminal radar systems for beacon decoding. It provides rapid target identification, reinforcement of the primary radar target, and altitude information from Mode C.
(See AUTOMATED RADAR TERMINAL SYSTEMS). (See TRANSPONDER).

TRACK—The actual flight path of an aircraft over the surface of the earth.
(See COURSE). (See ROUTE). (See FLIGHT PATH). (See ICAO term TRACK).

TRACK [ICAO]—The projection on the earth's surface of the path of an aircraft, the direction of which path at any point is usually expressed in degrees from North (True, Magnetic, or Grid).

TRAFFIC—
1. A term used by a controller to transfer radar identification of an aircraft to another controller for the purpose of coordinating separation action. Traffic is normally issued:
   a. in response to a handoff or point out,
   b. in anticipation of a handoff or point out, or
   c. in conjunction with a request for control of an aircraft.
2. A term used by ATC to refer to one or more aircraft.

TRAFFIC ADVISORIES—Advisories issued to alert pilots to other known or observed air traffic which may be in such proximity to the position or intended route of flight of their aircraft to warrant their attention. Such advisories may be based on:
1. Visual observation.
2. Observation of radar identified and non-identified aircraft targets on an ATC radar display, or
3. Verbal reports from pilots or other facilities.

The word "traffic" followed by additional information, if known, is used to provide such advisories; e.g., "Traffic, 2 o'clock, one zero miles, southbound, eight thousand."

Traffic advisory service will be provided to the extent possible depending on higher priority duties of the controller or other limitations; e.g., radar limitations, volume of traffic, frequency congestion, or controller workload. Radar/nonradar traffic advisories do not relieve the pilot of his responsibility to see and avoid other aircraft. Pilots are cautioned that there are many times when the controller is not able to give traffic advisories concerning all traffic in the aircraft's proximity; in other words, when a pilot requests or is receiving traffic advisories, he should not assume that all traffic will be issued.

(Identification), TRAFFIC ALERT, ADVISE YOU TURN LEFT/RIGHT (specific heading if appropriate), AND/OR CLIMB/DESCEND (specific altitude if appropriate) IMMEDIATELY.—(See SAFETY ALERT).

TRAFFIC ALERT AND COLLISION AVOIDANCE SYSTEM—An airborne collision avoidance system based on radar beacon signals which operates independent of ground-based equipment. TCAS-I generates traffic advisories only. TCAS-II generates traffic advisories, and resolution (collision avoidance) advisories in the vertical plane.

TRAFFIC INFORMATION—(See TRAFFIC ADVISORIES).

TRAFFIC IN SIGHT—Used by pilots to inform a controller that previously issued traffic is in sight.
(See NEGATIVE CONTACT). (See TRAFFIC ADVISORIES).

TRAFFIC MANAGEMENT PROGRAM ALERT—A term used in a Notice to Airmen (NOTAM) issued in conjunction with a special traffic management program to alert pilots to the existence of the program and to refer them to either the Notices to Airmen publication or a special traffic management program advisory message for program details. The contraction TMPA is used in NOTAM text.

TRAFFIC MANAGEMENT UNIT—The entry in ARTCC's and designated terminals responsible for direct involvement in the active management of facility traffic. Usually under the direct supervision of an assistant manager for traffic management.

TRAFFIC NO FACTOR—Indicates that the traffic described in a previously issued traffic advisory is no factor.

TRAFFIC NO LONGER OBSERVED—Indicates that the traffic described in a previously issued traffic advisory is no longer depicted on radar, but may still be a factor.

TRAFFIC PATTERN—The traffic flow that is prescribed for aircraft landing at, taxiing on, or taking off from an airport. The components of a typical traffic pattern are upwind leg, crosswind leg, downwind leg, base leg, and final approach.
1. Upwind Leg. A flight path parallel to the landing runway in the direction of landing.
2. Crosswind Leg. A flight path at right angles to the landing runway off its upwind end.
3. Downwind Leg. A flight path parallel to the landing runway in the direction opposite to landing. The downwind leg normally extends between the crosswind leg and the base leg.
4. Base Leg. A flight path at right angles to the landing runway off its approach end.

The base leg normally extends from the downwind leg to the intersection of the extended runway centerline.

5. Final Approach. A flight path in the direction of landing along the extended runway centerline. The final approach normally extends from the base leg to the runway. An aircraft making a straight-in approach VFR is also considered to be on final approach.

(See STRAIGHT-IN APPROACH-VFR). (See TAXI PATTERNS). (See ICAO term AERODROME TRAFFIC CIRCUIT).

TRANSCRIBED WEATHER BROADCAST—A continuous recording of meteorological and aeronautical information that is broadcast on L/MF and VOR facilities for pilots.

TRANSFER OF CONTROL—That action whereby the responsibility for the separation of an aircraft is transferred from one controller to another.

(See ICAO term TRANSFER OF CONTROL).

TRANSFER OF CONTROL [ICAO]—Transfer of responsibility for providing air traffic control service.

TRANSFERRING CONTROLLER—A controller/facility transferring control of an aircraft to another controller/facility.

(See ICAO term TRANSFERRING UNIT/CONTROLLER).

TRANSFERRING FACILITY—(See TRANSFERRING CONTROLLER).

TRANSFERRING UNIT/CONTROLLER [ICAO]—Air traffic control unit/air traffic controller in the process of transferring the responsibility for providing air traffic control service to an aircraft to the next air traffic control unit/air traffic controller along the route of flight.

Note: See definition of *accepting unit/controller.*

TRANSITION—

1. The general term that describes the change from one phase of flight or flight condition to another; e.g., transition from en route flight to the approach or transition from instrument flight to visual flight.

2. A published procedure (SID Transition) used to connect the basic SID to one of several en route airways/jet routes, or a published procedure (STAR Transition) used to connect one of several en route airways/jet routes to the basic STAR.

TRANSITIONAL AIRSPACE—That portion of controlled airspace wherein aircraft change from one phase of flight or flight condition to another.

TRANSITION POINT—A point at an adapted number of miles from the vertex at which an arrival aircraft would normally commence descent from its en route altitude. This is the first fix adapted on the arrival speed segments.

TRANSMISSOMETER—An apparatus used to determine visibility by measuring the transmission of light through the atmosphere. It is the measurement source for determining runway visual range (RVR) and runway visibility value (RVV).

(See VISIBILITY).

TRANSMITTING IN THE BLIND—A transmission from one station to other stations in circumstances where two-way communications cannot be established, but where it is believed that the called stations may be able to receive the transmission.

TRANSPONDER—The airborne radar beacon receiver/transmitter portion of the Air Traffic Control Radar Beacon System (ATCRBS) which automatically receives radio signals from interrogators on the ground, and selectively replies with a specific reply pulse or pulse group only to those interrogations being received on the mode to which it is set to respond.

(See INTERROGATOR). (See ICAO term TRANSPONDER).

TRANSPONDER [ICAO]—A receiver/transmitter which will generate a reply signal upon proper interrogation; the interrogation and reply being on different frequencies.

TRANSPONDER CODES—(See CODES).

TRSA—(See TERMINAL RADAR SERVICE AREA).

TURBOJET AIRCRAFT—An aircraft having a jet engine in which the energy of the jet operates a turbine which in turn operates the air compressor.

TURBOPROP AIRCRAFT—An aircraft having a jet engine in which the energy of the jet operates a turbine which drives the propeller.

TWEB—(See TRANSCRIBED WEATHER BROADCAST).

TVOR—(See TERMINAL-VERY HIGH FREQUENCY OMNIDIRECTIONAL RANGE STATION).

TWO-WAY RADIO COMMUNICATIONS FAILURE—(See LOST COMMUNICATIONS).

UDF—(See DIRECTION FINDER).

UHF—(See ULTRAHIGH FREQUENCY).

ULTRAHIGH FREQUENCY—The frequency band between 300 and 3,000 mHz. The bank of radio frequencies used for military air/ground voice communications. In some instances this may go as low as 225 mHz and still be referred to as UHF.

ULTRALIGHT VEHICLE—An aeronautical vehicle operated for sport or recreational purposes which does not require FAA registration, an airworthiness certificate, nor pilot certification. They are primarily single occupant vehicles, although some two-place vehicles are authorized for training purposes. Operation of

an ultralight vehicle in certain airspace requires authorization from ATC.
(See Part 103).

UNABLE—Indicates inability to comply with a specific instruction, request, or clearance.

UNDER THE HOOD—Indicates that the pilot is using a hood to restrict visibility outside the cockpit while simulating instrument flight. An appropriately rated pilot is required in the other control seat while this operation is being conducted.

UNICOM—A nongovernmental communication facility which may provide airport information at certain airports. Locations and frequencies of UNICOMs are shown on aeronautical charts and publications.

UNPUBLISHED ROUTE—A route for which no minimum altitude is published or charted for pilot use. It may include a direct route between NAVAIDS, a radial, a radar vector, or a final approach course beyond the segments of an instrument approach procedure.
(See PUBLISHED ROUTE). (See ROUTE).

UPWIND LEG—(See TRAFFIC PATTERN).

URGENCY—A condition of being concerned about safety and of requiring timely but not immediate assistance; a potential *distress* condition.
(See ICAO term URGENCY).

URGENCY [ICAO]—A condition concerning the safety of an aircraft or other vehicle, or of person on board or in sight, but which does not require immediate assistance.

USAFIB—(See ARMY AVIATION FLIGHT INFORMATION BULLETIN).

UVDF—(See DIRECTION FINDER).

VASI—(See VISUAL APPROACH SLOPE INDICATOR).

VDF—(See DIRECTION FINDER).

VDP—(See VISUAL DESCENT POINT).

VECTOR—A heading issued to an aircraft to provide navigational guidance by radar.
(See ICAO term RADAR VECTORING).

VERIFY—Request confirmation of information; e.g., "verify assigned altitude."

VERIFY SPECIFIC DIRECTION OF TAKEOFF (OR TURNS AFTER TAKEOFF)—Used by ATC to ascertain an aircraft's direction of takeoff and/or direction of turn after takeoff. It is normally used for IFR departures from an airport not having a control tower. When direct communication with the pilot is not possible, the request and information may be relayed through an FSS, dispatcher, or by other means.
(See IFR TAKEOFF MINIMUMS AND DEPARTURE PROCEDURES).

VERTEX—The last fix adapted on the arrival speed segments. Normally, it will be the outer marker of the runway in use. However, it may be the actual threshold or other suitable common point on the approach path for the particular runway configuration.

VERTEX TIME OF ARRIVAL—A calculated time of aircraft arrival over the adapted vertex for the runway configuration in use. The time is calculated via the optimum flight path using adapted speed segments.

VERTICAL SEPARATION—Separation established by assignment of different altitudes or flight levels.
(See SEPARATION). (See ICAO term VERTICAL SEPARATION).

VERTICAL SEPARATION [ICAO]—Separation between aircraft expressed in units of vertical distance.

VERTICAL TAKEOFF AND LANDING AIRCRAFT—Aircraft capable of vertical climbs and/or descents and of using very short runways or small areas for takeoff and landings. These aircraft include, but are not limited to, helicopters.
(See SHORT TAKEOFF AND LANDING AIRCRAFT).

VERY HIGH FREQUENCY—The frequency band between 30 and 300 mHz. Portions of this band, 108 to 118 mHz, are used for certain NAVAIDS; 118 to 136 mHz are used for civil air/ground voice communications. Other frequencies in this band are used for purposes not related to air traffic control.

VERY HIGH FREQUENCY OMNIDIRECTIONAL RANGE STATION—(See VOR).

VERY LOW FREQUENCY—The frequency band between 3 and 30 kHz.

VFR—(See VISUAL FLIGHT RULES).

VFR AIRCRAFT—An aircraft conducting flight in accordance with visual flight rules.
(See VISUAL FLIGHT RULES).

VFR CONDITIONS—Weather conditions equal to or better than the minimum for flight under visual flight rules. The term may be used as an ATC clearance/instruction only when:

1. An IFR aircraft requests a climb/descent in VFR conditions.
2. The clearance will result in noise abatement benefits where part of the IFR departure route does not conform to an FAA approved noise abatement route or altitude.
3. A pilot has requested a practice instrument approach and is not on an IFR flight plan.—All pilots receiving this authorization must comply with the VFR visibility and distance from cloud criteria in Part 91. Use of the term does not relieve controllers of their responsibility to separate aircraft

in Class B and Class C airspace or TRSA's as required by FAA Order 7110.65. When used as an ATC clearance/instruction, the term may be abbreviated "VFR;" e.g., "MAINTAIN VFR," "CLIMB/DESCEND VFR," etc.

VFR FLIGHT—(See VFR AIRCRAFT).

VFR MILITARY TRAINING ROUTES—Routes used by the Department of Defense and associated Reserve and Air Guard units for the purpose of conducting low-altitude navigation and tactical training under VFR below 10,000 feet MSL at airspeeds in excess of 250 knots IAS.

VFR NOT RECOMMENDED—An advisory provided by a flight service station to a pilot during a preflight or inflight weather briefing that flight under visual flight rules is not recommended. To be given when the current and/or forecast weather conditions are at or below VFR minimums. It does not abrogate the pilot's authority to make his own decision.

VFR-ON-TOP—ATC authorization for an IFR aircraft to operate in VFR conditions at any appropriate VFR altitude (as specified in FAR and as restricted by ATC). A pilot receiving this authorization must comply with the VFR visibility, distance from cloud criteria, and the minimum IFR altitudes specified in Part 91. The use of this term does not relieve controllers of their responsibility to separate aircraft in Class B and Class C airspace or TRSA's as required by FAA Order 7110.65.

VFR TERMINAL AREA CHARTS—(See AERONAUTICAL CHART).

VHF—(See VERY HIGH FREQUENCY).

VHF OMNIDIRECTIONAL RANGE/TACTICAL AIR NAVIGATION—(See VORTAC).

VIDEO MAP—An electronically displayed map on the radar display that may depict data such as airports, heliports, runway centerline extensions, hospital emergency landing areas, NAVAID's and fixes, reporting points, airway/route centerlines, boundaries, handoff points, special use tracks, obstructions, prominent geographic features, map alignment indicators, range accuracy marks, minimum vectoring altitudes.

VISIBILITY—The ability, as determined by atmospheric conditions and expressed in units of distance, to see and identify prominent unlighted objects by day and prominent lighted objects by night. Visibility is reported as statute miles, hundreds of feet or meters.

1. Flight Visibility. The average forward horizontal distance, from the cockpit of an aircraft in flight, at which prominent unlighted objects may be seen and identified by day and prominent lighted objects may be seen and identified by night.

2. Ground Visibility. Prevailing horizontal visibility near the earth's surface as reported by the United States National Weather Service or an accredited observer.

3. Prevailing Visibility. The greatest horizontal visibility equaled or exceeded throughout at least half the horizon circle which need not necessarily be continuous.

4. Runway Visibility Value (RVV). The visibility determined for a particular runway by a transmissometer. A meter provides a continuous indication of the visibility (reported in miles or fractions of miles) for the runway. RVV is used in lieu of prevailing visibility in determining minimums for a particular runway.

5. Runway Visual Range (RVR). An instrumentally derived value, based on standard calibrations, that represents the horizontal distance a pilot will see down the runway from the approach end. It is based on the sighting of either high intensity runway lights or on the visual contrast of other targets whichever yields the greater visual range. RVR, in contrast to prevailing or runway visibility, is based on what a pilot in a moving aircraft should see looking down the runway. RVR is horizontal visual range, not slant visual range. It is based on the measurements of a transmissometer made near the touchdown point of the instrument runway and is reported in hundreds of feet. RVR is used in lieu of RVV and/or prevailing visibility in determining minimums for a particular runway.

a. Touchdown RVR. The RVR visibility readout values obtained from RVR equipment serving the runway touchdown zone.

b. Mid-RVR. The RVR readout values obtained from RVR equipment located midfield of the runway.

c. Rollout RVR. The RVR readout values obtained from RVR equipment located nearest the rollout end of the runway.

(See ICAO term VISIBILITY). (See ICAO term FLIGHT VISIBILITY). (See ICAO term GROUND VISIBILITY). (See ICAO term RUNWAY VISUAL RANGE).

VISIBILITY [ICAO]—The ability, as determined by atmospheric conditions and expressed in units of distance, to see and identify prominent unlighted objects by day and prominent lighted objects by night.

Flight Visibility.—The visibility forward from the cockpit of an aircraft in flight.

Ground Visibility.—The visibility at an aerodrome as reported by an accredited observer.

Runway Visual Range [RVR].—The range over which the pilot of an aircraft on the centre line of a runway can see the runway surface markings or the lights delineating the runway or identifying its centre line.

VISUAL APPROACH—An approach wherein an aircraft on an IFR flight plan, operating in VFR conditions under the control of an air traffic control facility and having an air traffic control authorization, may proceed to the airport of destination in VFR conditions.
(See ICAO term VISUAL APPROACH).

VISUAL APPROACH [ICAO]—An approach by an IFR flight when either part or all of an instrument approach procedure is not completed and the approach is executed in visual reference to terrain.

VISUAL APPROACH SLOPE INDICATOR—(See AIRPORT LIGHTING).

VISUAL DESCENT POINT—A defined point on the final approach course of a nonprecision straight-in approach procedure from which normal descent from the MDA to the runway touchdown point may be commenced, provided the approach threshold of that runway, or approach lights, or other markings identifiable with the approach end of that runway are clearly visible to the pilot.

VISUAL FLIGHT RULES—Rules that govern the procedures for conducting flight under visual conditions. The term "VFR" is also used in the United States to indicate weather conditions that are equal to or greater than minimum VFR requirements. In addition, it is used by pilots and controllers to indicate type of flight plan.
(See INSTRUMENT FLIGHT RULES). (See INSTRUMENT METEOROLOGICAL CONDITIONS). (See VISUAL METEOROLOGICAL CONDITIONS).

VISUAL HOLDING—The holding of aircraft at selected, prominent geographical fixes which can be easily recognized from the air.
(See HOLDING FIX).

VISUAL METEOROLOGICAL CONDITIONS—Meteorological conditions expressed in terms of visibility, distance from cloud, and ceiling equal to or better than specified minima.
(See INSTRUMENT FLIGHT RULES). (See INSTRUMENT METEOROLOGICAL CONDITIONS). (See VISUAL FLIGHT RULES).

VISUAL SEPARATION—A means employed by ATC to separate aircraft in terminal areas. There are two ways to effect this separation:

1. The tower controller sees the aircraft involved and issues instructions, as necessary, to ensure that the aircraft avoid each other.

2. A pilot sees the other aircraft involved and upon instructions from the controller provides his own separation by maneuvering his aircraft as necessary to avoid it. This may involve following another aircraft or keeping it in sight until it is no longer a factor.

VLF—(See VERY LOW FREQUENCY).

VMC—(See VISUAL METEOROLOGICAL CONDITIONS).

VOR—A ground-based electronic navigation aid transmitting very high frequency navigation signals, 360 degrees in azimuth, oriented from magnetic north. Used as the basis for navigation in the National Airspace System. The VOR periodically identifies itself by Morse Code and may have an additional voice identification feature. Voice features may be used by ATC or FSS for transmitting instructions/information to pilots.
(See NAVIGATIONAL AID).

VORTAC—A navigation aid providing VOR azimuth, TACAN azimuth, and TACAN distance measuring equipment (DME) at one site.
(See DISTANCE MEASURING EQUIPMENT). (See NAVIGATIONAL AID). (See TACAN). (See VOR).

VORTICES—Circular patterns of air created by the movement of an airfoil through the air when generating lift. As an airfoil moves through the atmosphere in sustained flight, an area of area of low pressure is created above it. The air flowing from the high pressure area to the low pressure area around and about the tips of the airfoil tends to roll up into two rapidly rotating vortices, cylindrical in shape. These vortices are the most predominant parts of aircraft wake turbulence and their rotational force is dependent upon the wing loading, gross weight, and speed of the generating aircraft. The vortices from medium to heavy aircraft can be of extremely high velocity and hazardous to smaller aircraft.
(See AIRCRAFT CLASSES). (See WAKE TURBULENCE).

VOR TEST SIGNAL—(See VOT).

VOT—A ground facility which emits a test signal to check VOR receiver accuracy. Some VOT's are available to the user while airborne, and others are limited to ground use only.

VR—(See VFR MILITARY TRAINING ROUTES).

VTA—(See VERTEX TIME OF ARRIVAL).

VTOL AIRCRAFT—(See VERTICAL TAKEOFF AND LANDING AIRCRAFT).

WA—(See AIRMET).
(See WEATHER ADVISORY).

WAKE TURBULENCE—Phenomena resulting from the passage of an aircraft through the atmosphere. The term includes vortices, thrust stream turbulence, jet blast, jet wash, propeller wash, and rotor wash both on the ground and in the air.
(See AIRCRAFT CLASSES). (See JET BLAST). (See VORTICES).

WARNING AREA—(See SPECIAL USE AIRSPACE).

WAYPOINT—A predetermined geographical position used for route/instrument approach definition, or progress reporting purposes, that is defined relative to a VORTAC station or in terms of latitude/longitude coordinates.

WEATHER ADVISORY—In aviation weather forecast practice, an expression of hazardous weather conditions not predicted in the area forecast, as they affect the operation of air traffic and as prepared by the NWS.
(See SIGMET). (See AIRMET).

WHEN ABLE—When used in conjunction with ATC instructions, gives the pilot the latitude to delay compliance until a condition or event has been reconciled. Unlike "pilot discretion," when instructions are prefaced "when able," the pilot is expected to seek the first opportunity to comply. Once a maneuver has been initiated, the pilot is expected to continue until the specifications of the instructions have been met. "When able," should not be used when expeditious compliance is required.

WILCO—I have received your message, understand it, and will comply with it.

WIND SHEAR—A change in wind speed and/or wind direction in a short distance resulting in a tearing or shearing effect. It can exist in a horizontal or vertical direction and occasionally in both.

WING TIP VORTICES—(See VORTICES).

WORDS TWICE—

1. As a request: "Communication is difficult. Please say every phrase twice."

2. As information: "Since communications are difficult, every phrase in this message will be spoken twice."

WORLD AERONAUTICAL CHARTS—(See AERONAUTICAL CHART).

WS—(See SIGMET).
(See WEATHER ADVISORY).

WST—(See CONVECTIVE SIGMET).
(See WEATHER ADVISORY).

Appendix I. Office of Personnel Management Addresses and Telephone Numbers

ALABAMA
Huntsville
Building 600, Suite 347
3322 Memorial Pkwy., South
35801-5311
(205) 544-5802

ALASKA
Anchorage
222 W. 7th Ave., #22
99513-7572
(907) 271-5821

ARIZONA
Phoenix
Century Plaza Bldg., Rm. 1415
3225 N. Central Ave., 85012
(602) 640-5800

ARKANSAS
(See San Antonio, TX listing)

CALIFORNIA
Los Angeles (For Southern California)
9650 Flair Dr., Ste 100A
El Monte 91731
(818) 575-6510

Sacramento (For Northern California)
1029 J Street, Rm 202
95814
(916) 551-1464

San Diego (For the San Diego area)
Federal Bldg., Room 4-S-9
880 Front St., 92188
(619) 557-6165

San Francisco (For Central California)
P.O. Box 7405, 94120
(Located at 211 Main St.,
2nd Floor, Room 235)
(415) 744-5627

COLORADO
Denver
P.O. Box 25167, 80225
(303) 969-7050
(Located at 12345 W. Alameda Pkwy.,
Lakewood)

CONNECTICUT
(See Massachusetts listing)

DELAWARE
(See Philadelphia listing)

DISTRICT OF COLUMBIA
Metro Area
1900 E St., N.W., Rm. 1416
20415
(202) 606-2700

FLORIDA
Miami
Claude Pepper Federal Bldg.
Room 1222, 51 SW 1st Ave.
33130
(305) 536-6738

Orlando
Commodore Bldg., Suite 125
3444 McCrory Pl., 32803-3701
(407) 648-6148

GEORGIA
Atlanta
Richard B. Russell Federal Bldg.,
Room 940A, 75 Spring St., S.W.,
30303
(404) 331-4315

HAWAII
Honolulu (and other Hawaiian Islands
and Overseas)
Federal Building, Room 5316
300 Ala Moana Blvd., 96850
(808) 541-2791
Overseas Jobs – (808) 541-2784

IDAHO
(See Washington listing)

ILLINOIS
Chicago
175 W. Jackson Blvd., Rm. 530
60604
(312) 353-6192
(For Madison and St. Clair Counties,
see St. Louis, MO listing)

INDIANA
Indianapolis
Minton-Capehart Federal Bldg.
575 N. Pennsylvania St., 46204
(317) 226-7161
(For Clark, Dearborn, and Floyd
Counties, see Ohio listing)

IOWA
(See Kansas City, MO listing)
(816) 426-7757
(For Scott County, see Illinois listing)

KANSAS
Wichita
One-Twenty Bldg., Room 101
120 S. Market St., 67202
(316) 269-6794
(For additional information services
in Kansas, see Kansas City,
MO listing)

KENTUCKY
(See Ohio listing; for Henderson
County, see Michigan listing)

LOUISIANA
New Orleans
1515 Poydras St., Suite 608, 70112
(504) 589-2764

MAINE
(See Massachusetts listing)

MARYLAND
Baltimore
Room 101
300 West Pratt St., 21201
(410) 962-3822

MASSACHUSETTS
Boston
Thos. P. O'Neill, Jr. Federal Bldg.
10 Causeway St., 02222-1031
(617) 565-5900

MICHIGAN
Detroit
477 Michigan Ave., Rm. 565, 48226
(313) 226-6950

MINNESOTA
Twin Cities
1 Federal Drive, Room 501
Bishop Henry Whipple Federal Bldg.
Ft. Snelling, Twin Cities, 55111
(612) 725-3430

MISSISSIPPI
(See Alabama listing)

MISSOURI
Kansas City
Federal Building, Rm. 134
601 E. 12th St., 64106
(816) 426-5702
(For Counties west of and including
Mercer, Grundy, Livingston, Carroll,
Saline, Pettis, Benton, Hickory, Dallas,
Webster, Douglas, and Ozark)

St. Louis
400 Old Post Office Bldg.
815 Olive St., 63101
(314) 539-2285
(For all other Missouri Counties not
listed under Kansas City above)

MONTANA
(303) 969-7052
(See Colorado listing)

NEBRASKA
(See Kansas listing)

NEVADA
For Clark, Lincoln, and Nye Counties,
see Los Angeles, CA listing. (For all
other Nevada Counties not listed
above, see Sacramento, CA listing.)

NEW HAMPSHIRE
(See Massachusetts listings)

NEW JERSEY
Newark
Touch Screen Service available at:
Peter W. Rodino, Jr., Federal Bldg.
970 Broad Street, 07102
(For additional information services
in Atlantic, Burlington, Camden,
Cape May, Cumberland, Gloucester,
Mercer, Monmouth, Ocean, and Salem
Counties see Philadelphia)

NEW MEXICO
Albuquerque
505 Marquette Ave.,
Suite 910, 87102
(505) 766-2906

NEW YORK
New York City
Jacob K. Javits Federal Bldg.,
2nd floor, Room 120
26 Federal Plaza, 10278
(212) 264-0422

Syracuse
P.O. Box 7257
100 S. Clinton St., 13260
(315) 423-5660

NORTH CAROLINA
Raleigh
4407 Blend Rd.
Suite 202, 27609-6296
(919) 790-2822

NORTH DAKOTA
(See Minnesota listing)

OHIO
Dayton
Federal Building, Rm. 506
200 W. 2nd St., 45402
(513) 225-2720
(For Van Wort, Auglaize, Hardin,
Marion, Crawford, Richland, Ashland,
Wayne, Stark, Carroll, Columbiana
Counties and all Counties north of
these, see Michigan listing)

OKLAHOMA
(See San Antonio, TX)

OREGON
Portland
Federal Bldg., Room 376
1220 S.W. Third Ave., 97204
(503) 321-3141

PENNSYLVANIA
Harrisburg
Federal Bldg., Room 168
P.O. Box 761, 17108
(717) 782-4494

Philadelphia
Wm. J. Green, Jr., Federal Bldg.
600 Arch Street, 19106
(215) 597-7440

Pittsburgh
Federal Building
1000 Liberty Ave., Rm. 119, 15222
(Walk-in only, for mail or
telephone see Philadelphia listing.)

PUERTO RICO
San Juan
Federico Degetau Federal Bldg.,
Rm. 340
150 Carlos E. Chardon Avenue
Hato Rey, P.R. 00918-1710
(809) 766-5242

RHODE ISLAND
(See Massachusetts)

SOUTH CAROLINA
(See Raleigh, NC listing)

SOUTH DAKOTA
(See Minnesota listing)

TENNESSEE
Memphis
(Walk-in only)
200 Jefferson Avenue, Suite 1312
(For mail or telephone, see Alabama
listing)

TEXAS
Corpus Christi
(See San Antonio listing)
(512) 884-8113

Dallas
1100 Commerce St., Rm. 6810,
75242
(214) 767-8035

Houston
(See San Antonio listing)
(713) 759-0455

San Antonio
8610 Broadway, Rm. 305, 78217
(210) 805-2423

UTAH
(303) 969-7053
(See Colorado listing)

VERMONT
(See Massachusetts listing)

VIRGIN ISLANDS
(See Puerto Rico listing)
(809) 774-8790

VIRGINIA
Norfolk
Federal Building, Rm. 220
200 Granby St., 23510-1886
(804) 441-3355
(Walk-in only)
Norfolk VEC Job Service Office
5145 E. Virginia Beach Blvd.

WASHINGTON
Seattle
Federal Building, Room 110
915 Second Ave., 98174
(206) 553-4365

WEST VIRGINIA
Phone only: (See Ohio)
(513) 225-2866

WISCONSIN
For Dane, Grant, Green, Iowa,
Lafayette, Rock, Jefferson, Walworth,
Milwaukee, Waukesha, Racine, and
Kenosha Counties, call (312) 353-6189;
for all other Wisconsin Counties not
listed above, see Minnesota listing.
(612) 725-5430

WYOMING
(303) 969-7054
(See Colorado listing)

APPENDIX II. FAA EMPLOYMENT OFFICES

Regional Employment Offices

Areas of Jurisdiction

Alaska Region
Federal Aviation Administration
Human Resource Management
Division (AAL-14)
222 West 7th Avenue #14
Anchorage, Alaska 99513
(907) 271-5747

Alaska and Aleutian Islands

Eastern Region
Federal Aviation Administration
Human Resource Management
Division (AEA-14)
JFK International Airport
Jamaica, New York 11430
(718) 917-1060

Delaware, Maryland, New Jersey,
New York, Pennsylvania, Virginia,
West Virginia, District of Columbia

Central Region
Federal Aviation Administration
Human Resource Management
Division (ACE-14)
601 East 12th Street
Kansas City, Missouri 64106
(816) 426-3304

Iowa, Kansas, Missouri, Nebraska

Great Lakes Region
Federal Aviation Administration
Human Resource Management
Division (AGL-14)
2300 East Devon Avenue
Des Plaines, Illinois 60018
(312) 694-7731

North Dakota, South Dakota, Illinois,
Indiana, Minnesota, Michigan, Ohio,
Wisconsin

New England Region
Federal Aviation Administration
Human Resource Management
Division (ANE-14)
12 New England Executive Park,
Box 510
Burlington, Massachusetts 01803
(617) 273-7345

Connecticut, Maine, Massachusetts,
New Hampshire, Rhode Island,
Vermont

Northwest Mountain Region
Federal Aviation Administration
Human Resource Management
Division (ANM-14)
1601 Lind Avenue, SW
Renton, Washington 98055-4056
(206) 227-2014

Colorado, Montana, Utah, Idaho,
Oregon, Washington, Wyoming

Regional Employment Offices (continued)	**Areas of Jurisdiction**
Southern Region Federal Aviation Administration Human Resource Management Division (ASO-12) P.O. Box 20636 East Point, Georgia 30320 (404) 763-7812	Alabama, Florida, Georgia, Kentucky, Mississippi, North Carolina, South Carolina, Tennessee, Puerto Rico, Virgin Islands
Southwest Region Federal Aviation Administration Human Resource Management Division (ASW-14) 4400 Blue Mound Road Fort Worth, Texas 76193-0014 (817) 624-5014	Arkansas, Louisiana, New Mexico, Oklahoma, Texas
Western-Pacific Region Federal Aviation Administration Human Resource Management Division (AWP-14) P.O. Box 92007 Worldway Postal Center Los Angeles, California 90009 (213) 297-0207	Arizona, California, Nevada, Hawaii, American Samoa

Other Major Field Employment Offices

Federal Aviation Administration
Human Resource Management Division (AHR-150)
800 Independence Avenue, SW
Washington, D.C. 20591
(202) 267-8007

Federal Aviation Administration (Technical Center)
Human Resource Management Division (ACM-140)
Atlantic City International Airport
Atlantic City, New Jersey 08405
(609) 484-6623

Federal Aviation Administration
Mike Monroney Aeronautical Center (AAC-14)
P.O. Box 25082
Oklahoma City, Oklahoma 73125
(405) 954-3011

Special Examining Office

Federal Aviation Administration
Mike Monroney Aeronautical Center
Aviation Careers Examining Division (AAC-80)
P.O. Box 26650
Oklahoma City, Oklahoma 73125
(405) 680-4657